Multinational enterprise in historical perspective

Edited by

ALICE TEICHOVA

Professor of Economic History, University of East Anglia

MAURICE LÉVY-LEBOYER

Professor of Economic History, Université de Paris – Nanterre

and

HELGA NUSSBAUM

Institut für Wirtschaftsgeschichte, Akademie der Wissenschaften der DDR

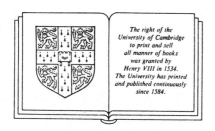

The right of the
University of Cambridge
to print and sell
all manner of books
was granted by
Henry VIII in 1534.
The University has printed
and published continuously
since 1584.

CAMBRIDGE UNIVERSITY PRESS

Cambridge
London   New York   New Rochelle   Melbourne   Sydney

& ÉDITIONS DE LA MAISON DES SCIENCES
DE L'HOMME

Paris

Published by the Press Syndicate of the University of Cambridge
The Pitt Building, Trumpington Street, Cambridge CB2 1RP
32 East 57th Street, New York, NY 10022, USA
10 Stamford Road, Oakleigh, Melbourne 3166, Australia
and Editions de la Maison des Sciences de l'Homme
54 Boulevard Raspail, 75270 Paris Cedex 06

First published 1986
Reprinted 1987, 1988

Printed in Great Britain by
Antony Rowe Ltd, Chippenham, Wiltshire

British Library cataloguing in publication data

Multinational enterprise in historical perspective.
1. International business enterprises – History
I. Teichova, Alice   II. Lévy-Leboyer, Maurice   III. Nussbaum, Helga
338.8'8'09   HD62.4

Library of Congress cataloguing in publication data

Multinational enterprise in historical perspective.
1. International business enterprises – Addresses,
essays, lectures. I. Teichova, Alice. II. Lévy-Leboyer,
Maurice. III. Nussbaum, Helga.
HD2755.M83425   1986   338.8'8   86–2253

ISBN 0 521 32040 2
ISBN 2 7351 0151 7 (France only)

UP

Contents

PART II: GOVERNMENT AND MULTINATIONALS

Home and host countries

viii   *Contents*

Preface

This volume is published as part of the preparation for the Ninth International Economic History Congress, which will be held in Berne, Switzerland, in August 1986, and will devote one of its main themes, in the section 'Debates and controversies', to 'Multinational enterprise: international finance, markets and government in the twentieth century'. The papers that are presented were discussed at a preparatory conference convened at the University of East Anglia, Norwich, England, attended by 43 scholars from 14 countries. The project was started in the Autumn of 1983, when the authors agreed to produce papers emanating from their research. We wish to thank them for meeting the deadlines so that their papers could be circulated to participants. This helped to raise the level of the discussion. Warm thanks are due to the rapporteurs, Bernard Alford, Philip Cottrell, Richard Davenport-Hines and Clemens Wurm, and to the commentators, Tony Corley, Rhys Jenkins, Francesca Sanna-Randaccio and Mikuláš Teich, for their constructive critical review of the papers and the searching questions they raised, thus stimulating rewarding exchanges of ideas in discussion. For competently steering the sessions, we are also grateful to the chairmen, Bernard Alford, Wacław Długoborski, Peter Mathias and Barry Supple.

Without the financial support of several institutions for the Conference this publication could not have gone to the press. We therefore gratefully acknowledge the generous support of the Economic and Social Research Council and the Nuffield Foundation as well as the support from the British Academy and the Norfolk and Norwich Chamber of Commerce. We owe a great debt to the School of Economic and Social Studies of the University of East Anglia, not only for the financial support but also for the constant assistance and encouragement received from the Dean, Professor Martin Hollis, and the administrative and academic staff. To the graphic artist and cartoonist Benny Kandler we should like to express our appreciation for the attractive and fitting logo he produced for the Conference and which appears also on the jacket of this volume. Above all, we extend our heart-felt thanks to the Conference Secretary, Valerie Striker, without whose untiring care and attention the whole project of the Conference and of publishing this volume could hardly have been attempted. Finally we want to thank the University of East Anglia for acting as host to the participants of the Conference.

A.T.

August 1985

M.L.-L.
H.N.

Introduction

MAURICE LÉVY-LEBOYER

For reasons that initially received general acceptance, multinational enterprises (MNEs) have been allowed, for a long period of time, less than a fair treatment. They developed dramatically in the 1960s and 1970s. And, since their policy was not simply to enlarge foreign markets by opening sales agencies, but also to substitute overseas production to home exports, they were made responsible (together with other domestic factors) for the economic stagnation that set in during those years in the USA and Western Europe. Using arguments reminiscent of the pre-1914 period, when capital was exported for the first time on a very large scale, studies were published taxing the MNEs of diffusing new technologies too freely and rapidly, of investing capital abroad at the expense of their country of origin, and of exporting jobs. Obviously, some of these criticisms were too extreme and had to be rectified at a later stage. All the more so, because business historians and economists had been conducting research at that time to get a closer view, and a more concrete one, of MNEs' operations. The documentary evidence they have accumulated so far has contributed to bring out two major reassessments. Firstly, they have shown that international firms have had a longer and more positive experience in the past than was first assumed: there were, for instance, trade companies operating in more than one country that propagated the cotton industry on the Continent as early as the 1780s and manufacturing firms (in plate-glass, metals, chemicals, machine-building) that have had foreign plants since the 1850s and 1860s, with beneficial results both for home and host-countries. As a matter of fact, each acceleration of world trade has been accompanied by waves of such undertakings. Secondly, they have added a new dimension to the concept of capital export, by making a sharp distinction between portfolio investments that allocate capital at home and abroad according to risks and rates of return, and foreign direct investment, i.e. the setting up of foreign subsidiaries by a company to gain greater efficiency through the internalisation of market operations and to reduce transactions costs. Business analysis has progressed in time-coverage and insight.

1

But, even though a more balanced view has emerged, there is still no consensus on a fair range of issues, such as the possibility of building up a typology of MNEs, according to the characteristics of their country of origin, in the latter part of the nineteenth century; their operations and relationship with other firms through the cycle, and specifically in the 1930s depression; their influence on wage structure and employment in the home and host-countries, when direct foreign investments are made backwards and forwards, as a way to protect supplies or to expand markets; the financing of MNEs and their organisational structure as they reach maturity, on the assumption that there are common patterns of change to which all firms have to conform; and the existence of stages in international involvement. It is to clarify these problems and bring them in historical perspective that this volume is being published. It contains the proceedings of the conference Multinational Enterprise in Historical Perspective, held at the University of East Anglia, Norwich, 26–9 March 1985. It follows the same order: the papers that were presented are organised in two parts – the growth of multinationals, and the response they faced in countries where their operations were located – to illustrate and answer the controversial aspects which the concept has raised from the start, and which are discussed, as a general introduction, in David Fieldhouse's report.

Three main themes, among those that came up for debate – the early steps, market control and external impact of multinational enterprise – stand out as of major concern to the participants in the conference; and it seems convenient to take them in succession.

1. *Early experience* Rather than analysing in detail the specific advantages (in terms of access to capital and new techniques) that allowed industrial firms to seek additional outlets and production facilities abroad, the discussion centered – following Alfred Chandler's presentation of the American early-twentieth-century experience – on the constraints that made it compelling for manufacturers, in a few key sectors from oil and processed food to light machinery, to expand their operations by integrating mass production with distribution and exploit the massive-scale economies that technology made possible or else run the risk of not reaching a minimum-scale efficiency and be left out of the market drive. The dynamics of competitive advantage, even in the 1880s and 1890s when the first American MNEs were starting, were such that those firms which did not try to increase their share of a sector by enlarging their productive facilities and building up mass market organisations at home and abroad would lose to others. This makes plain that there were true risks at stake, in spite of the oligopolistic structure of modern industries, and that the system developed first in America, as industries there had used at an early date capital-intensive methods, and could 'run out their success at home, in a huge domestic market, before incurring the transactions costs of going abroad'.

This presentation suggests that firms should not have had any incentive to develop foreign subsidiaries, when scale economies were either too high (as in steel and capital equipment, since minimum-efficient plants would overstep local demand; and, to a certain extent, this is warranted by the two case-studies that G. Kurgan-van-Hentenryk and Cl. Beaud have presented), or too low (as in the case of consumer goods made by traditional methods, where foreign subsidiaries had no cost advantage over local producers). MNEs should have been most efficient in those sectors where they brought manufactured goods in large batches to the consumer. Still, one should not feel that American methods were the only ones open to develop international operations. The review that Mira Wilkins has made of European MNEs in the USA – as an introduction to her forthcoming book – demonstrates that alternative ways were used before 1914, for instance 'free standing companies', set up near a financial centre to do business abroad but with no real operations in their own country, and more traditional firms, adding up new production units to extend their markets in what were still labour-intensive sectors, and with great efficiency, because of the quality and reliability of their workmanship. In a similar way, one would find the old expertise of merchant bankers in John McKay and Ph. Chalmin's accounts of the operations in and out of industry of the Rothschilds, setting up refineries and distribution networks in the metals and oil markets at the end of the nineteenth century, and of Tate and Lyle, diversifying after the 1920s into engineering, shipping and trading, with a desire, in both cases, not to run against the market and be stuck with frozen assets.

This means that adaptation to the market, in contradiction with the more rigid methods imposed by highly mechanised plants and sales drives, should not be left out of the picture. That is the lesson, at any rate, which comes out of Roy Church's account of the British car industry: the subsidiaries of American MNEs led the market in periods of sustained growth (before 1914 and after the 1950s) because of their superior resources and productivity; but they were overtaken in the intervening years by the local car makers to such an extent that Ford had to take back British managers and models to cut losses. One would conclude that there were variants to the Chandlerian model, for the obvious reason that large-scale enterprises had to look for efficiency, but also to cope with business fluctuations, local consumption habits, labour skills and incentives and so on.

2. *Market organisation and finance* The international experience of the German dyestuffs and electro-technical industries, which are covered here by four papers, was of a completely different nature, since overseas transfers of production in their case were kept to a minimum – firstly in the pre-1913 period because of the necessity to maintain plants near laboratories and research centres (the ratio of exports to overseas production, in the IG Farben group, was 6:1) and after the war, once surplus capacities plagued

industry in ex-belligerent countries, because of the competition they were to face when trade reopened. Market organisation, i.e. negotiated agreements, exchange of shares and patents, joint-ventures, and later cartels, assumed a role unheard of in the past; 40% of world trade in 1929–37, as recalled by Helga Nussbaum, was conducted through concerted action.

But did this situation prevent the development of new ventures on a multinational basis? In a broad historical perspective, according to Peter Hertner's paper, the good performance of the German electrical industries had been due firstly to their technical achievements; Siemens, for instance, changed three times and with equal success its main foreign operations between the 1860s and the 1920s; and secondly to their ability to mobilise large amounts of capital once they had set up holding companies, in the mid 1890s, to finance their long-term projects. These two factors should still have been operative in the interwar period, particularly since research and investment had increased in cost, and called for amortisation through sales on an international scale. This readily applies to IG Farben's American operations, as described by Verena Schröter: the concern had kept diversifying into new markets (dyestuffs accounted for no more than 45% of its exports in 1926, as against 80% in 1913); and so it was able to enter 'several crucial fields', set up new financial holdings, move manufacturing to the USA in 1929–34, when tariff and devaluation raised barriers to entry, and regain a strong position in the American industry. Actually, the same process would fit in even better with the Swedish experience, as Ragnhild Lundström has convincingly demonstrated: if MNEs became a major factor in Sweden's industrialisation, from the 1890s, this is to be accounted for by the country's strong engineering tradition and by the active support of the local bankers, who managed to attract capital, domestic and foreign, by setting up holding companies in 1901–18 and who kept the industry going in the consolidation period that followed.

One would be tempted to explain on the same dual basis (a market and finance) the early-twentieth-century experience of direct investment that developed through 'long-term supply contracts, franchises, licenses, agents', and with the short-term credit facilities made available to trade by the foreign branch networks of the British banking system; they are described here by S. Nicholas and A. Rowley. But the two papers that deal with banking in the Danubian basin and the Middle East are good reminders that, besides their location in low technical sectors, these loose institutions were up against local nationalist pressures, organisational progress (the internalisation of markets), and American competition. This section of world trade, under proto-MNEs, was doomed to failure, even if its disappearance since the 1930s has attracted less attention than other developments.

3. *Appraisals* In spite of the quicker diffusion of new technologies and beneficial effects that can be ascribed to MNEs, as on trade and domestic

growth, their operations became an object of public concern in the early 1970s, to such an extent that a code of conduct, along the lines recalled in Horst Heininger's paper, was drafted at the UN; their control of industry in small host countries, the artificial pricing that intra-trade made possible, and the danger they represented for local culture and environment were among the issues which came up for discussion and which are still relevant in a long-term perspective. Along the same lines, three sources of hostility were highlighted in the conference: firstly, wage discrimination (against women employees) and a lack of concern for the long-term position of the labour-force, when it was uprooted and paid by foreign companies; this explains some of the workers' unrest, despite a real improvement in their living conditions, as in the oil fields of Mexico and the sugar plantations of colonial Zimbabwe; secondly, the feeling that excessive (and hidden) profits were accumulated in depression periods and transferred abroad, with damaging effects on government receipts and on the balance of external payments, as in Poland during the 1930s; and thirdly, the need to protect scarce natural resources, when they were unduly depleted by foreign individuals or companies, as in Finland in the late nineteenth century.

These are clearly evils that have always been associated in the past with the activities of new manufacturing firms, domestic and foreign, because their operations acted upon life and work conditions. Most textbooks in economic history have chapters dealing with public alarm, Luddism and other forms of resistance to technological change. But they also teach that change applies to industrial firms, that MNEs tend to concentrate in industrial countries, that they are less resource-based and more market oriented, and, to revert to Finland again, that they settled in that country (after the Second World War) to compete for the Finnish market, with imported raw materials, foreign capital and new technical expertise. Hostility, therefore, is still a historical fact. However, when considering the wide variety of experience, origin, structure, performance they display, and the gap that exists between their subservience to market changes and, by contrast, 'the multi-national operations of state-bureaucracies in territories opened up by conquest', as recalled in Richard Overy's paper on the Reichswerke during the Second World War, one cannot help feeling that people often look at modern enterprise not realistically, in a true historical perspective, but with the memory of past political oppression.

Part I

Growth of multinational enterprise

1   The multinational: a critique of a concept

D. K. FIELDHOUSE

Collective terms are a useful shorthand if they encapsulate an idea or thing with some degree of accuracy; but they are dangerous if they are thought to be self-definitive or explanatory. The shortest possible definition of a multinational corporation (MNC) is a business enterprise which 'owns and controls income-generating assets in more than one country'.[1] This essay investigates how it was that the many different types of business, whose only common feature was that they conformed to that definition, came to be grouped together under a single generic name (together with its later aliases, transnational enterprise, international firm, etc.); and whether the use of such a collective concept has caused confusion rather than clarity of thought. Four basic questions will be considered. First, on the assumption that the genesis of a term of art may throw light on its significance, why, by whom and when was the term 'multinational corporation' first used? Second, if the name came into existence long after the enterprises themselves, how was the reality seen and analysed previously? Third, if the term originally attempted merely to indicate a corporation operating across national boundaries, how and why did it acquire the complex bundle of connotations with which it has long been burdened? Finally, is the concept of the MNC a useful analytical tool for the historian; and, if not, how should he study the realities to which it refers?

The birth of the multinational

Perhaps the most surprising feature of the MNC is that it achieved a collective name and therefore potentially a defined identity so late in time. The date of birth was 1960 and the father David E. Lilienthal, once head of the Tennessee Valley Authority, then of the Atomic Energy Authority and, from 1955, chief executive of the Development and Resources Corporation of New York, set up with Lazards to provide loans to less developed countries (LDCs). In April 1960 he gave a paper to the Carnegie Institute of Technology on 'Management and corporations, 1985', which was published later that year as *The multinational corporation*. Talking of the special managerial problems of American corporations with 'industrial or commercial operations abroad which directly involve managerial responsibility', he provided the following definition: 'Such corporations – which have their home in one country but which operate and live under the laws and customs of other countries as well – I would like to define here as multinational corporations.'[2] He was proud of this term. In his journal for 20 April 1960 he commented that he and his assistant, David Schwartz, had been working on the paper for months; and on 23 January 1962 he recorded his pleasure that the *Wall Street journal*'s leading article on the European Common Market had used the word 'multinational'. Lilienthal continued:

So far as I know, my talk at the Carnegie Tech. in 1960 ...was the first time the word had been used; I rather think I coined it, to mean that form of internationalization that is more than the conventional meaning of international. In any case, it is good to see that wholesome and meaningful term get into Newspaper use.[3]

Lilienthal can probably be left with the credit for coining the term: the New York journal *Business week* for 25 April 1963 accepted his authorship and followed his argument in suggesting that the MNC had three definitive features. First,

It has a manufacturing base or some other form of direct investment that gives it roots in at least one foreign country. It has a genuinely global perspective; its management makes fundamental decisions on marketing, production, and research in terms of the alternatives that are available to it anywhere in the world.[4]

Second, top management now took full responsibility for all overseas operations, so that 'the old "international division", as a separate and self-contained unit into which all off-shore operations are bundled, tends to wither away'. Third, and above all, the MNC had to be seen as a whole, an integrated operation. 'The goal...is the greatest good of the whole unity, even if the interests of a single part of the unity must suffer.'[5]

As a concept, then, the multinational was born in 1960 and in circulation a couple of years later, though it was not until later in that decade that it became widely known and used.[6] It is significant that in this original form it related very specifically to the characteristic US corporation of the later 1950s: that is, its overseas activities were an extension of its domestic functions and its decision-making centre remained at home. It was not therefore conceived as a firm whose home base was merely the source of financial investment in one or more overseas enterprises, still less as one engaged in portfolio investment. If one is a terminological purist, the later extension of the concept to include virtually any form of overseas investment still under home control involved serious dilution. It is important also that at the start the concept implied that the MNC was beneficent, since it very soon lost this innocence and became mainly a term of abuse. But before examining these semantic changes an important question must be asked. How far had the existence and implications of an integrated international firm of this type been grasped before 1960? If there was then no accepted name for such a firm, how was its underlying reality treated? Two established intellectual traditions seem likely to provide evidence: analysis of the causes and effects of foreign direct investment (FDI); and studies of the business corporation.

1 *Foreign direct investment*

In its simplest form an MNC is merely a form or agent of FDI; and one would therefore have expected that the very considerable literature on foreign investment would have reflected interest in its special features long before 1960. The surprising thing is that, on the whole, it did not. Despite a long tradition of interest in the causes and effects of foreign investment within the capital-exporting countries, attention was mostly concentrated on the macro-economic aspects of the problem, rather than on the particular agents of capital export.[7] Thus it seems that analysis of the special features of investment by an MNC arose in capital-receiving rather than capital-exporting countries; and it is possible that the first considered analysis of its significance for a host economy was made as late as the 1950s and in Australia.

Australia had, of course, received large amounts of FDI long before the 1950s; yet there is no evidence of Australian concern either at the near-monopolistic position of some British firms (such as Levers in detergents)[8] or at the implicit balance of payments problem, before the mid 1950s; and then it was the sudden expansion of General Motors-Holden (GM/H) as the only locally based company making, as distinct from assembling, cars, coupled with a meteoric rise of its transferred profits, that stimulated economists in Australia to examine some of the fundamental issues involved.

The facts, briefly, are as follows.[9] GM had established a wholly owned subsidiary in Australia in 1931, buying out Holden Motor Body Builders. From 1948 GM/H began the complete manufacture of an 'all-Australian' car; and since it was specially designed for Australian conditions and benefited from tariffs on imported cars or parts, it was very popular and sold at a large profit. In 1953 GM/H made an accounting profit of £A9.8m., of which £A4.5m. was transferred to America as a dividend. This sum represented 8% of total Australian dollar earnings in 1954/5 (when the transfer was made), 560% of the ordinary capital (the original dollar investment), and 39% of the shareholders' funds, excluding locally sold preference shares. Such large profits and so great a drain on dollar earnings at a time of reduced commodity export prices brought such matters to the attention of the Australian public for the first time. E. V. Evatt, leader of the opposition Labour Party, criticized this American 'Colossus'. H. W. Arndt, Professor of Economics at the then Canberra University College, stated in a broadcast that the Holden case 'may induce some caution in giving indiscriminate encouragement' to FDI. Australia might be wise to 'concentrate less on attracting American capital and more on hiring American technical and managerial know-how'.[10]

After that first reaction Arndt (and also Edith Penrose) published articles which may well provide the first serious analysis of the special economic consequences of the activities of MNCs for host countries. Arndt distinguished this 'New Model' investment by a foreign-owned firm from portfolio and other types of investment common in Australia, primarily on the ground that it could not be controlled by Australians and that its exportable profits, unlike fixed-interest liabilities, were theoretically unlimited. His analysis of its potential effects on the host country previewed many of the concepts and criteria that became common in the next decade, distinguishing direct from indirect effects and balancing costs against benefits. In the last resort, however, his test of the balance of advantage was the effect on the balance of payments. Despite possible additional capital inflow after the initial investment, 'the growth in the borrowing country's dividend commitment on overseas direct investment, viewed on its own, is equivalent to the certain prospect of a long-term decline in its terms of trade'.[11] Thus, if a projection was made on the basis of 1948/9–1954/5, the profits on American direct investment might, during the next ten years, rise from 0.71% to 5% of Australia's national income, and to 25% of her export earnings. His conclusion was that the Australian government should reduce these risks by encouraging export-oriented FDI, insist on a minimum share of the equity's being locally owned, and make greater use of technology imported by Australian firms on licence, borrowing the capital at fixed interest.

Two points stand out from this analysis. First, while Arndt recognized that FDI might involve a number of 'indirect costs', particularly those relating to sovereignty and autonomy, he did not emphasize these as later critics of the MNC were to do. Second, and more important, he showed no interest in the nature of the foreign investing firm: what its motives were, how it operated, whether it represented a new economic phenomenon. Whatever the reasons for the investment, from the host country's point of view, all that really mattered was the balance of payments effect of acting host to companies owned abroad whose success would involve an open-ended Australian commitment to find sufficient foreign exchange to fund transfers. Much the same approach was adopted by the British economist (Sir) Donald MacDougall, who became interested in the GM/H case when on a visit to Australia. In an article published in 1960 he did not discuss the special character of this enterprise, talking rather of 'foreign firms' merely as distinct from Australian, and allocating them no special characteristics apart from possession of technology and know-how not otherwise available in Australia, except on licence.[12] Other contemporary writers on the subject adopted a similar approach.[13] This suggests the conclusion that, right or wrong, analysis of the economic significance of FDI did not find it necessary to conceptualize the foreign agent of investment as a special sort of economic 'beast', to use Stephen Hymer's later term;[14] that macro-economics did not need to invent the multinational to measure its economic effects on host countries. It is mainly for this reason that the concept of the multinational had to grow from micro-economic studies of the growth of the firm.

2 *The growth of the firm and the multinational corporation*

The genesis of contemporary conceptions of the MNC lies in the belief that this modern, large-scale capitalist enterprise is a unique phenomenon, different in kind from earlier business organizations such as the partnership and the small 'Marshallian' firm (to use A. D. Chandler's term),[15] and that, as a result, modern FDI cannot be understood merely in terms of international capital movements and the balance of payments. Growth is the primary characteristic of the large modern business; and in the process of indefinite growth some firms find it necessary to expand beyond their national bases, changing their character in the process. But who first perceived that the MNC was born from the inexorable growth of the firm, that overseas expansion had become a necessary part of corporate strategy? Such questions can never be answered with certainty. Some would give the credit to F. A. Southard's *American industry in Europe* (Boston, 1931); but an equally strong claim can be made for Alfred Plummer, Vice-Principal of Ruskin College, Oxford, who published his *International combines in modern history* in 1934.

Plummer distinguished two special types of combine that were more integrated than a cartel; the 'international concern' and 'international trusts'. Following R. W. Liefmann,[16] he defined an international concern as 'combined businesses under unified financial control, but falling short of complete fusion', that is, the component parts, which might be in different countries, remained 'juridically independent of one another'.[17] One stage beyond the concern lay the international trust: 'when to centralised and unified control there is added the complete merger and ownership of the constituent undertakings, in two or more countries, we have an international trust'.[18] Plummer then set out to explain why concerns and trusts had developed as they had, and this is where he can be seen as the pioneer of modern conceptions of the MNC:

International concerns and trusts developed first from the desire to have branches – factories, warehouses, offices – in two or more countries; a line of advance which is no doubt attributable partly to the pressure of heavy import duties, and partly to the desire to have a closely controlled unit 'on the spot', making a special study of the local market requirements and peculiarities.[19]

But there was a second method and motive for the creation of international trusts:

While one international trust may bring together under unified control a number of *existing* undertakings, another may begin as a single national undertaking and spread *itself* and its activities out into other countries. This type of international business does not have to achieve unified control for control is unified from the beginning, but it has to create its foreign undertakings before it can control them.[20]

Either way, there were three main conditions or reasons for the establishment of international combines and trusts: the need to keep plants fully employed; desire to escape from severe competition, price-cutting and so on; and, most interesting, 'the desire to substitute certainty for the uncertainties of business as previously conducted'.[21]

Here, in embryo, is the concept of 'internalization'. The main reason why Plummer does not get credit for this conceptual leap is that, having got so far, he seems to have lost interest in the institutional aspects of the growth of the international firm, saying nothing more about it in this book or, so far as I know, elsewhere. Where he stopped, the evolution of a special theory of international companies also stood still until the mid 1950s, and those who then picked up the problem seem not to have been aware of his pioneering efforts, though Hymer knew and referred to Southard. But again, the roots of a new theory lay in studies of the internal dynamics of the firm; and, without any suggestion that they held a monopoly of the subject, four names are commonly associated with the evolution of the concept of internalization between 1954 and 1960: Edith Penrose, Maurice Byé, J. H. Dunning and Stephen Hymer.

In 1955 Penrose published an article, 'Limits to the size and growth of firms',[22] which formed the basis of her book, *The theory of the growth of the firm* (Oxford, 1959), and in which she suggested that the key to expansion in a large corporation lay in the nature of its management, particularly on the planning side. The supply of managers limited the amount of expansion that could be undertaken, but also provided an incentive to use them for further growth. The following year, in commenting on the GM/H case, she developed a parallel argument.[23] The continued growth of foreign firms in host countries was better seen in terms of factors governing the growth of firms than in relation to foreign investments. Since there was no reason why a firm should not expand indefinitely, a foreign subsidiary could best be seen initially as much the same as a branch of the firm in its home country. But once established overseas, the subsidiary was likely to develop a life and logic of its own, following the normal laws governing growth of firms: 'growth will continue in response to the development of its own internal resources and the opportunities presented in its new environment'.[24]

While Penrose was developing this concept of the international firm as a self-creating octopus, the French economist Maurice Byé was evolving what can now be seen as the germ of the idea that the key feature of such firms was their ability to transcend the limitations inherent in geographical boundaries and also conventional economic constraints. He was probably also the first to emphasize the potentially sinister features of such large firms. In a paper published in 1957 as 'L'Autofinancement de la Grande Unité Interritoriale et les dimensions temporelles de sa place',[25] his central argument was that such big firms were able to stand outside the accepted patterns of business activity and to act in ways not predicated by normal economic theory. He defined his 'large unit' as 'an organized set of resources depending on a single decision centre capable of autonomous activities in the market'.[26] Its special feature was ability to control many factors internally which would be exogenous to smaller firms; for example, capital formation and planning rates of output. On evidence drawn mainly from the big American petroleum companies, he based a critique of the general effects of large international companies on host countries. Two were predominant. First, in relation to their balance of payments, the MNC largely determined the rate of exports and the use of export earnings. It did not compensate for this by importing significant amounts of capital, since most expansion was financed out of local earnings. All investment decisions of this kind were autonomous to the MNC: 'it operates like a world distribution centre of the capital funds for its subsidiaries'.[27] Second, the MNC generated a 'dual economy'. It did not transfer to the domestic sector of the host economy significant proportions of its savings, or buy much of its inputs locally.

Byé's arguments were largely speculative because based on very limited data and they related almost exclusively to the extraction of commodities by MNCs in LDCs. The first really informed study of American overseas investment in manufacturing in a developed country was J. H. Dunning's book on American investment in Britain, published in 1958.[28] His central argument, based on extensive empirical research, which led eventually to his concept of 'location-specific' motives for FDI,[29] was that American expansion into Britain must be seen in terms of the growth of firms, not the export of capital. There had, indeed, been very little transfer of new capital from America to Britain: since most large US corporations already had agencies or subsidiaries in Britain, they were able to finance acquisitions and expansion largely from retained profits, local partners, local borrowing or government grants.[30] Thus their aim was to expand their total market in a country which offered many special advantages – economies of scale through using existing American technology, brands, management etc., internal access to a highly protected market, the ability to export their products to America and elsewhere. This added up to profit maximization: in 1955 US companies in Britain had an average rate of return of 19.5%, as compared with 15% on all overseas investment and 10% at home.[31]

It is clear, then, that by 1960, when Lilienthal gave his paper in Pittsburgh, the concept of the MNC as the product of the growth of the firm was well advanced. This was also the year in which Stephen Hymer completed his Ph.D. dissertation, 'The international operations of national firms'.[32] He may therefore be regarded primarily as the man who pulled together a number of existing strands and gave them at least the appearance of logical coherence. His main contribution was to define the specific motives which induced firms to undertake direct rather than portfolio investment overseas. Differential interest rates alone could not explain this and FDI seemed characteristic of some types of American firms, but not others. His explanation was related to an idea floated by R. H. Coase in 1937, that under certain circumstances it was desirable for a firm to create and use an internal market rather than face the high transaction costs of an external market, made worse by government intervention in the form of trade controls, taxes etc.[33] Coase had restricted his argument to domestic markets, but Hymer extended it to overseas investment. The basic advantage of FDI was that it enabled the firm to retain control of its capital, with two alternative objects: product control, which gave safety as well as a satisfactory return; and 'to remove competition between that foreign enterprise and enterprises in other countries' or 'to appropriate fully the return of certain skills and abilities'. Thus the motive for FDI must be higher profit from a monopolistic rent, and hence the study of FDI ' is part of the theory of the firm... It is a problem of determining the extent of vertical and horizontal integration of firms. The tools used to analyse international operations are the same, essentially, as those used to analyse the firm in its operations.'[34]

By about 1960, then, there was a rapidly growing appreciation that FDI in its contemporary form posed significant problems. Yet it is clear that there was no necessary connection between the two main lines of investigation. Arndt and others showed that one could analyse the economic consequences of FDI for the host country without studying the motives of the investing enterprise, while to the growth of firms specialists these macro-economic aspects were secondary or merely inferred. A first conclusion might therefore be that effective study of FDI did not require a unifying concept such as the MNC provided. A second is that these early studies of the MNC as a logical consequence of corporate evolution contained the seed of future misunderstanding. Extrapolating from the assumed internal logic of corporate growth to overseas investment, these writers (apart from Dunning) tended to assume that the MNC sprang from universal causes; and in this, as will be seen, many of those who publicized or developed the concept during the next two decades followed them. The result was a double distortion. First, rationalization from the logic of recent American corporate behaviour ignored fundamental diversity in different types of enterprise, both from the USA and other investing countries and at various times. Second, on the assumption of uniformity, those who disliked certain features of the MNC as defined by writers such as Byé developed a hostile critique which tarred all MNCs with the same black brush. The consequences become clear if we survey the main trends in the literature since 1960.

The monstrous regiment of the multinational

Endowed with a collective name and with an apparently universal rationale, the MNC was now ready for intellectual take-off. The main food of literature did not start until the later 1960s, and thereafter we can distinguish four central responses: those of popular alarmists, theorists hostile to international capitalism, applied economists and specialists in the theory of the firm. In surveying these in turn one central theme will emerge: that, while most early writers tended to accept the alleged universality of the MNC as a form of capitalism, many also asserting that its effects were harmful to both home and host countries, by the later 1970s both assumptions were in serious doubt. As a result, the utility of the MNC as an organizing concept was called into question, leaving the field open to the empirical historian to test its validity.

1 *Popular alarmists and publicists*

Inevitably an exciting new concept which could arouse nationalist emotions stimulated a flood of general accounts of the MNC, which ranged from journalism to semi-scholarly writing for non-academic audiences. It is conventional wisdom that the first influential debunker of the MNC was the French journalist, J.-J. Servan Schreiber, who published *Le Défi Américain* in Paris in 1967: it appeared in English as *The American challenge* in 1969. His argument was simplistic. Pointing to the rapid growth of US corporate investment in Europe, which he wrongly ascribed to the creation of the EEC in 1958, he held that this gave the Americans dangerous dominance in the critical and expanding field of high technology. The book got more publicity than it deserved, as Raymond Vernon later remarked;[35] but it acted as a catalyst, stimulating a rash of similarly alarmist accounts, whose common theme tended to be that the MNC was a challenge to national sovereignty. Among the best known and generally more respectable were Louis Turner's *Invisible empires* (1970), K. Levitt's *Silent surrender: the multinationals and Canada* (1970), C. Tugendhaft's *The multinational* (1971) and R. J. Barnet and R. E. Müller's *Global reach* (1974). *Global reach* is a useful example because it was written when ideologues and economists had established many of the central debating issues, and also because it demonstrates the common relationship between an a priori position and treatment of the alleged main features of the MNC.

The standpoint of the authors of *Global reach* was that of many American liberals who were concerned with American 'imperialism' during the Vietnam war, believed that this reflected the interests of the power of capitalism and the 'military-industrial complex' to dictate public policy, and wanted to show that these things were related both to unemployment in America and to poverty in the Third World. Their central message, reflecting a conventional populist attitude, and inverting the position adopted by Lilienthal, was that big was probably bad. The MNCs and their 'world managers' aimed to create a 'Global Shopping Center', which involved the establishment of uniform world-wide tastes. These managers had no national loyalties, were prepared to work with any sort of regime and attempted to camouflage their overseas activities by appearing to be 'good citizens' wherever they operated. The consequences were equally serious for the host LDCs and USA. Summarizing the growing stock of accusations then being made by economists, Marxists and other critics (some of which are outlined below), they concluded that MNCs were the main cause of or contributor to Third World poverty. Paradoxically, despite the profits they funnelled back, they were equally bad for America, causing 'the obsolesence of American labor', regional under-development, increasing class stratification and growing dependence on the export of primary products rather than advanced manufactures. Thus it was in America's interests as much as those of the Third World that the MNCs should be tamed.

2   *The ideologues: Marxists and dependency theorists*

The first specific Marxist critique of the MNC appears to have been P. Baran and P. Sweezy's *Monopoly capitalism* (New York, 1966), which was itself partly a reaction to the 1963 *Business week* article quoted above. The lack of any previous Marxist analysis seems likely to be explicable in terms of commitment to the Leninist view of imperialism as characterized by undiff-erentiated export of capital and to excessive concern for the relations between capitalism and the bourgeois state. These preoccupations continued to influence the writings of many Marxists during the following decade: for example R. Murray, Bill Warren, F. Mandel and H. Magdoff.[36] In fact, it was again Stephen Hymer, now a Marxist, who provided the first specifically Marxist critique of the MNC based on developments in the theory of the firm. In a series of essays published between 1970 and his death in 1974 he established a hostile critique which was to have very wide influence.[37] Briefly, he now argued that the MNC, in pursuit of monopoly profit and by internalizing its world-wide activities, created a hierarchical world order and an international division of labour. The result was a global realization of Marx's diagram of reproduction in which the MNCs owned most of the world's capital, took the surplus value from those countries in which they operated to their home base, and reduced the rest of the world to the position of an exploited proletariat. Hence, despite the undeniable ability of the

MNC to increase the sum of the world's wealth by its relative efficiency, it was socially dangerous and must be controlled.

By the 1980s, however, there was a quite different Marxist attitude to the MNC. From a fundamentalist position based on Marx rather than Lenin, Bill Warren, in his posthumously published *Imperialism: pioneer of capitalism* (London, 1980) and Arghiri Emmanuel's *Appropriate or underdeveloped technology* (London, 1982) both criticized the conventional assumption that the MNC, as the agent of capitalism, was bound to cause immiseration in the Third World. Both, from different standpoints, held that MNCs were part of a historically essential process of establishing capitalism in LDCs. While admittedly producing class stratification, they also generated wealth; and ultimately true socialism and affluence could only come as the end product of this process. Third World governments should therefore aim to use but to harness and control MNCs, minimizing their potentially bad effects while making full use of their ability to introduce modern technology and efficient business management.

The influence of Hymer and other Marxist critics of the MNC on Latin American 'dependency' theorists, who had previously shown very little interest in this phenomenon in analysing the causes of poverty, was striking. Essentially the new concept of an international division of labour and a global hierarchy created by the MNCs provided them with at least a partial explanation of how what they called 'underdevelopment' had been created and was sustained. As early as 1972 O. Sunkel, writing in the American journal *Foreign affairs*, adopted Hymer's concept of an international hierarchy and argued that MNCs 'contribute significantly to shaping the nature of the economy, society and polity, a kind of "fifth column", as it were'.[38] From the later 1960s especially MNCs had moved from exporting commodities to controlling key sectors of the domestic economy. They tended to monopolize rather than diffuse their skills and technology. They blocked opportunities for indigenous enterprise. Their 'complete package' of capital, skills etc. was likely to be 'inappropriate' and to have weak linkages with the local economy. They had undesirable ability to influence consumption patterns. They could use monopoly power to extract excessive profits, much of them hidden and protected from local taxation by transfer pricing. Such accusations, many of which were drawn from the then evolving critique provided by development economists, were widely reproduced in dependency literature and were later synthesized by A. G. Frank in *Dependent accumulation and underdevelopment* (London, 1978).

But not all Latin Americans agreed that the MNC was all loss to host countries, or that there was a simple alternative. Celso Furtado, for instance, took a much less deterministic view. Posing the question 'would the Latin American countries have registered the high rates of growth characterising their manufacturing sectors in the post-war period if they had not been able to count on the effective cooperation of international groups, primarily North American, with considerable industrial experience and easy access to the sources of financing?', he suggested that the answer must be 'no'.[39] This points to an important division that had developed not only within the ranks of Latin American theorists, but more generally among left-wing critics of the MNC by the later 1970s. Much the same trend can be seen among most serious students of the MNC, particularly development economists.

3 Development economics and the 'nationalist' critique of the MNC

Largely because of the growth from the early 1950s of a brand of 'development economics' which concentrated on the assumed special 'structural' problems of LDCs, it was inevitable that specialists should attempt to build the MNC into their development models. It was around 1969 that the first serious studies of the role of the MNC in the Third World began to be published, with J. N. Behrman's *Some patterns in the rise of the multinational enterprise* (Chapel Hill, NC, 1969), C. P. Kindleberger's *American business abroad* (New Haven, 1969) and R. E. Rolfe's *The international corporation* (Paris, 1969); but only from 1971 that the debate really got going. It is not practicable to list even the main participants in this continuing and expanding debate: two useful surveys are N. Hood and S. Young, *The economics of multinational enterprise* (London, 1979) and R. E. Caves, *Multinational enterprise and economic analysis* (Cambridge, 1982). Instead it is proposed to use S. Lall and R. Streeten's sensitive survey of the intellectual argument in *Foreign investment, transnationals and developing countries* (London, 1977) as a guide to this type of study, particularly in relation to LDCs, since it provides both a catholic overview of the concepts which development economists were then using and a balanced critique from the 'nationalist' standpoint of host countries.

   Their starting point is that, in assessing the impact of MNCs on LDCs, both the normal profit and loss measurement of the corporate accountant and the neo-classical Paretian welfare paradigm are inappropriate. The weakness of what Lall elsewhere calls the 'Business School Approach'[40] lies in the unacceptability of the following assumptions: that FDI must increase the host country's growth; that patterns of growth characteristic of an open market economy are desirable; that international economic integration is good for all parties; and that the 'externalities' resulting from MNC activity, such as the dissemination of skills in management, marketing, finance and technology, are desirable, but that other externalities are economically unimportant. Equally inapplicable are conventional welfare assumptions: that individual preferences are beyond question; that there is a basic harmony of interests in a society; and that the state is neutral as between social groups, benevolently pursuing the 'national interest'. Thus these, as many other development economists, have argued that one must approach analysis of the impact of the MNC on developing countries with initial suspicion. Even if their activities raised the national income, 'it would not necessarily follow that economic welfare…is increased, unless a number of other conditions are also satisfied'.[41]

Not all development economists, even those who took welfare rather than commercial accounting or crude growth rates as their criterion, agreed with this approach, or with the underlying assumption that most LDC governments lacked the will or ability to assess the pros and cons of FDI. In particular, I. M. D. Little, a pioneer of welfare theory and the cost–benefit approach to LDC development, has provided a considered critique of the MNC in LDCs as part of his general study of the theory and practice of development economics since 1945.[42]

He makes two main points. First, any adverse effects MNCs have on modern post-colonial LDCs are likely to be the responsibility of the host government, since it is normally their incompetence, anxiety for prestigious industrialization or 'autonomy', and the ill-advised macro-economic policies they adopt as a consequence, that create conditions under which foreign firms can operate in ways one might regard as 'undesirable'. Second, there is in many cases very little difference between the way in which subsidiaries of MNCs and locally owned enterprises operate: the mere fact of an MNC being foreign is not in itself a reliable guide to its character or economic effects. It is not necessarily either beneficial or harmful: one must test particular enterprises and investment proposals, as Little did in his seminal study of the social costs and benefits of the Kulai Oil Palm Estate in Malaysia.[43]

Little's critique effectively deflates the more emotive arguments of hostile 'nationalist' critics of the MNC. It underlines, moreover, that the main trend in studies of the MNC since 1960 has been in the wrong direction. The MNC must not be assumed to be unique or dangerous, simply because its activities transcend national frontiers. Its effects can properly be assessed in terms applicable to any form of productive investment, as was done by economists before the concept was invented and taken up. Similar conclusions were by then being reached by those who approached the MNC from the standpoint of the growth of firms.

4 *Growth in the theory of the firm*

'As trade follows the flag, so does applied economics follow the newspapers.' So, in 1971, Richard Caves began an influential article, 'International corporations: the industrial economics of foreign investment'.[44] It is certainly true that once the concept of the MNC was established applied economists specializing in the theory of the firm gave it considerable attention. There were two roots from which new and more sophisticated theories to explain the existence and character of MNCs developed: first, Hymer's concept of a monopoly rent to the overseas investment of large firms; second, Vernon's 'Product Cycle Theory'. The first, based on the still unnamed concept of 'internalization', was given much of its present shape in 1969 by Kindleberger's *American business abroad.* He argued that big firms possessed five special assets: access to both patented and generally available technology; team-specific managerial skills; plant economies of scale; superior marketing skills; and generally popular brand names. In these things a firm had monopoly; and in exploiting its assets abroad it could either license others to use its patents etc. or use them itself. The former involved no risk but also produced lower profits both because of imperfections in the market and also because the firm could not then obtain a return for its other non-transferable assets. Other benefits of direct investment were ability to exploit differences in factor prices and tariff protection, using local knowledge and avoiding transport costs.

From this point the concept of internalization became more refined. In 1971 Caves suggested (in the article quoted above) as a variation of Kindleberger's formulation the ability of oligopolistic firms to differentiate either the same product across different regions or to differentiate a wide range of products in one region, or mix of the two. By the mid 1970s a group of economists at Reading University were playing a leading role in the further development of this approach. In 1976 P. J. Buckley and M. Casson first applied the term 'internalization' to the concept and this was further developed by Casson in 1979.[45] In the mean time Dunning had produced what he originally called 'an eclectic theory' of international production, integrating internalization theory (which concentrated on the firm's 'owner-specific' advantages) with other factors, such as 'location-specific' factors, which influenced FDI.[46] Internalization theory has since been further refined and it seems likely that this process will continue indefinitely.[47]

Although internalization theory seems to have become predominant, account must also briefly be taken of Vernon's 'Product Cycle Theory'. As first publicized in 1966,[48] and based primarily on the evidence of recent US investment overseas, the theory defined three stages in the cycle which might generate FDI. During the 'new product' stage a firm in a developed country evolved new products and new technology at home for the home market: overseas demand would be satisfied by exports. The second 'maturing product' stage started when the 'differentiation' that had given the new product much of its initial value began to dissipate and the innovating firm began to look for larger sales and lower production costs. This made it consider a shift in the location of production, particularly to those overseas markets served by exports, with tariffs, the threat of rival local producers, transport costs and the need for special adaptation of the production to local needs acting as additional stimulants. At this point the firm became an MNC, operating in relatively affluent countries. In the final stage, when the product had lost almost all its differentiation, the company might either give up the attempt to control or share all markets, or use some part of its assets in establishing factories in Third World countries. At that point the initial product cycle would end, leaving the MNC as a relic of an earlier phase of the firm's needs.

Vernon's theory generated much interest and a considerable literature.[49] But, although many of its predictive assumptions were sound, it was seen from the start that its applicability was largely restricted to the American industrial experience after 1945. By the later 1970s it was losing its relevance even for the more advanced industries of the USA; and Vernon recognized this in his 1979 article in which, as Caves put it, 'The product cycle…was laid to rest by its progenitor.'[50] Vernon claimed some continuing virtues for his original hypothesis;[51] but in retrospect it now seems that the product cycle was a side-stream in which the concept of a 'differentiated' product merely replaced that of a monopoly rent.

Prediction is rash; but it would seem that by 1985 application of the theory of the firm to the MNC had reached a plateau. Highly sophisticated and endowed with a glossary of specific terms, it had become a rarified and somewhat esoteric approach to the MNC. Although theorists still had room to manoeuvre, to some it seemed that the debate would become increasingly arid unless fuelled by new empirical evidence. As one economic historian, reviewing a recent collection of essays which centred on the theory of internalization, has commented, while much of the best work on the theory of the firm had been based on empirical evidence,

such data do not exist in the case of multinationals… It is not true that the 'documentation of the growth of international business is already well established'. Remarkably little is known, for example, about the history of non-American multinationals… Only archivally-based studies of multinationals can reveal the full complexity of business life, and present a real 'test' for economists' abstraction.[52]

Even so cursory a survey of how the concept of the MNC evolved after 1960 supports the main point made above. Assumed to be both a recent and uniform phenomenon, the MNC was taken up by a variety of interest groups and made to fit their patterns of thought or objectives. Particularly by popularizers, radicals and some development economists, it was made to carry a huge burden of guilt as proxy for hitherto inexplicable weaknesses in the economic and social development of the Third World and as the expression of predatory modern capitalism. But by the later 1970s a reaction had set in: the earlier certainties were under question. This, therefore, is the point at which to turn from the theorists to the historians and to consider whether historical research so far suggests that the concept of the MNC as a discrete and uniform phenomenon is consistent with known facts.

The multinational and the economic historian

Historians have studied MNCs at three main levels: the general or statistical, looking at very broad trends over time and on a world scale; an intermediate level, involving more or less specialized research into the activities of MNCs based on particular countries or operating in certain host countries or regions or, alternatively, on different types of MNC differentiated by the nature of their operations; and, finally, at the level of individual corporations or their subsidiaries. Without specific reference let us summarize some of the general conclusions that have emerged from work done since about 1960.

1 *The chronology of the MNC*

One obvious point is that the assumption that the MNC was essentially a post-war phenomenon pioneered by a hegemonic USA is quite wrong. Even by rigorous criteria, manufacturing FDI can be dated back to at least 1867, other forms earlier still; and until the 1940s the majority of FDI came from Europe, not the USA. By 1914, at 1972 prices, known accumulated FDI has been calculated at \$72.5 b.: it was only \$91.8 b. in 1960. Only thereafter was there a major increase, with a world total of \$257.4 b. in 1978.[53]

2 *The unity of the concept*

Research has shown that the MNC is neither homogeneous in function nor consistent in character over time. It has taken at least four main forms: public utilities; extraction or production of commodities; manufacturing for consumption in a host country; and manufacturing overseas for the world market. Although all these forms have existed since the mid nineteenth century, their relative importance has changed drastically with the world economy. The proportions differ for each capital-exporting country; but Mira Wilkins, in her invaluable surveys of US investments, shows a very marked shift between 1914 and the 1970s, broadly from utilities and commodities to manufacturing and petroleum.[54] There are no directly comparable figures for Britain, but Dunning's estimate for 1971 suggests similar trends.[55]

All this demonstrates that the conventional image of the MNC as a primary-producing or plantation-owning enterprise, largely insulated from a host economy and able to dictate to governments, a challenge to their sovereignty, has long ceased to be realistic. Even the character of petroleum investment has changed from extraction, involving large territorial concessions and near autonomy, to refining and distribution, which do not. The very model of a modern MNC is a factory; and this means a fundamental change in the relations of foreign capital with host governments. What may have been true of foreign-owned plantations or mining concessions before, say,

1950, when such enterprises might constitute baronial enclaves largely exempt from control by a sovereign state or colonial government, has little or no relevance to high-technology factories, which depend on the goodwill of the host government for every aspect of their activities.

3 *The sources of foreign investment*

In this also there have been major changes over time. In 1914 Europe was by far the largest collective overseas investor, with 76.9% of known FDI, and Britain the largest single investor with 45.5%. In 1960 the USA had 52%, and this was a major factor in the polemics of the next decade. But by 1978 the American share was down to 43.5%, that of Europe had risen to 41%, Japan was up to 6.9%, and even developing countries were entering the field, with 3.2% between them.[56]

4 *Motives for foreign direct investment*

Perhaps most important for the argument of this essay, historical research has shown that the tidy logic of growth of firms theory, the main intellectual foundation for the concept of the MNC, simply does not fit the unruly variety of corporate motivation. It is critical that most early theorizing was based on recent American experience, mainly in manufacturing and petroleum, and even this was not uniform. Still more variable were the historical reasons for US and European investment in overseas mining, plantations and utilities. In none of these last did FDI commonly or necessarily flow from the growth patterns of metropolitan firms. In many of them capitalists established new corporate enterprises without a previous home base, specifically to produce a commodity which could only be obtained elsewhere, or to exploit an evident overseas need for public services, such as railways or telecommunications in Latin America. Motives for FDI were therefore infinitely more complex than any unitary theory of the MNC could possibly comprehend, and had no necessary connection with the internalization concept. If one were to attempt a very crude classification based on empirical evidence, a fundamental distinction would be drawn between FDI made in response to a variety of overseas obstacles to export of goods (Dunning's 'location-specific' factors), of which tariffs and import controls would be pre-eminent; and FDI undertaken as a necessary means of extracting foreign commodities or providing services. Once such fundamental contrasts are perceived, the spurious unity of the concept of the MNC disintegrates, leaving only the single and non-explanatory common fact of transnational control of income-generating assets. It has been the main contribution of historians during the past two decades to demonstrate this fact.

A conclusion

A short answer to the question posed at the start – whether the concept of the MNC has proved a useful analytical tool – must therefore be that it has proved stimulating but in many respects misleading. Although initially related to a particular type of mostly American business enterprise, the suggestion that any capitalist enterprise operating across national frontiers was likely to have special characteristics opened the way for theorists and historians to see a much wider range of activities from this new perspective. In so far as this resulted in an immense incentive for the study of business enterprise, it was pure gain. To the extent that it led to the assumption that this one common feature was definitive of the nature of essentially diverse enterprises, it did much harm. But by the early 1980s the heady early days were over. It was now widely, if not universally, accepted that Multinational is merely shorthand for a wide range of capitalist enterprises which share only one common and non-definitive feature: that beyond there is fundamental diversity camouflaged under an umbrella term. Dunning has recently provided a suitable epitaph for the salad days of the concept: 'it now seems generally accepted that, because of the very different motives for FDI, a single predictive theory of international production is just not possible'.[57]

NOTES

1 J. H. Dunning (ed.), *Economic analysis and the multinational enterprise* (London, 1974), p. 13.
2 D. E. Lilienthal, *The multinational corporation* (New York, 1960), p. 1. Italics in original.
3 D. E. Lilienthal, *The harvest years 1959–63* (New York, 1971), p. 86.
4 *Business week*, 25 April, 1963, 63.
5 *Ibid.*, 35, 80.
6 The earliest example quoted in the 1976 Supplement to the *Oxford English dictionary* is from *The economist* for 17 October 1964.
7 Neither the classical nor the neo-classical economists examined the issue in detail; nor did under-consumptionists such as J. A. Hobson. R. Hilferding in *Finanzkapital* (Vienna, 1910) emphasized the special character and importance of FDI, but Lenin and other later Marxists treated capital export as an undifferentiated feature of capitalism in its 'highest stage'. It is, however, true that there was occasional reaction to foreign ownership of industries in Britain and elsewhere long before the 1950s. See for example M. Wilkins, *The emergence of multinational enterprise: American business abroad from the colonial era to 1914* (Cambridge, Mass., 1970), pp. 215–17.
8 See D. K. Fieldhouse, *Unilever overseas* (London, 1978), ch. 3.
9 Based on E. Penrose, 'Foreign investment and the growth of the firm', *Economic journal*, LXVI (1956), 64–99; H. W. Arndt, 'Overseas borrowing – the new model', *Economic record*, XXXIII (1957), 247–61.
10 Penrose, 'Foreign investment', 65.

11 Arndt, 'Overseas borrowing', 256.
12 D. MacDougall, 'The benefits and costs of private direct investment from abroad', *Economic record*, XXXVI (1960), 13–25.
13 E.g. J. H. Dunning, *American investment in British manufacturing industry* (London, 1958).
14 R. B. Cohen *et al.* (eds.), *The multinational corporation: a radical approach* (Cambridge, 1979), p. 140. As Hymer remarked, 'People call it many names: Direct Investment, International Business, the International Firm, the International Corporate Group, the Multinational Firm, the Multinational Family Group, La Grande Enterprise Plurinationale, La Grand Unité Plurinationale; or, as a French Foreign Minister calls them, "The U.S. Corporate Monsters".' He might later have added 'The Transnational Enterprise', which was taken up by the United Nations Centre to suggest that such corporations were not truly multinational in ownership and control. In this essay such verbal quibbles are ignored.
15 A. Chandler, *Strategy and structure* (Cambridge, Mass., 1962).
16 R. W. Liefmann, *International cartels, combines and trusts* (London, 1927); *Cartels, concerns and trusts* (London, 1932).
17 A. Plummer, *International combines in modern history* (London, 1934), p. 25. It must be remembered that 'concern' was a term widely used before and during the inter-war period to indicate a business built up from a number of firms which had not lost their legal or productive identity. Thus William Lever always refused to allow the individual companies he added to his 'concern' to lose their corporate identity: 'no scrambled eggs' was his repeated phrase.
18 Plummer, *International combines*, pp. 25–6.
19 *Ibid.*, p. 26.
20 *Ibid.*, p. 41.
21 *Ibid.*, p. 54.
22 E. Penrose, 'Limits to the size and growth of firms', *American economic history review*, XLV (2) (1955).
23 See Penrose, 'Foreign Investment'.
24 *Ibid.*, 70.
25 M. Byé, 'L'Autofinancement de la Grande Unité Interritoriale et les dimensions temporelles de sa place', *Revue d'economie politique*, June 1957; published in English as 'Self-financed multiterritorial units and their time horizon' in *International economic papers*, VIII (London, 1958). References are to the English edition.
26 Byé, 'Self-financed multiterritorial units', p. 148.
27 *Ibid.*, p. 171.
28 Dunning, *American investment in British manufacturing industry*.
29 J. H. Dunning, 'Trade, location of economic activity and the MNE: a search for an eclectic approach', in B. Ohlin *et al.* (eds.), *The international allocation of economic activity* (London, 1977).
30 Dunning, *American investment*, p. 287.
31 *Ibid.*, p. 310.
32 Published as S. Hymer, *The international operations of national firms: a study of direct foreign investment* (MIT Press, Cambridge, Mass., 1976). In his introduction C. P. Kindleberger, who had supervised the dissertation, explained that the delay in publication was the result of initial rejection by the MIT Press on the ground that it was too simple and straightforward. References are to the published version.
33 R. H. Coase, 'The nature of the firm', *Economica* (1937), 386–405.

34 Hymer, *The international operations*, p. 28.
35 R. Vernon, *Sovereignty at bay* (London, 1971), p. 196.
36 E.g. F. Mandel, 'International capitalism and "Supra-nationality"' in R. Miliband and J. Saville (eds.), *The socialist reporter* (1967) and his *Late capitalism* (London, 1975). There is a useful collection of essays by Murray, Warren and other Marxists in H. Radice (ed.), *International firms and modern imperialism* (Harmondsworth, 1975).
37 These were published by Cohen *et al.* (eds.) as *The multinational corporation*. References are to that book.
38 O. Sunkel, *Foreign affairs*, L (3), 519. Other influential publications by Latin American dependency theorists on the MNC include: T. dos Santos, 'The crisis of development theory and the problems of dependence in Latin America', in H. Bernstein (ed.), *Underdevelopment and development* (London, 1973); F. Cardoso, 'Dependent capitalist development in Latin America', *New left review*, LXXIV (1972); J. J. Villamil (ed.), *Transnational capitalism and national development* (Atlantic Highlands, 1979); C. V. Vaitsos, 'Bargaining and the distribution of returns in the purchase of technology by developing countries', *Institute of development studies bulletin*, III (1) (1970).
39 C. Furtado, *Economic development of Latin America* (1970; rev. edn., London, 1976), pp. 202, 299. References are to the revised edition.
40 S. Lall, *Developing countries and the international economy* (London, 1981), pp. 53–67.
41 S. Lall and R. Streeten, *Foreign investment, transnationals and developing countries* (London, 1977), p. 53.
42 I. M. D. Little, *Economic development: theory, policy and international relations* (New York, 1982), chs. 10 and 12.
43 I. M. Little and D. G. Tipping, *Social cost benefit analysis of the Kulai Oil Palm Estate* (Paris, 1972).
44 R. Caves, 'International corporations: the industrial economics of foreign investment', *Economica*, XXXVIII (1971), 1.
45 P. J. Buckley and M. Casson, *The future of the multinational enterprise* (London, 1976); M. Casson, *Alternatives to the multinational enterprise* (London, 1979).
46 J. H. Dunning, 'Trade, location of economic activity and the MNE: a search for an eclectic approach', in Ohlin *et al.* (eds.), *The international allocation of economic activity.* See also Dunning's *International production and the multinational enterprise* (London, 1981).
47 For recent refinements see A. M. Rugman, *Inside the multinationals: the economics of international markets* (London, 1981); A. M. Rugman (ed.), *New theories of the multinational enterprise* (London, 1982), particularly chs. 1–5; and M. Casson (ed.), *The growth of international business* (London, 1983), particularly chs. 1–4, which also point to lines of inquiry now under way or needed.
48 *Quarterly journal of economics*, LXXX (1966), 190–207. The theory was later refined and restated many times, notably in W. Gruber, D. Mehta and R. Vernon, 'The R. & D. factor in international trade and international investment of United States industries', *Journal of political economy*, LXXV (1967), 20–37. See also Vernon's more popular expositions in *Sovereignty at bay* (New York, 1971) and *Storm over the multinationals* (Cambridge, Mass., 1977).
49 See in particular Gruber, Mehta and Vernon, 'The R. & D. factor', which attempted an empirical test of the theory; and Vernon, 'The product cycle hypothesis in a new international environment', *Oxford bulletin of economics and statistics*, XLI (1979), 255–67. For a short survey of some of the main investigations

sparked off by the theory see R. E. Caves, 'Multinational enterprises and technology transfer', in Rugman (ed.), *New Theories*, pp. 263–6.

50 Rugman (ed.), *New Theories*, p. 263.

51 Vernon, 'The Product cycle hypothesis', 267.

52 G. Jones, reviewing M. Casson (ed.), *The growth of international business* in *Economic history review*, second series, XXXVI (4) (1983), 668–9.

53 Based on J. H. Dunning, 'Changes in the level and structure of international business', table 5.1, p. 84, in Casson (ed.), *The growth of international business*. Current prices have been adjusted by the implicit price deflator for US gross national product in Department of Commerce, *National income and product accounts of the U.S., 1929–76 and 1976–79*.

54 Wilkins, *The emergence of multinational enterprise*, table 5.2; and *The maturing of multinational enterprise* (Cambridge, Mass., 1974), tables 8.2 and 13.1.

55 Dunning, *International production*, table 6.5.

56 Dunning, 'Changes in the level and structure'. For an interesting comment on the rise of Third World MNCs, see S. Lall, *Developing countries as exporters of technology* (London, 1982). See also T. Agmon and C. P. Kindleberger (eds.), *Multinationals for small countries* (Cambridge, Mass., 1977); L. T. Wells, 'Foreign investment for the "Third World"; the experience of Chinese firms from Hong Kong', *Columbia journal of world business* (1978), 39–49.

57 Dunning, 'Changes in the level', pp. 103, 134–5.

2 Technological and organizational underpinnings of modern industrial multinational enterprise: the dynamics of competitive advantage*

ALFRED D. CHANDLER JR

Modern multinational enterprise has taken on several forms since the coming of the railroad, steamship, telegraph and cable transformed transportation and communication and made possible modern forms of production and distribution. The defining mark of a multinational is that it makes and manages direct investments (as differentiated from portfolio investments in stocks, bonds and other securities) in foreign countries. Of the different types of multinational enterprise the best known and certainly the most influential have been large managerial enterprises that operated both at home and abroad. At home they operated on a national scale. Abroad they usually had direct investments in several countries, often in both advanced and less developed regions. Such foreign facilities and personnel were administered from the central or corporate home office. They were legally and administratively integral parts of an extensive managerial hierarchy. Such multinationals are those that in recent times have been listed in *Fortune*'s 500 largest American and 300 non-American industrial companies and by such scholars as John H. Dunning and John M. Stopford. They dominate the commanding sectors of the global economy as they do their own domestic economies.

It is on such enterprises that this paper concentrates. Because the large majority of these global enterprises are industrial firms, the paper focuses on the beginnings and continued growth of such industrial companies. Explanations abound on why such industrial enterprises became multinational by making direct investments abroad.[1] They did so, some economists say, to exploit their capital advantages, or their technological strengths including their abilities to develop and differentiate products, or their specialized labor or managerial skills, or their market power. Other scholars argue further that such investments were made to reduce the cost of the many transactions involved in getting the materials to their manufacturing plants and their products to their customers including costs created by tariffs and other transborder transactions.

30

Rather than review the already massive literature by economists on the different theories of multinational enterprise, let me suggest a historical framework of analysis. The large modern industrial enterprise from its earliest years operated more than one unit or, to use the United States Census's term, one establishment; that is it was multiunit, operating a number of plants and offices. It quickly became multi-functional; that is it established units to carry out distribution, research, and sometimes transportation as well as production.[2] The multinational enterprise differs only from such modern industrial enterprises in that it established operating units abroad as well as at home.

The primary goal of these capitalist enterprises has been long-term profit. The surest way to attain and maintain this goal has been to reduce unit costs. Such reductions came from lowering costs *within* the operating units by improving technology and organization and from lowering costs of transactions *between* operating units by joining (internalizing) such units within a single enterprise. Such transactions costs included not only government levies on such transactions – taxes, tariffs and other transborder charges – but also those costs resulting from human fallibility which economists have described as opportunism and bounded rationality. The argument of this paper is that cost reductions achieved from lowering transactions costs between units were of a less magnitude than those obtained by improving technology and organization within units. Therefore an understanding of the competitive advantages resulting from technological and organizational developments is essential in any explanation of why the modern industrial enterprise initially made and continued to expand direct investment abroad, why some firms were more constrained than others in making this investment and why some were more successful than others in maintaining profit and market share through such investment.

Common characteristics of the modern industrial enterprise

Historically large, multiunit industrial enterprises have had three common characteristics no matter what was their country of origin.[3] They appeared quite suddenly in the 1880s and 1890s in western Europe and the United States, and a little later in Japan because Japan industrialized later. They appeared and continued to grow in industries with similar technologies of production. Finally they expanded their activities in much the same manner. In nearly all cases they became large, first, by taking over the functions of the wholesaler and other commercial intermediaries by investing in marketing, distribution and purchasing facilities and personnel; then by obtaining units producing raw and semifinished materials and, though much less often, by investing in research and development. At the same time many, though not all, became multinational by investing abroad, first in marketing and then

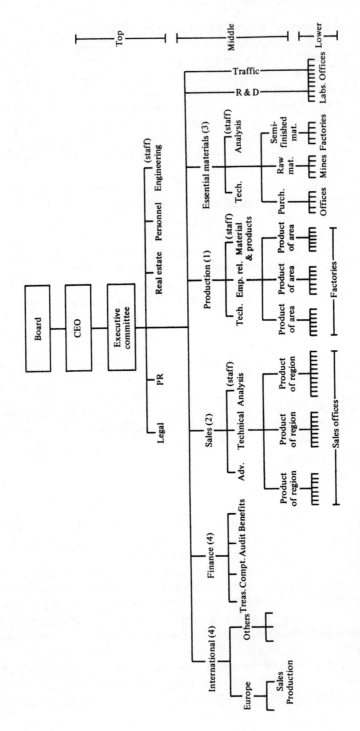

Figure 2.1 Multiunit, multi-functional enterprise

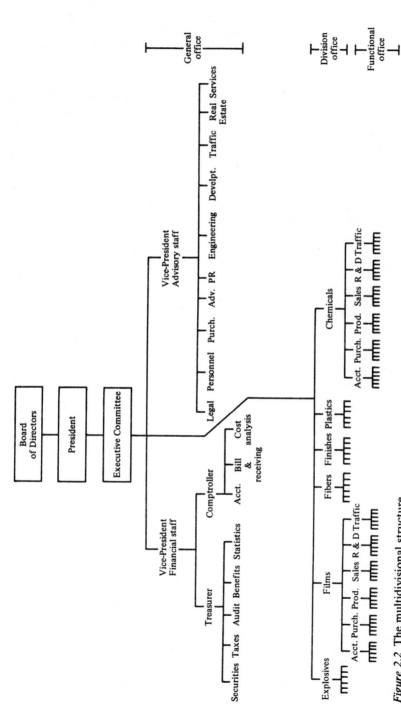

Figure 2.2 The multidivisional structure

Table 2.1. *The distribution of the largest manufacturing enterprises with more than 20,000 employees, by industry and nationality, 1973*

SIC		US	Outside the US	UK	Ger-many	Japan	France	Others	Grand Total
20	Food	22	17	13	0	1	1	2	39
21	Tobacco	3	4	3	1	0	0	0	7
22	Textiles	7	6	3	0	2	1	0	13
23	Apparel	6	0	0	0	0	0	0	6
24	Lumber	4	2	0	0	0	0	2	6
25	Furniture	0	0	0	0	0	0	0	0
26	Paper	7	3	3	0	0	0	0	10
27	Printing and publishing	0	0	0	0	0	0	0	0
28	Chemical	24	28	4	5	3	6	10	52
29	Petroleum	14	12	2	0	0	2	8	26
30	Rubber	5	5	1	1	1	1	1	10
31	Leather	2	0	0	0	0	0	0	2
32	Stone, clay and glass	7	8	3	0	0	3	2	15
33	Primary metal	13	35	2	9	5	4	15	48
34	Fabricated metal	8	6	5	1	0	0	0	14
35	Machinery	22	12	2	3	2	0	5	34
36	Electrical machinery	20	25	4	5	7	2	7.	45
37	Transportation equipment	22	23	3	3	7	4	6	45
38	Measuring instruments	4	1	0	0	0	0	0	5
39	Miscellaneous	2	0	0	0	0	0	0	2
	Diversified/ conglomerate	19	3	2	1	0	0	0	22
	Total	211	190	50	29	28	24	58	401

In 1970 the 100 largest industrials accounted for more than a third of net manufacturing output in the US and over 45% in the UK. In 1930 they accounted for about 25% of total net output in both countries.

Source: Fortune, May 1974 and August 1974

in production. In this way they created the organization that is shown in Figure 2.1. Finally they continued to expand their activities by investing in product lines related to their existing businesses, thus often creating the organization shown in Figure 2.2.

The similarities in location, as illustrated by Tables 2.1–2.5, are particularly striking. Table 2.1 indicates the location by country and by industries of all

Table 2.2. *The distribution of the 200 largest industrial enterprises in the United States, by industry**

SIC		1917	1930	1948	1973
20	Food	30	31	26	22
21	Tobacco	6	5	5	3
22	Textiles	5	3	6	3
23	Apparel	3	0	0	0
24	Lumber	3	4	1	4
25	Furniture	0	1	1	0
26	Paper	5	7	6	9
27	Printing and publishing	2	3	2	1
28	Chemical	20	18	24	27
29	Petroleum	22	26	24	22
30	Rubber	5	5	5	5
31	Leather	4	2	2	0
32	Stone, clay and glass	5	9	5	7
33	Primary metal	29	25	24	19
34	Fabricated metal	8	10	7	5
35	Machinery	20	22	24	17
36	Electrical machinery	5	5	8	13
37	Transportation equipment	26	21	26	19
38	Measuring instruments	1	2	3	4
39	Miscellaneous	1	1	1	1
	Diversified/conglomerate	0	0	0	19
	Total	200	200	200	200

* Ranked by assets

industrial corporations in the world which in 1973 employed more than 20,000 workers. (The industries are those defined as two-digit industrial groups by the US Census's Standard Industrial Classification [SIC].) In 1973, 263 (65%) of the 401 companies were clustered in food, chemicals, oil, machinery, and primary metals. Just under 30% were in three-digit subcategories, such as cigarettes in tobacco; tires in rubber; newsprint in paper; plate glass in stone, glass, and clay; cans and razor blades in fabricated metals; and mass produced cameras in instruments. The remaining 21 companies (5.5%) were in apparel, lumber, furniture, leather, publishing and printing, instruments and miscellaneous.

A second point that Table 2.1 illustrates is the predominance of American firms among the world's largest industrial corporations. Of the total of 401 companies employing more than 20,000 persons over a half (211 or 52.6%) were American. The United Kingdom followed with 50 (12.5%), Germany with 29 (7.2%), Japan with 28 and France with 24. Only in chemicals, metals,

Table 2.3. *The distribution of the 200 largest industrial enterprises in the United Kingdom, by industry**

SIC		1919	1930	1948	1973
20	Food	63	64	52	33
21	Tobacco	3	4	6	4
22	Textiles	26	24	17	10
23	Apparel	1	3	2	0
24	Lumber	0	0	0	2
25	Furniture	0	0	0	0
26	Paper	4	5	6	7
27	Printing and publishing	5	10	6	7
28	Chemical	11	9	19	21
29	Petroleum	3	3	3	8
30	Rubber	3	3	2	6
31	Leather	0	0	1	3
32	Stone, clay and glass	2	6	7	16
33	Primary metal	35	18	24	14
34	Fabricated metal	2	7	9	7
35	Machinery	8	7	10	26
36	Electrical machinery	11	18	12	14
37	Transportation equipment	20	14	20	16
38	Instruments	0	1	1	3
39	Miscellaneous	3	4	3	1
	Diversified/conglomerate	0	0	0	2
	Total	200	200	200	200

* Ranked by sales for 1973 and by market value of quoted capital for the other years

and electrical machinery were there as many as four or five more firms in the top 401 outside of the United States than there were within it.

Table 2.2 shows that in the United States the large industrial corporations had clustered throughout the twentieth century in the same industries in which they were concentrated in 1973. The pattern depicted in Tables 2.3, 2.4 and 2.5 is much the same for the United Kingdom, Germany and Japan. Other data document what is indicated here, that the American firms were larger, as well as more numerous, than those in other countries. For example in 1948, only 70 to 80 of the British firms had assets comparable to those of the top 200 in the United States. In 1930, the number was about the same. For Germany and Japan it was smaller. Well before the Second World War the United States had more and larger multinational industrial enterprises than did any other nation.

Why then did these large integrated hierarchical enterprises appear in some industries and not in others? Why did they appear at almost the same

Table 2.4. *The distribution of the 200 largest manufacturing firms in Germany by industry**

SIC		1913	1923	1953	1973
20	Food	23	28	23	24
21	Tobacco	1	0	0	6
22	Textiles	13	15	19	4
23	Apparel	0	0	0	0
24	Lumber	1	1	2	0
25	Furniture	0	0	0	0
26	Paper	1	2	3	2
27	Printing and publishing	0	1	0	6
28	Chemical	26	27	32	30
29	Petroleum	5	5	3	8
30	Rubber	1	1	3	3
31	Leather	2	3	2	1
32	Stone, clay and glass	10	9	9	15
33	Primary metal	49	47	45	19
34	Fabricated metal	8	7	8	14
35	Machinery	21	19	19	29
36	Electrical machinery	18	16	13	21
37	Transportation equipment	19	16	14	14
38	Instruments	1	2	4	2
39	Miscellaneous	1	1	1	1
	Diversified/conglomerate	0	0	0	1
	Total	200	200	200	200

* Ranked by sales for 1973 and by assets for the other three years

historical moment in the United States and Europe? Why did these industrial enterprises in advanced economies grow in the same manner first, by taking on distribution, purchasing and other functions, next by becoming multinational and then multiproduct?

Because these enterprises initially grew larger by integrating mass production with distribution, answers to these critical questions require a careful look at both these processes. Mass production is an attribute of specific technologies of production. In some industries the primary way to increase output was to add more workers and more machines; in others output was more rapidly expanded by improving and rearranging the inputs, by improving the machinery, furnaces, stills and other equipment, by reorienting the process of production within the plant, by placing the several processes of production required for a finished product within a single works, and by increasing the application of energy (particularly fossil fuel energy).

The first set of industries remained 'labor intensive', and the second set

Table 2.5. *The distribution of the 200 largest manufacturing firms in Japan by industry**

SIC		1918	1930	1954	1973
20	Food	31	30	26	18
21	Tobacco	1	1	0	0
22	Textiles	54	62	23	11
23	Apparel	2	2	1	0
24	Lumber	3	1	0	1
25	Furniture	0	0	0	0
26	Paper	12	6	12	10
27	Printing and publishing	1	1	0	2
28	Chemical	23	22	38	34
29	Petroleum	6	5	11	13
30	Rubber	0	1	1	5
31	Leather	4	1	0	0
32	Stone, clay and glass	16	14	8	14
33	Primary metal	21	22	28	27
34	Fabricated metal	4	3	6	5
35	Machinery	4	4	10	16
36	Electrical machinery	7	12	15	18
37	Transportation equipment	9	11	18	20
38	Instruments	1	1	3	5
39	Miscellaneous	1	1	0	1
	Diversified/conglomerate	0	0	0	0
	Total	200	200	200	200

* Ranked by assets

became 'capital intensive'. In this second set of industries – the capital intensive industries – the technology of production permitted much larger economies of scale than was possible in the first, the labor intensive set of industries; that is it permitted much greater reduction in cost per unit of output as volume increased. So in these capital intensive, large batch or continuous process technologies large plants, operating at minimum efficient scale (scale of operation that brought the lowest unit costs) had a much greater cost advantage over small plants than was the case in the labor intensive technologies. Similarly costs per unit rose much more rapidly when production fell below minimum efficient scale (of say 80–90% of capacity) than was true in labor intensive industries.

What is of basic importance to an understanding of the coming of the modern managerial industrial enterprise is that the cost advantage of the larger plants cannot be fully realized unless a constant flow of materials through the plant or factory is maintained. The decisive figure in determining costs and profits is then the throughput – that is the amount of output processed during a single day or other unit of time. The throughput needed to maintain minimum efficient scale requires careful coordination not only of the flow through the processes of production but also of the flows of inputs from the suppliers and of the flow of outputs to the retailers and final consumers. Such coordination cannot happen automatically. It demands the constant attention of a managerial team. Thus economies of scale are only technological; those of throughput require an organizational input. The latter depends on knowledge, skills and teamwork – on the organization of human inputs essential to exploit the potential of the technological processes.

A well-known example illustrates these generalizations. In 1881 the Standard Oil 'alliance' formed the Standard Oil Trust. The purpose was not to obtain control over the industry. That alliance, a loose federation of 40 companies each with its own legal and administrative identity but tied to John D. Rockefeller's Standard Oil Company through interchange of stock and other financial devices, already controlled close to 90% of the American output of kerosene. Instead the purpose was to provide a legal instrument to rationalize the industry and to exploit more full economies of scale. The Trust provided the essential legal means to create a corporate or central office that could, first, reorganize the processes of production by shutting down some refineries, reshaping others, and building new ones and could then coordinate the flow of materials, not only through the several refineries, but from the oil fields to the refineries and from the refineries to the consumers. The resulting rationalization made it possible to concentrate close to a quarter of the world's production of kerosene in three refineries, each with a 6,000 to 7,000 barrel daily throughput, with two-thirds of that product going to overseas markets. (At this time the refined petroleum products were by far the nation's largest non-agricultural export.) Imagine the diseconomies of scale and the resulting increase in unit costs that would result from placing close to one-fourth of the world's production of shoes, textiles or lumber into three factories or mills!

The reorganization of the Trust's refining facilities brought a sharp reduction in average cost of production of a gallon of kerosene. It dropped from 1.5 cents a gallon before the reorganization to 0.54 cents in 1884 and 0.45 in 1885 (with the resulting increase in the profit margin from 0.53 cents in 1884 to 1.003 cents in 1885), the costs of the giant refineries being still lower – costs far below those of any competitor. However, to maintain this cost advantage required that these large refineries had a continuing daily throughput of from 5,000 to 7,000 barrels, or a three- to four-fold increase over the earlier 1,500 to 2,000 barrels daily flow, with concomitant increases in transactions handled and in the complexity of coordinating the flow of materials through the process of production and distribution.

In the 1880s and 1890s, processes of production with comparable economies of throughput appeared in other industries besides oil. They came in the processing of food and chemicals (both consumer and industrial), the production of rubber, glass, abrasives, and other materials and in the making of a wide variety of machinery and metals. In most of these industries, new technologies and their organization led to the building of the plants of such high minimum efficient scale that a very small number of (in some cases just one or two) plants satisfied a sizable share of existing national and even global demand. The structure of these industries quickly became oligopolistic at home and abroad. Indeed in the smaller European economies a single firm often came to dominate. Oil and rubber oligopolies quickly became global. A very small number of producers of cigarettes, matches, breakfast cereals, whiskies, and other grain products, sugar, vegetable oil, chocolates, confectionery (even chewing gum), biscuits, jams, and soft drinks, soon dominated their industries at home and abroad. There were even fewer members in the global oligopolies in the production of recently invented light machinery mass produced by means of fabricating and assembling interchangeable parts – machines such as sewing machines; reapers, harvesters, and other agricultural machinery; typewriters, cash registers, adding machines and other office equipment. For example by the mid 1880s Singer Sewing Machines' two factories, one in New Jersey and one in Glasgow and each producing 8,000 machines a week, probably absorbed as much as three-fourths of world demand.

In metal making the coming of the Bessemer and open-hearth process for the mass production of steel and the electrolytic processes in the refining of copper, aluminum and nickel greatly increased the throughput of individual production units which, when operating at minimum efficient scale, brought impressive, often spectacular declines in unit costs. Thus the cost of steel rails fell from above $100 a ton in the 1870s to $12 a ton in the 1890s, and the price of aluminum from 87.5 fr. in 1888 to 47.5 fr. the next year, to 19 fr. by the end of 1890 and 3.75 fr. by 1895.

Even more skilled and technically trained managerial teams were needed to achieve the potential economies of throughput in the production of complex industrial machinery, particularly the recently invented equipment to generate, transmit and use electricity, and industrial chemicals, particularly dyes, fibers, nitrates and alkalis produced by new brand methods of chemical synthesis and chlorines, carbons, and gases by the new electrolytic methods. The first three firms to build the new synthetic dye works that brought the price of alizarin down from 200M in 1870 to 23M in 1878 and 9M in 1886 – Bayer, Hoechst and BASF – are a century later Germany's three largest chemical companies. On the other hand in the older, technologically simple, labor intensive industries such as apparel, textiles, leather, lumber and publishing and printing, neither technological nor organizational innovation substantially increased minimum efficient scale. The opportunities in these industries for cost reduction through managerial coordination of high volume throughput remained limited.

The differentials in potential scale economies of different production technologies indicate not only why the large hierarchical firms appeared in some industries and not in others, but also why they appeared suddenly in the last decades of the nineteenth century. Only with the completion of the modern transportation and communication networks – those of the railroad, telegraph, steamship, and cable – could materials flow into a factory or processing plant and the finished goods move out at the rate and in the volume required to achieve substantial economies of throughput. Transportation that depended on the power of animals, wind, and current was too slow, too irregular, and too uncertain to permit the level of throughput necessary to achieve modern economies of scale.

The economies of scale as measured by throughput help to explain why the large firms appeared in the industries that they did and why they appeared when they did, but they do not explain why they initially grew by integrating forward into distribution and backward into purchasing. The new mass producers might well have continued to buy from and sell to commercial intermediaries – wholesalers, retailers and manufacturers' agents. By so doing they would have been spared the expense of investing in expensive distribution and purchasing facilities and personnel. An explanation of such vertical integration requires a more precise understanding of the processes of volume distribution; particularly why the wholesale, retailer, or other commercial intermediaries lost their cost advantage vis-à-vis the volume producer.

The intermediaries' cost advantage – and the economic reason for their being – lay in their ability to exploit the economies both of scale and of scope. Because they handled the products of many manufacturers, they achieved a greater volume (*scale*) and lower per unit cost than any one manufacturer in the marketing and distribution of a *single* line of products. Moreover, they increased this advantage by the broader *scope* of their operation; that is by handling a number of *related* product lines through a single set of facilities. As a manufacturer expanded output the intermediary began to lose his cost advantage. In the words of one economist: 'provided that such a minimum efficient scale in transactions exists, the intermediary will have a cost advantage over his customers and suppliers only as long as the volume of transactions in which he engages comes closer to that scale than do the transactions volumes of his customers or suppliers'.[4] This rarely happened in retailing, except in heavily concentrated urban markets; but it often occurred in wholesaling. In addition, the advantages of scope were sharply reduced when marketing and distribution required specialized, costly product-specific facilities and skills that could not be used to handle other product lines. By investing in such product-specific personnel and facilities, the intermediary not only lost the advantages of scope but also became dependent on what were usually a small number of producers to provide those suppliers essential to making his investment pay. On the other hand the manufacturer, by making the same investment, obtained direct access to a wide number of retailers.

Competition as well as cost reduction from volume and the need for product-specific investment in distribution provided the manufacturer with an incentive to have his own sales force, for the new production technologies with their historically unprecedented output created a new type of competition. In those industries where a few large plants could meet existing demand, the few companies operating those plants quickly came to compete for a sizable share of national and often international markets. To maintain their cost advantages of throughput the manufacturers had to retain their market share. The loss of share to a competitor not only increased one's production costs but also decreased those of one's competitor.

In the new capital intensive, oligopolistic industries the few large competitors could not afford to depend on commercial intermediaries who made their profits by handling products from many manufacturers. They needed a sales force of their own to concentrate *full-time* on advertising; canvassing for customers; assuring delivery on schedule; and providing installation, continuing service and repair, customer credit and other services for their particular line of products. Such a force became the only dependable instrument to obtain and hold a market share large enough to assure the cost advantages of throughput. A final incentive for a manufacturer to build a sales force of his own was that it provided a steady flow of information about markets and customer needs and tastes.

Thus the modern industrial enterprise first appeared and continued to grow in industries with two characteristics. The first and most essential was a technology of production in which the realization of the cost advantage of that technology demanded close and constant coordination of material flows by experienced management teams. The second was that the marketing and distribution of the products in the volume required to maintain the market share needed to achieve these cost advantages called for investment in specialized product-specific human and physical capital.

Where this was *not* the case, that is in industries where technology did *not* require specialized skills and facilities, there was less incentive for the manufacturer to integrate forward into distribution or backwards into purchasing. There was less need for a unifying hierarchy in such industries as publishing and printing, lumber, furniture, leather, apparel and textiles, and specialized instruments and machines. In these industries the large integrated firm had fewer competitive advantages. In these industries economies of scale and scope did bring cost reductions, but not enough to permit a few firms to dominate the industry. Small, even single unit, firms continued to prosper. These industries stayed fragmented. Competition remained based more on price determined by the relationships of supply and demand than was true in industries in which the large integrated firm came to cluster.

Because of the importance of the economies of scale and scope for understanding the growth of multinational industrial enterprises, a few more words need to be said about both. As to scale let me begin by repeating for emphasis that different production technologies create different opportunities for the exploitation of scale economies. Cost decreases and increases more rapidly in relation to volume in some than in others. Second, manufacturers quickly appreciated the importance of this relationship between cost and volume. By the early twentieth century managers, particularly in the United States, were using the concept of over- and underabsorbed burden as a way to place these variations in cost resulting from fluctuation in throughput on their accounting sheets. If the plant operated at below standard volume (i.e. minimum efficient scale), the resulting loss was listed as unabsorbed burden; if it operated at above the scale, the resulting gain was listed as overabsorbed burden. By the 1920s such over- and underabsorbed burden became one of the critical items on the costs sheets of individual plants and on the profit and loss accounts of the enterprise as a whole.

A third point is that 'minimum efficient scale' refers to that of a unit (a census 'establishment'), and not the total output of a multiunit enterprise. As important, the minimum efficient scale for a specific plant or facility is related as much to existing demand as to potential output of a technology. The number of plants that can operate at a minimum efficient scale is limited by the size of the market. If demand did not permit a plant to operate at minimum efficient scale, its unit cost rose, becoming higher than those of a smaller plant running at its minimum efficient scale. Therefore the efficient size of plant and its location in a multiplant enterprise depends on a complex equation including costs of production based on the minimum efficient scale of that technology, the location and expected size of markets and the expectations of what share of those markets might be obtained, plus transportation, distribution and supply costs. If placed in foreign lands the costs of tariffs and other restrictive legislation also need to be computed. In other words, the relationship between an efficient scale and the size of a multiunit enterprise is a complex one indeed.

As to the economies of scope (that is those that come from processing several products within a single unit or set of facilities), they exist in manufacturing, in research and development and other functional units as well as in distribution and within the administrative and functional staffs of the corporate headquarters. In manufacturing often the same intermediate materials and processes can be used to produce different end products. In product engineering and in research and development the same facilities can be used to improve several existing products or processes and at the same time to develop new ones. In selling, a facility can market and distribute several products that go to similar markets. If the exploitation of economies of scale provided the basic incentive behind the strategy of vertical integration, the exploitation of those of scope have been the dynamic force behind a strategy of diversification.

The impact of technological differences on continuing growth of multinationals

Differences in the potential economies of scale and scope help to explain why the modern multinational appeared when it did, in the industries that it did, and grew in the manner that it did. They also make more understandable why the timing, location and amount of direct investment abroad, particularly in production facilities and personnel and the resulting relationships between foreign subsidiaries and the central corporate office, differed from industry to industry.

The first direct investment abroad was almost always in marketing and distribution; and it was made for precisely the same reasons that it was made at home. Manufacturers quickly replaced foreign commercial agents with sales forces of their own. Many set up branch offices in major foreign commercial centers almost as soon as they did those in their home-country cities. The more costly investment in product-specific storage, transportation and other facilities and personnel soon followed.

Investment abroad in production which came after that in distribution was still more costly, more permanent and usually required managers and supervisory staff with a greater variety of skills. The high initial costs and the relatively long time period required to get such facilities on stream forced the executives making these investment decisions to review carefully the long-term foreign demand for their product and to carry out the complex calculations involved in determining the size and location of plants to meet this demand. For these reasons a review of the evolution of a direct investment abroad in production facilities and personnel by multinationals in the major industries in which such firms have always clustered – oil, rubber, chemicals, machinery, metals and branded packaged food and consumer chemicals – from their beginnings in the 1880s until the Second World War reveals much about the impact of the economies of scale and scope on the continuing growth and the resulting organizational structure of modern multinational enterprise.

In oil the Standard Oil Trust (later the Standard Oil Company of New Jersey) dominated world markets from its formation until at least after the First World War. After the organizers of the Trust had rationalized the domestic production, they made an extensive investment in a world-wide marketing and distributing organization. Thanks to this investment, Standard held off the challenge of the Nobels and the Rothschilds – refiners and distributors of Russian oil – in the large and profitable European market. In a proposed treaty in 1895 between Standard and the Nobels and Rothschilds the American company was allocated 75% of the world's export trade.[5] At that time, when kerosene was the primary product, Standard and its European competitors concentrated production in giant refineries either close to the crude oil fields or at pipeline or rail terminals, shipped the refined products in their own tankers or rail cars and packaged and branded the product for the final consumer close to the markets.

At the turn of the century the oil industry was revolutionized by the opening of new sources of crude oil in the United States, Europe and the Far East and by the almost simultaneous transformation of markets resulting from the coming of electricity that reduced the demand for kerosene, and the automobile and oil-powered ship that vastly enlarged the market for gasoline, lubricants and fuel oil. Even before the break-up of Standard Oil under the Supreme Court decision in 1911, several integrated competitors had appeared in the United States including Texaco and Gulf. Abroad, however, only two seriously challenged Standard's dominance – the European Petroleum Union, the German dominated combination formed in 1907 of the older Nobel and Rothschild enterprises and the new refiners and producers, and Royal Dutch Shell, a merger in the same year of the refiner and the distributor of oil from the Dutch East Indies.

To meet the new markets these major oil companies invested extensively in facilities for the distribution of gasoline, lubricants and fuel oil for home heating as well as for ship propulsion. Although these companies preferred to concentrate production in refineries with massive throughputs – as late as 1928 78% of Jersey Standard's refining in the United States (and produced in large part for foreign markets) was concentrated in three refineries[6] – the increasing number of markets and sources of supply and the increasingly differentiated demand and growing alternative sources of supply led to the building of refineries closer to major markets. Such investments in refining required the balancing of minimum efficient scale to local and regional demand against the costs of transportation and storage as well as tariffs and other transborder restrictions. Because the consistency of crude differed from field to field – that of each field requiring a somewhat differing refining process – and because the demands for the different products in different regional markets were constantly changing, the coordination of the flow from the field to the refineries and then to the markets became an increasingly complex task, and one that had to be taken over by the central corporate office. The following description written in October 1927 of the function of Standard Oil's recently formed Coordination Department makes this point effectively:

In general, the Department assists in currently determining the policies to be adopted so far as the activities of the producing, transportation and manufacturing branches of the Company are concerned, and cooperates with the subsidiary companies to see that these policies are carried out. This entails arranging for refinery crude supplies; Crude transportation and allocation; production, purchases and movements of certain finished products, i.e., napthas [gasoline], refined oil, gas and fuel oils; coordination of refining manufacturing operations from the standpoint of Crude's run and products required, stock on hand, etc. and the allocation of business among the various subsidiary companies.[7]

After spelling out the complexities of global coordination in crude oil production, transportation and refining, the memorandum reviewed the intricacies of coordinating globally the distribution of refined products. In this way the need for tightly scheduled coordination reduced the decision-making autonomy of the managers of the operating subsidiaries and increased that of the executives at corporate headquarters.

In rubber the production of apparel (boots, gloves and rainwear) and industrial products (belting, hose, insulation and the like), particularly the vulcanizing process, offered cost advantages of scale. It was, however, the coming of the automobile and with it the pneumatic tire that quickly determined the players in the global oligopoly. Those who built factories large enough to exploit the massive scale economies offered in automobile tire manufacturing between 1899 and 1906 remained for the rest of the century the dominant members of that oligopoly. (The only major new entrant, Bridgestone, built its giant plant in the late 1950s just before the Japanese automobile industry began its large-scale expansion.) These firms – four in the United States (Firestone, Goodyear, US Rubber and Goodrich) and one in each of the major European countries – Dunlop, Michelin, Continental and Pirelli – quickly built national and then international sales networks.[8] However, because of scale economies these companies hesitated to build tire plants in those markets where such a factory had already been established. If they did, neither they nor their competitor could operate at minimum efficient scale. The Americans did make direct investment in Canada to get under the tariff barrier and inside the British Empire. Only when automobile production began to boom in Britain in the 1920s did three of the four American leaders build plants there.[9] Not only did the growing demand appear to permit the operation of plants at minimum efficient scale, but also the tires for that market were made to quite different specifications from American truck and car tires and so would have required separate production facilities even if produced in the United States. Because tire production abroad did not require the coordinating control to maintain a stable throughput as did foreign oil refineries, the subsidiaries of these rubber companies operated more independently than did those of major oil companies. However in rubber, as in oil, product and process improvement was carried on in the home country's central offices and laboratories.

In machinery, differences in the timing and location of direct manufacturing investment abroad reflected even more than in other industries differences in potential economies of scale and scope. In light machinery mass produced by the fabricating and assembling of interchangeable parts American firms completely dominated the international markets until well after the Second World War. These producers of sewing machines, of office machinery such as typewriters, cash registers, adding machines, and of agricultural machinery including harvesters and reapers and later tractors, and also the makers of automobiles, all had extensive sales organizations which provided specialized marketing services such as demonstration, installation, after sales service and repair and consumer credit. Such firms as Singer, National Cash Register, Burroughs Adding Machine and International Harvester built plants at minimum efficient scale in Europe well before the First World War, usually to meet regional (that is European) rather than national markets.[10] On the other hand, in the production of automobiles where there were greater scale economies in fabricating than in assembling, fabrication remained concentrated in large plants at home and assembling plants were built abroad. Thus, Ford concentrated production at the Highland Park, then the River Rouge Works, sending parts in CKO (complete knocked down) units to branch plants at home and abroad.[11] Even before 1920 Ford's Canada Works at Windsor just across the river from Detroit began some fabrication for parts to be shipped to markets within the British Empire system. Only at the end of that decade did Ford begin building a fabricating plant abroad near London to supply the European subsidiaries with their bodies and engines (and they did so on a scale larger than the market required). Thus, while the subsidiaries at the sewing, office and agricultural machinery firms operated quite autonomously, those at Ford were much more centrally controlled in order to ensure the coordination of the flow of shipments essential to maintain the continuous operation of many scattered assembly plants.

Americans also excelled in the production and distribution of standardized volume-produced industrial machinery, such as elevators (Otis), heating equipment (American Radiator), printing presses (Mergenthaler), boilers (Babcock & Wilcox), pumps (Worthington), and air brakes (Westinghouse). These leaders soon supported their marketing organizations abroad by setting up, usually in Europe, one or two plants to cover that Continental market and sometimes Africa and Asia. As in the case of light machinery, day-to-day operations remained quite independent in the home office, although product design and development continued to be carried out at home.

In the production of new electrical machinery including transforming and generating equipment and more specialized products such as storage batteries and magnetos, the Germans (Siemens, AEG, AFA, and Bosch) and the Americans (General Electric, Westinghouse, Electric Storage Battery) shared world markets. In the first decade of this century the Germans built plants in eastern and southern Europe, while both Germans and Americans had factories in western Europe, particularly in Britain. Although the managers of these subsidiaries operated their day-to-day operations quite autonomously, they were more closely tied to the corporate office than machinery makers because the all-important, ever-changing product design as well as process improvement in this technologically dynamic industry continued to be carried out in central offices and laboratories in the home country.

In the production and distribution of more specialized processing and materials-handling machinery used in the new oil, rubber, machinery, chemicals, electrical, metal and food processing industries, as well as in mines, shipyards, transportation junctions and the like, the Germans excelled. Here such firms as Borsig, Humboldt, DEMAG, MAN, and BAMAG exploited the economies of scope. That is they used the same foundries, forges, sheet making and other fabricating equipment, dies, presses, milling and perforating equipment and coating processes to produce a variety of end products. To achieve these economies they carried on their operations in one or two giant works. Although they had worldwide marketing organization, they made little attempt to manufacture for abroad. Such economies of scope were rarely transportable. They could not be obtained in small plants.

Europeans, particularly the Germans, also excelled in chemicals. In some products, such as artificial fibers, the cost advantages that brought global oligopoly came from scale. In others, such as dyes and other coal-based chemicals and also electro-chemicals, they came more from scope. In rayon the pattern was much the same as in rubber. The first to build a large plant and then a marketing organization continued to dominate in each of the major European nations for decades. The difference from rubber was that in rayon the Europeans built plants in the United States before Americans began to make the product. The British firm, Courtaulds, led the way and other members of the global oligopoly followed during the boom of the 1920s. Of the American producers only Du Pont, an explosive maker who diversified into rayon shortly after the First World War, was able to obtain a substantial market share. As there was little need to coordinate the activities of the subsidiaries, and because the European producers made little investment in product development, the subsidiaries remained quite independent of the home office. Indeed, the home offices of Courtaulds and the others did little more than rake in the profits from their American subsidiaries, much to the detriment of their long-term competitive advantage.

In organic and electro-chemicals the members of the global oligopoly were those German companies which had built in the 1870s the first large plants that so greatly reduced unit costs and had then supplemented these by creating powerful world-wide marketing organizations. However, in both, the large firms continued to grow more by exploiting the economies of scope than those of scale. The dye companies, particularly Bayer, Hoechst and BASF, after greatly expanding their product lines producing literally hundreds of different dyes, quickly moved into the production of pharmaceuticals and film that used the same intermediate products and processes as did dyes. So too did DEGUSSA and Griesheim-Elektron diversify, going from the electrolytic production of caustic soda to that of liquid chlorine, liquid gases, magnesium and other alloys, acetate, sodium and other chemicals produced by the same basic processes and with many of the same ingredients. Like the German machinery companies these enterprises concentrated production in one or two huge plants in order to exploit the cost advantages of scope. So they rarely invested in foreign manufacturing except for small facilities for packaging and finishing pharmaceuticals and dyes. Even in the United States where high tariffs, heavy transportation costs and the rapidly growing continental market all encouraged such investments, only DEGUSSA and Bayer built and operated major works. On the other hand, leading German pharmaceutical firms with less diverse product lines (and so with smaller cost advantages of scope) and producing more widely distributed consumer goods invested more extensively in foreign production facilities. Before the First World War Merck and von Heyden had factories in the United States, as did Schering in Britain and Russia. As the subsidiaries of these German chemical firms, except possibly that of DEGUSSA, relied on the home plants for many of their basic materials, they remained rather tightly controlled from their corporate offices.

In metals it was the requirements of the economies of scale, not scope, that restrained investment in manufacturing facilities abroad. In non-ferrous metals the new electrolytic refining technologies perfected around 1890 that revolutionized production brought massive-scale economies. By 1900 four aluminum producing plants – Alcoa's at Niagara Falls, that of Aluminium Industrie AG at Neuhausen in the Alps and the two smaller works of a French and a British company produced all the aluminum the world called for. Indeed, the two leaders spent the next decades concentrating on developing a wide variety of products to expand the use of this once precious metal. In copper, with the adoption of a new powerful generator in 1891, minimum efficient scale became so high that only 21 refineries were built in the United States in the 90 years between 1890 and 1980 and a smaller number elsewhere, even though there was in these decades an enormous growth in the market for copper wire for electrical transmission and copper pipes and tubes in growing industries and cities.[12] The resulting global oligopoly came to include until well after the Second World War four American companies – American Smelting and Refining, Anaconda, Phelps-Dodge and Kennecott and one German, Metallgesellschaft. While the American firms had worldwide sales forces, they made no attempt to increase capacity greatly by building refineries abroad. The German firm did build in 1891 – the year of the innovation – a small refinery at Perth Amboy (later dismantled because of its size) and bought into a much larger one on Long Island constructed that same year.

Since the days of Andrew Carnegie and Alfred Krupp the production of steel has been cited as a classic example of the cost advantages of scale. Yet neither the Bessemer nor open-hearth processes developed as striking economies as did the electrolytic technique in non-ferrous metal processing. Moreover, as iron and steel were the basic metals used in modern transportation, industry and urban development, their market was much greater than that for copper, aluminum, or other non-ferrous metals. Nevertheless, in all major countries, the industry quickly became oligopolistic. The leading steel makers, particularly German and American, set up branch offices in foreign countries; but they rarely invested in plants abroad, even though both transportation and tariff costs were often high. The little investment that was undertaken was made in less developed regions where no modern works existed. Again, as in copper, aluminum, heavy and light machinery, chemicals and even rubber, the building of a plant of the size to assure operation at minimum efficient scale in a foreign market would have so increased that nation's capacity that neither the new plant nor the existing ones could have maintained the throughput necessary to achieve that scale.

If the metal makers had few foreign manufacturing subsidiaries, multinationals producing branded packaged food and consumer chemical products had many. In sugar, vegetable oil and grain, scale economies alone brought concentration, even before the processors began to do their own packaging and therefore their own branding. However, in most food and consumer chemicals (soap, pills, paint and the like) the large firm and with it oligopolistic competition appeared when new processing and packaging techniques permitted high daily throughput. This was true in cigarettes (but not in cigars), in beer (but not in wine), in chocolate and cocoa products, in biscuits, confectionery, canned meats, soups and bottled sauces, soft drinks and spirits. These goods required little in the way of complex technological skills and facilities in production or extensive product-specific investment in distribution. Product differentiation was maintained primarily by advertising. The leaders in these industries were quick to establish sales offices abroad. Because the cost advantages of scale were smaller in these industries than the others in which the large firm clustered; because local tastes shaped demand more; and because materials to be processed were more likely to be obtained locally, the producers of such branded, packaged products invested in plants abroad more quickly and in greater numbers than did those in the other industries just examined. These plants usually served national rather than large regional markets. Nevertheless, where demand was limited in relation to minimum efficient scale, one works often served several national markets; or two companies might form a joint venture to build one plant at that scale, as the British chocolate makers Cadbury and Fry did in Australia. Because coordination of purchasing, production and marketing was done most effectively at local or regional levels, there was little need for corporate office coordination. The firm's central office did, however, provide advertising and other marketing skills and strategies.

These same factors relating to scale and scope in production and product-specific requirements in distribution can also account for the timing, number, location and size of foreign direct investment in manufacturing in such materials-producing industries as glass, paper, abrasives and tin cans and also in mass production and distribution of dairy, meat and other perishable products. On the other hand, in industries with few economies of scale or scope in production and few product-specific needs in distribution – industries such as apparel, textiles, leather, lumber, furniture, publishing and printing, and seasonal food products – manufacturers invested less extensively in world-wide marketing organizations or foreign production facilities. (The obtaining of off-shore factories for cheap labor is a post-Second World War phenomenon.) In these industries there were few global oligopolies. They long remained competitive. Manufacturers in these labor intensive industries did invest abroad, but as they had few competitive advantages, they rarely achieved long-term dominance or even maintained a sizable share of foreign markets. In these industries the distant plant operated almost independently of the corporate office.

Conclusion: technologies and transactions as shapers of multinational strategy and structure

Historically the pattern of direct investment abroad by modern multinationals has differed from industry to industry. The most significant step in the evolution of the modern multiunit, industrial enterprise was the internalizing of marketing, distribution and purchasing functions of wholesalers and other commercial intermediaries. Such enterprises then invested in research, moved backward into owning and operating units producing raw and semifinished materials and expanded geographically by investing in operating units abroad only after the internalization of such commercial activities. That critical move into marketing, distribution and purchasing reflected a balance between the cost advantages of scale and scope enjoyed by distributors. The timing, location and size of direct investment in production facilities that followed reflected the balancing of the cost advantages of scale and scope and those of the transportation and transactions involved in reaching distant markets. In these calculations the cost advantages or disadvantages of scope and scale remained the primary consideration. Thus in some industries such as branded packaged products these technologically based considerations led to the building of a number of relatively small plants, usually for national markets.

In others, like mass produced machinery, it led to the investment in fewer but larger plants, usually for regional markets (or where scale economies were high in fabrication to concentrating fabrication in large plants, usually at home, and assembling in smaller ones for national markets). In chemicals and heavy machinery the economies of scope restrained investment abroad except occasionally in distant continents. In others the restraint came as it did in metals because minimum efficient scale was so high and in others like furniture, apparel and leather because it was so low.

Although the story is not reviewed in this brief essay, the modern industrial enterprise also made direct investments abroad in units producing raw and semifinished materials. The motives for such backward integration were not primarily to reduce costs by exploiting the economies of throughput based on scale and scope. Such investments were made more to assure a constant flow of materials into the processing and manufacturing plants on a precise schedule and to precise specifications – a flow that was essential to maintain throughput at minimum efficient scale. They were essentially a form of insurance to reduce potential high transactions costs resulting from the failure of suppliers or transporters to carry out their contractual agreements. However, the size and significance of such investment were closely related to the scale of operation within an industry. The greater the volume of output, the greater the need for such insurance. So these costs also varied from one technology of production to another. Supply-related foreign investments were, therefore, much larger in oil, rubber, paper and metals than they were in branded packaged products, or even chemicals and machinery – industries that relied on smaller amounts of raw materials obtained from foreign sources. Thus in accounting for these supply oriented investments in which transaction cost reduction was a much more important consideration than was the case in market oriented investments, an explanation of the differences in their timing, location and size must take into account the technology of production used by the investing enterprise.

For these reasons I argue that an understanding of technological and organizational differences and changes within operating units is essential to an explanation of the beginnings and continued growth of the industrial multinational enterprise. It was the organization created to exploit the cost advantages of scale and scope of certain technologies that generated the transferable capital and skills and provided the market power that gave the multinational industrial enterprise competitive advantage in distant markets. And the cost advantages of scale and scope remained the major consideration in decisions that determined when, where and how much to invest abroad. At least these differences in timing, location and size of direct investment abroad can be more precisely explained in terms of differences in technologies employed within units than by the differences in the costs of transactions between units.

Most of the leading industrial multinationals of the 1950s – those that were among the top 200 in their economies – had their beginnings well before the First World War. Their founders were the first to recruit the management teams essential to exploit the new high speed, high volume production technologies that were made possible by the coming of modern transportation and communication and the first to make the necessary investment in product-specific distribution facilities and personnel. These first mover advantages were so powerful that the pioneers continued to dominate the resulting global oligopolies for decades. They competed with a small number of competitors for the market share essential to maintain the cost advantages of scale and scope economies. They did so functionally and strategically, that is they competed by improving their marketing and purchasing and their process of production, by their research and development, and by moving more quickly into new markets and out of old ones; or they maintained their share through contractual agreements with one another. Such cartel arrangements occurred most often in continental Europe where such contracts were enforceable in courts of law. The strategies of specific companies in international markets reflected their position in the oligopoly and the historical evolution of the enterprise and of that industry. In defining and carrying out their strategies their senior executives normally took account of the availability of capital, human skills, the costs of transportation, tariffs and other government levies and the risks of high transaction costs resulting from human frailties. Even more central to their calculations, however, were the competitive advantages resulting from the economies of scale and scope and from extensive product-specific investment abroad in distribution as well as production.

NOTES

* This paper has greatly benefited from the comments of Richard S. Tedlow, Louis T. Wells, Mira Wilkins and particularly William H. Lazonick, and from financial support received from the Alfred P. Sloan Foundation, the German Marshall Fund and the Division of Research, Graduate School of Business Administration, Harvard University.

1 A useful summary of the extensive literature of the many explanations and theories of multinational enterprise can be found in Jean-François Hennart, *Theory of multinational enterprise* (Ann Arbor, 1982), particularly ch. 1. More concise are Richard E. Caves, *Multinational enterprise and economic analysis* (Cambridge, 1982), ch. 2, A. L. Calvert, 'A synthesis of foreign direct investment theories and theories of the multinational firm', *Journal of international studies* XII (Spring/ Summer, 1981), 43–59 and P. J. Buckley, 'A critical review of theories of the multinational enterprise', *Aussenwirtschaft*, XXXVI (March 1981), 70–87.

2 Alfred D. Chandler Jr, *The visible hand: the managerial revolution in American business* (Cambridge, Mass., 1977), pp. 1–4.

3 The following few pages closely follow my 'Emergence of managerial capitalism', *Business history review*, LVII (Winter 1984), 473–503. Because they present my basic views on the beginnings of modern industrial enterprise as concisely as I can define them and because these views are essential to the arguments of this paper, some paragraphs are taken verbatim from that article. Documentation on specific facts for pp. 31–44 in this article can be found there.

4 Scott J. Moss, *An economic theory of business strategy* (New York, 1981), 110–11.

5 Robert W. Tolf, *The Russian Rockefellers* (Stanford, Calif., 1976), p. 117.

6 Henrietta M. Larson *et al.*, *New horizons: history of Standard Oil Company* (*New Jersey*), *1927–1950* (New York, 1971), p. 200.

7 Quoted in Alfred D. Chandler Jr, *Strategy and ~tructure: chapters in the history of the industrial enterprise* (Cambridge, Mass., 1962), p. 190.

8 These comments here and elsewhere in this paper on British, French and Japanese multinational enterprise summarize what is discussed in detail in my forthcoming study tentatively entitled *Scale and scope: the dynamics of global enterprise – a history*, on the evolution of modern industrial enterprise in these three nations and in the United States.

9 Mira Wilkins, *Maturing of multinational enterprise* (Cambridge, Mass., 1974), p. 75.

10 Mira Wilkins, *Emergence of multinational enterprise* (Cambridge, Mass., 1970), pp. 212–13 lists the location of such light and heavy machinery producing plants. Often a factory in the United Kingdom served the British empire.

11 Wilkins, *Maturing of multinational enterprise*, pp. 72–3; and Mira Wilkins and Frank Ernest Hill, *American business abroad: Ford on six continents* (Detroit, 1964), pp. 189ff and 435.

12 Thomas R. Navin, *Copper mining and management* (Tucson, Arizona, 1978), pp. 65–9.

3 European multinationals in the United States: 1875—1914*

MIRA WILKINS

'It is by now a cliché to observe that, though foreign direct investment in the United States accelerated dramatically in the 1970s, foreign involvement in the business affairs of this country has been a central ingredient of economic growth since the founding of the Republic.' So wrote David McClain, in an article published in 1983.[1] 'A cliché', 'a central ingredient': these are strong words. Yet no full-length book has ever been published documenting the role of foreign investment in America,[2] and while the typical American economic history textbook mentions foreign investments in the 1830s and may note foreign investments in US railroads, it certainly does not consider the subject as central to American economic growth. But McClain is right. It was central.

McClain is a specialist on multinational enterprise and not American economic history, and it has been such specialists, in the main, who have looked back in time and seen the significance of foreign investment in America's past. There now exists a literature on European direct investment in the United States, which includes the older and important work of Cleona Lewis and the newer materials of John Dunning, T. C. Coram, David McClain, John Stopford, Larry Franko, Francesca Sanna Randaccio, Peter Buckley and Brian Roberts, and Thomas R. Kabisch.[3] These contributions (with the exception of Kabisch's) all had their genesis in studies of foreign direct investment and multinational enterprise. I, along with these authors, use the phrase 'foreign direct investment' to indicate foreign investments made with an eye to management and control – that is, the type of foreign investment that is made by multinational enterprises. Throughout this paper, I am discussing non-resident foreign direct investment. The capital of an immigrant who migrated to America is excluded, since there remained no foreign claim on US assets. A number of students of American history have dealt with specific aspects of British direct investments in the United States (W. Turrentine Jackson, W. G. Kerr, Roger V. Clements, Clark C. Spence, and Larry McFarlane, for example).[4] Likewise, the growing literature on European multinational enterprises is relevant.[5] In short, there are substantial materials on these businesses in America.

55

In the late nineteenth and early twentieth centuries, when the modern American multinational emerged,[6] European enterprises invested in the United States. Lower costs of transportation and speed in communication, made for an integrated world economy.[7] More important, in terms of prospects for profits, America was irresistible. Across the country thousands of miles of railroad track were being laid. Visitors reported on the wonders. Immigrants filled the country. There was construction. There were demands for producer and consumer goods. There were also high tariffs, limiting imports of a broad range of articles.

Frequently, European companies that exported to the United States saw their markets dwindling, as Americans made the products previously imported. In the post-civil war years, and especially 1875–1914, European enterprises in many industries made decisions on whether to invest in the United States or to accept diminishing sales. Their decisions were not uniform. Some retreated; some appointed agents and reconciled themselves to filling an ever smaller market segment; others developed extensive marketing organizations and fought US tariffs that discriminated against their products; still others licensed Americans to produce, obtaining from zero to controlling interest in the American venture. Many invested in one or more plants in the United States. Some acted on the initiative of Americans, some on their own. Some remained, others left.

While far more European multinationals invested to reach the American market than to obtain sources of supply, some European companies that had imported from the United States integrated backward. Such investments were unaffected by US tariff considerations. America was a rich country, rich in agricultural land and minerals, and generally rich in natural resources. Some European direct investments were associated with that great wealth. The many involvements, the different industries, and the different nationalities are striking.

In addition to what we have come to accept as the 'typical' multinational, that is, a firm with operations in one country that expands into other foreign lands, there were investing in America what I call 'free standing' companies, ones normally set up in Europe (very typically in England) to do business in the United States. These free standing firms had a board of directors and a secretary, but no operations in the home country. They were direct investments in that the firm extended over borders and there was the intention of control.

Rather than repeat what others have written, in this paper I want to consider European multinational enterprise in America, 1875–1914, industry-by-industry. I am going to be brief and schematic, moving quickly through the industrial spectrum. Were there differences by industry? Were there differences by nationalities? How important was European direct investment in America? I debated footnoting each point and decided that this would not be feasible in view of the publication requirements. Since the findings of this paper will be treated in far greater detail in my forthcoming book on the history of foreign investment in the United States, full documentation will be available in that study. Here, I will summarize the 1875–1914 evidence and then extract from the data some overall conclusions relating to the commercial and industrial structure of European business in the United States, 1875–1914.

Agriculture, forestry, and fisheries: Europeans invested in growing cotton, wheat, sugar, and rice in the United States, in cattle ranches and timberlands. With some miscellaneous exceptions (for example, A. W. Faber, German pencil makers, had in 1875 among its other US investments some tracts of timberland; the Fine Cotton Spinners' and Doublers' Association acquired in 1911 cotton plantations in Mississippi), most of the investments in agriculture, cattle raising, and timberlands involved 'free standing companies'. Foreign investments in fisheries were trivial. Only in cattle lands was the size of the investment formidable vis-à-vis US enterprises. British cattle companies in the United States had multiplied, especially in the early 1880s. There were Dutch stakes, also of the 'free standing' variety. In the main, the large cattle company investments were notoriously unsuccessful, that is, they did not fulfil the profit expectations of the investors. Many such investments did not persist into the twentieth century, because of the lack of profit and because Argentina became a far superior source of beef for the British.

Mining and oil production: Sizable foreign direct investments went into America's iron ore, copper, gold, silver, coal, oil, and so forth. As in the case of agriculture, many of these were by 'free standing companies', set up to develop a particular mine or oil property. A number of investments were made by free standing companies in iron ore properties, associated with planned iron and steel production. In copper, in the late 1890s, foreign-controlled enterprises produced more than 25% of American output. While most of the foreign investment in gold mining was by free standing companies (with British and French involvements), the large British firms active in South African gold participated in American gold mining. Multinational trading companies (from the British Balfour, Williamson to the German Metallgesellschaft) invested in coal mines, associated with related activities. Americans developed their own borax mines; but in time Borax Consolidated, a British multinational enterprise, came to control this entire industry. The American companies established or acquired by Royal Dutch Shell made that firm one of the major enterprises in America's oil industry.

Construction: Only in very specific, limited niches (tunnel building, for example) were European enterprises in evidence. Here the contribution was primarily British. Particular foreign investments (in land, iron ore, and so forth) required the investor to engage in construction and this, of course, occurred. In the United States, the large construction industry was unquestionably American. Only when specialized technology and talents were needed, or when the demand stemmed from a related investment, were foreign companies involved.

Food and beverage manufacture: Numerous and significant European investments were made by both free standing and operating enterprises in meatpacking, flour milling, breweries, chocolates, and other food products. Investors occupied important positions in American industry. British, Swiss, and German companies were involved. The huge free standing companies in meatpacking, flour milling, and the breweries proved unprofitable to the shareholders.

Tobacco manufacture: American Tobacco was supreme. British-American Tobacco, formed in 1902, was in these years American-controlled, so its investments in the United States (for export) cannot be considered foreign ones. There were some other minor interests, but it is fair to say that for all practical purposes, foreign investment in US tobacco manufacturing in 1875–1914 was minimal.

Textile mill products: Here came the surprise. Since in this era American investment abroad in textiles was trivial, many have assumed that the same would be true of European enterprises. By contrast, I have found a whole battery of British, German, French, and to a lesser extent, Swiss investments in yarn, thread, woven fabrics, carpets, dyeing and finishing operations, lace goods, and so forth. The investments were in cotton, linen, wool, and silk manufactures. They were not made by free standing companies, but extensions of existing enterprises. Some firms had multiplant operations in the United States. J. & P. Coats Ltd and English Sewing Cotton Company Ltd became the most prominent of the investors. After 1898, the American cotton thread industry was, in fact, dominated by foreign investment. Other British enterprises with US stakes in textiles included Linen Thread Co. Ltd; Sir Titus Salt, Bart., Sons & Co. Ltd, of Saltaire; Alfred Sykes, Huddersfield; T. F. Firth & Sons, Heckmondwike; and the Bradford Dyers' Association Ltd. German manufacturers of fine worsted yarns and specialized wools set up operations in Passaic, New Jersey (Stoehr & Co., for example). Five German-controlled enterprises in that city came to employ some 15,000 people. Other German companies invested in lace making and in silk weaving, dyeing, and finishing facilities. H. E. Schniewind, Elberfeld, was a large investor. French wool textile makers headquartered in Roubaix and Tourcoing established woolen mills in the vicinity of Woonsocket, Rhode Island. Likewise, French companies, located in Lyon, invested in manufacturing silk in America. Swiss investments in silk (Robert Schwarzenbach) also existed. The interests appear to have been by companies that saw their US export markets disappear as tariffs protected American industry. In addition, rayon, a high technology (for this period) textile product, covered by patents, was produced in the United States in the years 1911–14, exclusively by a subsidiary of the British Courtaulds Ltd in a 'modern' plant, built especially to make viscose yarn.

Apparel manufacture: Virtually no foreign direct investment in apparel manufacturing existed in the United States. The German firm Wilhelm Benger Soehne was exceptional; its US company produced widely advertised, trademarked woolen underwear (Jaeger Underwear).

Lumber and wood manufacture: Foreign stakes existed, but were not of major importance.

Furniture and fixtures: I have identified no foreign direct investments in this manufacturing activity, 1875–1914.

Pulp, paper and board mill; converted paper products; boxes and containers: There were minor interests, but not of significance.

Printing and publishing: Some British and German publishing companies had American houses. The investments were not large and did not play a major role in this American industry.

Chemicals: Here foreign direct investments were pervasive, with the Germans pre-eminent. In many branches of the chemical industries – in industrial and consumer chemicals – German, British, Belgian, Swiss, and French firms invested. There were Austrian investments in fertilizer production. Foreign direct investments had more impact on this American industry than any other. The effects were formidable. It is impossible in this short paper to document the proliferation of activities. These companies were not free standing ones, but always associated with parent businesses. The investors introduced new technology and often trademarked goods. Licensing arrangements accompanied foreign direct investments. Sometimes (as in the case of certain German dye companies), the investment in a US marketing network was larger than in manufacturing. A number of companies had multiplant establishments in the United States. From alkalies to dyes, from miracle drugs to nostrums, from perfumes to flavors to soaps, European multinationals participated in shaping and forming the American chemical industries.

Petroleum refining: There were some (not terribly important, when judged by the size of their US market), free standing foreign-owned companies with oil refineries. In 1914, Shell owned several small refineries, but its huge new refinery at Martinez, near San Francisco, was not yet on stream.

Rubber products: Michelin made tires in the United States. Dunlop had started to, sold out, and had not by 1914 regained entry. Other rubber and rubber-type products made by British multinationals in the United States included belts, primarily for industrial use.

Leather and leather goods: Alfred Booth & Co., a British trading firm, became involved in manufacturing gloves and shoe leather in the United States. In kid leather, it found a special niche. It was atypical as a foreign investor in this industry.

Glass, stone, clay, concrete, gypsum, etc.: There were a number of foreign direct investments, but highly miscellaneous and specialized, involving either a unique technology or some particular demand requirements (thus, foreign-owned land companies often set up a small plant to provide for land development needs). German firms owned certain cement plants.

Primary metals, ferrous and non-ferrous: Important British investments helped develop the iron and steel industry in the American South; and there were British direct investments in several companies – or their predecessors – that were later absorbed by the US Steel Corporation. In the ferrous metals, free standing companies seemed more in evidence that European-operating ones (especially in the British case), but German international businesses such as Mannesmann were present in the United States. As for the non-ferrous metals, highly significant German interests existed in smelting and refining of copper, lead, and zinc and the associated trade in these metals. There was one important, multinational-type French investment in the American aluminum industry.

Fabricated metal products: In a range of metal products, there were foreign investments in US manufacturing, among them those of the Sheffield steel producers.

Non-electrical equipment and machinery: A British company (Howard & Bullough) became an important textile machinery manufacturer in the United States; other British investments in machinery were made, in boilers, for instance. German and Swedish firms invested in making machinery in America. Orenstein & Koppel-Arthur Koppel, AG, Berlin, had a number of factories in the United States and branch sales offices in Pittsburgh, New York, Chicago, and San Francisco. It produced in the United States equipment for such American customers as Westinghouse, US Steel, and Du Pont. American companies abroad had been active in sewing machines, harvesters, and office machinery. No European investor in the United States made this type of machinery.

Electrical equipment and machinery: For a short time, the predecessor of General Electric was German-controlled. In various specialized segments of the American electrical equipment industry, multinational enterprise-type investments existed. Siemens had important investments, albeit shortlived. The Swedish L. M. Ericsson began to make telephone equipment in the United States in 1904, but soon discovered it was not competitive in this industry and switched to making automobile ignitions. In many of the electrical industries, the strong American presence made survival for foreign business precarious. The British-controlled Marconi company was exceptional in finding a particular market in which it could eventually surpass its US competitors. (It was basically a service company, involved in radio commu-nication, but in 1905 it had begun to manufacture apparatus in the United States.)

Transportation equipment: Several French automobile companies manufactured in America in the early twentieth century. A subsidiary of the German Daimler company made Mercedes in the United States (1905–13). Likewise, in 1906, Giovanni Agnelli (head of Fiat) visited America, and three years later Fiat started to produce cars in Poughkeepsie, New York. This last was a rare Italian direct investment in the United States. All the European automobiles made in America were for the wealthy consumer. The British invested in the American bicycle industry. British and German firms made direct investments in manufacturing railroad equipment. There were British and German stakes in America's early submarine industry. So, too, there were some abortive British attempts to enter into American shipbuilding.

Instruments, optical and ophthalmic goods, photographic equipment, watches and clocks: Kny-Scheerer Corporation (100% German-owned) was the largest seller and manufacturer of surgical instruments in the United States. It advertised widely. The Germans had stakes in the US photographic and optical goods industry. The Carl Zeiss works in Jena, Germany, had a 25% interest in 1914 in the Bausch & Lomb Optical Co., which received valuable technological information and licences from the German firm.

Miscellaneous manufacturing: German direct investments existed in a range of miscellaneous activities, from piano making to lead pencils.

Transportation, communication, and public utilities: Much of the giant foreign investment in US railroads was portfolio rather than direct investment. Marconi in radio communication was an innovator. In public utilities, there were sizable portfolio investments and far smaller European direct investments.

Wholesale and retail trade: European multinationals that exported to the United States often integrated into selling on a wholesale level. Some firms in producer goods (the dye companies, the machinery makers) sold directly to their customers, without going through a retailer. On the other hand, most foreign sellers of consumer goods used American retail channels. A few tried to have their own 'shops' in America and then rejected such an approach. None of the large retailers in Great Britain developed retail networks in the United States. Lipton considered doing so, but decided against it. Shell apparently started to sell gasoline through company outlets on the West Coast before the First World War.

Finance, insurance, and real estate: A number of European direct investments in banking and finance existed, but deposit banking in the United States was American. In 1875–1914, European stakes in American domestic banking were negligible. British investment trusts and mortgage companies did make direct investments in providing American farm loans. The Dutch were also involved. Many European fire and marine insurance offices had branches or affiliates in the United States. While British companies were predominant among the foreign insurance companies, many European nationalities were represented, including Russian- and Bulgarian-headquartered firms. In real estate, from farm lands to urban properties, European direct investments existed.

Other services: Multinational enterprise-type investments were present in a range of services, among the most important being accounting services, where British partnerships extended themselves into America, offering a model for Americans.

To conclude, substantial European direct investment existed in the United States in the years before the First World War. While the investments of free standing companies may have been more a late-nineteenth- than a twentieth-century phenomenon in America, European-operating multinational enterprises clearly expanded in the United States in the early twentieth century. A number of the more important investments of this type took place in the two decades before the First World War.

The only 'two-digit' industrial classification in which I could not identify any European direct investment in the United States was 'furniture'. The nearest I got to furniture was 'floor covering', and one important British firm did make linoleum in the United States. Why was furniture excluded? Probably because there were no technological breakthroughs in furniture making; it was a local, technologically unsophisticated industry. Small companies predominated. Often, furniture was made of wood. Europeans had no advantage in this industry. Furniture was, moreover, in 1870–1914 generally sold without trademark. Otherwise, the range of industrial involvement is very broad.

What is evident, however, is that there was far from equality in the industrial distribution of investments. Some industries attracted more investment than others. The sizable foreign direct investments in the United States in textiles is one of my most notable discoveries. As I pushed for details, I found that a number of the textile products made in the United States were differentiated goods (trademarked cotton thread), technologically difficult to make (the woolen products of the Germans and French appear to have involved special knowhow), new industries (the silk industry was new to America), or patented processes (viscose yarn). Others before me have commented on the contributions of German investors to the American chemical industry. As I looked at the industries in which Europeans made investments in the United States, they turned out to be ones where the direct investor had some kind of identifiable advantage. And, for success, the advantage had to be retained. Sometimes, there was an initial perceived advantage that did not prove an advantage, or was dissipated over time. The advantage for some of the free standing companies was capital – and this was rarely an adequate advantage in and of itself.

I found major differences in the investments in the United States from one European country to the next. The British free standing companies were involved in agriculture (predominantly cattle), mining, manufacturing from steel to breweries, transportation, and finance. Companies that operated in Britain were visible in America in branded consumer goods (grocery products, textiles, medicines) and in specialized producer goods (textile machinery, chemicals, railroad equipment, and wireless apparatus). The British-Dutch Royal Dutch Shell entered the American oil industry. Some, but not many, British products that were manufactured by British firms in America involved new technology – from rayon to wireless equipment. The British had no investments in the new American automobile industry. British companies made many service-type investments in the United States.

The Germans specialized in high technology products, but also stood out in trademarked and branded goods. There has been substantial discussion about German advantages in chemicals and specialized machinery (electrical and non-electrical). There has been less stress on the fact that Germans developed name products that established the quality and integrity of the goods. This was true of goods sold to consumers (from underwear to aspirins to chocolates) as well as goods sold to producers (from dyes to machinery). German executives in the United States were well versed on both patent and trademark issues. The existence in the United States of a large German immigrant community provided management, labor, and also, on occasion, markets for German companies. German enterprises in America were particularly evident in the metal trades, where foreign markets became key.

French free standing companies existed in US mining and oil production. In the woolen yarn and silk, automobile, rubber tire, consumer chemical, and aluminum industries, French multinational enterprises were present in the United States. Likewise, in insurance and to a small extent in banking, there were French multinational companies in America. I was surprised at the extent of French business involvement.

Large and longstanding Dutch portfolio investments in the United States were very much in evidence. Dutch direct investments appear to have been more limited – some in oil, including those by Royal Dutch Shell, some in other minerals, some in cattle and land holdings, some in mortgage banking, and then not much else in the way of direct investments.

Companies controlled by Swiss, Belgians, Italians, Austrians, Swedes, Bulgarians, and Russians were all present in one or more industries with important direct investments (the Swiss in prepared foods, textiles, and chemicals; the Belgians in chemicals; the Italians in automobiles; an Austrian in fertilizers; Swedes in electrical and non-electrical machinery; the Bulgarians and Russians in insurance). All these were multinational-type investments.

There were more European direct investments in the United States in the years 1875–1914 than has been previously recognized. In some industries, they played highly significant roles. In many instances, they introduced new technology and new goods and services, as well as added capital to America.

NOTES

* I wish to thank the John Simon Guggenheim Memorial Foundation for support of the research for this paper.

1 David McClain, 'Foreign direct investment in the United States: old currents, "new waves", and the theory of direct investment', in Charles P. Kindleberger and David B. Audretsch (eds.), *The multinational corporation in the 1980s* (Cambridge, Mass., MIT Press, 1983), p. 219.

2 I am in the process of writing such a history.

3 Cleona Lewis, *America's stake in international investment* (Washington, Brookings, 1938). John Dunning in 1959–60 undertook a study of the history of British manufacturing in the United States; his student, T. C. Coram, in 'The role of British capital in the development of the United States c. 1600–1914', unpublished master's thesis, University of Southampton, 1967, used Dunning's data. David McClain, 'Foreign investment in United States manufacturing and the theory of direct investment', unpublished Ph.D. dissertation, MIT, 1974, ch. 1, relied heavily on Lewis's work. John Stopford, 'The origins of British-based multinational manufacturing enterprises', *Business history review*, XLVIII (1974), 303–35 and Lawrence Franko, *The European multinationals* (Stamford, Conn., Greylock Publishers, 1976) covered European foreign direct investment in the United States, as did Francesca Sanna Randaccio, 'European direct investments in U.S. manufacturing', unpublished B. Litt. thesis, University of Oxford, 1980. Peter Buckley and Brian Roberts, *European direct investment in the USA before World War I* (London, Macmillan Press, 1982) is a book riddled with errors; Thomas R. Kabisch, *Deutsches Kapital in den USA* (Stuttgart, Klett-Cotta, 1982) deals with German direct investments.

4 W. Turrentine Jackson, *The enterprising Scot* (Edinburgh University Press, 1968). W. G. Kerr, *Scottish capital on the American credit frontier* (Austin, Texas State Historical Association, 1976). Roger V. Clements has written several relevant articles, among them 'British controlled enterprise in the west between 1870 and 1900', *Agricultural history*, XXVI (1953), 132. Clark C. Spence, *British investments and the American mining frontier, 1860–1901* (Ithaca, Cornell University Press, 1958). Larry A. McFarlane has prepared a number of articles on British direct investments in land and land mortgages in the American West, for example, 'British investment and the land: Nebraska, 1877–1946', *Business history review*, LVII (1983), 258–72. Dorothy Adler, *British investment in American railways 1834–1898* (Charlottesville, University Press of Virginia, 1970), has some material on direct investment.

5 In my forthcoming 'The history of European multinationals – a new look', *Journal of European economic history*, I document this new literature.

6 Mira Wilkins, *The emergence of multinational enterprise: American business abroad from the colonial era to 1914* (Cambridge, Harvard University Press, 1970).

7 Professor Alfred D. Chandler Jr has made this point.

Industrial multinationals

4 The groupe Philippart: an experience of multinational enterprise in railway and banking business in western Europe: 1865–80

GINETTE KURGAN-VAN HENTENRYK

When studying the building of the multinational groupe Philippart, we have to look at the peculiar way in which the Belgian railways developed in the nineteenth century.[1] For the first time in Europe, a government conceived the construction by the state of a network connecting the country with its main neighbours. The reasons were political, strategical and economical. The new-born Belgian state had to consolidate its independence and to link its industrializing economy with the rest of Europe.

During a first stage, from 1835 to 1843, the state monopolized railways construction and operation. Once the trunk lines had been built, the secondary lines were left to private contractors without any public scheme. English, then Belgian capitalists rushed to get concessions, mostly in the industrial areas. The Rothschilds of Paris succeeded also in linking their line from Paris to the Belgian frontier with the main Belgian industrial towns of Mons, Charleroi and Liège.

In 1865, the network was cut up into 47 concessions on a territory of scarcely 30,000 square kilometres. Numerous short lines were conceded, especially in the Hainaut province, a very important coal and industrial area. These lines were so tangled, and the competition between the operating companies so tense, that the need for reorganization of the conceded lines into more competitive and profitable networks became urgent.

The initiative came from the private sector: the Société générale, the foremost bank of the kingdom, on the one hand, and a textile manufacturer, Simon Philippart, on the other.

At this time the second bank of the country, the Banque de Belgique, was changing its investment policy and replaced some members of its board of directors by businessmen who were in touch with the liberal cabinet. Simon Philippart and the Banque de Belgique negotiated with the government the constitution of a *société anonyme*, the Compagnie des Chemins de fer des

Bassins houillers du Hainaut. They intended in the first instance to issue 50 million francs of capital shares; but the administration somewhat feared the ambitions and appetites of the promoters, and so limited the capital at 25 million. Thus the company was founded on 1 February 1866.

Four years later the new company controlled the railways conceded to 19 companies in Belgium, including 1,000 km in operation and 500 km to be built. It must be remembered that the two major networks of the time, the Belgian state network and the Grand-Central, controlled by the Société générale, operated 869 km and 605 km respectively. Thus the Bassins houillers were running a third network mainly located in the western part of the country and based on the rationalization and development of transport in the three coalfields of the Hainaut province.

How did the company achieve such rapid growth, by Belgian standards? The answer is that it benefited from the financial crisis of 1866 which hardly hit the railway shares market. The Bassins houillers had no difficulty in getting control of companies unable to carry on the construction work because of lack of funds. Bidding the shareholders to exchange the shares of the railway companies for old or new bonds issued by the Bassins houillers was the company's favourite ploy. Afterwards, a special operating company leased the lines which fell under control of the Bassins houillers.

After merging the lines in operation and completing the railways in construction, it still did not have an autonomous network. Thus the Bassins houillers was unable to rival its main competitor, the state. Moreover, the merging activity and financial commitments slowed down the growth of profitability. Simon Philippart was assuming the exclusive responsibility for that policy.

Since the spring of 1868, indeed, he had obtained full control of the Bassins houillers. Reluctant to tie up too much capital, the Banque de Belgique had withdrawn. It was followed by all the influential members of the board. Philippart systematically replaced them in the various boards of the companies; the Bassins houillers was dominated by his own town relatives or friends and the managers of lines he had leased. These managers had often helped Philippart to obtain the lease of their lines because he offered them more favourable conditions in his own companies.

Simultaneously Philippart extended his operations in France and the Grand Duchy of Luxemburg by the scheme which he was following in Belgium, i.e. the promotion of goods transport between the industrial areas in the process of reconstruction in this part of western Europe. In these two countries he was running into powerful vested interests: the monopoly of the six big railway companies in France, and the iron industrialists in Luxemburg. But at the same time he turned the French 'mystique of small companies' of the end of the Second Empire to account and was welcomed by the Luxemburg government for national reasons. By the same methods as he used in Belgium, he obtained several hundred kilometres of railways in the two adjacent countries; but for many French lines he had still not obtained a decree of public utility.

To ease his financial trouble, he systematically issued bonds of the new companies which he built up without providing any capital. In these circumstances, Philippart tried to give up his Belgian railway network to the state.

At the end of the sixties, the Belgian state faced an increasingly pressing dilemma. It resulted from its twofold responsibility of protector of public interest on the one hand and that of entrepreneur on the other. The rising concentration of railway networks parallel to its own imperilled its traffic and receipts. As an industrialist, the state could not admit that its share of the market was being reduced. But as administrator of the Treasury, it could no longer accept a merciless struggle with private companies. Philippart's network, while not profitable, was nevertheless embarrassing.[2] Its competition had disastrous results on the state railways traffic and numerous conflicts occurred between the contractor and the administration.

It was in these conditions of struggle and financial trouble that Philippart offered his Belgian railway network back to the state. The liberal government was divided. The problem was to find a solution which would not cost the budget anything. Finally, with the help of two ministers, an agreement was reached on 25 April 1870: the state took back the operation of 601 kilometres consisting of the most profitable lines and those which were the most tangled in its own network. The state neither bought nor leased the railways, but associated itself with Philippart's company to share the receipts. The agreement rested on the principle of a financially self-supporting operation with nevertheless a fixed annual instalment of 7,000 francs per km guaranteed by the state in case of a receipt insufficiency. The guarantee was intended for paying the interests to the bondholders of the conceded railways. It was calculated on the assumption that goods traffic would increase. Philippart undertook to complete the conceded lines which were not yet built.

However, the Franco-Prussian War of 1870 had a profound effect on Philippart's enterprises. In Belgium, the Banque de Belgique came back into his business to capitalize the annual instalments owed by the state for the operation of the lines it had taken over. Very extensive speculation was starting on the prospect of increasing receipts and construction of new lines. Philippart failed in the creation of a Belgian-Luxemburgian railway consortium, but succeeded as an intermediary in the repurchase by the Belgian state of the Great Luxemburg Railway in 1873. Thus he gained admission to several banks and extended his interests in the Grand Duchy of Luxemburg. In France, with the support of local notables, he went on trying to obtain concession of branch lines. That enterprise was not easy because of the French government's hostility to foreign entrepreneurs and the

Table 4.1. *Capital issued at face value in 1875 (million fr.).*

	Belgium		France		Luxemburg		Total	
	Shares	Bonds	Shares	Bonds	Shares	Bonds	Shares	Bonds
Banking	54	—	60	—	—	—	114	—
Railways	22	238.6	138.5	258.7	17.5	50	178	547.3
Tramways	15	—	5.1	—	—	—	20.1	—
Mines, metalworks	30	—	—	—	5	—	35	—
Total	121	238.6	203.6	258.7	22.5	50	347.1	547.3

notables' fierce opposition to any agreement with the Compagnie du Nord, their main competitor.

Many contractors were giving up their projects for small railway companies. Philippart, however, persevered and during the summer of 1873 conceived the plan of an autonomous secondary lines network with international connections, the so-called *septième réseau*. Less than two years later he controlled more than 4,000 km of secondary railways. Had they been definitely conceded and built, his network would have been able to compete seriously with those of three big companies, the Compagnie du Nord, the Compagnie de l'Ouest, and the Compagnie d'Orléans. But there were only 2,705 km definitely conceded and 980 km in operation.[3] The war between the operating services was increasingly merciless.

From mid 1873 onwards Philippart left his career of railway contractor to become a financier. His huge capital needs persuaded him to take over banking houses and to reorganize and integrate his business under the control of one holding company. Thus at the beginning of 1875 he controlled a group of some twenty joint-stock companies in Belgium, France and Luxemburg, including banking and financial business, railways and tramways, mines and metal works, and sugar refineries. The issued capital amounted to 900 million francs at face value from which half a billion were in railway bonds, as can be seen in Table 4.1.

At this juncture we need to analyse the organization and the working of the group, which depended largely on the local conditions of the different countries in which Philippart was operating.

In Belgium special companies were formed to carry out the agreements concluded with the state, which implied the construction of several hundred kilometres of track. All the operating railway companies were liquidated and any remaining operations were transferred to one Bassins houillers service. The various mining and industrial properties, acquired when Philippart dominated the different railway companies before 1870, were grouped in one subsidiary company.

In the Grand Duchy of Luxemburg, where the Prince-Henri railway network was conceded to it, the Bassins houillers managed to monopolize the supplies of rolling stock and rails and the railway bonds sale. At the same time it created a new company to operate mining concessions which the Luxemburgian government had granted by way of subsidy and to produce part of the rolling stock and other supplies which its business needed.

In France, the Bassins houillers office of Paris centralized all Philippart's interests in French railway companies. It performed the various duties of stockholder, general contractor and banker, while the different networks' operating activities were merged in one single service.

In this way, the daily management was shared between several directors. The ability of the Bassins houillers to extend its activities was unrestricted by converting its statute into that of the very liberal 1873 law on the *société anonyme*. All these rationalizing arrangements alleviated the financial burden and reduced administrative costs, but they did not resolve the financial problems completely.

The industrial crisis in Belgium jeopardized all the sophisticated schemes worked out with the Banque de Belgique. Moreover, in France access to the stock market was very difficult because of the attitude of the public authorities and big companies towards the secondary railways. Philippart decided to overcome these obstacles by acquiring banks in order to get better access to small investors.

He used a method that had often been successful: massive purchase of shares to form a docile majority at the shareholders' meeting designed to replace the board of directors, and that with the help, if possible, of some manager of the company concerned. He succeeded without too many difficulties in dominating two French and one Belgian bank.[4] The conquest of the French Crédit mobilier in March 1875, however, was to be dearly paid for.

Thanks to the judicial archives, it is possible to know with accuracy how the group was working. As far as the groupe Philippart is concerned, there are four major items to be considered: the decision-making process, methods of financing, stock exchange operations and external relations.

When broadening his ventures, Philippart eliminated his friends and relatives from the boards of his companies. Furthermore the reorganization and the modification of the statute were giving him great autonomy in managing the Bassins houillers. He introduced on to the boards of the companies he controlled men whose docility and/or technical ability he appreciated. To begin with there were two categories of collaborators: the technicians, who were busy with the railway, mining and metallurgical enterprises, on the one hand, and the administrators on the other. Among the technicians there were some strong personalities, but Philippart carefully put them aside from his numerous financial deals. None of the administrative managers was in a position of influence or wished to influence him.

Philippart's control of banks introduced a third category, the financiers, whose part was much more ambiguous. In Paris, he left the daily banking management and speculating to two directors of the Banque Franco-Hollandaise although one of them, Auguste de Laveleye, while very docile, committed some very costly mistakes. In March 1875, for instance, Laveleye badly underestimated the entire purchasing policy of Philippart's banks at the stock exchange with the consequence of a catastrophic financial gap. In Brussels, on the contrary, Philippart met stronger opposition to his policy of merging all the banks' assets in his ventures.

When looking at the division of responsibility and Philippart's near circle, we need to consider his own position in the decision-making process. It is beyond all question that he identified himself with his companies. He told a judge:

Quand je dis 'Je', ou 'Nous', je parle en général au nom de la *Compagnie des Bassins houillers* dont je suis l'un des administrateurs-délégués et au nom de groupes financiers qui gravitent autour de cette société et qui traitent concurremment des affaires avec elles.[5]

That identification had a very concrete result. From 1869 onwards he was transferring to the Bassins houillers all his personal ventures and used the company as an intermediary when personally speculating in the interest of his enterprises. To that identification must be added an extraordinary ascendancy within his own circle.

In such conditions it is not surprising that with Philippart's overwhelming power and his collaborators' relative docility a bad lack of coordination imperilled a system of multiple, rather scattered ventures gravitating around two decision-making centres, Brussels and Paris. The connection between them was quite arbitrary, depending either on Philippart's or on one of his collaborators' movements. While using the most modern legal forms to build his business, Philippart had a fundamentally paternalistic management style which did not fit in with the size and dispersion of his ventures.

The methods of financing deserve some attention too. Notwithstanding the scarcity of information, one main trend appears – the diversion to the highest degree of resources towards the Bassins houillers and sharing out the charges between the companies it controlled. Furthermore, from 1873 the Bassins houillers was repurchasing its own stock, thus accumulating the profits in a reserve fund, with the object of tightening its control. Thus very little of the profits was distributed outside the group.

The way the company financed the repurchase is characteristic. The Banque de Belgique gave it a credit on guarantee of shares of one subsidiary company. Legally Philippart took some precautionary measures. In May 1873 the stockholders' meeting authorized the board of directors to use the profits exceeding 625,000 fr. and a quarter of the reserve fund to buy the stock back. The repurchased shares had to be destroyed. But Philippart neglected to obtain ratification of the repurchases and speculated with the Bassins houillers shares in the same way as with the other ones.

Philippart's squandering when he decided to acquire a new enterprise was also a typical feature of his business methods. Among several examples is the purchase at 1,500,000 fr. of an Austrian coalmine from a Belgian businessman who had paid only 100,000 fr. for it. That squandering may be explained partly by the large number of his achievements during the years 1873 and 1874.

Philippart rarely paid cash. On the whole he proceeded either by purchasing with the securities of his own societies, using the resources of the just-bought or newly created enterprises, or contango operations. But as ventures expanded, the need for cash increased. To provide the group with liquid funds, four methods were utilized: issuing securities of the Philippart's companies, selling securities to the banks which had been taken over, borrowing from those banks, and borrowing from the outside.

Nevertheless the group was always short of cash: a dozen million francs at least. Getting credit became increasingly difficult. Consequently transfers of funds and securities, and book-keeping operations between the various companies and Philippart himself were accelerating. A veritable communication system was set up between the financial institutions, each one resting on the other ones to obtain credit at the cheapest terms and to multiply the possibilities of access to it. Sometimes the same securities were used twice. Philippart juggled with the securities to get firms to supply his holding company with cash provided by the recently acquired banks or to obtain credit from outside. A third item of the groupe Philippart's working must be mentioned: the stock exchange operations. They constituted the main indictment during the preliminary investigation of Philippart's and his collaborators' case. Before his judges, Philippart kept on arguing firmly that he had speculated either to support the price of the securities of his companies at the stock market or to further the operations of companies with which he wished to be connected. Notwithstanding their disastrous results, his speculations were legally unquestionable. The problem was that by their volume and their aims they were giving rise to anxiety, then hostility in financial circles.

From the summer of 1874 onwards, speculating was Philippart's favourite method of carrying out his plans. He engaged in frantic struggles at the Paris Bourse to conquer the Crédit mobilier. He got the support of many brokers by numerous speculations with them. But his eagerness to compel the speculators selling securities of his companies to deliver these gave rise to much enmity.

External relations also played an important part in the activities of the Bassins houillers. Notwithstanding the controversies about the cession of railways in operation to the Belgian state, Philippart enjoyed the support of important bankers and secondary financial institutions. After 1870, the Banque de Belgique increased its interests in his business. The latter provided valuable support at the Brussels stock exchange and in the financial press. While he started his ventures with the support of liberal politicians, Philippart got some assistance from the conservative catholic ministers too.

In the Grand Duchy of Luxemburg, thanks to his financial links with some influential politicians such as the previous conservative prime minister baron de Blochausen, he could obtain the favour of the government.

In spite of repeated efforts, Philippart never obtained the benevolence of the leading circles towards his enterprises in France. On the contrary, his greed for acquiring a position in the stock market, his numerous speculations with the Parisian brokers, and his munificence towards the newspapers attracted dubious businessmen such as the well-known Erlanger, but alienated those influential business interests connected with the political leaders in power. These obstacles contributed to his collapse.

By conquering the Crédit mobilier, Philippart was becoming an embarrassing competitor for the big railway companies and their supporters; when he collapsed, he presented himself as a victim of powerful opponents. The reality was more complex. Certainly the big companies and the 'haute banque' played an important part in the newspaper campaign of 1875, but the main opponents at the stock exchange, the parliament and the courts were the directors of the Crédit mobilier and Erlanger, who was also aiming to dominate the Crédit mobilier. His obstinacy to defeat his opponents at the stock exchange led to Philippart's disaster in May 1875 with international repercussions on the Berlin and Brussels stock markets. For eighteen months Philippart fought to survive, but without giving up his methods. From January 1877 almost all his companies were going bankrupt.

Thus the groupe Philippart's venture finds a place in a particular stage of railway history in Belgium and in France. In both countries, by different ways, the operation of the main networks was monopolized. But under the pressure of economic liberalism, public authorities conceded railways to other entrepreneurs, starting harsh competition and increasing anarchy and squandering. In Belgium, private entrepreneurs, among them Philippart, tried to reorganize the networks. In France the big companies undertook to extend secondary networks to eliminate competition.

The final result of Philippart's action in Belgium was the repurchase by the Belgian state of more than 1,150 km of operating lines in the seventies. In France the attempt to create a *septième réseau* anticipated the *plan Freycinet*, and hence as in Belgium it contributed to strengthen the monopolies established at the beginning of the railway era. However, by aiming to develop an international industrial railways network to promote communications between the traditional industrial areas and the new coalfields and iron beds in western Europe, Philippart encountered powerful interests but raised strategical problems too. The fear of Germany after the Franco-Prussian War was often expressed in the controversies about Philippart's business in Luxemburg and France.

On the other hand Philippart's passage in the French stock market participated, according to M. Lévy-Leboyer, in the speculation wave initiated by the Pereire's Crédit mobilier which led to the crash of the Union générale in 1882.[6] His struggle with the big companies was an episode of the *haute banque* obstructing access to the Paris stock market during the Second Empire. Notwithstanding the victory of economic liberalism in Belgium and France, whatever mistakes Philippart committed, the power of vested interests cannot be denied.

Finally the groupe Philippart's experience illustrates how difficult it is to pass from industrial capitalism to financial capitalism, from leadership of a family business to that of a financial group, especially in a market where banking was playing a growing part in business financing.

NOTES

1 This paper is based on copious unpublished material collected in several archives deposits in Belgium and abroad. This material is listed in G. Kurgan-van Hentenryk, *Rail, finance et politique: les entreprises Philippart (1865–1890)* (Brussels, 1982). For more details on the subject-matter of this paper, the reader may usefully refer to that book.

2 In 1869 the receipts of Philippart's railways amounted to 14,000 francs per kilometre; those of the state railways reached 52,000 francs.

3 The French network included the lines of several companies:

Nord-Est	300 km
Lille à Valenciennes	761 km
Lille à Béthune	53 km
Orléans à Rouen	1,441 km
Chemins de fer normands	30 km
Chemins de fer du Rhône	7 km
St Nazaire au Croisic	30 km
Bressuire à Poitiers	604 km
Chemins de fer de la Vendée	815 km

(For more details see Kurgan-van Hentenryk, pp. 189–90.)

4 They were the Banque franco-autrichienne-hongroise, Banque franco-hollandaise and Banque belge du commerce et de l'industrie.

5 Quoted in Kurgan-van Hentenryk, p. 227. See also the quotations on p. 228.

6 M. Lévy-Leboyer, *Histoire économique et sociale de la France*, (Paris, 1976), III.1, pp. 448–51.

5   The House of Rothschild (Paris) as a multinational industrial enterprise: 1875–1914

JOHN McKAY

When one looks at both scholarly and polemical writing on the historical development of multinational enterprise, it is obvious that large corporations with wholly owned (or closely controlled) foreign subsidiaries have attracted most of the attention. Thus there has been great interest in US direct corporate investment, originating in the late nineteenth century and growing rapidly after the Second World War, as well as in early and subsequent efforts of European and Japanese giants to catch and match the American pioneers. Yet this is at best only part of the story.

Historically, multinational business activity more traditionally considered under such rubrics as 'foreign entrepreneurship' or 'the export of capital' was also important, especially for western European companies. Indeed, Mira Wilkins sees the common western European practice in the late nineteenth century of establishing an ostensibly independent, 'free-standing company' as a striking departure from the 'American model' of major corporations expanding out of domestic operations to create foreign branches.[1] To borrow from organization theory to frame an initial hypothesis, it seems likely that prior to 1914 the foreign and domestic portions of the typical European multinational enterprise were more 'loosely coupled' than their American counterparts.

At the same time, scattered evidence also suggests a second hypothesis, namely, that in numerous cases ostensibly free-standing European multinationals were actually clustered around some common patron (or combination of patrons) and constituted an informal group of international firms, a pattern rarely stressed by students of US direct foreign investment. In my own work on foreign entrepreneurship in pre-revolutionary Russian industry, for example, it was sometimes possible to distinguish industrial firms clustered together in an organic relationship, like those in the Bonnardel Group, as well as those linked by more easily recognized financial ties.[2] Unfortunately, since ties between group-related firms of European origin were frequently obscure and hard to evaluate, this important phenomenon has in recent times attracted more attention from ideologues than from serious historians.

74

This study addresses some of these broad questions through an examination of the development of one such important group – the multinational firms in mining and refining controlled by the French Rothschilds between 1875 and 1914. Recognized vaguely by some contemporaries and an occasional historian, this group of related companies has never been seriously investigated, or even discussed.[3] Therefore three questions seem appropriate within the context of this volume. First, what was the basic history of the industrial holdings and firms that came to form what I shall call 'the Rothschild Group'? Second, what were the business strategies of the Paris Rothschilds and their related free-standing companies? Third, how does the growth of the Rothschild Group offer fresh insights into the history of multinational business enterprise?

To avoid misunderstandings we must first be clear what we are talking about. As is well known, the House of Rothschild rose to prominence as a multinational family firm *sui generis*. The five gentlemen of Frankfurt formed a tight-knit partnership with operations in Frankfurt, London, Paris, Vienna, and Naples (liquidated in 1863). This legal framework was maintained throughout the nineteenth century, although the different branches also operated in their own names and experienced varying fortunes. By the 1870s the French division of the firm was apparently the most active and the most important quantitatively. A surviving balance sheet for 27 July 1877 shows a total capital for all branches of the firm equalling £30,200,000, or 755,000,000 francs. Of that total £16,800,000 was at work in Paris, £6,100,000 in London, £4,200,000 in Frankfurt, and £3,100,000 in Vienna.[4] The capital shares of the individual houses and partners were much more nearly equal, and the pre-eminence of Paris reflected large deposits from Frankfurt and Vienna, though apparently not from London. These financial arrangements continued into the twentieth century, so that the partners in Paris managed a large portion of the extended family's great fortune.

When the Paris Rothschilds built an informal group of free-standing multinational companies in the 1880s and 1890s, they were basically striking out in a new direction. As Bertrand Gille has shown, under James de Rothschild (1792–1868) the Paris branch generally avoided industrial ventures as risky and inappropriate. Such industrial loans and participations as there were aimed mainly at facilitating major investments in state-supported railroads, which were a logical extension of the bank's primary and highly profitable focus on government loans and public finance.

Suspicious of industrial commitments, the French House of Rothschild had like many private bankers a strong and long-standing interest in international commerce, particularly the trade in precious and non-ferrous metals. According to Gille, the underlying strategy was to focus on selected commodity markets which had few buyers and sellers, and where opportunities for profitable manipulation were believed greatest. Thus, as sales representative of the Demidovs of Russia, the House of Rothschild dominated the French market for copper until 1838. Becoming exclusive sales agent for the Spanish government's mines at Almadén in conjunction with underwriting a state loan, it effectively monopolized the world market for mercury until the 1850s. By the 1860s lead from Spain and petroleum from the United States were also particularly important items of commerce.[5] Of special interest for our purposes, by the mid 1860s the firm also owned and operated two refineries in France as part of its interest in metals.

In the 1870s the powerful French branch of the firm began to face serious long-term challenges as a viable enterprise, as distinct from wealthy rentiers living royally on returns from accumulated capital. Above all, competition from joint-stock deposit banks began to undermine the House's position in the government loan business, which eventually did lead to a large relative decline in French (and European) public finance. The firm's international commerce also suffered in the 1870s, buffeted by falling prices, increased competition, and shifting markets. In precious metals the response of the French Rothschilds was quite limited; the business declined and the precious metals refinery in France was subsequently liquidated. In lead, however, the firm chose to fight, which proved to be a critical decision.

A first, possibly inadvertent step was taken in 1872, when the Paris partners – Alphonse, Gustave, and Edmond de Rothschild – hired a skilled metallurgist and recent graduate of the Paris School of Mines named Jules Aron as the House's consulting engineer. Combining practical experience of managing a major Spanish lead foundry and a flair for trading metals on international markets, Aron was well suited to supervise both the industrial and commercial aspects of the Rothschild lead business.

Although there are gaps in the surviving records, by 1870 that business apparently consisted of purchasing silver-bearing lead pig from Spanish founders through an agent at Cartagena in southern Spain. The agent also advanced working capital in accordance with delivery of stipulated quantities of silver lead, which was then refined at the Rothschild plant at Le Havre, prior to sale of the purified merchant lead and the silver by-product in the Paris market. Charging Spanish founders a complicated mixture of interest, refining fees, and selling commissions, the firm's lead business had apparently grown out of its general interest in commerce and its powerful position in Spanish public finance and railroad building. From all indications the business had customarily earned solid returns while incurring only modest risks.[6]

In the 1870s, sharply falling and increasingly volatile prices for lead and progressively demonetized silver shook the industry and combined with aggressive English competition to put heavy pressure on the fees which the refinery at Le Havre could charge. Moreover, Spanish founders resisted lower prices, sometimes reneging on contracts and striving to hold the price of silver at Cartagena above that prevailing on world markets. Aid from the Spanish government for its embryonic refining industry, through an inflated mint price for domestically refined silver and an export tax on silver-lead pig, strengthened their resolve.

The Rothschilds' first move, planned and implemented by Aron, was defensive investment at Le Havre of roughly 250,000 francs. Designed to being 'the transformation of productive equipment which was as defective as it was insuffisant', the installation of an improved refining technology dramatically cut the cost of refining Spanish silver-lead and made the plant at Le Havre marginally profitable once again.[7]

Turning next to serious problems on the commercial side, Aron conducted a thorough on-the-spot investigation in southern Spain in 1876. There he became convinced of the need to introduce (or possibly reintroduce) 'the system of direct purchase' of silver-lead requirements. Rather reluctantly, his bosses agreed. Seconded by Bauer and Weisweiller, the Rothschild financial agents at Madrid, Aron negotiated long-term contracts to purchase a total of 500 tons of silver lead per month from two or three medium-sized founders, who also obtained Rothschild loans secured by first mortgages on their properties. Significantly, all settlement prices were now based on the London market, and a solid rate of return on total commercial capital of more than 2,000,000 francs was virtually guaranteed by the complicated pricing and refining schedules built into the contracts. By bargaining directly with hard-pressed founders the Rothschilds had subverted market-rigging manipulations in Spain, and their revitalized lead business passed through the 1870s without suffering the heavy losses experienced by many firms.

Yet the Paris Rothschilds remained reluctant investors in industry in the 1870s. Operations in lead – the biggest 'industrial' activity (excluding railroads) as far as one can judge – absorbed less than 2% of total capital at the Paris branch, which consisted mainly of commercial credits backed by first mortgages. The partners rejected Aron's recommendation in 1877 to invest in a Spanish foundry or refinery, in order to get behind the protectionist measures being erected by the Spanish government. And they continued to reject various offers to invest in mining properties around the world. Fears of being trapped in spiraling illiquid investments, apprehensions about blackmail threats from disgruntled shareholders, and a limiting desire to transform industrial-commercial operations into banking operations all played a role in their cautious approach.[8]

Yet other considerations militated in favor of a major reorientation toward industrial ventures. First, as a talented salaried expert seeking to promote his career while loyally serving the House, Aron skillfully pressed for a more active industrial policy and stood eager to manage certain kinds of investments. Second, the mining industry in Spain (and elsewhere) presented enticing opportunities: mine owners and founders were notoriously short of capital;

and their mines and stocks of metal provided potentially good security for both loans and partnership arrangements. Third, the House's commercial section (*bureau des marchandises*) had the expertise necessary to finance such stocks and sell them effectively in sophisticated international markets, occasionally in conjunction with successful speculative maneuvres. Finally, the House's declining position in public finance and the gradual recouping of some earlier investments in Italian and Spanish railroads meant that ample capital was available for promising new ventures.[9]

A first result of this orientation was Rothschild participation in the founding of the Peñarroya Mining and Metallurgical Company (Société minière et métallurgique de Peñarroya), which with almost simultaneous investment in Spanish petroleum (see below) marked the beginning of a decade of entrepreneurship in industrial undertakings. At the origin of its Peñarroya involvement in 1880, the House went beyond the system of direct purchases and loaned money to a major mine owner named Carlos Huelin. In return, the House leased Huelin's vast lead-mining concessions on a royalty basis and became the exclusive selling agent for all the metal produced. Intending to develop Huelin's mines, the Rothschilds were nevertheless hesitant to build and operate the necessary foundries and refinery in their own name. A solution was reached when they agreed to transfer their leases on Huelin's properties to a new corporation formed in conjunction with the French-owned Belmez Coal Company after extensive negotiations.

Belmez was a major Spanish coal producer which had grown out of French railroad building in Spain, and it was controlled by the Mirabaud Bank and Cahen d'Anvers, banker and dealer in non-ferrous metals.[10] Belmez had also acquired lead mines it wished to develop and, like Aron, its directors believed that the future lay in large-scale founding and refining of silver lead in Spain itself. Moreover, Charles Ledoux, outstanding mining engineer and Belmez's chief executive, was eager to build and manage such operations. The Rothschilds were no less eager to serve as the new company's banker and exclusive selling agent, while charging Aron to collaborate closely as Peñarroya's consulting engineer. The firm was officially founded in late 1881 with the House of Rothschild taking 40% of the capital stock.

Easily surviving the depression of 1882, Peñarroya went on to prosper mightily. Producing 80% of Spain's silver and 60% of its lead in 1913, Peñarroya was the undisputed leader in the Spanish lead industry, the most important in the world along with that in the United States. Using Peñarroya as one source of supply for its refining operations at Le Havre, the Paris branch steadfastly maintained its initial investment position and continued as Peñarroya's exclusive selling agent (until 1909). With several representatives on the board of directors, the House of Rothschild was commonly identified as the power behind Peñarroya in the financial press.[11]

The second Rothschild venture in non-ferrous metallurgy was the Nickel

Company (la Société de nickel), formed in early 1880 by an Australian-born entrepreneur named John Higginson to develop rich nickel deposits which he had acquired on the French island of New Caledonia in the Pacific Ocean. Lacking adequate liquid capital to develop the production and sale of what was still a semi-precious metal, Higginson turned to the Rothschilds. As with their Spanish venture, in 1881 the Rothschilds lent the mine-rich, cash-poor Higginson development funds secured by his property (Nickel Company shares), provided trade credits, and marketed nickel output on an exclusive basis. In the 1880s the Paris branch purchased about 25% of the firm's stock, mainly from an overly extended Higginson. Combined with its advances as banker, this minority ownership permitted effective but by no means exclusive control of the widely held company.

The Nickel Company's progress was less even than Peñarroya's. Striving to dominate completely the world market for nickel, the company gathered up New Caledonia's principal deposits. In 1884 it acquired the European nickel refineries of its two main competitors in Great Britain and Germany, which complemented the firm's foundry operations in New Caledonia. But world-wide monopoly was short-lived. In 1891 American and Canadian capitalists opened rich nickel mines in Ontario near Sudbury, which led to a crisis of overproduction and sharply lower prices. The result was a large loss on inventory, which the Nickel Company chose to cover in 1896 by abruptly reducing the par value of its capital stock by 50%. Shortly thereafter a market-sharing arrangement with what soon became the International Nickel Company was finally worked out, and the firm again entered a period of profit and steady growth as senior partner of the world duopoly.

Finally, rounding out their participation in non-ferrous metallurgy, the Paris branch played a major role in turning virtually unexploited mineral deposits on Mexico's Lower California peninsula into an important copper producer, which operated as the Boléo Company (Compagnie du Boléo).[12] The initiative in the Boléo venture was taken by the Mirabaud Bank, whose directors were already partners with the Rothschilds in Peñarroya. After careful follow-up studies the Rothschilds subscribed 37.5% of Boléo's initial 1885 capital of 6,000,000 francs, and they received a substantial portion of the founders' parts.

In addition to solid Rothschild representation on Boléo's board of directors, similar to that found at Peñarroya and the Nickel Company, Aron served once again as the firm's consulting engineer for almost thirty years. He made a major contribution to Boléo's ultimately brilliant financial success which demanded imaginative technical solutions to difficult production problems. Specifically, Aron and his Boléo associates chose advanced American water-jacket technology for smelting copper in Mexico, engaged a leading Chicago firm to build the installation, and trained French specialists to use the unfamiliar techniques effectively. Boléo's all-French managerial team further demonstrated its ability to adapt to foreign conditions by wisely placing Mexicans in some supervisory positions, thereby escaping the intense antipathies aroused by some North American mining companies in Mexico because of their exclusive hiring practices.[13]

Petroleum was the second pole of multinational industrial activity for the Paris Rothschilds before 1914. Since the Rothschild petroleum adventure has a complex history and has already attracted a fair amount of scholarly attention, I shall focus mainly on unsuspected or misunderstood aspects of the story in this brief paper.[14]

First, contrary to a common impression, Rothschild interest in petroleum did not originate with their famous investments in Russia. Rather, building upon a substantial import trade in American petroleum in the late 1860s and close ties with the French refiner Deutsch de la Meurthe, the Paris branch accepted a proposition from that firm in late 1879 to form a fifty–fifty partnership to manufacture kerosene in Spain.[15] According to the Deutschs, recently enacted protectionists legislation promised large profits to whomever seized the opportunity; and despite inevitable vicissitudes the joint refining venture in Spain was quite successful until 1914.

Experienced petroleum industrialists and trusted associates, the Deutschs participated as investors and managers in all subsequent Rothschild petroleum ventures. They were a valuable though seldom suspected asset for the petroleum group. Thus in 1882 Deutsch was charged with constructing at Fiume on the Austrian Adriatic a second Rothschild-related refinery, one-third of which was owned by the Paris and Vienna branches acting in concert.

Second, the Rothschilds were initially attracted to Russia's Baku petroleum industry as a source of raw materials, and the refinery at Fiume was profitably supplied with Russian feed-stocks for many years. But, as is generally known, they soon saw more exciting opportunities in financing and managing the sale of rapidly growing Russian kerosene exports to European markets. Unable in 1883 and 1884 to negotiate a merging of interests with the Nobel Brothers Petroleum Company, far and away the industry's leading enterprise, the Rothschilds purchased in 1886 a smaller but still quite important Russian firm orientated toward export markets, the Batum Oil Refining and Trading Company, commonly known by its Russian acronym of Bnito.[16]

The Paris branch then proceeded to market Russian kerosene aggressively in the late 1880s, linking a growing network of Russian suppliers with western European distributors, some of which were subsidiary firms. These were the Rothschild marketing companies outside Russia that subsequently joined with the Royal Dutch Petroleum Company and the Shell Oil Company in 1903 to form the famous Asiatic syndicate, thereby unintentionally paving the way for the sale of the Rothschild Russian petroleum companies in Russia to Royal Dutch in 1912. Marketing was unquestionably one of the principal themes in the Rothschild Russian petroleum business.

Third, initially interested in Russian oil almost exclusively in terms of European markets for raw materials and refined products, the Paris branch moved in the mid 1890s to take a much stronger position in Russia's internal petroleum trade. The critical step was creating a second Russian company for the large-scale shipment and distribution of bulky fuel oil to the Russian national market, in conjunction with Russian partners who held a minority interest. This firm, the Mazout Petroleum Company, enabled the Rothschilds better to balance Bnito's substantial output of crude and residual oil at Baku with the foreign demand for refined kerosene. Moreover, by fashioning a serious Russian marketer for their petroleum interests, the Rothschilds were at last able to challenge effectively the Russian Nobels on their own ground, and thereby lead them to favor mutually advantageous market-sharing arrangements at home and abroad. Unlike the oft-mentioned story of Rothschild kerosene exports, the strategy of developing marketing capacity for the Russian market has gone largely unnoticed. I intend to treat it fully at a later date.

Leaving aside substantial investments in electricity, which were mainly confined to France, this completes our historical overview of the known multinational industrial enterprises that were closely related to the Paris Rothschilds between 1871 and 1914. By way of summary, it would be desirable to make precise quantitative statements about total capital invested in these firms. Unfortunately, no single listing of all industrial participations at a given moment before 1914 has been uncovered, and the historian must rely on fragmentary and sometimes contradictory evidence which will require careful processing and heavily qualified presentation. Nevertheless, even rough calculations show that substantial sums were involved.

The best data relate to the Russian petroleum business. Circa 1900, de Rothschild frères and Rothschild family members (and a few trusted employees) had invested roughly 35,000,000 francs in the capital stock of Bnito, Mazout, and the marketing companies in western Europe. In addition, the House had loaned these firms 19,000,000 francs, which combined with losses on a Russian drilling venture in liquidation meant a total Rothschild investment of about 58,000,000 francs. With less precision one may say that by 1900 the House and family members had invested in the capital stock of Peñarroya at least 2,500,000 francs (with a market value more than twice as great) and at least 4,500,000 francs in the Nickel Company, as well as Boléo. At an absolute minimum original investment in the capital stock of these firms totaled 11,500,000 francs, which (even including the Nickel Company's reversals) had a market value at least twice as great. Nor does this include working capital advances of unknown size. Thus, circa 1900, total Rothschild capital in these petroleum and non-ferrous metals companies was at least 80,000,000 francs, and possibly more than 100,000,000 francs. This compares with a total capital for all branches of the House of Rothschild of £41,500,000 (1,037,500,000 francs) on 31 December 1899, of which £25,000,000 (625,000,000 francs) was being used in Paris and of which £15,000,000 (375,000,000 francs) was the share of Alphonse, Gustave, and Edmond de Rothschild.[17] It seems that the industrial companies were not only profitable achievements in their own right, but that they also had come to loom large in the life of the family and especially its French branch.

Turning now to the question of business strategy as revealed in explicit documentary evidence and deduced from observed behavior, it is first of all clear that the Paris Rothschilds were extremely selective in their industrial participations. With a long interest in metals, they nevertheless were extremely suspicious of all mines and mining promoters. At the same time, they refused to scatter their shots, seeking instead those rare big ventures that were, as Aron once put it in 1879, 'serious', 'sure', and 'worthy of the House'.[18] Moreover, the Rothschilds were chronologically selective: their *grandes affaires* in industry came mainly in the 1880s, a concentration that is rather puzzling.

As for the few big undertakings that actually were realized, they grew out of and harmonized with the firm's considerable experience in financing and selling selected high-value commodities on international markets. Indeed, one might well argue that the strategic common denominator was the adaptation and capitalization of rather traditional but sophisticated marketing skills to an emerging corporate world: above all, the Rothschilds skillfully maneuvred to make themselves the exclusive selling agent of large industrial undertakings on a guaranteed commission basis. More generally, the goal was to realize profits from several sources, so as to increase the effective total return on the underlying risk capital. Thus the Paris partners anticipated solid dividends (and capital gains) on their joint-stock investment, but they also expected commissions on sales and interest on working capital advances, both of which were assured by the investment in capital shares.

Capitalizing on their marketing skills, the Paris Rothschilds continued to concentrate on product markets where they intended to play a large, possibly dominant role through the international enterprise in question. With the possible exception of copper (Boléo), they planned at a minimum to weigh heavily, as in the international lead market through a leading firm in the main producing country in Europe. At a maximum they hoped to command an effectively international trade, notably that in nickel through the New Caledonian undertaking. Initial strategies in petroleum centered on domination of a well-defined sub-sector – kerosene produced within Spain, Russian kerosene marketed in western Europe. Investment was thus confined to multinational enterprises which seemed potentially capable of exercising real market power, the presumed source of exceptional profits that justified purchase of risky capital shares.

Seeking instinctively to regulate markets, the Paris Rothschilds were warm partisans of interfirm understandings, market-sharing agreements, and cartels. This was especially true from the 1890s onward, when the ambitious goals of the 1880s proved illusive. Thus great efforts were devoted to negotiating such agreements, and considerable success was eventually achieved in petroleum and nickel.[19] But, as one might expect from what is known of late-nineteenth-century European enterprise, even when attempts temporarily floundered the Rothschilds were not much interested in the contemporaneous American model of monopolization through the merger of competing firms into a single trust or holding company.

A revealing example concerned the Nickel Company in the 1890s. Having ended the French firm's monopoly and also ruined the world price after 1891, the firm controlling the industry in North America offered to merge the two competitors in 1895 and painted a rosy picture of probable profits. A skeptical Alphonse de Rothschild refused, arguing instead that a more modest market-sharing agreement would better respect the various interests involved and was therefore more practical.[20]

One of those interests was financial control. At least until the death of Alphonse de Rothschild in 1905, it seems certain that the Paris branch normally invested major sums only in firms in which it had a controlling interest and expected to retain a long-term commitment. Dilution of their 25% ownership share in the Nickel Company would expose the Paris Rothschilds to the danger of becoming mere passive investors, a condition they were not prepared to accept for several reasons.

Financial control was necessary to insure subsidiary sources of profits as banker and exclusive selling agent. It was also necessary for close supervision and/or day-to-day management by Rothschild partners and trusted employees. Intimate involvement also guaranteed strict financial orthodoxy in the French corporate tradition for all these firms. This orthodoxy featured limited initial investments, rapid depreciation, modest dividends, and growth through reinvested profits. Finally, the Rothschilds had a fear of criticism and a sense of accountability: zealously guarding their reputation, they long wanted control to prevent any business disaster for which they felt the public would be quick to hold them responsible.[21] Perhaps this also explains why they apparently showed little interest in short-term gains from underwriting newly formed industrial companies.

Since market considerations were of primary significance in Rothschild decisions to invest in the different firms we have considered, the technological factor, which scholars (including myself) have often seen as critical in the development of multinational enterprise, appears distinctly secondary in this instance. Nevertheless, these multinational companies shared a common technological base in extractive industry, where the expertise of experienced engineers like the firm's Jules Aron was absolutely crucial for the evaluation and development of mines and refineries. Along with other Rothschild representatives, Aron participated as consulting engineer in the daily management of all these companies and helped plan and implement sophisticated and effective technical policies. Moreover, with the bank's interests ever in mind, Aron helped coordinate the recruitment and promotion of the top technical personnel of the different firms, thereby building up valuable human resources that could be shared between the related companies.

To conclude with a broader and more tentative perspective, the Rothschild-related firms highlight some neglected dimensions in the history of multinational enterprise. First, these firms were excellent examples of free-standing European multinational enterprise before 1914, and as such they clearly departed from the more frequently studied 'American model' of direct corporate investment. Second, these nominally independent free-standing firms were, in fact, loosely tied to the House of Rothschild, as other congeries of multinationals of European origins might also be linked to a common patron, often a financial institution. Yet the Rothschild experience suggests that much more was usually involved in such groups than simply a portfolio of passive investments. Rather, these firms formed a clearly discernible Rothschild Group of multinational mining and refining companies. With two different but related components – one in petroleum and one in non-ferrous metals – the Group had rather striking similarities to some contemporary multinational (and national) conglomerates.

As with such freer-form firms today, the Group delegated most 'line' operations related to day-to-day production to local managers of the different firms, while a core 'staff' of Rothschild employees monitored or performed certain specialized functions at the centre. For each firm these functions included marketing and commercial negotiations, financial policy, technological policy, and continuous evaluation of operating company managers. More generally, Rothschild partners and employees exercised a decisive voice in each firm's major decisions and long-term strategic planning.

While this characterization of the Rothschild Group is accurate as a schematic generalization, one must remember that there were substantial variations in the specific details between the individual companies, each of which had its own history and legal identity. Certainly the distribution of staff functions was not neatly standardized, reflecting the diverse origins of the firms, the degree of Rothschild ownership, the assertiveness of minority partners, the demands of managing directors, and so on. Many aspects of the closely held Russian oil business were run from Paris on a daily basis, for example, while Peñarroya with its Belmez partners and autocratic but competent managing director operated with more autonomy.

This diversity of arrangements suggests that one of the long-term appeals of the loosely coupled, free-standing enterprise was its enormous flexibility, permitting divergent interests to combine in an effective entrepreneurial cadre

under many different circumstances. For the Rothschilds, as perhaps for some
enlightened multinational corporations in the Third World today, only
underlying or even only latent control was the absolutely essential prerequisite.
By way of epilogue, it was such control that enabled Guy de Rothschild,
Alphonse's grandson, to merge Peñarroya and the Nickel Company together
after the Second World War, creating in the resulting Inmetal Company one
of the world's principal multinational enterprises in non-ferrous metals.[22]
It was an achievement that confirmed the Group's long-standing existence
while giving it a new form.

NOTES

1 Mira Wilkins, 'The history of European multinationals – a new look', *Journal of European economic history*, forthcoming, an excellent guide to current research. For an example of a 'free-standing' firm of American origin, see discussion of the French Thomson-Houston Company in John P. McKay, *Tramways and trolleys: the rise of urban mass transport in Europe* (Princeton University Press, 1976), pp. 125–62.

2 John P. McKay, *Pioneers for profit: foreign entrepreneurship and Russian industrialization, 1885–1913* (University of Chicago Press, 1970), pp. 62–71, 337–67.

3 Jean Bouvier, *The Rothschilds* (Paris, Fayard, 1963), pp. 255–8. I am currently writing a monograph on the industrial participations of MM de Rothschild frères from 1875 to 1914. The history of the French branch from 1815 to 1870 has been exhaustively studied by the late Bertrand Gille, *Histoire de la maison Rothschild* (2 vols., Geneva, Librairie Droz, 1965, 1967), which provides a guide to existing sources.

4 Archives nationales, Paris (cited hereafter as A.N.), 132 AQ, 2.

5 Gille, *Maison Rothschild*, I, pp. 407–15; II, 547–57, 564.

6 Large portions of the business records of the Paris branch, now housed in the French National Archives under 132 AQ, have been lost. Many dossiers on industrial firms and sixty-two volumes of Aron's out-going correspondence from 1875 to 1913 survive, however. On the Spanish lead business in the 1870s, see A.N. 132 AQ, primarily 116 and 823–31. Complete documentation on this and other questions will be provided in my forthcoming book.

7 A.N., 132 AQ, 825, Aron to MM de Rothschild frères, 10 June 1876, is particularly informative.

8 A.N., 132 AQ, 826–9, especially Aron to Weil, 16 August 1877 and 9 January 1878.

9 In addition to the fragmentary account in Gille, *Maison Rothschild*, II, pp. 507–8, 520–1, 531, and 537, see his unpublished 'Inventaire' of Rothschild papers at the French National Archives.

10 On Belmez and Peñarroya, see Albert Broder, 'Le Rôle des intérêts économiques étrangers dans la croissance de l'Espagne au XIXe siècle, 1767–1924', Ph.D. dissertation, University of Paris, n.d., vol. v, pp. 1517–34, 1586–91.

11 See the sample in A.N., 65 AQ, L 2601 (1–2). Abundant if incomplete material on Peñarroya's formation is in 132 AQ, 831–5.

12 Some contemporaries also believed that the Rothschilds may have been involved in the speculations leading up to the collapse of the Société des métaux and the

copper crash of 1889, a complicated subject well beyond our scope. See Bouvier, *Rothschilds*, p. 228.

13 Crédit Lyonnais, Paris, Études Financières, 'Cie du Boléo', unpublished study, Oct. 1899.

14 In addition to an article on early Rothschild activities by Bertrand Gille, 'Capitaux français et pétroles russes (1884–1894)', *Histoire des entreprises*, Nov. 1963, 9–94, see F. C. Gerretson, *History of the Royal Dutch* (4 vols., Leiden, E. J. Brill, 1953–7).

15 The firm operated ostensibly in Deutsch's name, while de Rothschild frères quietly furnished the entire capital of 3,000,000 *en commandite*. Profits were divided equally. A. N., 132 AQ, 139.

16 In addition to n. 14 above, see John P. McKay, 'Baku oil and Transcaucasian pipelines, 1883–1891: a study in Tsarist economic policy', *Slavic review*, XLI, no. 4 (Winter 1984), 604–23, and sources cited there.

17 In A. N., 132 AQ, see especially 136 (for oil in 1900), 335 (for non-ferrous metals), and 2 (for balance sheet of 31 December 1899).

18 A. N., 132 AQ, 832, Aron to his uncle, 26 November 1879.

19 The fullest information of this type in A. N., 132 AQ, is on petroleum; that on lead is weakest.

20 A. N., 132 AQ, 859, Aron to Ruef, 25 October 1895.

21 For example, see Aron's correspondence on a diamond-venture in Borneo in A. N., 132 AQ, 850, especially Aron to Gansl, 4 August 1887. Judging by Aron's letters, the Dreyfus affair heightened the House's sensitivity to the threat of attacks, particularly anti-Semitic attacks.

22 Guy de Rothschild, *Contre bonne fortune* (Paris, Pierre Belfond, 1983), pp. 251–64.

6 Investments and profits of the multinational Schneider group: 1894–1943

CLAUDE PH. BEAUD

With the international expansion at the end of the nineteenth century, the process of multinationalisation of the Société Schneider et Cie began. Financial intervention in industrial companies sited abroad progressed at the same time as the commercial expansion. The foreign share of the turnover in the total turnover more than doubled between 1894 and 1912, increasing from nearly 14% to more than 31%. During the first half of the twentieth century, the Schneider group, Penelope-like, twice wove multinational networks tightly bound to the diplomatic and military history of France. Before the First World War, a first multinational group, specially constituted in Russia, was to collapse together with the tsarist regime. It was replaced, in the aftermath of that war, by a second multinational company located in central Europe; but it was ruined by the French capitulation at Munich.

A succinct but difficult study of the accounts[1] shows three periods of important investments abroad before the First World War: at the extreme end of the nineteenth century in Spain and Russia, about 1905 in South America and Morocco, and just before 1914 in Belgium and again in Russia.

Most companies in which Schneider had interests had a particular commercial purpose: they were intended to supply insufficiently provided services with preference orders. The first attempts were very disappointing; the long-standing participation in the Channel Bridge and Railway Co., the relations set up in Italy with the Terni steel works, and the Cie franco-chilienne du port d'Iquique.

From 1895 a new strategy of international expansion asserted itself in Europe. Schneider contributed to found the Sté des procédés Harvey in order to exploit the Harvey patent of armour-plate cementation. The Creusot firm took important interests in the English Harvey Continental Steel Co.; but this participation was rather a burden until its sale in 1912.

In 1898, Schneider also contributed to found the Sté franco-suisse pour l'industrie électrique. This participation of 8% to secure commercial influences shows Schneider's early interest in new technologies. It was intended to supply with orders the electrical works at Le Creusot, then after 1901 those at Champagne-sûr-Seine.

After 1899 several documents show a new interest for Italy: relations were renewed with the Terni company; but these negotiations only led to a small participation in the Sta del minieri e alti forni Elba.

Much more important were the investments effected in the Spanish iron-mines and in Russia; but in both cases the losses were in keeping with the invested sums.

In the Conjuro and Moncorvo iron-mines in 1898, Schneider alone effected direct investments which, in two years, consumed more than three million francs, that is 30% of the total investments. These important investments did not prove profit-earning; and the Spanish mines were no longer mentioned.

The same is true of the more important portfolio investments effected by Schneider in Russia for the first time.[2] In 1897 the Sté minière et métallurgique de Volga-Vichera was established in the Urals; in 1900 the Chaniters de Paratoff were separated from this company. Schneider allowed himself to be led, with de Wendel, into a consortium managed by Paribas. These participations swallowed up more than five million francs. The situation in the Urals and the technique of charcoal cast-iron were badly chosen. The Russian ventures were written off as early as 1901. The loss, therefore, amounted to nearly five million francs for Le Creusot and more than 41 million francs for the whole Paribas group.

This lesson was to cause, in the future, a great repulsion to operations managed by high finance, and even to large investments effected in Russia. At the same period, Schneider engaged in more remote Chinese Railway enterprises, but risking small capital.

The investments effected abroad at the end of the nineteenth century amounted to about 10 million francs. We can estimate that two-thirds of them were lost, and these losses were not compensated for by the profits from the cheapest and most profitable investments.

It is easy to understand why the strategy of international financial expansion was reduced to a minimum at the beginning of the twentieth century. The proportion of foreign participations decreased from nearly 9% in 1899 to less than 5% in 1901.

From 1903 the expansion abroad started again in two directions, South America and north Africa, principally Morocco. The first business deserving of interest in north Africa was the Sté d'études de l'Ouenza in Algeria. With more than 16% of a small capital, Schneider securely installed himself in a great European industrial consortium.

From 1903 Schneider tried to establish in Morocco a network of diversified companies, connected to each other and depending on Le Creusot for the smallest expenses. Schneider was a joint founder with the quite new Banque de l'Union parisienne, of the Compagnie marocaine, which was to be the main relay and lever for a great industrial strategy in Morocco. It was the first real

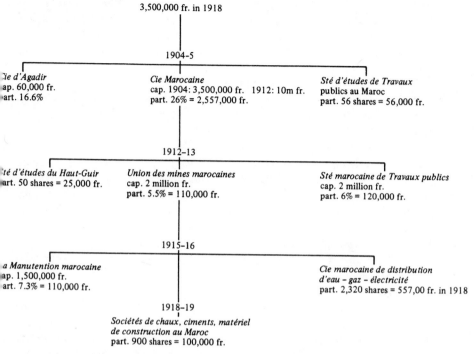

3,500,000 fr. in 1918

1904-5

Cie d'Agadir
ap. 60,000 fr.
art. 16.6%

Cie Marocaine
cap. 1904: 3,500,000 fr. 1912: 10m fr.
part. 26% = 2,557,000 fr.

Sté d'études de Travaux
publics au Maroc
part. 56 shares = 56,000 fr.

1912-13

té d'études du Haut-Guir
art. 50 shares = 25,000 fr.

Union des mines marocaines
cap. 2 million fr.
part. 5.5% = 110,000 fr.

Sté marocaine de Travaux publics
cap. 2 million fr.
part. 6% = 120,000 fr.

1915-16

a Manutention marocaine
ap. 1,500,000 fr.
art. 7.3% = 110,000 fr.

Cie marocaine de distribution
d'eau – gaz – électricité
part. 2,320 shares = 557,00 fr. in 1918

1918-19
Sociétés de chaux, ciments, matériel
de construction au Maroc
part. 900 shares = 100,000 fr.

Figure 6.1 The network of Schneider's participations in Morocco
(Source: C. Beaud, 'Schneider en Russie 1896–1914', in *Colloquium of the European University Institute on the early phase of multinational enterprise*, organised in Florence by Professor P. Hertner in October 1984 (forthcoming))

subsidiary company, but too weak financially for the economic conquest of Morocco, since it had to face the double competition of German concerns and French high finance, preferred by the government.[3]

Schneider formed around the Cie marocaine an aureola of specialised firms in which the company had interests: the Sté marocaine de travaux publics, the Union des mines marocaines, the Manutention marocaine, and the Cie marocaine de distribution d'eau, de gas et électricité. At the end of the First World War, Schneider had invested 3,500,000 francs in Morocco, and his group at least 18 million francs. Unlike others, that network of subcompanies, added to by new companies, was to last until after the Second World War.

Schneider's second expansion area was South America, in Argentina, Chile and Bolivia. In its search for supplies and orders, the Schneider-Hersent group founded the Sté du port Rosario in 1902. The purpose of this company was the building and exploitation of the Rosario harbour. Total estimated expenditure amounted to about 55 million francs, enabling Le Creusot to deliver some 11 million francs of supplies. Schneider could take advantage of the importance of the orders as well as of the company's excellent financial situation, attested by the spectacular rise of the share prices. This business proved to be the most profitable and so contrasts with other foreign enterprises.

It is also in search of orders that Schneider was interested in the Sté des hauts-fourneaux, forges et aciéries du Chili, founded in 1906; but this company rapidly encountered difficulties and in 1914 Schneider had no interest in that business any more.

It also seems that the Schneider group had important interests in the Bolivian Rubber and General Enterprise. This Bolivian company, established in London with French assets, operated in Bolivia. After serious losses in 1913, Schneider imposed a total financial reorganisation; but this reorganisation did not avoid the complete disaster of the Bolivian company. The group lost about 15 million francs in this episode.

So the investments effected in South America at the beginning of the twentieth century amounted to nearly 16 million francs. For the Sté Schneider et Cie, we can estimate that the losses of the Bolivian undertaking were compensated for by important profits from the Rosario.

Just before the First World War, there was a new launching of investments abroad. The strategy was moving towards a more durable establishment abroad, taking advantage of the international boom and of the support of the French government. That investment took place in neighbouring Belgium, in Italy which was turning towards the Entente cordiale, and especially in remote Russia again.

Since Schneider's establishment in 1912 on the iron-mines in Lorraine near Droitaumont, it was urgent to look for new supplies of coking coal. The Winterslag collieries in the Belgian Campine were chosen. In 1913 and 1914 more than 13 million francs was directly invested in Winterslag.

At the same period, Italy again was the object of great interest. In 1910 a simple technical and industrial agreement was signed with the Sté Gio Ansaldo, Armstrong et Cie with a view to artillery material supplies. Numerous missions led in 1917 to the formation of the Unione industriale Italo-francese, with a capital of 10 million francs and more than forty Italian and French participants, including E. Schneider as vice-chairman. That union can be considered as the beginning of close industrial collaboration between Italy and France. Nevertheless, whatever its interest, it was chiefly a circumstantial institution and was not to survive the war.

The third and most important expansion area was again Russia.[4] To break with the past, the method consisted in multiplying technical agreements against heavy dues, and in developing, in the cheapest way, a durable network of Russian subcompanies contributing to the manufacture of war supplies.

The centre of that network was the Poutilow organisation. In 1911

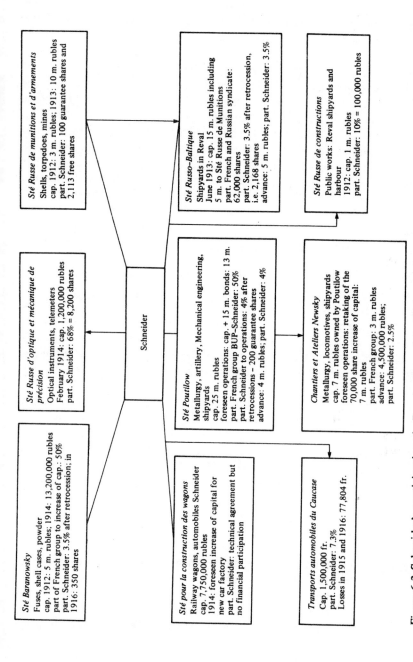

Sté Baronowsky
Fuses, shell cases, powder
cap. 1912: 5 m. rubles; 1914: 13,200,000 rubles
part of French group to increase of cap.: 50%
part. Schneider: 3.5% after retrocession: in 1916: 350 shares

Sté pour la construction des wagons
Railway wagons, automobiles Schneider
cap. 7,750,000 rubles
1914: foreseen increase of capital for new car factory
part. Schneider: technical agreement but no financial participation

Transports automobiles du Caucase
Cap. 1,500,000 fr.
part. Schneider: 7.3%
Losses in 1915 and 1916: 77,804 fr.

Sté Russe d'optique et mécanique de précision
Optical instruments, telemeters
February 1914: cap. 1,200,000 rubles
part. Schneider: 68% = 8,200 shares

Schneider

Sté Poutilow
Metallurgy, artillery, Mechanical engineering, shipyards
cap. 25 m. rubles
foreseen operations: cap. + 15 m. bonds: 13 m.
part. French group BUP–Schneider: 50%
part. Schneider to operations: 4% after retrocessions – 200 guarantee shares
advance: 4 m. rubles; part. Schneider: 4%

Sté Russe de munitions et d'armements
Shells, torpedoes, mines
cap. 1912: 3 m. rubles; 1913: 10 m. rubles
part. Schneider: 100 guarantee shares and 2,113 free shares

Sté Russo–Baltique
Shipyards in Reval
June 1913: cap. 15 m. rubles including 5 m. to Sté Russe de Munitions
part. French and Russian syndicate: 62,000 shares
part. Schneider: 3.5% after retrocession, i.e. 2,168 shares
advance: 5 m. rubles; part. Schneider: 3.5%

Sté Russe de constructions
Public works: Reval shipyards and harbour
1912: cap. 1 m. rubles
part. Schneider: 10% = 100,000 rubles

Chantiers et Ateliers Newsky
Metallurgy, locomotives, shipyards
cap. 7 m. rubles owned by Poutilow
foreseen operations: retaking of the 70,000 share increase of capital: 7 m. rubles
part. French group: 3 m. rubles
advance: 4,500,000 rubles;
part. Schneider: 2.5%

Figure 6.2 Schneider's participations in Russia, December 1914
(Source: Beaud, 'Schneider en Russie 1896–1914')

Schneider succeeded in setting up essential relations between three companies: Poutilow received help from Le Creusot for artillery material without the ammunitions, the Sté russe de munitions et d'armements made the shells without the fuses, which were reserved to the Baranowsky organization.

After 1912, Schneider was obliged to engage further; the capital, however, was to be provided mainly by the French financial group managed by the Banque de l'Union parisienne, dominated by Le Creusot, and by the Banque russo-asiatique under French influence and presided over by Mr Poutilow. The investments in Russia had to obey a strict rule: they had to be financed by Russian profits and cause no loss of capital. In the end, they had to be reduced to a minimum. In 1913, however, the very bad financial situation of the Poutilow organisation compelled Russian and French banks to increase their credits. But Schneider succeeded again in limiting his intervention.

Just before the war, Schneider organised, around Poutilow, a network of associations often complementary to each other. In 1914 the Baranowsky organisation added to the fuses the building of a powder-factory. The capital of the Sté russe de munitions was increased to 7 million rubles in 1913; but the shipyards of this company, being built at Reval, were committed to a new Sté russo-baltique. Schneider provided 10% of the capital of a Sté russe de construction created to manage the works of Reval harbour and shipyards. In 1914 Schneider also wanted to start building motor-cars in Russia, thanks to a contract of technical collaboration with the Sté pour la construction des wagons. Finally he took the initiative in creating a Sté russe d'optique et mécanique de précision in order to meet the requirements of artillery-making, particularly the manufacture of telemeters.

Let us sum up the amount of investments made in Russia at the end of 1914: the shares in portfolio represented somewhat over 2 million francs. If we take into account the contributions to the guarantee syndicates and the advances to some companies, it is a total of 4,800,000 francs that Schneider invested in Russia in various forms.

After January 1915, the mission of de Saint-Sauveur, sent by Schneider to Russia in order to coordinate the war effort of the different establishments, played a considerable part. The production of the groupement Poutilow developed at a spectacular tempo. But such an effort needed increases in capital.

Very late, Schneider even engaged in a new electricity business, Samour Bakou, founded by a consortium, including the BUP; for this very important funds, blocked in Russia by the revolutionary governments, had to be used.

The possible losses, however, could be amply compensated for by the enormous profits drawn from the payments for orders placed with the various companies. According to a telegram from de Saint-Sauveur to Schneider dated July 1917, the funds blocked in Russia amounted to 27,200,000 rubles, or more than 50 million francs. That was a considerable war-treasure which Schneider was to give up.

Since the end of the nineteenth century, Schneider had invested abroad comparatively important capital for poor profits or weighty losses. It was just when, in Russia, moderate investments were proving particularly valid that the hazards of history were to prevent him from collecting the profits.

In the aftermath of the First World War, Schneider took advantage of the French supremacy both in the area of the Franco-German borders and, even more, in a dislocated central Europe.

On the left bank of the Rhine, he took hold of the German spoils of the Gelsenkirchen AG and controlled, with a participation exceeding 20%, the Sté métallurgique des Terres rouges, the plants of which were situated in Luxemburg and the Aachen basin. In conjunction with the Banque de Bruxelles he also took an 11% share in the powerful Belgo-Luxemburger ARBED Co.

But it was above all in central Europe that Schneider amply compensated for the Russian losses. In April 1920, he founded with the BUP a holding company l'Union européenne industrielle et financière,[5] in order to control the industrial and banking participations organised over the remnants of the Austro-Hungarian Empire.

The establishment of this industrial empire in 1919 resulted from the convergence of the interests of the Schneider-BUP group, the French state and of the countries, particularly Czechoslovakia, which emerged from the Austro-Hungarian Empire. The impetus and driving force behind this certainly emanated from Ed. Beneš, the Minister of Foreign Affairs of Czechoslovakia. To carry out both the 'nostrification' and the reorganisation of the Czech economy, the Czech government needed foreign but friendly capital and management. It was therefore logical to prepare, through common economic interests, for the subsequent Franco-Czechoslovak alliance. In a note of March 1920, it is mentioned that: 'the French government has encouraged industrial and financial groups to plan strong positions mainly in countries where French sympathies are traditional'. But Schneider was not only the instrument of action for the French and Czechoslovak governments. Its policy fits into a general strategy which had been elaborated at the beginning of the twentieth century. The Union européenne fits into an extension of the Russian venture: Škoda was to become the arsenal of the 'Little Entente' and replace Poutilow. At that time central Europe represented an investment area for war profits; but it could well be thought too that Schneider had the ambition of contributing to national greatness.

Thus, by 1919, Schneider had acquired control of the Škoda works and the Berg- und Hüttenwerksgesellschaft, two important concerns in the heavy industry of central Europe. But the general policy of the Union européenne moved, like French diplomacy, between two poles, that of industrial Czechoslovakia and the new financial pole of a revisionist Hungary. In spring 1920, M. Paleologue, general secretary of the Quai d'Orsay, was inclined to favour a Danube confederation coordinated by Hungary. The Hungarian government considered the negotiations to be a real bargaining operation. But when one reads the Hungarian requirements with the general political and therefore economic arrangements in mind, one understands that the secretary of the Quai d'Orsay could not accept such excessive political terms even in exchange for large economic concessions. Thus it was during the summer of 1920 that the mission of the Union européenne obtained only a minority participation in the Hungarian General Credit Bank.

The abandonment of Hungary by French diplomats in October 1921 also prompted the Union européenne's swing towards Czechoslovakia. At the end of 1921 not only had the Union itself been consolidated, but the major lasting links of its network had also been set up in central Europe.

The organisation and mechanisms of action of this French interwar multinational company should first be clarified. As far as the internal structure of this holding company is concerned, the essential question must be asked: how could Schneider, with less than 14% of the invested capital, control one of the most important industrial and financial empires of the interwar period? Schneider dominated the Union by two practices common at that time:

1. that of making a distinction between the preferred, registered and above all plural-voting A shares, and the ordinary, single-vote B shares which were easier to disperse publicly. Thus with less than 4 million francs, Schneider possessed 52% of the A capital and 27.5% of the votes.

2. the practice of the Union of syndicating blocks of preferred A shares: the three groups taking part in the Union kept all the A shares for themselves and blocked them.

Thus the syndicate controlled the Union with more than half the votes and Schneider dominated the Union by holding more than half the A shares. The Belgian group Empain, a sleeping partner, was already overshadowed by the leading group of that time. The BUP group only looked on as a brilliant second; as in the Russian venture, the bank was dominated here by big industry and was to play increasingly the role of the milch-cow. Thus with 13.5% of the total capital, that is 10 million francs, Schneider controlled nearly a third of the votes and dominated the company because of its organisation of groups and the syndicate agreement.

The Union tried hard to build up a close-knit network throughout central Europe. Was it possible to create some form of unity, beyond hostile borders, in the face of the political and economic disintegration of central Europe?

Its two finest jewels were the Czech subsidiaries: the Škoda works, Berg und Hütten and their numerous dependent firms. The practice of the syndicating blocks established the Union's domination in Berg und Hütten and Škoda more firmly. At the same time, the Union sought to create a mutual system of interdependence amongst the controlled companies. The French company Huta Bankowa, established in Silesian Poland, was invited to participate also in Škoda's syndicate as well as in that of Berg und Hütten. But the Union's fundamental interests in Czechoslovakia represented not a springboard but an obstacle for the expansion of its influence in neighbouring territories. French influence in Poland had to be extended in a different manner through the increasing and direct formation of Schneider, particularly by the Cie franco-polonaise de chemins de fer after 1930.

The French financial links of the Schneider group with the BUP group were reflected in the links between banks and industry in central Europe. The Union endeavoured to maintain banking links with Vienna, particularly with the Boden Credit Anstalt and with the Niederösterreichische Escompte Gesellschaft. But the bank–industry links appear to have become tighter in the Czech framework, particularly with the Živnostenská banka in Prague. It must be acknowledged, therefore, that the endeavours of the Union to re-establish an economic unity in central Europe clashed with a virulent nationalism.

Did the Union européenne possess sufficient means to direct or help the subsidiaries? This becomes doubtful even if we take into account only the smallest numbers of staff in the company's service during its first years. However, in the 1920s the company expanded to such an extent that the question arose of reducing staff costs during the great crisis. In fact, many departments of the Union were run by Schneider et Cie's departments, which seconded experienced staff to be sent on assignments or to be employed in Czechoslovakia. Permanent French branches were set up after the missions. It seemed necessary to retain the control of the Union through attaching to the management of Škoda and Berg und Hütten a very small but highly qualified French management, after which a permanent office of the Union's departments in Czechoslovakia was organised in Prague.

Did these increasingly close links create domination and even exploitation or, on the contrary, were they fair collaboration? It must be admitted that during the 1920s, in face of the difficulties, the Union's managers felt the need to impose their men and their objectives and to safeguard their profits. After a rather bitter struggle, the agreement in April 1921 imposed on Škoda and on Berg und Hütten a contractual payment of 0.75% of the foreign turnover. During the great depression, A. Lepercq, the general manager, was to take the initiative for a reform which replaced the contractual allocation system with a more moderate set of various remunerations which corresponded to precise services rendered by the Union.

Once the services–profits relationship had been normalised, the correspondence between Prague and Paris revealed cordiality and straight-forward collaboration. Thus sympathetic relations between the French and the Czech leaders had gradually to be built up in order that the relations between the parent company and its subsidiaries could change from domination to friendly collaboration.

The Union's actions with regard to its subsidiaries remain to be considered. The Union put all its efforts into action, and used all its means and its French or international support first to rectify the poor situation of the companies, then to increase their prosperity. This worrying situation during the aftermath of the war explained the slight participation of the Czech managers in the discussions and the almost dictatorial nature of the safety measures imposed on them. Although the Union could not be the cement of scattered economic nuclei, it was, nevertheless, a cohesive factor in central Europe and provided a link between these countries and France. Indeed it increased, to the benefit of its subsidiaries, the various political or diplomatic interventions.

The most important task was still concerned with the reorganisation of the controlled companies in Czechoslovakia. The Union endeavoured to create reciprocal commercial links between the controlled Czechoslovak companies. The take-over of the United Plants by Škoda in 1922 should have made possible a reduction of staff in the offices. But it was more difficult to find a solution for the excessive number of workers; it was even more essential to increase the production of the workshops by carrying out the new programme of civil production. Certain products implied technical agreements between Škoda and Schneider. In order to compensate for the reduction of the neighbouring markets of central and eastern Europe, the links with the Union were intended to facilitate the opening of a French market. Besides agreement with Škoda in April 1921 the Union was granted the commercial representation of the firm for France, Belgium and their dependencies.

However, the solidarity between the Union and its subsidiaries did not go so far as to compete with products of the dominant company. This is why the artillery and sugar refineries equipment governed by particular agreements were excepted from the commercial representation contract in 1922.

The financial difficulties of the controlled enterprises provided the major preoccupation of the Union. It must be admitted that the Union did put in a maximum of effort at the time when its financial means were greatly reduced. A much greater burden resulted from the accounts difficulties of Škoda. The Union constantly intervened to increase and speed up the payments of supplies for the Czechoslovak government and foreign orders. Despite these efforts, the bank overdrafts, especially at Živno, continued to increase until the beginning of 1923. Despite the increasingly important advances granted by the Union to its subsidiaries, the Pilsen firm thus risked falling into a position of subordination to this Prague bank. At the end of 1921, the difficulties of the subsidiaries brought the Union's financial situation to a very critical point. This situation was very likely to lead to an increased subordination of the Union to the BUP, in a similar manner to the subordination of Škoda to the Živno.

Still, neither a capital increase of the Union nor the issue of bonds could be thought of at that time on the Parisian market. Therefore there was no other solution than to call upon British credit. Indeed, when the floods of British capital came to Czechoslovakia, they were to facilitate spectacular expansion of the Škoda company, which developed its business and its whole network of subsidiaries. This expansion could be realised without an excessive financial effort either by Škoda or by the Union européenne which, until the great depression, collected the abundant profits of its empire.

The controlled companies of central Europe and the Union européenne obviously suffered from the crisis of 1929, but moderately and only during three years from 1931 to 1933. As early as 1934 re-armament efforts enabled them to recover rapidly, and collect copious profits. It can be estimated that the credits of the Union abroad secured France some 500 million francs in foreign currency between 1920 and 1938. But just when the Czechoslovak companies were getting prosperous again, Munich rang the knell of the Union européenne.[6]

The Union had been founded on the victory of France and had constituted the economic counterplan of the French alliance system in central Europe. It was logical that the capitulation in September 1938 should lead to the collapse of French economic positions, beginning with Škoda, the arsenal of the 'Little Entente'. In fact, it was necessary to foresee that Hitlerite Germany would make that arsenal work, with Czechoslovakia, under its influence. In such a case, facing German war orders, the position of the Union in Škoda would become untenable. The only solution was, therefore, the sale of Škoda in the least unfavourable conditions, which explains the Schneider group's proposal 'to transfer the whole of its Škoda shares to the Czechoslovak government or to a third party nominated by that government'.

These applications to the Czech government were made in close connection with the Quai d'Orsay and obtained the agreement of the army general staff. Finally, on 23 December 1938, the Union sold 315,000 Škoda shares, i.e. 46% of the capital of that company, to a syndicate consisting mainly of the Československá zbrojovka, a state armament manufactory in Brno. The total price amounted to $9,591,750, i.e. $30.45 or 1,156 francs for each share. In fact, the Union was to receive only $8,589,324, that is nearly 325 million francs and an accumulated profit of nearly 285 million francs. The balance was paid up with shares of a Polish subcompany of Škoda, the Warszawska-Wytwornia Kabli.

Most of the contracts and agreements existing between the Union or Schneider and Škoda were cancelled as soon as the shares were handed over.

Figure 6.3 The network of the Union européenne industrielle et financière (UEIF) (*source*: C. Beaud, 'The interests of the Union européene in central Europe', in A. Teichova and P. L Cottrell (eds.), *International business and central Europe 1918–1939* (Leicester, 1983), p. 382

Union européenne industrielle et financière

Holding company formed on 22 Apr. 1920

Capital 75 m.fr. in 150,000 shares of 500 fr; 15,000 blocking A shares and 135,000 B shares

	A shares %	B shares at formation %	B shares at end of 1921 %
Schneider group of which:	52.3	34.7	25.3
Framerican		19.2	14.3
BUP group	34.8	35.6	28.9
Empain group	12.8	16.3	10.9
Crédit lyonnais		13.3	
Shares sold by BUP syndicate			34.8

1 *Škoda Works*

1919: capital 144 m.Kč in 450,000 shares of 320 Kč
Factories at Plzeň: metallurgy and mechanical construction
Steel works subsidiary company at Hrádek (near Plzeň – 55% controlled by Škoda)

Participation of UEIF in 1920: 229,567 shares bought by Schneider at 104.6 fr each, i.e. 51% of the capital +42,800 to the blocking syndicate (32,000 of which to Huta Bankowa) +5,400 to the Živnostenská banka

In 1921 following purchases on the stock

exchange UEIF controlled 52.3% of the capital of Škoda.

2 United Engineering Construction Plants Co. Ltd

1919: Capital raised from 25 to 50 m.Kč by the creation of 125,000 shares reserved for Škoda which controlled more than 50% of the capital

4 mechanical construction works at:
Smíchov (suburb of Prague)
Plzeň
Doudlevec (near Plzeň)
Hradec-Králové

1922: Amalgamation of United Plants with Škoda which increased its capital by 156,250 shares, UEIF subscribing 78,125

3 Berg- und Hüttenwerksgesellschaft

The Austrian company became the Czech company Báňská a hutní společnost

1920: Capital 50 m.Kč in 125,000 shares UEIF controlled 24% of the capital and 48.4% with the blocking syndicate: Boden-Credit-Anstalt, Huta Bankowa and the American group Equitable Trust Co.

1921: Participation of UEIF in increase of capital from 50 to 76 m.Kč

Principal installations in Czechoslovakia in the Těšín region:
coal mines in
Ostrava-Karviná
steelworks at Třinec
sheet metal rolling mills
at Karlova Huť
in Slovakia: iron mines at Maria metallurgic works and at Bindt
in Poland: foundry at Węgierska Gorka, run as Polish company

4 Participation of UEIF as member of group of French steel manufacturers in an Austrian company, the Veitscher Magnesit Werke at Vienna, for the exploitation of magnesite products

The participation of the group of French steel manufacturers, initially a minority holding in 1919–20, gradually became a majority one; the VMW controlled 70% of MIAG (Magnesit Industrie AG) at Bratislava which owned three magnesia plants, two in Slovakia and one in Hungary.

5 UEIF participation of 4% in 1923 in the Niederösterreichische Escompte-Gesellschaft

6 Huta Bankowa Co. (Poland)

French company, the capital of which was raised in 1920 from 23 to 80 m.fr. by the issue of 114,000 shares of 500 fr., 22,000 of which, i.e. 13.7% of the capital, were subscribed by Schneider, then transferred to UEIF.

Iron mines and metal works at Drombrowa

Subsidiary companies in Poland:
Count Renard Coalmining Co.
Metallurgical industries company in Russia
Franco-Russian Mining Co.

Subsidiary companies in Russia:
Steel Foundry Co. of Donetz (with iron mines at Krivoi-Rog)

Participation of Huta Bankowa in Škoda and in Báňská a hutní společnost

7 Small participation by UEIF in the Polish Financial Union formed in 1928 under the aegis of the Banque belge pour l'Étranger, a subsidiary of the Société générale de Belgique

8 Hungarian General Credit Bank

1920: capital raised from 160 to 280 m.CH in 700,000 shares of 400 CH

Participation of UEIF with 100,000 shares, i.e. 14.3% of the capital, and BUP with 100,000 shares

Participation of UEIF in increases of capital in the Croatian General Credit Bank as well as in three timber companies reorganised in a Swiss Holding Co., the Lignum Trust
Hungarian General Timber Co.
Ehrlich Hungarian General Co. Ltd
Yugoslavian Forestry Co. Ltd of Zagreb

9 STEG participation in 1920–1

Participation of 10% taken by UEIF in the syndicate formed by the Cie française de Levant for the purchase of Staats-Eisenbahn-Gesellschaft (STEG) locomotives and their resale to the Romanian government

That rupture of the links between the Union and Škoda was to be dramatic for the French as well as for the Czech leaders, as attested in various correspondence; for everyone felt that it was much more than a mere rupture of economic interests.

The other great Czech company, the former Berg- und Hüttenwerksgesellschaft, whose Czech name was Baňská a hutní společnost, was compelled by Munich to create a Polish subcompany, Třinec-Karwina. which took over the subsidiary factories located on the Teschen territory annexed by Poland. Since the declaration of war in September 1939, the Union européenne had been completely cut off from its involvement in central Europe. A German bank consortium presided over by the Boehmische Union Bank, behind which stood the Deutsche Bank, proposed to buy the Union's share. Lepercq, its general manager, then a prisoner of war, was set free to lead the negotiations. In December 1940, after the agreement of the French Ministry of Finance, the Union européenne sold more than 110,000 Baňská a hutní shares, i.e. more than 44% of the capital for nearly 331 million francs. Although it represented less than half of the Bourse value of the company, that sum still left an account profit of more than 205 million francs.

In the Hungarian General Credit Bank the share of the Union was little more than 10%. At the beginning of 1941, the Dresdner Bank proposed to buy it; but the French Ministry of Finance only gave agreement in April 1941, after the intervention of the Wiesbaden Armistice Commission. The selling price of 86,430 shares was over 40 million francs, leaving an account profit of more than 30 million francs.

So these four sales represented a total of more than 700 million francs and a profit of more than 520 million francs, on which the Union paid nearly 89 million francs in tax. It was practically drained of most of its substance, but it had important financial means at its disposal, despite the successive reductions of capital from 140 million francs to 28 million francs, and the repayment of 350 francs for each share of 500 francs. The future, therefore, had to be looked to. Now since 1929 Schneider had controlled a business bank, the Banque des Pays du Nord, which lacked financial means. It therefore made sense to put the structure of the BPN in the service of the available assets of the Union européenne so as to elaborate a new strategy, far less directed abroad. Hence in June 1943, the fusion of the BPN with the Union européenne was at the origin of a Banque de l'Union européenne which was to enable the Schneider group to have, at last, a business bank of wider spread at its disposal.

Was the Union européenne more than a multinational capitalist company? Its name would seem to anticipate the economic unity of Europe.

As a multinational company, the Union showed two original features:

1. The holding company only controlled foreign interests and did not have

any proper major activity of its own in France. It only existed for the support of and thanks to the incomes of controlled companies, which determined a great solidarity of interests between the parent company and its subsidiaries, the former owing its prosperity only to that of the latter, thanks to the double collection of dividends and allocations on the turnover. The parent company had a great interest in serving its foreign activities; however, the development of these activities should not go too far against the dominant company of the Union, Schneider et Cie. One can even see between the two world wars a relative stagnation of Schneider's French business, for the benefit and expansion of foreign subsidiaries of the Union.

2. To real subcompanies with major participations, enjoying a relative autonomy, were added enterprises in which Schneider held minority participations. By these secondary participations, nearly independent, the Union reminds one of many French companies before 1914 which often held foreign portfolio investments. But by a much closer control of the two great Czechoslovak companies, the holding foreshadowed the multinational companies of today.

Could this multinational company be also an anticipation of the European Federation projected by A. Briand just before the great crisis and of today's Common Market? It could not and for two reasons:

1. The Union européenne was not even a confederation of freely associated enterprises; like all efforts of European concentration until the Second World War, it was founded upon a dominant position. Even if this dominant position gradually became an open and friendly collaboration in Czechoslovakia, the very foundations of the Union were initially vitiated.

2. The efforts to reinforce the links between the parent company and its subsidiaries and between the different companies of the network had failed to a large extent because of the political and economic partition of central Europe. In Europe more divided economically between the two wars than before 1914, the Union was a weak element of unification. The ulterior political evolution did not even enable western democracies to profit by the considerable economic and military power resulting from the close link of the firm of Creusot with that of Pilsen.

NOTES

1 C. Beaud, 'La Stratégie de l'investissement dans la Sté Schneider et Cie (1894–1914)', in *Enterprises et entrepreneurs – XIXème–XXème siècles*, VII (Presses de l'Université de Paris-Sorbonne, 1983), pp. 118–31.
2 C. Beaud, 'Schneider en Russie (1896–1914)', in *Colloquium of the European University Institute on the early phase of multinational enterprise*, organised in Florence by Professor P. Hertner in October 1984 (forthcoming).
3 P. Guillen, 'L'Implantation de Schneider au Maroc', *Revue d'histoire diplomatique*, no. 2 (1965).

4 Beaud, 'Schneider en Russie (1896–1914)'.
5 C. Beaud, 'The interests of the Union européenne in central Europe', in A. Teichova and P. L. Cottrell (eds.), *International business and central Europe, 1918–1939* (Leicester, 1983), pp. 357–97.
6 Archives Union européenne and A. Teichova, *An economic background to Munich: international business and Czechoslovakia, 1918–1938* (Cambridge, 1974).

7 The strategy of a multinational in the world sugar economy: the case of Tate and Lyle: 1870–1980

PH. CHALMIN

Sugar has always occupied a very specific place among commodities. The sugar, and more broadly now, the sweetener economy relies on two complementary agricultural crops: cane from tropical areas and beet from temperate ones. More recently grains, and especially corn, should be counted among the sources of sweetening agents.

Till 1850, sugar production in the 'cane islands' was a typical example of a colonial system. Since then, the development of beet cultivation in temperate areas has slowly but regularly taken over cane's market share.

Industrial organisation in beet and cane has always been quite different: on one side (beet), powerful national oligopolies achieving rapid production of the finished product (white sugar), but generally limited to their local market, on the other (cane), cane producing estates selling their raw sugar to refiners in the importing countries. The beet economy was to be at the origin of some powerful industrial firms on a general national basis. The more extrovert cane economy gave more scope to a multinationalisation of the companies engaged in the production, trade and processing activities: the most interesting case is Tate and Lyle of the United Kingdom.

The analysis of Tate and Lyle's evolution during this last century is a good example of the strategy of a firm staying within the boundaries of a system, itself in evolution: the sugar economy. To be accurate, Tate and Lyle has only been international for half a century and a real 'multinational' for twenty years. But it seems interesting to show how a British industrial concern has evolved into a multinational enterprise embracing all aspects of the sugar economy.

First, I shall give a brief account of Tate and Lyle's history before trying to outline the main conditions which enabled the company's development on a multinational basis.

Brief history of Tate and Lyle[1]

The context of the origin of Tate and Lyle is the British sugar refining industry in the second half of the nineteenth century. At that time, Britain, which was the biggest sugar consumer in the world, was importing all its sugar either from the cane producing countries, its traditional suppliers, or from the heavily subsidised beet-sugar industries of the Continent. In a context of disappearing tariff protection (with suppression of all barriers on sugar from 1874), the refining industry had to struggle for its survival against fierce competition from imported refined sugar.

It was a period of rapid changes in the organisational structure of industry during which a few truly large individual corporations emerged among numerous small firms. The enterprises which survived and grew during that very difficult period (without any help from the government) did so through their ability to exploit technical innovation and mass production. Such were the firms founded in Greenock by a Scottish shipowner, Abram Lyle, in 1865 and in Liverpool by a grocer, Henry Tate, in 1859. At the turn of the century they were among the biggest sugar refiners in the country, with refineries in London and Liverpool for Tate, in London for Lyle. Henry Tate, particularly, became quite wealthy and is now more famous for the Tate Gallery than for sugar cubes.

For the two companies, the First World War was an occasion of consolidating their position in enjoying for the first (but not the last!) time the protecting umbrella of the state at war.

In 1914, the imports of sugar, coming primarily from Germany and Austria-Hungary, were something of a problem for the British government, which had to take over the whole sugar system which was to be handled for the next seven years by a Royal Commission on Sugar Supplies. The Commission did guarantee the refining margin and apart from shortfalls in production, the war period was a very prosperous one for the refiners.

After the war, probably with some inducements from official quarters, Abram Lyle and Sons and Henry Tate and Sons merged into Tate and Lyle. The alliance between the two family-owned firms can be interpreted in many ways: the most important seems to be that, as the market was to regain its former freedom with the disappearance of the sugar commission, the government wanted a company to exercise a certain control on an important industry (there is a certain parallel to be seen with the mergers giving birth at the same period to ICI). Indeed, from that time on, Tate and Lyle has always enjoyed a high level of protection for its refining activities in Britain and complete support by the government, from the 1928 refining agreement to the negotiations for the entry of the UK into the EEC (apart from the brief nationalisation campaign of 1949–51).

From 1921 onwards the firm was thus in an almost monopolistic position in the British refining industry: it strengthened this position in buying the remaining refiners, the last being Manbre and Garton in 1976. During the twenties it tried to get into the emergent beet-sugar industry but was forced out in 1936 by the creation of the British Sugar Corporation, which was more or less a state company. Up to that time Tate and Lyle had remained a strictly British company. Trading in a commodity quoted on an international market, :t had of course to keep an eye on world problems. But the company had not yet set foot abroad: it was managed by directors who came from the founding families and who had all served a 'sugar apprenticeship'.

Shortly before the war, in order to use the men and the money now idle after the beet venture, Tate and Lyle bought some estates in Jamaica and Trinidad. From now on, Tate and Lyle was to embark, quite late by world standards, on the classic itinerary of a plantation company: from small beginnings in the thirties, it grew to become at the end of the sixties one of the biggest of such companies in the world owning estates and factories in Jamaica, Trinidad (80% of the local production), Belize, Zambia and Rhodesia. We are still far here from a 'multinational': Tate and Lyle's developments were limited to the British Empire, and a high proportion of the sugar it produced was to be refined in the group's refineries. Apart from its refineries in Britain, Tate and Lyle owned Canada and Dominion, since the end of the fifties one of Canada's biggest refiners. At that time, too, it began to diversify into engineering and sugar machinery.

In 1965, Tate and Lyle was a fairly conservative British company living on its sugar estates and refineries. Then it bought an international trading company: United Molasses, which at that time was the world's biggest trader in molasses, a by-product of sugar. Through the acquisition of United Molasses, the company made its first entry into the non-British world: it acquired a world-wide level of managing the sugar economy. In fact as an international trader, like Cargill or Philipp Brothers on another scale, United Molasses was surely a 'transnational corporation'. It was also active in shipping, here again a transnational activity by nature.

The next ten years were crucial for the evolution of the company. In a few years, it lost most of its estates in developing countries; and the diversification into sugar engineering (the elaboration of Turn-Key projects) after initial successes ended in failure. In shipping, too, the company was unable to escape the downturn of the market since 1976, and sold all its ships. In Britain, the refineries had to reduce their activities with the entry of the UK into the EEC, and another diversification into starch, glucose and isoglucose proved to be a further failure. Despite these setbacks, the company was extremely prosperous at least till 1977: the reason was its activities in commodity trading (sugar, but also molasses, alcohol and so on), in which Tate and Lyle earned almost two-thirds of its trading profit.

But this also was the period of the birth of a true multinational: links with

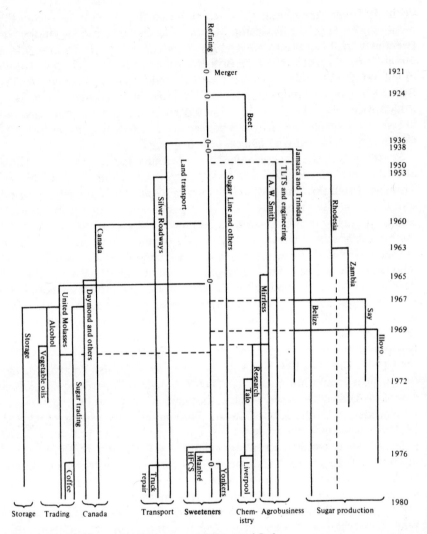

Figure 7.1 The diversification process of Tate and Lyle

Points marked 'O' identify the moments when, following a decision at headquarters, the group's general direction changed. Other diversifications have been seen as the results of earlier investment: for example sugar trading was a consequence of Canadian activity and of the acquisition of United Molasses. (source: Ph. Chalmin, *Tate and Lyle: géant du sucre* (Paris, Economica, 1983), p. 649) the Empire were severed as were psychological links with the British refineries, which were still important, especially as a bargaining tool with the British government (in a time of high unemployment) but which played only a marginal role in the business policy of the company. Tate and Lyle became in fact the association of a commodity trader and an international engineer (based on much R. and D.). Management became more international (the present CEO is a Canadian). Still the company has kept its sugar emphasis: in fact, the last few years have seen a rise in those interests with the acquisition of refineries in Portugal (soon to be in the EEC) and in the United States.

In fact, Tate and Lyle is by now probably the only company in the world having defined, quite painfully, a global strategy on a world-wide basis for the sugar complex. For this reason, it can really be called a multinational.

From industry to services and back

A first level of analysis is to examine the ways and means of Tate and Lyle's strategy in the world sugar economy (see Figure 7.2). The company's first moves out of refining arose from a will to integrate: sugar produced in English beet factories was to be refined in Tate and Lyle's British refineries. The move to the West Indies in 1937 was not at first motivated by an integration strategy: in fact, sugar produced in the West Indian estates was very likely to end up in the British refineries. But the contractual link and afterwards, through the Commonwealth Sugar Agreement, the price, were determined in fine by the government. In fact, there were many advantages on the logistics side in controlling a good part of one's raw materials, but the classical accusation against multinationals of transfer pricing cannot stand in Tate and Lyle's case.

Nevertheless, Tate and Lyle built quite an integrated sugar empire: estates in the West Indies and Africa, sugar cane factories, even wharves in the West Indies for the handling of bulk sugar, ships specially built for the transport of sugar (the 'Sugar Line'), refineries in Britain and then in Canada (the other export market of West Indian sugar), road transport to deliver the refined sugar, and engineering services to build sugar factories and refineries. Tate and Lyle was heavily involved in the hard core of sugar economy: production, transport, processing. The strategy was not very imaginative, but proved reasonably successful during the post-war period in a rather protected zone.

From 1965 onwards everything changed: strategies, men, environment. Until that time Tate and Lyle's management had been fairly conservative, limited in fact to the inheritors of the Tate and Lyle families and some outsiders who had spent all their careers with the company. The most dynamic elements of those, like Robert Kirkwood, a Lyle by his mother, who initiated the West Indian purchase, were quickly dismissed. Tate and Lyle's board was filled by 'amateurs' rather than by 'professionals'; they were tied

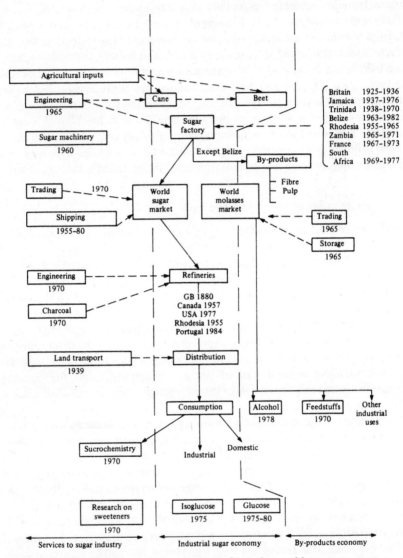

Figure 7.2 The withdrawal of Tate and Lyle from the world sugar economy

The first date is that of the entry of Tate and Lyle into a new activity. The second, if any, is the date of cessation from that activity (source: Chalmin, *Tate and Lyle*, p. 637).

to a tradition, a company spirit, much cultivated since the 'Mr Cube' campaigns of the early fifties.

And then the outside world changed. People in charge were not taken totally unawares, but for about fifteen years the company was to remain without a real strategy. Historians can always depict strategies after the event. Here one can see two contradictory moves: in the industrial economy, on the one hand, Tate and Lyle lost its estates and its monopoly over British sugar. The first nationalisation (Trinidad, 1970), took the company by surprise. Afterwards Tate and Lyle's managers took this as a lesson and tried to disengage themselves from their other ventures, which they did without much problem. But still they felt that they had to be sugar producers and tried their hand in France and in South Africa. On the refining side, on the other hand, Tate and Lyle had to reorganise its activities with the entry of the UK into the EEC: here again its managers chose to buy out the other British refining group Manbre and Garton and to dismantle it rather than to close too many of its factories. Through Manbre and Garton it got an entry into the glucose industry, which was to become a competitor of sugar with the development of isoglucose (high-fructose corn syrup). In 1977, too, Tate and Lyle entered the United States by buying a refinery near New York.

All those moves can be interpreted in the continuity of the former sugar strategy: most of them were ill-timed and ended in failure. However, a second level of initiatives was more successful and ended in the transfer of Tate and Lyle's dynamism from the industrial to the 'services' aspect of the sugar economy: it did not grow more sugar cane, nor did it produce raw sugar, but it built plantations and factories and often managed them.[2] The company processed less and less raw sugar but began to trade it on a world-wide basis. Shipping and transport services also became independent from the sugar business. Finally, the firm invested much money in research into sucrochemistry and new uses of sugar. The new Tate and Lyle emerging in those years was a mixture between an engineering shop, a trading room and a research laboratory.

The move away from the hard-core sugar economy to services at least seemed coherent, even if it was not so well strategically planned. In fact, the directors were taken by surprise by their success in trading activities. They thought that in a few years they could become 'a world of commodity services', as they described it in a brochure published in 1977. In fact at that time most multinational companies seemed to be engaged in such an evolution, away from production and industrial risks to the safer and more profitable world of services.

That picture, which I presented in my earlier work on Tate and Lyle and multinationals, was turned upside down in the last few years. Tate and Lyle wasn't able to hold its grip on services: engineering and agribusiness were almost brought to a standstill by the depression of agricultural markets:

research was too expensive to finance in the long run and, as no really decisive discoveries were made, was finally abandoned; the extension of trading to other commodities (alcohol, vegetable oils, coffee) turned out to be disastrous. Those results, coupled with problems on the industrial side, put the company in a severe financial and management crisis from 1978. Finally there emerged a completely different company: the founding family directors, and with them the company's tradition, were swept away. A financial diet resulted in the slimming of many activities.

Because perspective is lacking, recent times are always difficult for an historian to analyse. From the last five years a completely different Tate and Lyle has emerged. It is still a sugar-only company, but its management, now quite international, has tried a shift to North America, buying in addition to the previously mentioned refinery near New York a refinery in Louisiana and other agricultural interests. The EEC still plays a big role in its strategy: the refineries in Britain are now rationalised (however painful the closure of Liverpool's refinery was), and in 1984 the company bought a refinery in Portugal to gain another backdoor entry into the EEC sugar market.

So we are now back to industry. Tate and Lyle seems to have abandoned its ideas of a services multinational. After a ten years' parenthesis, the old imperial sugar company is evolving into a multinational sugar company, based on refineries and even some production. Its interests in the Third World have of course almost completely vanished: the company now limits itself to industrialised, 'safe' countries. This is also a good example of the disinvestment by multinational companies in less developed countries.

Tate and Lyle's case is thus quite interesting as its developments have almost always been confined to sugar and all its aspects. Its strategy can then be compared with those of other operators within the field.

Tate and Lyle: a multinational in perspective

Within the last twenty years, Tate and Lyle has evolved from a British industrial company to an industrial and services multinational firm.

First, we should look for other examples of this in related fields of activity. If we look first at the sugar sector, Tate and Lyle's evolution appears to be extremely unusual. In the beet-sugar industry as well as on the refining side, most big names have strictly confined their activities to their own countries: this is true for Continental Europe, for the United States, and Japan. The main reason for that situation can be found in the existence, back in the nineteenth century, of very strong national sugar policies and intervention from the different states. Those policies, generally quite protectionist, did not favour foreign intervention: a good example of it was provided when in 1967–73 Tate and Lyle tried to take control of one of France's biggest producers, Raffineries et sucreries Say, and was prevented from doing so by a 'French' solution. Tate and Lyle's expansion was only possible on the refining side when those forms of protection were not so strong (Canada, United States and now Portugal). The biggest refiners in the world, the American companies like Amstar, did not go for internationalisation in sugar, but looked rather to diversify in the general food industry.

It is only in the cane sugar industry that some form of internationalisation did exist. But, as I have already said, it was more in the form of estate companies operating within the boundaries of a colonial empire: this applied to, for instance, Booker McConnel (UK), Grands Moulins de Paris (France), HVA (Netherlands), and Colonial Sugar Refinery (Australia). The disappearance of those empires and the nationalisation that followed generally provoked the collapse of those companies. This was true not only for sugar but also for most agricultural and mineral commodities. The era of commodity production-based multinationals is gone (apart from some dubious cases like the banana companies in Central America): the British plantation houses so active in Asia (Sime Darby, Guthrie, Harrison and Crossfield) have been the last to resist but have generally been taken over by local interests in the last few years. Unilever in Asia, Africa and the Pacific is probably the most important survivor of that era, but its plantation division represents only a small part of its activities.

Gone are the foreign plantations. The companies that developed from them often tried to survive by adapting themselves to new activities in agribusiness, that is giving expertise and engineering skill to projects owned by local companies or governments. Such was the strategy of Tate and Lyle, Booker McConnel, HVA and so on. This required an international network but often remained tied to the national character of the financial packages of those projects: for a sugar estate financed by Dutch money or aid, it was thought that there should be a Dutch contractor! However, these activities did not flourish and most companies engaged in them were confronted with severe problems in the eighties.

It can be assumed, then, that the production side of agricultural or mineral (for this applies also to mining companies, apart perhaps from Rio Tinto Zinc) commodities has not been a very fertile field for the birth of multinationals. Nor was it on the whole the case for the sugar industry. In fact, Tate and Lyle became a multinational through its trading activities. International traders can be said to have been the first true multinationals: the Fuggers or the Ravensburger Gesellschaft were already multinationals at a time when nations were in formation. From the seventeenth to the nineteenth century, the development of trading companies was closely linked to colonial growth.

From the end of the nineteenth century, the main intermediaries of international trade were the brokers who channelled information and prices. But for some commodities, international merchants began to appear: for grains, companies like Louis Dreyfus, Bunge, Ralli Brothers; for metals,

Philipp Brothers and Metallgesellschaft, and for molasses, United Molasses. Those traders were by nature multinational, buying in one country to sell in another without much reference to the country of origin. However, until the 1960s their importance was fairly small.

In buying United Molasses in 1965, Tate and Lyle bought a small multinational. But the time was ripe for those companies. The great commodity boom of 1972–6 greatly enhanced the role of commodity traders in international trade. In a world characterised by instability, not only of the commodities but of the whole financial system, commodity traders became the most important operators on the markets. At the time of writing, one can say that about 20 international trading companies control more than three-quarters (rough estimate) of all commodity trade from petroleum to grains. Most of those companies are over a century old and were previously local merchants or brokers. Among them are Cargill, Continental Grain, Dreyfus, André, and Bunge y Born for grains; Philipp Brothers and Marc Rich for petroleum and metals; Gill and Duffus for cocoa; Ed. F. Man, Sucres et denrées, and Tate and Lyle for sugar (at least, during the seventies). All those companies have to manage their activities on a world-wide basis. They do not normally directly own processing or handling facilities, but are represented in every corner of the world.

The increased activity of those international commodity traders has rather set aside the more traditional general trading companies (UAC and Inchcape in UK, SCOA and CFAO in France, Internatio in the Netherlands and of course the sogo shosas of Japan). But those are more specialised in import and export: for example, the Japanese traders (Mitsui, Mitsubishi and the like) who probably have the biggest network of all, cannot be called multinational, but in fact are Japanese import–export companies (off-shore trade accounts for a mere 20% of their activities).

Far more than the general trading companies which have generally kept a strong national or ex-colonial basis, the international commodity traders are hence probably the purest form of multinationals now in existence.[3] In fact, their head offices are located either in great financial centres or in tax havens (like Zug in Switzerland or the Bermudas). Among those companies, Tate and Lyle is unusual as it is almost the only one to have gone over to trading from an industrial basis (there have been some other cases among grain millers and oil crushers in the United States like Pillsbury or Archer Daniel Midlands; in the mining field, most mining companies have set up their trading subsidiaries, but they generally remain quite minor compared to the global size of the firms). For Tate and Lyle, as shown in Table 7.1, the trading activities very soon represented more than two-thirds of the company profits: a handful of traders (ten at the most) earned the major part of the profits of a 10,000-employee company!

Table 7.1. *Breakdown of Tate and Lyle's trading profit* (%)

	1965	1970	1975	1980
Sugar refining	62.7	63.7	22	31
Sugar production	6.0	−12.9	9	6
Trading	12.5	26.8	61	76
Shipping	9.0	26.5	1	5
Engineering	9.8	−4.1	3	−16
Glucose	—	—	—	−2
Others	—	—	4	—

Source: Ph. Chalmin, *Tate and Lyle: gèant du sucre* (Paris, 1983) p. 641.

Like other trading companies, Tate and Lyle invested heavily in shipping and in storage capacities, all managed on a world-wide basis. It did not divert into financial services as did companies like Continental Grain or Philipp Brothers when it bought the US commission house and broker Salomon Brothers.

So Tate and Lyle's evolution as a multinational is in general classical and characteristic of international trading companies: the only uncharacteristic feature is that this was the evolution of an industrial company.

If we look now at the more general field of food companies (Tate and Lyle ranks among the 20 major food companies in the world), the firm's choices of the last years are clearly explained. The main purpose of internationalisation of food companies appears to have been the extension of consuming habits, of products and brands and eventually of processes: internationalisation has been far stronger in the food sector itself than in the first processing of agricultural products traditionally dominated by producer cooperatives on one side and by the grocer's own brands on the other. Since the appearance of the first food products trade mark during the interwar period in the United States and in Western Europe (with Coca Cola), a small number of companies have developed a strategy of international marketing of their brands: but it must be stressed that it has generally been a strategy limited to developed countries' markets: the United States and Canada, western Europe and some other spots with westernised dietary habits. If one looks, for example, at the American-based food companies, the percentage of their turnover realised abroad is surprisingly low: 15 to 25% for the biggest twenty, exceptions being, for 1976, Coca Cola (44%) and Corn Products Corporation (54%).[4]

Early internationalisation can only be found in the cases of the two biggest food companies in the world, originating from small markets: Unilever (UK-Netherlands with 71% of turnover realised out of its national markets) and Nestlé (95%). More recently, in a reverse trend during the years 1930–70

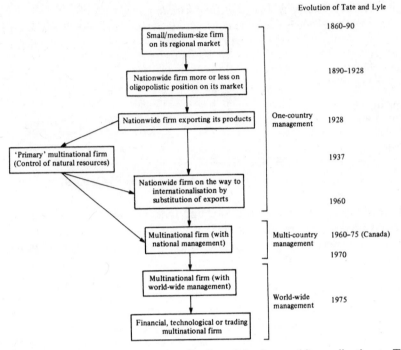

Figure 7.3 Theory of the internationalisation of the firm and its application to Tate and Lyle

when American food companies invested in Europe, European food companies have tried to enter the United States (BSN-Gervais Danone, Nestlé and so on). Tate and Lyle is thus not a unique case.

Thus Tate and Lyle's evolution as a multinational appears rather haphazard: its international base is less the fruit of its history as a plantation or sugar refining company than the result of its developments for the last twenty years as a trading-oriented firm. It is only in recent years that Tate and Lyle seems to get back within the more general framework of food companies.

In conclusion: the company vs the state

Figure 7.3 shows a scheme of the history of Tate and Lyle from the point of view of its internationalisation. Unlike many other so-called 'multinationals' which are still managed from a national basis as American, British or French companies, Tate and Lyle very quickly operated on a world-wide basis, first in services and now on the industrial side.

As already noted, the originality of Tate and Lyle lay in its having limited its developments to the sugar economy. As a basic agricultural product, sugar has always been the object of direct regulatory interventions by public bodies in almost all producing countries (this means everywhere in the world as with the two crops, beet and cane, sugar can be produced in most climates). The main constraints of Tate and Lyle's 'strategy' have indeed been the different sugar policies: most sugar companies in the world have tried to solve that problem in diversifying away from sugar. Tate and Lyle's answer, which can be explained by the education and training of its managers, was to diversify into sugar in order to strengthen its hand against the 'state' ('Tate not state' was one of the slogans of the Mr Cube campaign in 1950).

Even if, during the seventies, Tate and Lyle's evolution was accelerated by its trading activities, the picture is quite clear: to become multinational was the only possible recourse against eventual public moves such as nationalisation and the organisation of markets. Operating in sensitive agricultural markets, the firm suffered more than its share from these. Lacking the will, or the opportunity, to get out of sugar at all, the only solution was to go across national borders on a multinational scale. The process of change was difficult and is still not yet stabilised. The historian must wait for a final judgment.

I have tried to answer one simple question: how does a company become a multinational? Answers come piecemeal but two main points appear: the first is a reaction against various hindrances on a national side and a desire to grow further; the second is linked to the necessity of a worldwide network for trading activities and more generally for services. By world standards Tate and Lyle (turnover in 1980 £1.4 billion) is a small company, but its evolution appears highly evocative of the evolution of multinational firms to a 'transnational' status.

NOTES

1 Here I shall only outline the history of Tate and Lyle. For more complete information, see my doctoral thesis, 'L'Émergence d'une firme multinationale au sein de l'économie sucrière mondiale: Tate and Lyle 1870–1980', Université de Paris-Sorbonne 1981, published as: *Tate and Lyle: géant du sucre* (Paris, Economica, 1983), soon to be published in English by Harwood Academic Publishers.

2 A sad irony of history is that in 1971, for the land, and in 1976 for the factories, Tate and Lyle was evicted from Jamaica, where an experiment with field cooperatives took place. In 1983/4, the Jamaican government, confronted with the collapse of its sugar production, called Tate and Lyle back to manage and rationalise its estates. In 1984, too, the Trinidadian government asked Tate and Lyle to manage Coroni Ltd, the former Tate and Lyle subsidiary, nationalised in 1970.

3 For literature on that subject, Ph. Chalmin, *Négociants et chargeurs, la saga du négoce international des matières premières* (2nd edn, Paris, Economica, 1984) (to be published in 1985 in English by Harwood Academic Publishers) and Dan Morgan, *Giants of grain* (New York, 1982).

4 UNCTC, *Transnational corporations in food and beverage processing* (New York, 1981).

8　The effects of American multinationals on the British motor industry: 1911–83

ROY CHURCH

Origins and innovations

A multinational presence has been a dominant factor in the history of the British motor industry since before 1914. In that year, Percival Perry, the English manager of Ford's British operations, remarked: 'Today we have near upon 1000 agents in our organisation...The car is established... It is far past the position of numerical domination in the English market. It takes the combined output of five of the next largest car manufacturers in this country to equal Ford sales.' The Model T, then assembled from imported kits, accounted for almost 29% of all passenger car production.[1] Ford's 1983 share was also 29%, compared with the share of GM's subsidiary, Vauxhall, of 15%, which brought the American MNE's total to a figure greater than at any time or than in any European country.[2]

The vision of Ford as a manufacturer supplying not only Britain but the Empire and Europe belonged not to Henry Ford but to Percival Perry, former agent, manager of Ford's early selling operations in London, and subsequently manager of the assembly plant at Trafford Park from 1911. Even before 1914 Henry Ford had been persuaded to agree in principle to Perry's plan for some form of manufacturing development, but the First World War hastened this process as a result of the imposition of the McKenna Duties in 1915. Aimed at safeguarding sterling and limiting shipping space available for non-essentials, a $33\frac{1}{3}$% duty was imposed on imported items, including cars and parts originating outside the Empire. As a result, the proportion of local content in vehicles assembled at Trafford Park, hitherto chiefly accessories and some special bodies, had risen to 50% by 1916. The continuation of the duties after 1918 provided the incentive to extend this policy of local content, which by 1924 amounted to 95%.[3]

America's lead in the innovation phase of product development enabled Ford to establish a lead over indigenous car producers by exploiting superior information relating to technology, finance, marketing and management.[4] In an industry which found little difficulty in raising capital from public issues

116

on the London Stock Exchange,[5] American investment was important to the industry more for the technology it embodied and the production methods thereby introduced than for the volume of capital expenditure. Mechanized chassis assembly introduced at Trafford Park in 1914 was the first in Britain, and directly related to this innovation was the establishment of a degree of managerial control over labour unique within the industry.[6] In British factories engine production had been affected by new machine method, interchangeability and the sectionalization of manufacture and assembly even before 1914, and considerable de-skilling had also occurred among production workers.[7] However, a critical difference between British manufacturers and Ford was that the former relied on piece rates; whereas immediately prior to the introduction of mechanized assembly Perry and Sorenson broke trade unionism at Trafford Park and imposed Fordism, which included job mobility, time wages and direct managerial control over the pace of production. The price of achieving this system was the payment of wages substantially higher than those of competitors.[8]

Engineering employers, and motor factory managers in particular, remained sceptical of Ford's methods even after moving assembly lines were in operation – by the mid 1920s at Morris's engine plant in Coventry and at Austin's Longbridge works for axles, and by 1928 for chassis assembly.[9] Managers of British factories continued to rely largely upon incentive at the shop floor level to determine labour productivity. One of Austin's senior officials expressed a widely held opinion that a 'driving works policy would not be acceptable either to English Labour or Management', a view which Lewchuck has adduced to explain British managers' inability to elicit labour effort – and consequently throughput – at levels sufficient to provide an incentive for a more rapid spread of mass production.[10] Under Anglo-American management, isolated from the principal centres of British car production and outside the influential Engineering Employers' Federation, the Ford enterprise exercised little direct influence on British production methods and approach. Morris and Austin learned and borrowed know-how and technology direct from Detroit.[11]

The major impact of Ford's operations in Britain was in demonstrating the existence of a home market for relatively low-priced family cars. Superior American resources, experience and productivity embodied in the Model T, combined with local assembly, enabled Ford to minimize the risks of launching a car of radical design on a relatively large scale.[12] Before Ford cars assembled at Trafford Park began to flood the market from 1911, the trend among British manufacturers had been away from small cars towards larger and more expensive models. The relative profitability of motor companies coupled with severe fluctuations had tended to obscure the potential rewards from volume production of the type of car which would find favour with families of modest incomes.[13] Although suited more to

American conditions, the Model T was relatively cheap to purchase, and by 1913 probably accounted for 60% of all cars priced below £200 sold in Britain.[14] The effect on British producers was swift, though limited to only a handful of companies which by 1914 were producing cars to compete in that class.[15] Morris's biographers describe the Morris Oxford as a direct response by Britain's first mass producer, who took the challenge personally 'to compete with Ford at his own game' and to diminish the dominance of Fords on British roads.[16]

Transformation in industrial structure

Morris was successful in achieving this goal in the 1920s, a decade which saw Austin, too, beginning to produce cars for the mass market. It is clear, however, that their achievements were facilitated by the myopic American management practised both at Trafford Park (where in 1919 Henry Ford had insisted upon Perry's replacement by American managers) and in Dearborn, which provided British producers with the time needed to recover from the war and to embark on mass production.[17] The Model T had been designed for American conditions and requirements, and to its high running costs was added the horsepower tax contained in the Finance Act of 1920, imposing a further disadvantage by comparison with the new British cars specially designed for the British market. These possessed low horsepower, were relatively cheap to run, and were more attractive in appearance.[18] From almost 30% in the post-war boom, the Ford's share in British production fell to 10% in the mid 1920s. By 1928 Perry had been recalled to spearhead Ford's revival in Britain. This involved the reorganization and formation of the £7m. Ford Motor Company Ltd as the major shareholder in the other European subsidiaries, and which monopolized the supply of Ford cars to the area, a strategy in which the large new plant built at Dagenham was central.[19]

By this time GM had taken over Vauxhall, initially as an experiment in overseas operations, and like Ford, in 1929 appointed an Englishman, Charles Barlett, hitherto employed at GM's assembly operations at Hendon, as manager.[20] This signalled the parent company's intention to develop vehicle production to suit British conditions. These two appointments suggest that by the late 1920s the multinationals had learned the value of indigenous managers to subsidiary enterprise, following a period when American finance had merely underwritten a dismal performance, notably by Ford.[21] A lack of commitment to their subsidiaries and managerial weakness in the 1920s allowed British volume producers to emerge and overtake Ford – despite contrasting styles of labour management – and transform the industrial structure. By 1930, 67% of all car production was shared between Morris and Austin, compared with Ford's 11% and Vauxhall's 10%.[22]

Rhys has argued that the subsequent revival of Ford and Vauxhall, which by 1935–8 shared 27% of car production, explains the lower level of concentration of the British as compared with other continental industries, and which by implication resulted in higher unit costs stemming from foregone scale economies.[23] Even though one effect of Dagenham's economies of scale was to intensify price competition, however, neither these nor direct control over labour were sufficient to counter the increasing competition from other British companies demonstrating a greater sensitivity to the character of the British market. Following their lead, Ford pursued a policy of model price competition designed to a price based on the 8 hp Ford – the first car specifically made for the British and Continental markets.[24] Vauxhall adopted a similar strategy, designing a 10 hp model in 1931.

Behind the MNE's revival in the 1930s lay capital investment which, except for initial investment or acquisition, was generated mainly internally from retained earnings; these were marginally lower as a proportion than those of British companies, while depreciation was very much higher. Ford showed the greatest increase in tangible net assets of all companies between 1929 and 1938, and raised external capital to finance Dagenham.[25] Part of this investment by the MNEs was directed to a switch from assembly to manufacture of commercial vehicles (CVs), following the extension of the McKenna Duties to this category in 1926. Resembling Ford's cultivation of the market for mass produced cars, Vauxhall developed the market for CVs in the 1 to 3 ton categories with the 'all British Bedford truck', introduced in 1932 accompanied by a highly organized marketing strategy.[26]

Did the MNE's success in the 1930s hamper rationalization of the British motor industry as Rhys has maintained?[27] It seems unlikely that this was the case. Industrial concentration might have been greater in their absence, though the successful growth and performance of relatively small British producers in the 1930s, notably Standard and Rootes, suggest that it is conceivable that these firms might have shared the market had not Ford and Vauxhall been present. Furthermore, while industrial concentration might have been greater without the MNEs, higher productivity from scale economies can only be achieved when managers actively pursue policies of rationalization. Yet the continuing personal rivalry between the companies of Morris and Austin ruled out merger after Morris's rejection of Austin's overture in 1924.[28] When merger did come in 1952, personal circumstances had altered; the American share of the British market was rising rapidly and Ford's assets were as large as those of Morris and Austin combined; the problem of managerial succession together with the threat of survival finally led to merger – in the form of BMC – though not to integration.[29]

Post-war expansion, competition and merger

Ford's post-war success was partly due to the company's ability to fill Dagenham's productive capacity for the first time. Dunnett has emphasized the freezing effect of the government's steel quota on industrial structure.[30] However, while this is valid for British companies, the most striking feature of the industry in this period is Ford's increased share in production – and in the government's export drive. A world-wide distribution network enabled the company to exploit the opportunities provided by sterling devaluation, while the government's release of dollars arising from the transferred ownership of Ford's European subsidiaries to the parent company facilitated the purchase of US machine tools and made it possible to introduce new models designed in Dearborn.[31] John Barber, at that time a senior manager at Dagenham, and later recruited as financial director of British Leyland, has emphasized the advantages enjoyed by Ford: access to American know-how and methods, to technical and instant engineering assistance when required, and to analytical techniques relating to production, marketing, planning, and finance. As in the period between the wars, Ford's British operations were in the hands of an outstanding British chief executive, Patrick Hennessey.[32] Staff advisers from Dearborn visited Dagenham to improve financial control, which was accompanied by a policy of continuing high depreciation and a higher proportion of retained earnings by comparison with BMC.[33] By the early 1950s, Ford's pre-war average of a 15% share in British production had risen to 27%, at which level it remained until the 1970s. Vauxhall's share continued at less than 10%. Ford and Bedford CVs together exceeded 40% of British output by 1960 and exceeded 50% in the 1970s.[34]

While Ford's £3.2m. acquisition of Briggs Bodies in 1953, which afforded a significantly higher degree of integration, diluted American ownership, in 1959 the American company acquired all £129m. of shares remaining in British hands.[35] This should be seen in the context of a shift in American consumers' preferences which began to favour cars of European type, though at the same time anticipation that Britain would soon enter the EEC may have been an additional consideration. When the brief boom in tied imports from European subsidiaries was ended, as parent companies began to produce sub-compacts in the US, decisions on which subsidiaries should meet the remaining limited demand for imports were made in American boardrooms. The British Ford Cortina was superseded by the German Capri; the Vauxhall Viva by the Opel.[36] Multinational competition in Europe intensified in 1964, when Chrysler, at that time owning a long-established small CV manufacturing operation, Dodge Brothers (Britain) Ltd, acquired a one-third share in Rootes, Britain's third largest car producer.[37] However, twice in the next twelve years British governments provided finance to rescue Chrysler UK. On the second occasion, in 1976, the government rejected an authoritative report on the industry by the government's own Central Policy Review Staff, which had concluded that there were too many manufacturers with too many models, too many plants and too much capacity.[38] Furthermore, in 1975 the government had placed BLMC at the centre of a strategy intended to recover a substantial share of the domestic market. Apprehensive concerning the anticipated effects of closure on unemployment, the government's action was against all precedent in Europe, and hindered the agreed policy of rationalization of vehicle production in Britain.[39] Three years later Chrysler UK was taken over by Peugeot.

Chrysler's attempt to salvage its international position by investing in the British market was doomed in part by the same developments which precipitated BLMC's rapid decline in the 1970s. Two major factors were the formation of Ford of Europe in 1967, presaging the regional integration of vehicle production based on international division of labour, and Britain's long-delayed entry into the EEC in 1973. By that time, the French and German industries had adjusted to a gradual reduction of tariffs within the EEC, a roughly symmetrical rivalry between French and German producers enabling the indigenous companies to preserve their shares in the market.[40] Slower, erratic growth of the British market, however, left the British industry with a degree of concentration and plant size which prevented production either at efficient levels yielding economies of scale, or at levels where economies of marketing or research and development might be achieved,[41] though Ford, possibly, was the exception.[42]

While differing in emphasis, reports commissioned by the government in 1975 agreed on the diagnosis explaining the weakness of the British motor industry: inadequate rationalization of productions and models, overmanning and restrictive labour practices, poor profitability and inadequate investment, ageing plant and a lack of new products.[43] These reports were precipitated by BLMC's imminent collapse, the banks finally refusing to lend. The first solution was the Ryder plan for recovery, involving direct government control through the National Enterprise Board, but a further crisis two years later saw the appointment of a new chairman and chief executive, Michael Edwardes, a member of the NEB who was seconded from Chloride, the major components manufacturer.

In many respects the Edwardes strategy was to achieve levels of productivity and profitability enjoyed by Ford UK, for which higher investment, improved (and fewer) models and more effective marketing were necessary;[44] but a key difference between Ford and the two American MNEs and the British manufacturers since 1914 had been the degree of management's control over labour and production. Without specifying precisely the benefits resulting from arrangements at Ford plants, in 1975 the chairman, Terence Beckett, observed: 'What we have had is a particular advantage in Ford that some of our competitors have not had...a wage structure that is on a time basis...and we have got a national joint negotiating committee which is charged with the total negotiations of hourly paid employees.'[45] Beckett was referring to advantages, shared with Vauxhall since 1956,[46] of measured day work, company-wide wage bargaining, and independence from the Engineering Employers' Federation, whose procedures for settlement dominated the conduct of industrial relations in the British motor industry. When Chrysler acquired Rootes in 1967 the adoption of a similar system to that of wage payment and labour relations identified with American firms was attempted but encountered fierce opposition. The new American management tried to insist that the right to control track speed must be transferred from shop stewards to managers, but the compromise that resulted fell short of complete managerial control over manning[47] and continued to present one of many other difficulties facing Chrysler UK. For the major MNEs, however, the closer direct managerial control associated with measured day work, combined with resistance to the power of workplace labour organization, was also accompanied by a superior record of labour disputes. Turner estimated the incidence of strikes at Ford to have been one-half that at BMC between 1945 and 1964, a contrast between the two major American MNEs (Vauxhall having been virtually strike-free throughout) and the British Federated firms which, according to one source, probably continued in later years.[48]

Measured day work was first introduced at BLMC in 1971, though the experiment was a failure. Its reintroduction by Edwardes ten years later was accompanied by bonus incentive payments, thus representing a major difference from the Fordist model of high day-wage payments. The bonus scheme was outside the control of the shop stewards, whose power was curbed by the imposition of tighter discipline at the shop floor level. 'From the start', Edwardes recalled, 'everything we did in employee relations was tested against the broader strategy of regaining management control of the business.'[49] Beginning in 1980, shop stewards' control over working practices – which differed in detail and degree from factory to factory ('the habits of two life times', as Edwardes described them) – was sharply reduced by the recovery plan, which incorporated flexibility in working to minimize costs and improve quality.[50] Another major difference between the American MNEs – though Ford in particular – and British manufacturers was the British manufacturers' lack of financial control. Model by model cost information did not exist, and even as late as 1973 the auditor of BLMC had registered dissatisfaction with inadequacies in the accounts, and inventory control. During the mergers of the 1960s Ford's reputation for sound management practice had led to the recruitment of considerable numbers of Ford managers by BLMC and by Chrysler UK, and this was repeated in the late 1970s. Edwardes felt that 'Ford lost good staff men and British Leyland gained inadequate line men'; nonetheless, both group chief executives who assumed Edwardes's own executive functions after the initial managerial transformation was completed had previously worked for Ford.[51]

Decline

By the 1970s Ford's implementation of a policy of regional integration of production and marketing throughout Europe, moving towards standardization of model range and allocation of vehicle and component production between subsidiaries, began to threaten the survival of firms which either rejected or lacked a similar policy option. The Ford Escort was conceived as a European car, while the Fiesta, planned jointly by an Anglo-German team seconded from Dagenham and Cologne, exemplified the even greater levels of regional integration in progress.[52] Assembly occurred in the UK, Germany and Spain; engine blocks were produced in Dagenham and carburettors in Northern Ireland, while the proportions of locally manufactured components in the three countries varied. When GM began to rationalize production in 1979, car production and marketing were concentrated in Germany, and commercial vehicles in the UK.[53]

Capital investment by the multinationals was limited by the parent companies' policy of internal subsidiary financing. Throughout the 1960s and 1970s neither of the major American subsidiaries in the UK reached the target rates of return set by the parent companies,[54] which helps to explain why much of the capital stock in their plants, as in those of British factories, was old by comparison with those on the Continent. Even Ford's real assets fell between 1963 and 1973.[55] Intra-UK comparisons, however, reveal that Ford continued to maintain its superiority in levels of productivity, financial performance and investment.[56] In 1974 Ford's UK fixed assets per man, gross output per man and value added per man were the highest of all vehicle manufacturers in Britain (with BLMC the lowest), though below every other European producer excepting Fiat.[57] On a rising trend, between 1973 and 1982 capital expenditure by Ford UK roughly equalled that of BLMC/BL and was on an upward trend, though that undertaken by GM was very small (see Table 8.1). Furthermore, Ford invested more in the UK than in any overseas region outside the UK, more than three times as much as in other European countries between 1976 and 1983, and more than double that elsewhere.[58]

During this period Ford replaced BLMC/BL as the largest CV producer and in 1980 almost achieved parity in car output. UK market shares reveal a similar dominance. After 1977 Ford cars exceeded BL's share, stabilizing at around 30% in the 1980s. Likewise in the CV market, Ford's share exceeded 30% (1979–83), as compared with below 20% for BL, and roughly 15% for Vauxhall.[59] When juxtaposed with the decline in the share of new

Table 8.1. *Capital expenditure and employment: Ford UK, GM, Chrysler UK and BL, 1973–82*

	Ford UK		GM		Chrysler UK		BL	
	Capital expen- diture (£m.)	Employ- ment (000)	Capital expen- diture (£m.)	Employ- ment (000)	Capital expen- diture (£m)	Employ- ment (000)	Capital expen- diture (£m.)	Employ ment (000)
1973	42	71	18	34	7	31	63	204
1974	52	70	32	33	2	31	108	208
1975	52	70	14	29	2	25	92	191
1976	56	72	7	27	14	19	114	183
1977	81	77	9	30	18	23	149	195
1978	163	78	32	33			233	192
1979	334	80	32	32			259	177
1980	324	80	22	30			284	157
1981	280	75	12	23			201	126
1982	398	70	11	21			230	105

Source: Krish Bhaskar *et al.*, *A research report on the future of the UK and European motor industry* (Bath, 1984), II, pp. 346, 534, 586.

Table 8.2. *Car sales: Ford UK and GM, 1976–83*

	Ford cars (000)			GM cars (000)		
	UK sales	Tied imports	Exports	UK sales	Tied imports	Exports
1976	325	29	108			
1977	340	87	132			
1978	392	138	102			
1979	486	237	130	141	46	
1980	465	217	85	133	51	
1981	459	203	82	127	59	
1982	474	230	61	182	103	
1983	518	240	40	262	139	

Source: Bhaskar *et al.*, *The future of the UK and European motor industry*, II, pp. 529, 591

car and CV registrations supplied by producers in the UK, the major role of the multinationals in defending the UK market appears to be unmistakable.

However, in two respects the reality is more complicated. Firstly, Ford's market share rose only because that company became the largest car importer into Britain; GM took second place (see Table 8.2). While Japanese imports rose from 9% to 11% between 1975 and 1983, the American multinationals' tied imports accounted for a substantial proportion of car imports from the EEC, notably Belgium and Spain.[60] Table 8.2 reveals the growth of tied imports by comparison with the UK car sales of Ford and GM, who together accounted for almost all in this category. The total was 1% in 1974, rising to 22% by 1984.[61] However, even these figures provide a misleading impression of the trend and degree of import penetration by the MNEs, for the second factor which complicates analysis of the effects of their policies since the early 1970s is the growing practice of importing parts and components for assembly in cars 'made' in the UK. Thus, whereas in 1973 Chrysler UK models sold in the UK market embodied 97% local content by value, by 1983 (as Talbot) the figure was 30%. Even more striking are the examples of GM and Ford. Over the same period the local content in Vauxhall cars fell from 98% to 22%, and that in Fords from 88% to 22%.[62] By taking into account local content D. T. Jones has calculated a tied car and component import figure of 4% in 1974 which rose to 31% ten years later. Estimating that the value of imported components was equivalent to 150,000 cars, Jones calculated a 'true import content' figure for the 1984 UK market of 66% – to be compared with the official car import figures which showed a stable 57% between 1979 and 1984.[63]

A corollary of tied imports and sourcing by multinationals has been restrictive export policies by the subsidiaries. Between 1966 and 1970 Ford UK's exports averaged 35% of production and Vauxhall's averaged 36%, as compared with 27% and 22% respectively during the succeeding five years – in both cases on a falling trend.[64] Yet the proportion exported by the ailing BLMC was 45%, falling to 41%. The explanation for these trends is parent company strategy. A detailed breakdown of intra-European trade in 1975 revealed that Ford UK sold no cars at all, either in West Germany or the Netherlands, and minimal numbers in France, Belgium and Italy.[65] Until 1975 GM prohibited direct overseas sales by Vauxhall, which was allowed to sell only to the GM subsidiary possessing marketing responsibility for the country concerned, which the subsidiary sold to dealers appointed to sell Vauxhall vehicles.[66] In 1975 no sales were made in either France or Italy. There is also reason to believe that similar restrictions on intra-European exports obtained at Chrysler UK.[67] The domestic fall in Ford exports since the mid 1970s, coupled with the equally rapid rise in tied imports, contributed negatively both to employment and to the UK balance of payments (see Table 8.3). So too did the trend share by the multinationals to increase output and exports of kits, the latter exceeding their exports of built-up cars by the mid 1970s.[68] By 1983, Ford's net trade deficit reached £700m., and that of GM £600m.[69] Thus, Britain's capacity for making built-up cars diminished her ability to meet demand in developed countries with high incomes, and at the same time increased vulnerability to higher import penetration in

Table 8.3. *Government subsidies: Ford UK, Vauxhall, Chrysler UK, 1976–83 (£m.)*

	Ford	Vauxhall	Chrysler UK
1976	0.2		
1977	0.8		1976–9:162
1978	8.9		
1979	42.4	5.2	
1980	44.2	5.9	
1981	30.0	3.1	
1982	26.0	4.8	
1983	6.0	6.5	

Source: Krish Bhaskar *et al.*, *State aid to the European motor industry: a report* (Norwich, 1984), pp. 74, 77

periods of strong short-term demand.[70] Whereas in 1973 the MNEs in the UK were net exporters of 200,000 cars, by 1984 they had become net importers of 350,000 cars, leaving BL and Jaguar as the only exporters of finished cars.[71]

It may be deduced that another effect of the considerably greater dominance of the multinationals as producers and importers in Britain by comparison with all other major vehicle-producing countries has been the poor record of expenditure on research and development. Ford relied on research and development undertaken in the US and Germany, though BL's expenditure had also been very low.[72] At the same time, the superior competitive potential of the MNEs, by comparison with the major British company, had led to state support being extended to the American firms in order to protect employment levels. It has been estimated that while in 1982 some 176,800 people were employed in vehicle manufacture in the UK, a further 270,000 found employment through input–output linkages with the assemblers.[73]

Whereas in 1967 the government underwrote the losses of Chrysler UK to prevent an American takeover (or closure), subsequent subsidization, mostly through regional development programmes and investment grants in the form of interest relief, has been one way of attracting direct investment into the industry. Of Ford's £182m. plant constructed at Bridgend in South Wales in 1972 about 40% is estimated to have been the government's contribution.[74] Since that time subsidies have been smaller but continuing (see Table 8.3).

Reinforcing the effects of multinational policies was the response of the major British component manufacturers, whose strength contrasted with the weakness of the assemblers. By comparison with the motor industry in other countries, a relatively low level of vertical integration has been characteristic of car production.[75] In 1973 bought-out components accounted for 65% of the material costs of BLMC cars, 70% of Ford UK, 71% of Chrysler UK and 85% of Vauxhall.[76] The firms which dominated the market, Lucas, GKN, Dunlop, Automotive Products, and Automotive Engineering, each dominated the domestic market for particular components, but the trend towards restricted exports and tied imports by the multinationals produced a drive for exports by the component and parts manufacturers – including, from the late 1970s, BLMC's spare parts division, Unipart. In the 1970s the deficit on the balance of trade in cars was more than offset by the surplus produced by components and parts.[77] However, the drastic fall in BL's production, combined with the rise in imported components and parts by the MNEs, caused a marked contraction of this branch of the industry in the UK. The reaction of UK producers was to undertake direct investment in component manufacture on the Continent, the source of the imports, in order to protect sales and retrieve profitability.[78]

Any assessment of the effects of the MNEs on the motor industry must take account of chronology. Before 1914, when balance of payments problems and unemployment levels gave little cause for concern, the emphasis must be on the demonstration effect achieved by the sale of the Model T, which nudged British manufacturers towards mass production of low-priced cars. Both Ford, and later Vauxhall, were enclaves of American enterprise, their methods of management and corporate strategy being largely ignored or rejected by British manufacturers. Protection which coincided with managerial myopia and indecision within the MNEs in the 1920s enabled British producers to develop competitiveness and to re-establish dominance. A turning point occurred when both Ford, and later GM, appointed British executive managers, who in the case of Ford were outstanding and proved successful too at Vauxhall. This policy heralded the Europeanization of the approach by the MNEs to the markets for cars and commercial vehicles, in which both companies re-established a major presence. After the Second World War they played an important part in Britain's successful export drive, Ford in particular recording a superior performance over the British firms by most criteria throughout the 1950s and 1960s. Once Britain entered the EEC the full effects of the MNE's policy of European – and subsequently global – integration were felt, for this involved sourcing, ostensibly on the basis of international division of labour and capital mobility. The weakness of Britain's manufacturers was compounded by Ford's relative strength, for by comparison with Ford Werke, Ford UK was a high-cost enterprise; an even more unfavourable comparison may be drawn between the achievements of Opel and the inferior performance of Vauxhall. Ford's major commitment to Britain, measured by investment and employment effects, had continued to offset the relative weakness of the British companies. The major proportion of Ford's European commercial vehicles came to be manufactured in Britain;

tractor production, too, was relocated to Britain's advantage, while the sizeable car and engine factories at Dagenham, Halewood and Bridgend also strengthened Ford's manufacturing position in the UK. For these reasons the multinational presence might still be judged as having been of net benefit to the industry in Britain – in the sense that had Ford withdrawn completely from vehicle manufacture in the UK at any time since the Second World War it seems probable that the course of development of the British industry would have been such as to hasten Britain's relative decline as an international competitor. Ford's comparative strength checked this for a period of more than twenty years after the Second World War and it is ironic that with the implementation by the MNEs of an integrated European policy Ford's strength in the market was a factor which adversely affected the sales of the British mass producer. However, the deleterious effects of a sharp rise in tied imports, a decline in exports, a drastic diminution in local content and a reduction in car manufacturing capacity combined to accelerate the drift towards industrial decline.

NOTES

1 Mira Wilkins and F. E. Hill, *American business abroad: Ford on six continents* (Detroit, 1964), p. 51.
2 Society of Motor Manufacturers and Traders, *The motor industry of Great Britain*, annually. Krish Bhaskar *et al.*, *A research report on the future of the UK and European motor industry* (Bath, 1984), II, ch. 7.
3 Wilkins and Hill, *American business abroad*, pp. 35–73.
4 Raymond Vernon, 'The location of economic activity', in J. H. Dunlop, (ed.), *Economic analysis and the multinational enterprise* (London, 1974), pp. 89–114.
5 A. E. Harrison, 'Joint stock flotation in the cycle, motor vehicle and related industries 1882–1914', *Business history*, XXIII (1981), 184–6. Wayne Lewchuck, 'The return to capital in the British Motor Vehicle industry, 1896–1939', *Business history*, XXVII (1985), 3–21.
6 Wayne Lewchuck, 'The economics of technical change: a case study of the British motor vehicle industry, 1896–1932', unpublished Ph.D. thesis, University of Cambridge, 1982, pp. 290–2.
7 *Ibid.*, pp. 228–44.
8 *Ibid.*, pp. 290.
9 Roy Church, *Herbert Austin: the British motor car industry* (London, 1979), p. 99.
10 Lewchuck, thesis, p. 361.
11 P. W. S. Andrews and Elizabeth Brunner, *The life of Lord Nuffield* (Oxford, 1955), pp. 72–5; Church, *Herbert Austin*, p. 70.
12 James Foreman Peck, 'The American challenge of the twenties: multinationals and the European motor industry', *Journal of economic history*, XLII (1982), 868–70.
13 Lewchuck, thesis, p. 277.

14 Roy Church, 'Markets and marketing in the British motor industry before 1914, with some French comparisons', *Journal of transport history*, third series, vol. III, no. 1 (1982), 17–18.
15 *Ibid.*
16 Andrews and Brunner, *Lord Nuffield*, p. 59.
17 Roy Church and Michael Miller, 'The Big Three: competition, management and marketing in the British motor industry, 1922–1939', in Barry Supple (ed.), *Essays in business history* (Oxford, 1977), pp. 163–93.
19 Wilkins and Hill, *American business abroad*, pp. 46–51.
20 L. T. Holden, 'Vauxhalls and the Luton economy', unpublished M.Phil. thesis, The Open University, 1984, pp. 36–46.
21 Church and Miller, 'The Big Three', pp. 163–83; Alfred P. Sloan, *My life with General Motors* (New York, 1969), pp. 316–20.
22 D. G. Rhys, 'Concentration in the inter-war motor industry', *Journal of transport history*, IV (1976), 247.
23 *Ibid.*, 247–8, 254; Foreman-Peck, 'The American Challenge of the Twenties', 881.
24 G. Maxcy and A. Silberston, *The British motor industry* (London, 1959), pp. 99–111; Church and Miller, 'The Big Three', pp. 163–82.
25 Maxcy and Silberston, *The British motor industry*, pp. 158–62.
26 Holden, thesis, p. 72.
27 D. G. Rhys, 'Concentration in the inter-war motor industry', 247–8, 254.
28 Church and Miller, 'The Big Three', pp. 162–83.
29 R. J. Overy, *William Morris* (London, 1976), p. 64; Graham Turner, *The Leyland papers* (London, 1971), pp. 94–5.
30 Peter J. Dunnett, *The decline of the British motor industry* (London, 1980), pp. 31–43.
31 Wilkins and Hill, *American business abroad*, pp. 365–8.
32 Transcript of interview with John Barber in connection with BBC 2 TV documentary 'All their working lives: the car industry', 1984.
33 Maxcy and Silberston, *The British motor industry*, pp. 161–3.
34 D. G. Rhys, *The motor industry: an economic survey* (London, 1972), p. 20. Bhaskar *et al.*, *The future of the UK and European motor industry*, II, p. 20.
35 Wilkins and Hill, *American business abroad*, pp. 386–8.
36 G. Maxcy, *The multinational motor industry* (London, 1981), p. 101.
37 Stephen Young and Neil Hood, *Chrysler UK, a corporation in transition* (1977), pp. 78–82.
38 Central Policy Review Staff, *The future of the British car industry* (HMSO, 1975), ch. 3.
39 Young and Hood, *Chrysler UK*, pp. 281–7.
40 Dunnett, *The decline of the British motor industry*, pp. 129–31.
41 *Ibid.*, pp. 22–3.
42 Krish Bhaskar, *The future of the British motor industry*, (London, 1979), pp. 36–7.
43 All are mentioned in D. Ryder, *British Leyland: the next decade* (HMSO, 1975); Central Policy Review Staff, *The future of the British car industry* (HMSO, 1975); Fourteenth report from the Expenditure Committee, *The motor vehicle industry*, HC 617 (HMSO, 1975).
44 Michael Edwardes, *Back from the brink* (London, 1983), pp. 131–45.
45 Fourteenth report from the Expenditure Committee, *The motor vehicle industry*, para. 900.
46 Holden, thesis, pp. 168–71.

47 Young and Hood, *Chrysler UK*, pp. 229–30.
48 H. A. Turner, G. Clack and G. Roberts, *Labour relations in the British motor industry* (London, 1967), pp. 236–45; J. Gennard and M. D. Steuer, 'The industrial relations of foreign owned subsidiaries in the United Kingdom', *British journal of industrial relations*, ix, no. 1 (1971), 158.
49 Edwardes, *Back from the brink*, p. 162.
50 *Ibid.*
51 *Ibid.*, pp. 53, 57; Young and Hood, *Chrysler UK*, pp. 229–30.
52 Maxcy, *The multinational motor industry*, p. 145.
53 *Ibid.*, pp. 144–6.
54 Fourteenth report from the Expenditure Committee, *The motor vehicle industry*, pp. 134–5.
55 *Ibid.*, pp. 94–6.
56 Rhys, *The motor industry: an economic survey*, pp. 363–71.
57 Fourteenth report from the Expenditure Comittee, *The motor vehicle industry*, pp. 94–6, 98.
58 Trade Union Research Unit, 'The decline of the UK motor industry' (mimeo, 1984).
59 Bhaskar *et al.*, *The future of the UK and European motor industry*, pp. 121, 327.
60 *Ibid.*
61 Daniel T. Jones, 'The import threat to the UK car industry' (SPRU research report, Brighton 1985), p. 4.
62 *Ibid.*
63 *Ibid.*
64 Young and Hood, *Chrysler UK*, p. 142.
65 *Ibid.*, pp. 142–5.
66 Fourteenth report from the Expenditure Committee, *The motor vehicle industry*, p. 268.
67 Young and Hood, *Chrysler UK*, p. 145.
68 Fourteenth report from the Expenditure Committee, *The motor vehicle industry*, p. 270.
69 Jones, 'The import threat', p. 6.
70 Fourteenth report from the Expenditure Committee, *The motor vehicle industry*, p. 271.
71 Jones, 'The import threat', pp. 2–3. This excludes the small specialist producers.
72 D. T. Jones, 'Technology and the UK automobile industry', *Lloyds bank review*, 148 (1983), 22–3, table 1.
73 D. J. Mackay, Janet P. Sladen and Margaret J. Holligan, *The UK vehicle manufacturing report: its economic significance* (1984), p. 37.
74 Krish Bhaskar *et al.*, *State aid to the European motor industry: a report* (Norwich, 1984), p. 74.
75 Maxcy and Silberston, *The British motor industry*, pp. 26–32.
76 Fourteenth Report from the Expenditure Committee, *The motor vehicle industry*, p. 19.
77 Bhaskar, *The future of the British motor industry*, p. 306.
78 Keith Cowling, 'The internationalization of production and de-industrialisation' (University of Warwick mimeo, 1984); Jones, 'The import threat', p. 6.

Market organisation

9 International cartels and multinational enterprises

HELGA NUSSBAUM

Attention similar to that focused on multinational enterprises in recent decades was paid in the period between the two world wars and in the years immediately after the Second World War to international cartels, the first of which came into being as early as the end of the nineteenth century. Numerous scientific, economic and legal studies were published, and economic journalism turned to them. In the government enquiry made at the end of the twenties in Germany on the production and sales conditions of the German economy they played no minor role;[1] in the USA they turned up in various anti-trust proceedings,[2] and also as subjects of investigation in congressional committees,[3] increasingly so in the Second World War, when the bottlenecks of wartime economy were under discussion.[4]

There was intense debate on them as far back as 1927 at the League of Nations' World Economic Conference. The Economic Committee of the League of Nations was concerned with international cartels in the following years and, among other things, commissioned several experts' reports.[5] A final memorandum on the work done by the League of Nations was published by the United Nations in 1947 'to render it more widely available to students of international cartel problems which have come to the fore in current economic discussion'.[6]

International cartels gave rise to widespread suspicion, but also hope. Some of these hopes are summarized in Oxford professor Alfred Plummer's book of the early thirties in which he discriminates between hopes concerning cartels and those relating to concerns:

It may prove possible to associate government representatives, and consumers' and workers' representatives, with the control and administration of international combines; to reduce greatly the fluctuations in the volume of employment, and to prevent wage reductions, which, by reducing the purchasing power of the many, help to cause or aggravate trade depressions. Further, a marked increase in the number of closely-knit international *concerns* may help to reinforce the influences making for world peace. For although cartels and other loosely-knit international organizations can, if the devil drives, readily dissolve into their component parts on the outbreak

131

of a great war, the majority of the more closely-knit international organizations find that war causes a disastrous disorganization entirely inimical to their interests.[7]

After such hopes had melted away Evans Clark, Executive Director of The Twentieth Century Fund, wrote in 1946 when introducing Stocking and Watkins's great work *Cartels in action*:

During the war it became clear that the problems of monopoly – both national and international – which had been temporarily submerged under the urgent necessities of armed conflict, would rise up to plague the world again after the fighting stopped. ...Early in 1944 the Fund selected this field as one of those most in need of an impartial factual review and in which constructive policies in the public interest would be most urgently called for.[8]

And Stocking and Watkins expressed their conviction that 'the trend toward concerted action or collective controls in economic affairs, with or without government sanction or direction, is unmistakable. But it is not, in our view, inevitable. Although time is running out, democratic societies still have room for choice. If they have the will to do, they can shape their own destinies.'[9]

Today, forty years after, 'the trend toward concerted action or collective controls in economic affairs' is even less 'unmistakable' than before. The question of 'choice' is still open. But the focus of attention has shifted from international cartels to multinational enterprises.

In a sense there seemed to be a repetition in the interwar period – at least in Europe – of the discussion that had been carried on before the First World War not only on the cartels on a national scale, which I shall call 'national' cartels for short, but on the other important form of horizontal associations, the trust, as well. They were regarded hopefully as preventers of crises by the Austrian Friedrich Kleinwächter, who was the first to bring out a book on the modern cartels,[10] by Lujo Brentano[11] and a number of other political economists. In Germany, there was heated controversy in the press, in parties and parliaments, and it was debated whether the lever of legislation should be applied. As we know, things went beyond mere discussion in the USA. At that time other forms of capitalist centralization or concentration, the vertical *Konzerne*, received far less attention than cartels and indeed were under the cross-fire of criticism in Europe, in spite of their powerful development everywhere. The main reason for this was the fact that in those days it was not possible for any one individual firm among these large enterprises to restrict or eliminate competition. It was the cartels by means of which the large enterprises – if necessary together with smaller and medium-sized firms – achieved monopolistic power on the market and were able to fix prices, distribute markets among themselves, and impose boycotts, embargoes, and dumping abroad. And so it was the cartels against which the opposition of a great many manufacturers, commercial houses and consumers was directed. There was a somewhat similar situation in the interwar period at an international level. Robert Liefmann, one of the best authorities in this field and a student of it since the 1890s, wrote the following in 1928, commenting on the World Economic Conference of the League of Nations (italics in original):

We may, in a sense contrast the international *cartels* with the great international *Combines*, which are usually *Trusts*. But while cartels are always on a monopolistic basis, the same is not always the case with combines or with trusts. The combines can only attain monopoly by means of *cartels*, and such cartels between international trusts are to-day of great and growing importance... Up to now, no single combine has enjoyed a *monopoly for the whole world*, in any major industry... Monopolies by any one combine in several countries are also rarities. But there are such; the chief is at the present time the *Swedish Match Trust*... But on the whole, monopoly is only obtainable by trusts internationally through cartels which are, of course, the more easily practicable the smaller the number of businesses (i.e., the greater the concentration of capital) concerned.[12]

Instructive surveys of existing cartels have been published,[13] as have the contents of agreements,[14] whole texts of agreements[15] and comprehensive and searching case studies.[16] The publications produce unequivocal evidence of what had already emerged as an experience from national cartelization: it is chiefly the homogeneous or highly standardized products that are within the reach of international cartelization. In the League of Nations memorandum Gertrud Lovasy argued that:

this is obviously true only of quota agreements; there is no cogent reason why mutual market reservation or the allocation of export markets should not be agreed upon, even if the commodities produced by the various cartel members show some variation... International cartels have actually been established in all branches of industry and at practically all stages of production, from industrial raw materials to different types of producers' and consumers' finished goods.[17]

One can readily agree with the last sentence. Nevertheless, it is easily seen that the 'different types of...finished goods' – even those listed in Lovasy's appendix – are standardized products such as incandescent lamps. Here, a successful and long-lived international cartel had been established[18] which, through the exchange of patents and mutual information, had itself advanced standardization. On the other hand, if you take a look at the Continental Linoleum Union, which is presented as a cartel in various surveys, you will be puzzled and may wonder if this could perhaps be an exception, if this particular cartel also worked in the case of a finished product that is hardly fit to be standardized to any high degree. At best, it is a crude state of the finished product that can be standardized here, a kind of standardization the Linoleum Union in fact prided itself on. But then colours, printing designs, fashion, and prevailing taste come into play. How can this work, this allocation of limited markets to individual cartel members so that consumers 'will have to accept the variety or varieties offered to them', as Lovasy visualized it? With the intensity of international trade relations as they have evolved in the twentieth century? A closer examination at the composition of this structure reveals that it was a cartel only in its initial stages. The international Convention originally founded in 1911 had, since 1925, quickly changed into a 'community of interests' with the pooling of profit by an extensive exchange of shares among the member firms and the establishment of a holding company in Switzerland. There were loose gentlemen's agreements only with the British linoleum industry. The German, Dutch, Swedish and Swiss enterprises entered the closer agreement just because the original cartel was not operable. In the newly shaped community of interests each individual firm took in the orders it was able to secure according to customers' tastes, and the profit was redistributed. It was possible to buy up outsiders. The following was stated in 1930: 'The Continental Linoleum Union at present possesses sixteen factories in seven different countries, including eight factories in Germany.'[19] Here the international cartel had become a multinational enterprise. In 1929 its output totalled 125 million reichsmarks and was estimated to be a quarter of world output.

This one example can elucidate the difference between cartelizable and non-cartelizable products. There were attempts at cartelizing non-standardizable finished products at an international level too, but they were as short-lived as the 'national' attempts or else were limited to fixing sales conditions.

In 1944 the Kilgore Committee compiled a list of 105 groups of commodities that had been established in anti-trust proceedings as subject to international cartelization (see Appendix to this paper). The list is not complete. Steel, for example, is not included as it certainly had not figured in anti-trust proceedings, for the cartelized Continental Europeans still exported only small amounts of steel into the USA at that time. When singling out an individual item such as 'dyes' or 'dye-stuffs', on the other hand, one has to consider that the IG Farbenindustrie AG alone produced about 2,000 paints and dyes at the end of the twenties. In 1939 this concern supplied the USA with 928 products in the paints and dyes business alone, '119 of which were competitive = 12.8%'.[20] In view of this list various statements to the effect that between 1929 and 1937 an estimated 40% of world trade was controlled by international cartels[21] do not seem implausible.

The particular development of the world production–world trade ratio in the interwar period has, of course, to be seen as general background. The figures in Table 9.1 are relevant to international cartels. They illustrate that in the period before the First World War world trade increased *somewhat* more quickly than world production and later, from 1949 to 1965, far more quickly, whereas it can be recorded even for the prosperous 1920s that world production increased more quickly than world trade. The problem of

Table 9.1. *Growth of world production and world trade, 1900–65*

	Mining	Industry	World production (incl. agriculture)	World trade
1. 1900	100	100	100	100
1913	196	170	**147**	**161**
2. 1913	100	100	100	100
1920	102	93	97	80
1929	150	146	141	130
1932	96	95	115	97
1937	148	165	156	122
1938	147	148	147	112
1939	144	173	**157**	(100)
1949	185	204	179	124
3. 1949	100	100	100	100
1965	196	256	**200**	**291**

Calculation based on Jürgen Kuczynski, *Die Geschichte der Lage der Arbeiter unter dem Kapitalismus*, xxxvii: *Weltübersicht über die Geschichte der Lage der Arbeiter*, without the USSR and other socialist countries.

overcapacity caused or intensified by war production and the consequences of war had already arisen in many branches of the economy at this period. It was aggravated enormously by the depression of the 1930s with its shrinkage in world trade. The majority of the international cartels in the interwar period, particularly those for industrial products, were 'European' cartels, as far as the registered seat of their members is concerned (but not the territorial extent of their marketing arrangements). At least, that is how things were officially supposed to be. US anti-trust legislation and its handling by the Department of Justice had enormous effects, at least in so far as the European cartelists most strictly avoided any allusion in public to the inclusion of either American firms or the American market. They, too, could be involved in anti-trust proceedings, as indeed they were.[22] Speaking of the late twenties Brewster describes

several cases which made few concessions to nationality in an effort to undergo foreign raw material cartels which were allegedly exacting monopolistic prices from American customers. Thus the proprietary interests of the French government in the potash syndicate did not deter United States prosecution over the protest of the French ambassador (United States v. Deutsche Kalisyndikat Gesellschaft, 31 F.2d 199).[23]

For this reason it says, for example, in the published business report of the IG Farben AG on the German-French-Swiss Dyestuff Agreement, known as the Three-Party Agreement, of 1929: 'The above agreement does not apply to business in the United States of North America.'[24] But the minutes of the signing ceremony of 27 April 1929 contain special regulations on sales quotas for the USA;[25] subsequently sales figures are exchanged every month, both within the Three-Party Agreement and the Four-Party Agreement existing since 1932 following the inclusion of ICI.[26] The files contain numerous references to concerted pricing in the USA. On the other hand United States firms strictly endeavoured, even when they were interested in agreements, to keep these as informal and secret as possible. This went so far that Lammot Du Pont, for example, who had become really interested in informal arrangements in the course of talks on the International Nitrogen Cartel and who wanted to come to Europe, committed himself on consultation with his lawyers to talks, but not at exactly the same time as the corresponding negotiations in Paris and not in that location.[27] During the government enquiry in Germany a cartel expert mentioned that it was known 'that for a while the Americans cleared their quota via the English'.[28] In other words, it is hardly possible to say exactly how far US American firms were associated with cartels for industrial products with seats in Europe. The associations of that kind which have been brought to light in anti-trust proceedings and analysed in the literature may well be only the tip of the iceberg in view of the behaviour described above.

The raw materials situation is described in the memorandum of the League of Nations as follows:

'World' cartels – including other than European and United States members – were very few in number and were limited, with a few exceptions, to raw materials. These raw material cartels are nevertheless of primary importance for the world economy, the (first) international copper cartel, for instance, being composed of European, United States, Chilean and African members, and the international lead and zinc cartels, comprising Canadian, Mexican, Northern Rhodesian and Australian producers. Chilean nitrate producers participated in the Nitrogen cartel. The international phosphate rock cartel combined United States, North African and Oceanian producers. The United Kingdom (tin mines in Cornwall) and Portugal were the only European members of the international tin cartel, an intergovernmental agreement controlling production in Malaya, the Netherlands East Indies, Siam, Indo-China, Nigeria, the Belgian Congo and Bolivia. The international rubber scheme, also an intergovernmental agreement, seems to be the only one which had no European or United States members.[29]

All this goes to prove that the international cartels played an important role in the world economy of the interwar period. The highly contradictory economic effects of this cartelization cannot be set out in full here. An interesting summary from the perspective of 1946 can be found in the League of Nations' memorandum.[30] But some of these effects are in need of discussion: those elucidating the connection with the development and expansion of trans- or multinational enterprise. Have the cartels facilitated or checked its expansion? Have they any effect whatever in this direction? Without doubt trans- or multinationals are at present those structures in which the process of concentration and centralization of capital is most advanced and in which therefore the degree of socialization of production within the capitalist mode of production is highest. Although Marxists are occasionally criticized for quoting Marx so frequently, I hope you will not mind my having recourse to some basic Marxian tenets. 'Centralization completes the work of accumulation by enabling industrial capitalists to extend the scale of their operations', Marx wrote in volume I of *Capital*. Again:

Everywhere the increased scale of industrial establishments is the starting-point for a more comprehensive organization of the collective work of many, for a wider development of their material motive forces – in other words, for the progressive transformation of isolated processes of production, carried on by customary methods, into processes of production socially combined and scientifically arranged... And whilst centralization thus intensifies and accelerates the effects of accumulation, it simultaneously extends and speeds those revolutions in the technical composition of capital which raise its constant portion at the expense of its variable portion, thus diminishing the relative demand for labour.[31]

Later Marx wrote in volume III of *Capital* that the joint-stock companies made possible 'an enormous expansion of the scale of production and of enterprises that was impossible for individual capitals' and that they were

a transition toward the conversion of all functions in the reproduction process which still remain linked with capitalist property, into mere functions of associated producers, into social functions... This is the abolition of the capitalist mode of production within the capitalist mode of production itself, and hence a self-dissolving contradiction, which *prima facie* represents a mere phase of transition to a new form of production. It manifests itself as such a contradiction in its effects. It establishes a monopoly in certain spheres and thereby requires state interference.[32]

The statement made above that today the great multinational corporations represent the highest degree of (capitalist) socialization of production is meant to include the contradictions mentioned by Marx. Here it was in the first instance the *mode of production* of capital that he had in mind. As to the power of acquisition and disposition, he wrote that stock and credit offer

to the individual capitalist, or to one who is regarded a capitalist, absolute control within certain limits over the capital and property of others, and thereby over the labour of others. The control over social capital, not the individual capital of his own, gives him control of social labour... There is antagonism against the old form [of credit] in the stock companies, in which social means of production appear as private property; but the conversion to the form of stock still remains ensnared in the trammels of capitalism; hence, instead of overcoming the antithesis between the character of wealth as social and as private wealth, the stock companies merely develop it in a new form.[33]

Thus, though multinational enterprise is to be regarded as progress in developing capitalist economic structures, it is progress that sharpens old contradictions and creates new ones at the same time.

What about the cartels? Have they checked or accelerated this kind of progress? Broadly speaking, some of each. It is, of course, difficult to separate analytically cartel effects from other factors. Just think of the stimulating effect of increasing customs barriers both on the growth of transnational enterprises and on the formation of 'national' cartels.

Basically, cartels – as written or oral contracts without capital transfer among the contracting parties – can delay the process of centralization. By preventing a loss of profits or facilitating extra profits by means of price fixing and the fixing of sales quotas they prevent less profitable firms from disappearing from the market. This is, of course, one of the chief arguments of bourgeois opponents against cartels. According to these opponents the 'normal' selection by free competition guarantees the survival of only the most efficient enterprises, and so they hold cartels to be detrimental. The application of this to the level of international competition and more especially to the conditions referred to in Table 9.1 could possibly mean having whole branches of industry of individual countries outrivalled and destroyed (say, the Chilean nitre industry). The survival of not very profitable industries which would be considered 'detrimental' in line with the concepts of economic liberalism could be of vital importance for individual national economies. No wonder, then, that in the thirties a number of governments favoured international cartels. Thus, if on the one hand the process of centralization may be delayed, the accumulation of member enterprises, i.e. 'normal' concentration, is on the other hand enhanced by preventing a loss of profits or by means of extra profits. This is of particular importance if giants waging war for individual products oppose each other but are unable to kill their respective rivals. In the interwar period IG Farben, ICI and Du Pont were associations of capital of about equal strength, each of an order of 1,000 million reichsmarks of stock capital. There was no chance of any of these enterprises being able to oust the others. The axioms of theoreticians of liberal competition would not work here. What is more, these giants were actually interlocked by division of labour. IG Farben, for instance, prepared analyses of enterprises abroad for the purpose of assessing possible strategies, all of them along the same pattern, like this for Du Pont: 'I. Du Pont as a customer of IG...II. Du Pont as a supplier of IG...III. Du Pont as IG's contracting party...IV. Du Pont as a competitor of IG...'[34] Under the condition of a balance of forces co-operation and cartel contracts were the only means for such giants of avoiding serious losses of profit, particularly with stagnant world trade.

The files on negotiations between representatives of these giants conducted in the late twenties and early thirties are quite impressive, say on the dyestuff cartels, the nitrogen cartel or the hydrogenation agreements between IG Farben and Standard Oil of New Jersey.[35] What impresses is the readiness for compromise, the conciliatory attitude, the endeavour to detect the claims lodged by the contractors and to reach really acceptable solutions. One is at first almost inclined to take this as a general model for international negotiations. Plummer's hopes as to the peace-promoting effects of international 'combines' do not by any means seem to be out of place when one reads of these negotiations. I shall return to this aspect later. The Second World War revealed a different picture.

Internal accumulation well or at least passably well secured by cartels enabled these giants – and the less gigantic enterprises too – to invest abroad in places where this was possible and strategically useful for them.[36] Moreover, internal accumulation secured by cartels also enabled the giants to initiate research and development projects which, with insecure markets, would probably not have been started. Although the frequently made statement that cartels obstruct technological progress cannot be generally refuted, it is equivocal under conditions in which very large R. & D. investment is required. In 1926 IG Farben, for instance, began to build a large-scale test plant for the hydrogenation of coal with an annual capacity of 100,000 tons of petrol, which swallowed up huge sums of investment. Because of the resulting high prices for the final product a smaller plant would not have paid in this case. *Without* the agreement with Standard Oil of New Jersey, the biggest supplier of fuel in the German market, IG would not have been able to launch such a project.

However, cartels with only co-operation but without interpenetration of capital have two important drawbacks for the participating enterprises also at an international level:

1. If they manage to fix profitable prices, they attract outsiders, market intruders, and thus aggravate the problem of overcapacity.

2. They are less stable than interpenetrated property; their continued existence will depend on the contractors' goodwill; should a participant terminate the contract, either in times of acute economic crisis or through a change in the balance of power within the cartel, a disastrous slump in prices can, in most cases, hardly be avoided.

This is the reason why at the time of an enormously expanding world market after 1949 there was a rapid expansion of international interpenetration of capital. In the final analysis, basing international production and world-wide marketing prospects on capital is the safer variant. This is also a more effective way of solving the problems of market intruders and of restricting overcapacity. At any rate, for finished products lending themselves less readily to cartelization the variant of transnational enterprise had already been increasingly developed before that time by the large firms concerned.

An example of how difficult it is to reach arrangements with complicated products is that of the relatively fragmented car industry in Germany, the country of cartels, where the enterprises were not even able to reach an agreement on limiting the number of models. On 24 November 1938 Göring's Plenipotentiary for the Motor Industry (*Generalbevollmächtigter für das Kraftfahrzeugwesen*), Colonel von Schell, addressed industrialists:

Present state obvious. Disastrous fragmentation. For the present, only a glance at lorries. In the first seven months of the year 41,407 lorries in 130 models, i.e. 320 lorries per model. From three to seven lorry models per factory...add to these the special models required by the communities and other great requiring bodies, above all the Wehrmacht. Desperate situation. Consequently intolerable for national defence, intolerable for industry itself, above all intolerable for the overall economic situation in Germany.[37]

With such medium-sized enterprises (compared to, say, General Motors) pressure by the state had to and could be applied to enforce streamlining as to the range of models in the interests of war preparations.

Things were quite different in the case of a giant like IG Farben. First of all, the problem of streamlining production (and that of overcapacity) had been solved by the industry itself. For the standardizable products of this branch cartels and loose associations of capital in the form of communities of interests had been founded at an early period. In 1927 IG Director Carl Bosch described the urgent necessity of a complete merger:

In 1904 we entered into the first community of interests in the chemical industry. Then there were certainly different reasons for this from those we have today for our merger. The intention behind the community of interests of that time was to eliminate the frequent arguments over patents etc., and also to eliminate such competition as existed in the form of new dyestuffs circumventing inventions and appearing daily on the market. After all, we were almost exclusively a dyestuff enterprise at that time. We have committed ourselves to leave certain areas to others, while they cede to us other areas for exclusive activity.

Bosch does not mention here that there had been proposals for a complete merger as far back as 1904, but which had not been accepted. He goes on to say that in the early 1920s sales had dropped to 50% of pre-war levels, which made it necessary to close factories. This and other factors 'made us see very soon that the form of a community of interests that we used to have is absolutely impossible as it does not enable us in any way to implement drastic measures. To enable us to go ahead with them in order to maintain our industry we have decided on a complete merger after overcoming much resistance and many misgivings.'[38] And contrary to the situation in the automobile industry it was IG itself that succeeded in getting its own concept of enforced armament in the chemical sector accepted by the government authorities.[39] The impressively peaceful tone of the above-mentioned cartel negotiations had now disappeared. IG Director Carl Krauch, who was appointed by Göring to act as Plenipotentiary for the Chemical Industry (*Generalbevollmächtigter Chemie*), said in April 1939:

To sum up, the great possibilities that the German chemical industry can offer to national defence in the fields of gun-powder, explosives and warfare agents cannot be emphasized clearly enough. The present programmes are nowhere near to exhausting that which the German chemical industry can achieve in purpose-oriented development. It is above all in the hydrogenation waste gases, in grid gas etc., which are produced as part of the growing German raw material basis within the framework of the mineral oil scheme, that the chemistry of warfare agents finds possibilities that can be called almost limitless.[40]

The international strategies developed in 1940 for the postwar period by this giant enterprise are again impressive.[41] Well to the fore was that: 'The emphasis in the struggle for a reorganization of the world market will be on the relationship to the *North American concerns.*' Above all this was with a view to the Latin American and South Asian markets. 'A glance backwards and forwards shows the necessity of focusing all planning work on safe-guarding success in this struggle and, in order to achieve it, of subordinating diverging interests in European industrial countries that can be influenced by Greater Germany in their economic policies to this very aim.' For France this planned subordination was presented in detail. The following is note-worthy for our topic:

1. Concerning the dyestuffs branch, the loss of six factories of the IG founder firms in France because of the First World War was characterized as very detrimental to sales development in the interwar period. 'To reach the desired reorganization and as partial reparation for damages suffered in and by France the most appropriate solution to the problem of safeguarding the integration and alignment of French production and sales for ever seems to be the capital-participation of the German dyestuffs industry in the French dyestuffs industry, in such a way that there can be no future impairment of German export interests.' The intended share was 50% of the capital.

2. IG made a vigorous attempt with various public authorities to have 'its method' accepted and brought its influence to bear to eliminate other ideas, among them those of the semi-governmental 'Wirtschaftsgruppe Chemie', for which the 'basic formative principle' was 'clearly the principle of cartelization'.

3. IG only intended to enter into cartel arrangements in the field of 'other chemicals', and that only 'by forming long-term interstate (*zwischenstaatlich*) syndicates... In contrast to hitherto prevailing forms of German-French agreement on the chemical industry these syndicates must, however, be under uniform and strict leadership which is to be in German hands and with its headquarters in Germany in line with the greater importance of the German chemical industry. Thus exports of French chemicals would be exclusively effected by these syndicates unless the French industry is decontrolled for the respective product and exportation into defined areas or on an exactly limited scale is permitted.'

Quite clearly under a changed power structure the relatively peaceful cartel compromise of the interwar period is only regarded as an enforced transition stage. The economic trend towards transnational enterprise as the most highly developed form of capitalist socialization was to be pushed through by brute force. *This* scheme for the postwar period did not get beyond the planning stage, but it reveals important possibilities.

APPENDIX

List of products involved in antitrust proceedings against international cartels by the department of justice[42]

acids
acrylic products
aircraft instruments
alcohols, synthetic
alkalis
aluminium
ammonia, synthetic
ammonia solutions, synthetic
ammunition
antiknock compounds
argon gas
arsenicals
atabrine
bicarbonate of soda
bismuths
borates, crude
borax
boric acid
brick, magnesite
calcium cyanide
calcium nitrate
cal-nitro
carbon
carburetors
cellophane
ceramic coloring materials
chemicals
chlorine
chlorine derivatives
citrates
cobalt
colors, dry
dies
drugs
dyestuffs
electrical automotive equipment
electric lamps, fluorescent
electric lamps, incandescent

explosives
fertilizer
fertilizer, nitrate
fertilizer, potash
films
flotation agents
fuel-injection equipment
gasoline, synthetic
glass bulbs, frosted
glass bulbs, unfrosted
glass cane
glass tubing
gyroscopic aircraft instruments
hormones
insecticides
iodides
iron
kernite
lacquers
lamp bases, machinery for
leather, artificial
lighting equipment
magnesite
magnesium
matches
medicinal chemicals
mercurials
methyl methacrylate
molybdenum
narcotics
newsprint paper
nickel
nitrate of soda
nitrogen fertilizer
oil
optical instruments, military
paints
patents

perfumes
pharmaceutical products
photographic materials
photoprinting films
pigments
plastics
potash
quebracho
quinines
rubber, synthetic
rubber accelerators
soda
sodium carbonate (soda ash)
sodium hydroxide (caustic soda)

solvents
sulphonamides
sulphate of ammonia
tanning materials
tantalum
textiles, synthetic fibre
titanium
titanium compounds
tungsten
tungsten carbide
tools
varnishes
vitamins, synthetic

NOTES

1 *Ausschuss zur Untersuchung der Erzeugungs- und Absatzbedingungen der deutschen Wirtschaft*. Verhandlungen und Berichte des Unterausschusses für allgemeine Wirtschaftsstruktur, 3. Arbeitsgruppe (1928–30), henceforth *Enquête*.

2 US Congress, *Senate Committee on Military Affairs*. Subcommittee on War Mobilization (Kilgore Committee), Report No. 4, 78th Congress, 2nd Sess., 1944, pp. 41–60; Kingman Brewster, Jr., *Antitrust and American business abroad* (New York, 1958); Corwin D. Edwards, *Control of cartels and monopolies: an international comparison* (New York, 1967).

3 George W. Stocking and Myron W. Watkins, *Cartels in action: case studies in international business diplomacy* (New York, The Twentieth Century Fund, 1946, 3rd edn. 1949).

4 Kilgore Committee.

5 League of Nations, Economic and Financial Section, *Review of the economic aspects of several international industrial agreements*. Prepared for the Economic Committee by Antonio St Benny (Italy), Clemens Lammers (Germany), Louis Marlio (France) and Aloys Mayer (Luxemburg) (Geneva, 1930); League of Nations, Economic and Financial Section, *Review of the legal aspects of industrial agreements*. Prepared for the Economic Committee by Henri Decugis (France), Robert Olds (USA) and Siegfried Tschiersky (Germany) (Geneva, n.d.)

6 United Nations, Department of Economic Affairs, *International cartels*. A League of Nations Memorandum (prepared by Gertrud Lovasy) (Lake Success, New York, 1947), p. iii.

7 Alfred Plummer, *International combines in modern industry* (London, 1934), p. 165.

8 Stocking and Watkins, p. vii.

9 *Ibid.*, p. ix.

10 Friedrich Kleinwächter, *Die Kartelle* (Innsbruck, 1883).

11 Lujo Brentano, *Über die Ursachen der heutigen sozialen Not* (Leipzig, 1889).

12 Robert Liefmann, *International cartels, combines and trusts: a record of discussion on cartels at the International Economic Conference and a summary of legislation on cartels*. With an introduction by Charles T. Hallinan (London, n.d.), pp. 66–71.

13 UNO, *International cartels*, Appendix; Paul Thomas Fischer and Horst Wagenführ, *Kartelle in Europa (ohne Deutschland)* (Nuremberg, 1929), appendix.

144   Helga Nussbaum

14 LoN, *Review of economic aspects.*
15 Plummer, appendices 1–5.
16 Cf. Stocking and Watkins; Yandel Elliot *et al.*, *International control in the nonferrous metals* (New York, 1937).
17 UNO, *International cartels*, pp. 2–3.
18 LoN, *Review of economic aspects*, pp. 65–75.
19 *Ibid.*, p. 59.
20 Zentrales Staatsarchiv Potsdam (henceforth ZStA), 80 IG 1, I. G. Farbenindustrie A. G., B1471, Aufstellung der nach den USA ausgeführten Farben, p. 1.
21 UNO, *International cartels*, p. 2.
22 Kilgore Committee, pp. 37–40.
23 Brewster, p. 23.
24 Spezialarchiv der deutschen Wirtschaft. Veröffentlichungen aus dem..., Chemie und Kali (Berlin, n.d.).
25 ZStA, 80 IG 1, A1202, Europäische Farbenkartelle, pp. 304–5.
26 *Ibid.*, B682, Viererkartell- (und Dreierkartell-) austauschzahlen über die Umsätze in Kanada und den USA.
27 *Ibid.*, A2127, Stickstoff, 1931, Ländermappe, p. 295.
28 *Enquête*, part 4, Kartellpolitik, second section (Vernehmungen) (Berlin, 1930), p. 101.
29 UNO, *International cartels*, p. 4.
30 *Ibid.*, pp. 12–32.
31 Karl Marx, *Capital*, I, translated from the third German edition by Samuel Moore and Edward Aveling and edited by Frederick Engels (Moscow, n.d.), p. 588.
32 *Ibid.*, III, edited by F. Engels (Moscow, 1971), pp. 436–8.
33 *Ibid.*, pp. 439–40.
34 ZStA, 80 IG 1, A99, Aktennotizen KA-Büro 1929–1931, pp. 31–41.
35 Stocking and Watkins, p. 491; Kenneth S. Mernitz, *Progress at a price: Research and Development of liquid motor fuels in the United States and Germany, 1913–1933* (Ph.D. Diss., University of Missouri-Columbia); Verena Schröter, *Die deutsche Industrie auf dem Weltmarkt 1929 bis 1933: Aussenwirtschaftliche Strategien unter dem Druck der Weltwirtschaftskrise*, European University Studies, third series, vol. 251 (Frankfurt, 1984).
36 Alice Teichova, 'Changing political constellations and the Anglo-American-German cartel relations in the chemical industry in the first decade of the interwar period', in Gustav Schmidt (ed.), *Konstellationen internationaler Politik 1924–1932: Politische und wirtschaftliche Faktoren in den Beziehungen zwischen Westeuropa und den Vereinigten Staaten* (Bochum, 1983), pp. 221–36.
37 Peter Kirchberg, 'Typisierung in der deutschen Kraftfahrzeugindustrie und der Generalbevollmächtigte für das Kraftfahrwesen', *Jahrbuch für Wirtschaftsgeschichte*, (Berlin, 1969), part 2, p. 133.
38 *Enquête*, part 1, Wandlungen in den Rechtsformen der Einzelunternehmungen und Konzerne (Berlin, 1928), p. 436.
39 Detailed documentary evidence in Dietrich Eichholtz, *Geschichte der deutschen Kriegswirtschaft 1939–1945*, vol. I: 1939–1941 (3rd edn. Berlin, 1984), p. 36 and appendix 1; Dietrich Eichholtz, 'Zum Anteil des IG-Farben-Konzerns an der Vorbereitung des Zweiten Weltkrieges. Ein Dokument zur staatsmonopolistischen Kriegsplanung des faschistischen deutschen Imperialismus', *Jahrbuch für Wirtschaftsgeschichte*, (Berlin, 1969), part 2, pp. 83–105.
40 Eichholtz, 'Zum Anteil des IG-Farben-Konzerns', p. 99.
41 Eichholtz, *Geschichte der deutschen Kriegswirtschaft*, appendix 1.
42 Kilgore Committee, pp. 40–1.

10 Financial strategies and adaptation to foreign markets: the German electro-technical industry and its multinational activities: 1890s to 1939

PETER HERTNER

The problem

In 1913, according to one estimate, the German electro-technical industry's share of world production approximated to 35%, compared to the United States' 29% and to the 16% claimed by Great Britain.[1] Another estimate accords 31% to the German industry, 35% to the American and only 11% to the British.[2] It is agreed, however, that German industry, with its comparatively limited home market, dominated world exports of electro-technical material with a share of 46%, followed by the British and US industries with shares of 22 and 16% respectively.[3] According to a contemporary observer German electro-technical industry exported 22% of its production; the corresponding values for its British competitors reached the level of 30% whereas the Americans remained at a level of about 7%.[4]

Since the crisis of 1901/2, which hit the German electro-technical producers especially hard,[5] a virtual duopoly had been established on the German market with the Siemens concern (Siemens & Halske in the low-voltage sector, Siemens-Schuckert in the high-voltage business) on one side and the Allgemeine Elektrizitäts-Gesellschaft (AEG) on the other.[6] In 1913 they were both larger than their principal competitors – the American firms of General Electric and Westinghouse on a world-wide scale. Whereas AEG achieved sales of about 453 million marks and the Siemens group even reached the figure of 472 million, General Electric claimed a corresponding figure of about 357 million marks and Westinghouse remained at a level of 160 million.[7] In 1913 the Siemens group employed 82,900 people, of whom nearly 17,000 worked in the group's factories in Austria, Hungary, Russia, France, Britain, and Spain.[8] During the previous year AEG's workforce had totalled 70,162, 6,551 of whom were employed abroad in its plants in Vienna, Milan, and Riga.[9]

If one considers these multiplant firms which control and manage 'production establishments...located in at least two countries', moreover, as companies that operate in an oligopolistically structured market, many 'conventional' arguments could be made to accept the two German groups as multinational enterprises (MNEs).[10] If, however, one takes a closer look at their development over several decades, and sees that their expansion abroad followed certain 'stages in foreign involvement' by changes in the mode of transaction,[11] one readily comes to accept the validity of the internalisation paradigm,[12] possibly employed in an 'eclectic' approach.[13] In the latter case the concept of 'comparative advantages', originating from theories of imperfect competition which developed in the beginning of theoretical discussions on the MNE, could be added;[14] this point should help us to explain not only 'degrees of multinationality' but also 'discrete acts of foreign investment'.[15] For these reasons this paper will, in the first instance, be dedicated to a – partial, and of necessity a rather provisional – reconstruction of the gradual process of multinationalisation in the German electro-technical industry up to the First World War. It will be followed by a brief explanation of the subsequent development during the inter-war period.

Multinationalisation from the beginnings until the crisis of 1901

By far the oldest German firm in this sector was Siemens & Halske, founded in 1847 in Berlin as a workshop for telegraph equipment by Werner Siemens, then a Prussian army officer, and by Johann Georg Halske, a gifted Berlin mechanic.[16] For more than four decades Werner Siemens remained the driving force behind the entire enterprise, combining considerable organisational abilities with a highly inventive mind in the field of engineering and electro-technology. Soon other members of his family became involved. The existence of those family ties offered special incentives to internalisation and certainly contributed to the firm's successful engagement abroad at a very early stage.

Hence, from 1852 onwards, when the Russian government first placed substantial contracts for telegraph equipment and its maintenance, the firm responded by establishing a local office and a workshop where, from 1855, components manufactured in Berlin were assembled. The Russian transaction was supervised on the spot by Carl Siemens, the brother of Werner, who became a partner of the Berlin firm in 1855 while staying in Russia. In 1864 Carl persuaded his brother to invest in a copper mine at Kedabeg in Transcaucasia, the first, and for a long time the only, raw material venture of the Siemens & Halske firm.[17] Another of Werner Siemens's brothers, Wilhelm, or William as he later called himself, represented the firm's interests in Britain and directed the British Siemens branch, founded in 1858, which was engaged in laying sea cables – a potentially very profitable but highly risky business. By 1863 production of these cables and of other electro-technical material was started at Woolwich near London. In 1865 the London branch changed its name to 'Siemens Brothers', the former partners having left and Werner and William remaining sole owners of the firm.[18] In order to settle disputes about responsibility and profit distribution which had come up between the brothers, in 1867 the whole firm was reorganised under the roof of a 'common business' (*Gesamtgeschäft*) with its head office in Berlin. The existence of two formally independent companies, Siemens & Halske in Berlin and Siemens Brothers in London, was acknowledged, while the Russian branch was given the status of an affiliate to the Berlin firm Siemens & Halske.[19]

At first sight this might appear to have been a multinational group with Berlin as its centre investing directly in Britain and Russia. However, closer scrutiny reveals that William Siemens operated quite independently despite the fact that, sea cables and telegraph equipment apart, all material originated from Germany since advantage was taken of the existing free-trade status of the United Kingdom. There was considerable dispute between the two firms because of Siemens Brothers' claim to control most overseas sales. Nor did the establishment of the British firm as a limited liability company in 1880 resolve this problem, and William's death in 1883 further aggravated it, since the manager who succeeded him refused to adopt any accommodating solution. The question was eventually resolved in 1888 when Werner Siemens replaced William's successor and re-established strict family control of the company.[20] Structurally this family enterprise was more akin to traditional models of international business such as the Huguenot, and later Jewish, bankers operating as family firms simultaneously in several European countries; it was certainly not co-incidental that Werner Siemens wrote to his brother Carl in 1887 that he had been enthusiastic from his early days about founding a 'world-wide business à la Fugger'.[21]

Apart from those in London and St Petersburg the foreign Siemens outposts grew rather slowly: a first subsidiary in Vienna, established in 1858, had to be closed down in 1864 and it was only in 1879 that a second (and finally successful) attempt was made in the Habsburg monarchy's capital.[22] Until the 1890s the standard type of representation abroad was an agent who had to buy Siemens material on his own account. In Europe this system of subsidiary representatives was started in the 1870s and agents were appointed for Holland, Belgium, Italy, Switzerland, and Scandinavia;[23] at about the same time a corresponding initiative was taken for Latin America, followed by the establishments of agents in China in 1879.[24] In France, the existing legislation required that patents be worked within the country; this is why – well before the outburst of protectionism in the guise of new tariffs – a French Siemens subsidiary was founded in 1878. Siemens frères, which was supposed to produce dynamos and arc lamps, failed to establish itself, probably because it depended on the London branch which neglected the high-voltage sector during the 1880s. In 1886 it was liquidated.[25] Another reason for this failure might have been increased anti-German feelings after 1871, which certainly did not favour sales and autonomous direct investment. Joint ventures proved to be a viable solution: accordingly in 1889 Siemens & Halske, Siemens Brothers (London), and the Société alsacienne de constructions mécaniques (Mulhouse) founded a common company to produce high-voltage material at Belfort, just inside the French border. The Mulhouse firm, which retained a 37.5% share, was to provide all the non-electrical mechanical equipment, while Siemens would furnish the electrical parts. In the long run, the Belfort company proved to be quite successful. However, Siemens was forced to abandon it in 1904, since the merger with Schuckert a year earlier had left Schuckert's French subsidiary – the Compagnie générale d'électricité de Creil, founded in 1897 – practically at Siemens's disposal. Consequently, Siemens-Schuckert rented the Creil works from the Schuckert holding E.A.G. vorm. Schuckert, which formally was still independent. A jointly owned cable factory at Belfort was nevertheless still managed with the Société alsacienne.[26] In Tsarist Russia Siemens started production of low- and high-voltage material on a larger scale as late as 1880-2. Up to that point its activities had been largely confined to repair and maintenance work.[27] The reason for this change of strategy was not so much increasing Tsarist tariffs as the growing pressure from a Russian administration insistent upon domestic production in exchange for the continuing placement of State orders.[28]

Though Siemens grew gradually, at home and abroad, it was quite circumspect in its involvement in the rapidly expanding high-voltage sector during the late 1880s and early 1890s; however, its main competitor, AEG, followed a more dynamic policy during these years.[29] It had only started in 1883 as the German licence-holder of Edison. Moreover, it had, during the first decade of its existence, been technically dependent on Siemens and financially on Siemens, and on a number of banks, particularly the Deutsche Bank. In 1887 it became independent of the Edison companies and its technological dependence on Siemens was somewhat lessened. Only in 1894 did it become completely independent of its principal competitor. During the first years of its existence AEG concentrated primarily upon the electrification of Berlin. Soon it began to handle other projects in Germany, creating the first three local offices at Munich, Leipzig, and Breslau in 1885/6.[30]

In contrast to Siemens, AEG abandoned the agent system comparatively early and established a network of 'bureaux' all over Germany and Europe. It adopted this policy essentially for two reasons: firstly the power station, lighting, and electrification of transport business dealt with a relatively large number of customers, whereas the early telegraph systems had the State as exclusive partner; secondly, growing product sophistication demanded personnel with commensurate sales training and training in repair and maintenance, in other words, the traditional sales agent had to be displaced by a sales engineer employed by the producer.[31]

In 1900, AEG could muster no less than 42 'bureaux' in Germany, 37 in other European countries, and 38 overseas.[32] Its activities were no longer confined to the finance and operation of electrical utilities and to the production of incandescent lamps, as it had been in the mid 1880s. Now it 'had expanded its manufacturing to include power equipment and had introduced a line of polyphase machinery', continuing, however, to finance and build power stations and electric tramway systems.[33] Yet, unlike Siemens, by 1900 AEG had virtually no production units abroad, even if one keeps in mind that it had participated with Siemens in founding the Accumulatoren-Fabrik-Actien-Gesellschaft in 1890, which was to become a small MNE in its own right.[34] Equally, one should not forget that AEG was one of the founders of the Neuhausen aluminium company in Switzerland (1889) and that it took part in the creation of the Edison General Electric Company in 1890 – giving up its shares, however, two years later when the American group merged with its main rival, the Thomson-Houston company.[35]

Incidentally, the general trend towards growing internalisation did not exclude the minor competitors of the two emerging giants. Despite its somewhat precarious financial structure which, two years later, was to become decisive in its loss of independence, the Nuremberg firm of Schuckert had by 1899/1900 almost rivalled the 'big two'. In terms of sales, 77 million marks, it slightly surpassed the corresponding Siemens figures (76.8), even if the latter figures exclude sales abroad. With 100.2 million marks AEG sales lay considerably but not spectacularly above these results.[36] Schuckert's sales organisation had also passed through a comparable evolution: founded in 1873, the firm had already established its first subsidiary abroad two years later in Vienna. By 1900 it possessed 36 agencies and technical bureaux in Germany, and it was represented in nine European and seven extra-European countries; it had no less than eight technical bureaux in Russia, and three in Spain.[37] Unlike AEG, Schuckert did own producing units abroad: in Austria in 1896/7 a Viennese factory was bought and transformed into the Österreichische Schuckert-Werke AG with the participation of the Böhmische Unionbank.[38] In France the Compagnie générale d'électricité de Creil, mentioned above, was founded jointly with a French construction firm in 1897. There appear to have been joint ventures with local firms in Stockholm and Oslo,[39] whereas the London and St Petersburg subsidiaries, both of them established in 1898/9, did not take up production but remained commercial outposts.[40]

Other medium-sized firms besides Schuckert expanded abroad in the 1890s: this was certainly true of the Union Elektrizitätsgesellschaft, founded in 1892 by the engineering firm of Ludwig Loewe & Co. and by Thomson Houston.[41] The Union owned two production units abroad, one in Austria, the other in Russia, which together accounted for approximately half of Siemens's total investment in these two countries and were about 40% higher in terms of value than those of the Schuckert plants in these same two countries.[42]

Reasons for these different modes of international expansion can be found without too much difficulty. In most of these cases one would easily identify State intervention in the form of tariffs or non-tariff trade measures, especially where the State was an important customer, as in the case of Tsarist Russia, where even at local level a contractual stipulation was made by such city councils as St Petersburg's, which from 1898 required all electrical firms to ensure that two-thirds of technical staff and all electro-technical materials used were of indigenous origin.[43] These facts explain quite well why most of the investment in producing units made by electro-technical manufacturers during the 1880s and 1890s went to typical high-tariff countries like Russia, Austria-Hungary or – if one takes also into account the national patent legislation – France. It could also explain the long hesitation of AEG before investing in plants abroad: apparently it felt that its 'ownership advantages' secured by the quality and price of its products were so considerable in the second half of the 1890s that it could easily overcome the rising tariff walls.[44] As to Britain, foreign electro-technical investment there was at first certainly influenced by its unique position at the centre of world trade.[45] After the turn of the century the advantages of imperial preference, introduced by Canada in 1897 and, followed by South Africa and New Zealand in 1903 and by Australia in 1906, did provide a certain incentive to foreign investors.[46]

Nevertheless, other factors must have been present and influential to account for the fact that in 1913, for instance, 87% of all electro-technical imports into Russia originated in Germany,[47] that in the same year the German share of Italian electro-technical imports reached 70%,[48] and that the Germans regularly succeeded, between 1903 and 1913, in providing about half of Argentina's imports in this field.[49] One of the principal causes of this development can be found in the nature of the so-called *Unternehmergeschäft*: this meant that the large German electro-technical producers created their own market by establishing local and regional power, tramway and lighting companies in those countries (e.g. Russia, Italy, Spain, Latin America) and for those customers (particularly local public authorities) which suffered from chronic lack of capital. Newly created companies were forced by statute to buy their electro-technical supplies from their big industrial founders.[50] Doubtless these operations were further steps in internalisation aimed at reducing the risks of selling in a foreign market. However, the electro-technical producers found themselves with the risks attendant upon accumulation of a growing volume of equity capital which they had to keep in their portfolios and which tended to reduce their liquidity quite dangerously. By creating financial holdings together with the great banks the producers found a solution to this problem. The financial holding companies were supposed to take over the shares and bonds of the newly created public utility companies, to keep them in their portfolios during the period of construction and initial development, and to sell most of these holdings to the general public as soon as they had 'matured' and were able to yield a profit. For the financial holding companies it was normally sufficient to retain afterwards only a controlling minority share.[51] Each of the German producers had such intermediate financial holdings at its disposal: AEG had among others the Bank für Elektrische Unternehmungen, which it had founded in 1895 at Zürich together with a group of mainly German and Swiss banks. Siemens could rely on the Basel-based Schweizerische Gesellschaft für Elektrische Industrie, formed in 1896, as well as on its Elektrische Licht- und Kraftanlagen, founded at Berlin in the same year. Schuckert and the larger of the minor electro-technical producers equally controlled their own *Finanzierungsgesellschaften*.[52] Some of the most important of these financial holdings took their legal seat in Switzerland or Belgium – in the latter country, for instance, the well-known AEG-controlled SOFINA was based. This was due mainly to the liberal company law and stock exchange regulations of the two countries; in part it was probably also due to the participation of important Swiss and Belgian banks in these holdings.[53]

The development from 1901/2 until the First World War

The decade that followed the crisis of 1901/2 was characterised by two fundamental developments:

1 There was an extraordinary process of concentration in this branch of German industry which led to the disappearance or subjugation of most of the medium-sized producers. The lesser firms in this group either went bankrupt (as did Kummer of Dresden) or were, at the point of failure, bought up by their larger rivals and simply shut down (as happened to Helios).[54] The two largest and technically certainly most advanced firms of this group were very rapidly taken over by AEG and Siemens: thus Schuckert merged with Siemens in 1903: their new common high-voltage division, the Siemens-Schuckertwerke, formally an independent unit, helped Siemens to overcome its relatively weaker position in that field.[55] AEG's take-over of the Union Elektrizitätsgesellschaft in two stages in 1902 and 1904 was more important for its consequences in the field of international contacts, the Union being closely connected with Thomson Houston from its beginnings and later on with General Electric.[56] The two remaining middle-sized companies which survived the immediate impact of the 1901/2 crisis succumbed at a later stage: although Lahmeyer had

in 1905 found a partner in the Felten & Guilleaume cable works, both of them lost their independence in 1910 and were – especially Lahmeyer – firmly integrated in the AEG group.[57] Siemens gained control of the Bergmann Elektrizitätswerke in 1912 when the Deutsche Bank, with whom both of them had worked so far, threatened to cut its credits to the Bergmann firm, which was not very soundly organised.[58]

As a consequence of this whole process of concentration, the two remaining large producers reorganised, among other things, their international network of agencies, technical bureaux, and plants. Thus, by taking over the existing factories of the Union Elektrizitätsgesellschaft, AEG finally became a producer in Russia and Austria-Hungary.[59] Its technical bureaux abroad were increasingly transformed into legally independent foreign subsidiaries; in 1911/12, for instance, a South-American AEG company, responsible for business in Argentina, Brazil, and Chile, and a Mexican AEG company were founded.[60]

After its merger with Schuckert, Siemens took over the plants possessed by the Nuremburg firm in Austria and Hungary and created the Öster-reichische Siemens-Schuckertwerke and likewise a Hungarian Siemens-Schuckert company, the latter with plants in Budapest and Bratislava.[61] In France, the Schuckert factory at Creil was, as we have already seen, leased to Siemens-Schuckert which, not very successfully, tried to reorganise it during the years just before the outbreak of the First World War.[62] In Russia, close collaboration between Russian Siemens and Schuckert subsidiaries was stipulated in 1904 for the high-voltage business, but only in 1913 was a common Russian Siemens-Schuckert company with considerable manufacturing capacities established.[63] Finally, the growing importance of exports to extra-European countries required better control and coordination, including the business of the British Siemens branch, over which Berlin had regained complete control after the turn of the century. In 1908, therefore, a common overseas department was created, since it was felt that the extra-European markets needed special care and monitoring.[64]

2 The second factor was the rapid increase in 'coordination', on a national and an international level, not only between AEG and Siemens but also between, for instance, AEG and General Electric (in 1903). Since this was a branch with rather heterogeneous products (light bulbs were a notable exception and there were permanent attempts to cartelise this product), the creation of cartels remained rather the exception than the rule. A more tangible result was the creation of common companies, for instance between Siemens and AEG in Russia, because in this case – the production of cables – the internal Russian market was considered to be too small for two competitors.[65] In Italy, AEG and General Electric – represented by one of the European Thomson Houston companies – in 1904 founded a joint

producing firm, since they had decided to share this market in common when 'dividing up the world' the year before.[66] The Italian firm of AEG-Thomson Houston started production on a larger scale only in 1909, but it was clear right from the beginning that it should produce only material which could not be delivered 'under more favorable conditions by AEG of Berlin or Thomson Houston of Paris'.[67] The German consul in Rome indicated another reason for direct investment in the Italian electro-technical industry in his annual report for the year 1910: 'Important firms such as AEG or Brown Boveri have established subsidiaries not only in order to save tariff duties but also for calming the protectionist lobby by offering national products.[68] Another country where production had to be started without much enthusiasm was Spain. There Siemens in 1910 took over an electro-technical plant from a local producer in the vicinity of Barcelona because of increasing Spanish tariffs and a new law for the protection of national industry.[69]

In most of these cases of direct investment in producing units there were only two alternatives. As Felix Deutsch, successor of the two Rathenaus at the head of AEG, once put it, they were 'either to renounce such business completely or to start part of the production in the foreign country itself'.[70] In the absence of such state-enforced multinationalisation the large producers preferred, however, to profit from increasing economies of scale in the big factories of their countries of origin. The growth of internalisation thus found its limits in certain technical constraints as long as typical location-specific factors – the protectionist policies mentioned above – did not prevail.

The interwar period

The loss of the war by Germany and the loss of most of their direct investments abroad confronted the German electro-technical producers with a radically changed situation. The old strategy, i.e. providing the product and at the same time its financing via the network of the international financial holdings, was no longer feasible after the Swiss and the Belgian holding companies slipped away from producers' control during the post-war inflation period. At that time neither AEG, Siemens nor the German banks were able to provide the necessary foreign exchange needed for maintaining the financial liquidity of these holdings.[71] Thus the high-voltage sector especially, with its long-term capital requirements, was hit particularly hard.[72] On the other hand, the telephone equipment and the wireless communications sector, in which a firm like Siemens traditionally had a strong position, could increase its share in German exports quite considerably during the 1920s.[73]

In any case, the dominant position held by the German electro-technical industry on the world market until 1914 could not be re-established. Its share of world exports – 46% before the war, as we have seen – fluctuated around 25-8% during the second half of the 1920s. Only in 1931, at the height of the crisis, did it reach the exceptional percentage of 32.7.[74] In 1927 the total volume of US production amounted to 7 billion marks against 2.7 billion marks for the German output of electro-technical material, which means that American production had grown almost five fold since 1912 whereas in the German case it had only somewhat more than doubled.[75] In 1929 Siemens's sales volume amounted to 850 million marks and AEG had a corresponding figure of 580 million. They were largely left behind by General Electric and Western Electric with 1,744 and 1,722 million respectively, whereas the second American producer of high-voltage material, Westinghouse, was not so far removed from the two German companies with its sales volume of 909 million marks.[76]

Under these conditions of reduced strength only certain strategies could guarantee a limited degree of success. A few of them will be mentioned here:

1 Despite serious financial constraints the German electro-technical producers could, in certain cases, try again to resort to limited direct investment. This was done, for instance, by Siemens in Italy and in Czechoslovakia in the communications sector, where the State as a customer for wireless and telephone equipment bought exclusively from 'national' producers.[77] Also in France a telephone producing firm was bought up by Siemens in order to get access to this specific market.[78] The situation was, of course, much more favourable for both Siemens and AEG in Austria and Hungary, where the previously established subsidiaries were not lost after the war and guaranteed therefore a strong position in these markets.[79] When, during the 1930s, the protectionist pressure grew in all these countries, an increasing scale of products could then be manufactured in these foreign producing units.[80]

2 Cartelisation proved to be only a rather limited possibility given the special character, already mentioned, of electro-technical goods. Nevertheless there were, beside the cartel of light bulb producers, founded in 1924, some efforts in the telephone sector in which Siemens participated against the powerful ITT.[81] Besides this, in the high-voltage business the big American, German, and British producers succeeded in signing the International Notification and Compensation Agreement in 1931 which covered the world outside Europe and which lasted until the outbreak of the Second World War.[82]

3 Technical co-operation, i.e. the exchange of patents and other types of know-how, with the large US companies was another chance for the German producers who wanted to get rid of the isolation caused by the First World War and its immediate aftermath. Thus in 1923 AEG renewed its traditional ties with General Electric, and Siemens chose in 1924 the

other important American producer, Westinghouse, as a partner for a ten-year technical agreement, renewed in 1934.[83]

4 The most promising solution seemed to be the search for new financial resources which in practical terms meant loans or equity capital from US investors. Siemens used this possibility quite extensively between 1925 and 1930,[84] and it is well known that in 1929 General Electric took a 25% share in AEG.[85] Where the German electro-technical producers lacked this financial support, competition with American industry became increasingly difficult, especially in the capital-intensive high-voltage sector. Argentina in 1926/7 illustrates this perfectly: Siemens and AEG tried to acquire control there of a considerable number of small power plants owned by the national Herlitzka group. The Brussels-based SOFINA, before the war controlled by AEG, hesitated to give the necessary financial support to this operation. It was therefore hardly surprising that the Electric Bond and Share Company, a financial holding of General Electric, succeeded in buying up the Herlitzka companies.[86]

As indicated in this brief analysis of the multinational activities of the German electro-technical industry, the processes of internalisation do not, historically speaking, have to be one-way developments by any means. The German case illustrates particularly well how the rapid growth of the electro-technical sector until the First World War and how the ensuing dramatic change in political and economic conditions affected the international strategies of the leading firms of this comparatively new industry.

NOTES

Abbreviations used: *ETZ = Elektrotechnische Zeitschrift* Siemens Archives = Siemens-Museum, München: Firmenarchiv

1 P. Czada, *Die Berliner Elektroindustrie in der Weimarer Zeit* (Berlin, 1969), p. 138.
2 G. Jacob-Wendler, *Deutsche Elektroindustrie in Lateinamerika: Siemens und AEG (1890–1914)* (Stuttgart, 1982), p. 11; 'Die Elektrizität auf dem Weltmarkt', *ETZ* (1913), 1016.
3 Czada, pp. 137ff; Jacob-Wendler, p. 11; see also the statistical tables in Siemens Archives, SAA 11/Lb 581 (Liedtke).
4 'Die Elektrizität auf dem Weltmarkt'.
5 J. Loewe, 'Die elektrotechnische Industrie', *Die Störungen im deutschen Wirtschaftsleben während der Jahre 1900ff.*, III, *Schriften des Vereins für Socialpolitik*, CVII (Leipzig, 1903).
6 See, among others, G. Siemens, *Geschichte des Hauses Siemens* (3 vols., München, 1947–52); *50 Jahre AEG* (privately printed, Berlin, Allgemeine Elektrizitäts-Gesellschaft, 1956).
7 I. C. R. Byatt, *The British electrical industry 1875–1914* (Oxford, 1979), p. 166.
8 Total figure from M. Levy, *Die Organisation und Bedeutung der deutschen*

156   Peter Hertner

Elektrizitätsindustrie (Berlin, 1914), p. 4. The figures for the foreign subsidiaries are taken from M. Waller, *Studien zur Finanzgeschichte des Hauses Siemens* (typescript in the Siemens archives), IV/2, pp. 142ff.; J. Scott, *Siemens Brothers 1858–1958* (London, 1958), p. 266; G. Siemens, *Carl Friedrich von Siemens: ein grosser Unternehmer* (2nd edn., Freiburg, 1962), p. 74.

9   H. von Sothen, *Die Wirtschaftspolitik der Allgemeinen Elektrizitäts-Gesellschaft* (doctoral thesis, University of Freiburg/Breisgau, 1915), p. 163.

10   R. E. Caves, *Multinational enterprise and economic analysis* (Cambridge, 1982), p. 1 (quotation), pp. 94ff.

11   S. Nicholas, 'The theory of multinational enterprise as a transactional mode', in P. Hertner and G. Jones (eds.), *Multinationals: theory and history* (London, 1985).

12   R. H. Coase, 'The nature of the firm', *Economica* (1937), 386–405; O. E. Williamson, 'The modern corporation: origins, evolution, attributes', *Journal of economic literature* (1981), 1537–68.

13   J. H. Dunning, *International production and the multinational enterprise* (London, 1981), pp. 25ff.

14   S. H. Hymer, *The international operations of national firms: a study of direct foreign investment* (Cambridge, Mass., 1976); C. P. Kindleberger, *American business abroad: six lectures on direct investment* (London, 1969).

15   J. H. Dunning, 'Explaining the international direct investment position of countries: towards a dynamic or developmental approach', *Weltwirtschaftliches Archiv* (1981), 30–64; quotation from p. 33.

16   See for the whole first phase of development Siemens, *Geschichte*, vol. I, and S. v. Weiher and H. Goetzeler, *Weg und Wirken der Siemens-Werke im Fortschritt der Elektrotechnik 1847–1972* (München, 1972), pp. 8ff.

17   S. v. Weiher, 'Carl von Siemens, 1829–1906: Ein deutscher Unternehmer in Rußland und England', *Tradition* (1956), 13–25.

18   S. v. Weiher, *Die Entwicklung der englischen Siemens-Werke und des Siemens-Überseegeschäfts in der zweiten Hälfte des 19. Jahrhunderts* (doctoral thesis, University of Freiburg im Breisgau, 1959), pp. 33ff.

19   Siemens, *Geschichte*, vol. I, p. 87.

20   v. Weiher, *Die Entwicklung der englischen Siemens-Werke*, pp. 115ff., 143f., 154ff., 180ff.; Scott, pp. 61ff.

21   Quoted in v. Weiher and Goetzeler, p. 9, n. 2.

22   v. Weiher, *Die Entwicklung der englischen Siemens-Werke*, p. 143, n. 4.

23   Waller, III, p. 130.

24   v. Weiher, *Die Entwicklung der englischen Siemens-Werke*, pp. 149ff.

25   Siemens archives, SAA 68/Li 177: 'Das Schicksal von Siemens frères, Paris...'.

26   *Ibid.* and SAA 4/LK 90 (Nachlass Wilhelm v. Siemens).

27   J. Mai, *Das deutsche Kapital in Russland 1850–1894* (Berlin, 1970), pp. 99ff., 197; G. S. Holzer, *The German electrical industry in Russia: from economic entrepreneurship to political activism, 1890–1918* (Ph.D. thesis, University of Nebraska, 1970), pp. 29ff., 41; W. Kirchner, 'The industrialization of Russia and the Siemens firm 1853–1890', *Jahrbücher für Geschichte Osteuropas*, n.s. 22 (1974), 321–57, particularly pp. 330f.; v. Weiher, 'Carl von Siemens 1829–1906', 13–25, particularly p. 23.

28   *50 Jahre AEG*, pp. 94f., 132, 158; Holzer, pp. 34, 41ff., 83; J. Mai, 'Deutscher Kapitalexport nach Russland 1898–1907', in H. Lemke and B. Widera (eds.), *Russisch-deutsche Beziehungen von der Kiever Rus' bis zur Oktoberrevolution* (Berlin, DDR, 1976), pp. 207ff.; V. Djakin, 'Zur Stellung des deutschen Kapitals in der Elektroindustrie Russlands', *Jahrbuch für Geschichte der UdSSR und der volksdemokratischen Länder Europas* (1966), 122f.

29 See especially J. Kocka, 'Siemens und der aufhaltsame Aufstieg der AEG', *Tradition* (1972), 125–42.
30 *50 Jahre AEG*, p. 70; T. H. Hughes, *Networks of power: electrification in western society 1880–1930* (Baltimore, 1983), pp. 175ff.
31 *50 Jahre AEG*, p. 83; Waller, III, pp. 131f.
32 H. Hasse, *Die Allgemeine Elektrizitäts-Gesellschaft und ihre wirtschaftliche Bedeutung* (Heidelberg, 1902), p. 35.
33 Hughes, p. 178.
34 *50 Jahre AEG*, pp. 81f.
35 *Ibid.*, pp. 89ff.
36 G. Eibert, *Unternehmenspolitik Nürnberger Maschinenbauer (1835–1914)* (Stuttgart, 1979), p. 372.
37 *Ibid.*, p. 267; [R. Cohen,] *Schuckert 1873–1923* [Würzburg, 1923], p. 58.
38 [Cohen,] *Schuckert 1873–1923*, p. 49. According to B. Michel (*Banques et banquiers en Autriche au début du 20e siècle* (Paris, 1976), p. 183) it should have been the Länderbank!
39 [Cohen,] *Schuckert 1873–1923*, p. 49; Eibert, p. 234.
40 Eibert, p. 234.
41 *Ludw. Loewe & Co. Actiengesellschaft Berlin, 1869–1929* [Berlin, 1929], pp. 37f.
42 F. Fasolt, *Die sieben größten deutschen Elektrizitätsgesellschaften* (Dresden, 1904), p. 174.
43 *ETZ* (1898), 230.
44 See for instance H. Nussbaum, *Unternehmer gegen Monopole* (Berlin, 1966), pp. 79ff.
45 v. Weiher, *Die Entwicklung der englischen Siemens-Werke*, pp. 149ff.
46 W. K. Hancock, *Problems of economic policy 1918–1939*, Part 1 (Survey of Commonwealth Affairs, vol. II) (London, 1940), pp. 86ff.
47 Djakin, pp. 142f.
48 P. Lanino, *La nuova Italia industriale*, II (Roma, 1916), p. XXVIII.
49 Jacob-Wendler, p. 69.
50 See R. Liefmann's important study, *Beteiligungs- und Finanzierungsgesellschaften: eine Studie über den modernen Kapitalismus und das Effektenwesen* (Jena, 1913), pp. 103f.
51 M. Jörgens, *Finanzielle Trustgesellschaften* doctoral thesis, University of München; Stuttgart, 1902), pp. 117ff.; Fasolt, pp. published 175ff.
52 A. Strobel, 'Die Gründung des Züricher Elektrotrusts: ein Beitrag zum Unternehmergeschäft der deutschen Elektroindustrie', in H. Hassinger (ed.), *Geschichte – Wirtschaft – Gesellschaft: Festschrift für Clemens Bauer zum 75. Geburtstag* (Berlin, 1974), pp. 303–32; H. Grossmann, *Die Finanzierungen der Bank für elektrische Unternehmungen in Zürich* (doctoral thesis, University of Zürich; published Zürich, 1918); K. Hafner, *Die schweizerischen Finanzierungsgesellschaften für elektrische Unternehmungen* (doctoral thesis, University of Friburg; published Genève, 1912).
53 A. Broder, 'L'Expansion internationale de l'industrie allemande dans le dernier tiers du XIXe siècle: le cas de l'industrie électrique: 1880–1913', *Relations internationales*, N°. 29 (printemps, 1982), 65–87, particularly pp. 173ff.; M. Dumoulin, *Italie-Belgique: 1861–1915: relations diplomatiques, culturelles et économiques* (doctoral thesis, Université Catholique de Louvain, published Louvain-la-Neuve, 1981), part 3, vol. II, pp. 619f.; Hafner, pp. 30ff.; Jörgens, pp. 73ff.
54 J. Loewe, 'Die elektrotechnische Industrie', pp. 103ff.; H. A. Wessel, 'Helios, A.-G. für elektrisches Licht und Telegraphenbau 1884–1913: Finanzierungsprobleme der deutschen elektrotechnischen Industrie', *Bankhistorisches Archiv* (1984),

no. 1, 35–53; J. Kocka, *Unternehmensverwaltung und Angestelltenschaft am Beispiel Siemens 1847–1914* (Stuttgart, 1969), pp. 327ff.

55 Eibert, pp. 260ff.; Siemens, *Geschichte*, I, pp. 281f.

56 *50 Jahre AEG*, p. 156; F. Pinner, *Emil Rathenau und das elektrische Zeitalter* (Leipzig, 1918), pp. 272ff.

57 *50 Jahre AEG*, pp. 178ff.; Pinner, pp. 296ff.

58 Kocka, *Unternehmensverwaltung*, pp. 328f.; Siemens, *Carl Friedrich von Siemens*, pp. 89ff.

59 *50 Jahre AEG*, p. 158.

60 *Ibid.*, p. 186.

61 R. Maass, *Die auswärtigen Geschäftsstellen der Siemens-Werke und ihre Vorgeschichte* (München, 1958), p. 137; V. Schröter, *Die deutsche Industrie auf dem Weltmarkt 1929 bis 1933* (Frankfurt a.M. 1983), pp. 414ff.

62 Siemens, *Geschichte*, I, p. 386.

63 *Hermann Görz 1861–1930: eine Erinnerungsschrift anlässlich seines 100. Geburtstages am 31. Januar 1961* (privately printed; in Siemens Archives), pp. 20, 28f.; Holzer, CIT. pp. 83ff.

64 Maass, pp. 138f.; W. Eitel, *Die historische Entwicklung des Übersee-Geschäftes des Hauses Siemens und seine Organisation* (Siemens Archives, SAA 12/Lm 910), pp. 74ff.

65 P. Hertner, 'Fallstudien zu deutschen Multinationalen Unternehmen vor dem Ersten Weltkrieg', in N. Horn and J. Kocka (eds.), *Recht und Entwicklung der Grossunternehmen im 19. und frühen 20. Jahrhundert* (Göttingen, 1979), pp. 388–419, particularly p. 412.

66 *Bollettino ufficiale delle Società per Azioni*, ed: Ministero di Agricoltura, Industria e Commercio (Roma, 1904), fasc. 13quater, pp. 3ff.

67 *Ibid.* (1907), fasc. 42, p. 318.

68 Zentrales Staatsarchiv Potsdam, AA Nr. 5804, Bl. 120a.

69 Siemens Archives, SAA 68/Li 144: Spanien (Werk Cornellá); for Spanish protectionism see also J. Harrison, *An economic history of modern Spain* (Manchester, 1978), pp. 84f.

70 'Zum 70. Geburtstag Dr. Felix Deutsch', *Die AEG-Umschau* (16. Mai 1928), 33f.

71 B. Fehr, *Zusammenschluss und Finanzierung in der Elektrizitätsindustrie* (doctoral thesis, University of Bern) (Bern, 1939), pp. 46f.; *Bericht des Verwaltungsrats der Bank für elektrische Unternehmungen an die ordentliche Generalversammlung der Aktionäre vom 31. Oktober 1921*, pp. 4ff.; *Der AEG-Konzern 1928* (Das Spezial-Archiv der deutschen Wirtschaft, Sonderausgabe) (Berlin, 1928), p. 18; *50 Jahre AEG*, pp. 235; L. Michel, *L'électricité en Belgique: organisation économique et financière* (Liège, n.d.), p. 182.

72 Waller, V, pp. 81ff.

73 A. Glardon, *Die deutsche Elektroindustrie und der Absatz ihrer Erzeugnisse in der Nachkriegszeit* (Hamburg, 1933), p. 61; H. Schröter, 'Siemens and central and south-east Europe between the two world wars', in A. Teichova and P. L. Cottrell (eds.), *International business and central Europe 1918–1939* (Leicester, 1983), pp. 173–92.

74 Glardon, p. 17; Czada, p. 317; K. Schröter, *Die aussenwirtschaftliche Stellung der deutschen Elektroindustrie* (doctoral thesis, University of Frankfurt, 1940), pp. 52ff.

75 Calculated on the basis of Glardon, p. 15; F. Gapinski, *Die Stellung der deutschen Elektroindustrie innerhalb der internationalen Elektro-Wirtschaft in der Gegenwart* (doctoral thesis, University of Cologne; published Berlin, 1931, pp. 85, 90).

76 A. Gebhardt, *Die Expansion der amerikanischen Elektro-Konzerne in Europa* (doctoral thesis, University of Heidelberg, published Wertheim am Main, 1932), p. 8.

77 H. Schröter, pp. 181f.; V. Schröter, pp. 437ff.; P. Hertner, *How they changed their strategy: German electro-technical industry in the Italian market before 1914 and between the two wars* (contribution to the conference 'The early phase of multinational enterprise in Germany, France, and Italy', Florence, 17–19 October, 1984) (European University Institute, Florence, EUI Colloquium Papers 159/84 (col. 28)).

78 Waller, v, p. 231; V. Schröter, p. 424.

79 V. Schröter, p. 415; H. Schröter, p. 180.

80 In the Italian case see, for instance, the *Officine Lombarde Apparecchi di Precisione* (OLAP), founded in 1927 (Siemens Archives, SAA 68/Li 182 (note on the SAM, 12 December, 1945)); *ibid.*, SAA 47/Lk 843 (note on Siemens in Italy, 9 September 1944).

81 V. Schröter, pp. 263, 332ff.

82 Waller, v, p. 189.

83 K. Wilhelm, *Die AEG* (Berlin, 1931), p. 90; V. Schröter, pp. 258f.; Waller, v, pp. 80f.

84 Waller, v, p. 151ff.; V. Schröter, pp. 394ff.

85 E. Hess, *Elektropolitik und Weltvertrustung* (Amsterdam, 1931), p. 9; V. Schröter, p. 258.

86 Siemens Archives, SAA 20/La 969–971; M. Wilkins, *The maturing of multinational enterprise: American business abroad from 1914 to 1970* (Cambridge, Mass., 1974), pp. 131f.; G. Tacke, *Kapitalausfuhr und Warenausfuhr: eine Darstellung ihrer unmittelbaren Verbindung* (Jena, 1933), pp. 157ff.; J. Del Rio, *Politica argentina y los monopolios electricos* (Buenos Aires, n.d.), pp. 20f.

11 A typical factor of German international market strategy: agreements between the US and German electrotechnical industries up to 1939

HARM SCHRÖTER

The development of multinational activities[1] of German industry cannot be traced as easily as, for instance, that of its US counterpart. Twice – in the two World Wars – German foreign investments were seized by the victors. As a result this side of multinational activities was relatively underdeveloped. But German industry tried to secure a substantial share of the world market by other means too: up to 1945 cartels played an important rôle in the German economy. It has been suggested that industrial cartel policy should be investigated as one aspect of international activity.[2]

The purpose of this paper is to investigate German industrial policy with regard to the international market. As the electrical industry has been one of the fastest growing sectors of the German economy, its two leading representatives, AEG and Siemens,[3] have been selected for special scrutiny. Other similar export-orientated industries pursued comparable strategies.[4]

At the Versailles Peace Conference in 1919 a major aim of the French Government's policy was to make French industry superior to German. As early as 1921 neutral observers stated, however, that this aim had not been attained.[5] In order to find out to what extent the strategy of international agreements adopted by the German industry was responsible for its surprising performance on the world market in the 1920s a closer look has been taken at the years following the Versailles Peace Treaty when US and German electrical industries formulated their strategies.

Before 1914 the USA and Germany were the most important countries in the electrotechnical field. While General Electric (GE) and Westinghouse concentrated more on their home market, the German industry dominated the world's export market by a share of 46.4% (US: 15.7%) in 1913.[6] Up to 1900 the big US and German enterprises had been expanding on the same pattern, the chief component of which was to establish foreign subsidiaries

160

in key countries, especially in the USA, Germany, Great Britain, France, Italy and Russia.

At the turn of the century the policy of fierce competition between the above-mentioned companies gradually changed to a more moderate one. Westinghouse and GE were the first to enter into a patent licensing agreement in 1896. In 1903 Siemens & Halske together with AEG founded the important Telefunken company in the field of wireless production. GE and AEG agreed in 1903 to exchange patents and licences and to allocate foreign markets. The relations between Siemens and GE became friendly, too. In an understanding reached in 1903, GE renounced its rights to patents which it had acquired by buying up the majority of shares of the Siemens & Halske Electric Company of America in Chicago.[7] In 1912 an agreement by GE, AEG and Siemens was drafted covering the exchange of patents and the payment of compensation.[8] This contract was never signed, because Siemens suggested the inclusion of Westinghouse, while AEG opposed the strengthening of Westinghouse which this step would undoubtedly have entailed.[9]

Whereas before 1914 the US electrical industry with its vast home market was the larger, the German industry was more active in the international field. In order to promote sales to public utilities AEG in particular worked out new patterns: it gave to its customers credits covering the entire investment. This meant that all the electrical equipment required had to be bought from AEG. This policy was applied to both the home and the international market. For this purpose AEG later set up several national and international financing institutions of which the Swiss Bank für elektrische Unternehmungen, Zurich, was the best known.[10] Siemens too established a system of international financing. In areas of great importance and scale, e.g. in the South American market, their financing bodies cooperated with each other.

The First World War changed the international balance of power in favour of the USA and its electrical industry, which grew very fast during those years. Its German counterpart, being cut off from the world market, lost most of its foreign investments. Not only public utilities companies but manufacturing ones were seized by the victors. The biggest losses which AEG and Siemens suffered were their Russian investments, Siemens Brothers in Great Britain, and their influence upon international companies financing electrical investments. Immediately after the war, German industry made great efforts to expand again on foreign markets. Because of anti-German feeling within the states of the Entente, the few neutral countries such as the Scandinavian states became the preferred areas of international activity for the German electrical industry.[11] What was left of their foreign investments was mainly in central and south-east Europe, especially in Austria; the Österreichische Siemens-Schuckertwerke AG (1930 share capital: $5 m.) and AEG-Union Elektrizitätsgesellschaft (1930 share capital: $1 m.). With these 'stepping stones' AEG and Siemens managed to build up their predominance again in this area of Europe.[12] But the world-wide system of electrotechnical exports and enterprises had to be reorganized after the war. This could not be done without the US companies, which were undoubtedly the trendsetters: everyone else had to react to their policies. The reaction of the two German enterprises on which I have chosen to concentrate is described in the following pages.

The representatives of AEG and Siemens in the USA, Herr Lissau and Mr K. G. Frank, monitored every action taken by GE and Westinghouse after the First World War. Since they were anxious for German industry to regain influence, some of their early reports show signs of nervous interpretation, even contradiction.[13] Indeed things of great importance happened in the USA. Moreover, because of the war GE had already acquired a world-wide dominant rôle 'at least for some years' (Gerard Swope).[14] In 1919 it founded the International General Electric Co. to promote foreign business and chose Mr Gerard Swope as its head. Besides establishing contact with various enterprises in Great Britain and France Swope also approached both AEG and Siemens in order to arrange international agreements. He was personally well known to Siemens, for it was he who had negotiated a pre-war agreement between Western Electric and Siemens. In a conversation with Frank, Swope pointed out that, though GE had a long-standing partnership with AEG, he himself would prefer an agreement with Siemens.[15] Above all he wanted to know whether the German enterprises would combine their efforts for future exports. A fortnight later, on 25 June 1920, Frank and Swope had another talk. Swope expressed his wish to negotiate directly with a high ranking Siemens executive during his trip to Europe. When asked, he revealed that his aims were:

> reconstruction of the pre-war bulb cartel
> general understanding with AEG and Siemens, including the 'exchange of all patents and experience of a scientific and technical nature, allocation of the world market etc.'[16]

On receipt of this information, Carl Friedrich von Siemens immediately replied to Frank that Swope would be welcome.

With the background of world-wide structural overcapacity Siemens, like most German enterprises, favoured cartels as a strategy of market regulation in those days: 'In principle we take the view that we prefer an understanding to open competition if the share of the world market we have had so far is not to be crippled by the new agreement...'.[17] Furthermore, Siemens thought it was entitled to claim a bigger share in an export cartel than that of AEG as a conditio sine qua non. Siemens knew very well that its products were of high quality. Bearing this in mind, the enterprise was even prepared to fight GE if necessary: 'As I said, we prefer agreements but we do not fear to set foot on the path of open competition. In view of the technical superiority of our products, we hope to secure for us a sufficient turnover in spite of the depression which the war has brought upon our country.'[18] It was quite clear that Siemens was not prepared to let the mighty GE have it all its own way. Like a flashlight this instance showed characteristic traits of Siemens with its typical German concern for high quality standards.[19]

AEG tried on its own initiative to re-establish the good relations it had had with the USA before the war. It wanted to renew its old ties with GE. Therefore, when Swope and Anson W. Burchard, Chairman of International GE, came to Europe, they took up negotiations with Rathenau, President of AEG, and not with Siemens. One of the reasons for doing so was to counteract Westinghouse's attempts to come to an agreement with the German electrotechnical industry.[20] The US banking house of Kuhn, Loeb & Co. discussed the possibility of US loans to AEG in the summer of 1920. These talks were facilitated by the fact that the two men concerned happened to know each other personally.[21] However, these negotiations were interrupted by the GE talks.

AEG – like Siemens – was fully prepared to sign an agreement with GE, but both sides asked for too much. Having travelled back without any results, Swope tried to put pressure on AEG for a more positive attitude towards GE by playing off Siemens against AEG. But the two German companies, though in competition with each other maintained good communications. Swope had told Rathenau about the negotiations with Siemens and about a telegram he claimed to have received from Carl Friedrich von Siemens. Thereupon Rathenau asked Carl Friedrich von Siemens about these negotiations with GE and the telegram to Swope. As there had been neither negotiations nor such a telegram, C. F. von Siemens grew very angry. He did not hesitate to write Swope a four-page personal letter. Though moderate in tone, it expressed considerable astonishment at the methods adopted by GE and set the relationship between the two companies to rights.[22] Furthermore he informed Swope that he now felt compelled to reveal to Rathenau a secret pre-war understanding between GE and Siemens about future cooperation. He closed his letter with the remark that he no longer felt obliged to keep to this agreement. All in all, it was a very cool letter which showed no sign of intimidation in facing the mighty GE. The secret understanding mentioned in this letter derived from a conversation between Mr Burchard and Mr Rice of GE and C. F. von Siemens shortly before the war. At that time GE and AEG had an agreement on the exchange of patents. As the techniques of Siemens were thought to be more advanced than those of AEG, GE wanted to change partners in order to obtain access to Siemens techniques. The three men agreed that this should be done when the existing contracts had run out; until then, they agreed to maintain silence.[23] Rathenau was of course impressed by C. F. von Siemens's revelation. A partnership with GE was very important to AEG, but the possibility that Siemens might be the new partner and AEG be left out in the cold was too serious a menace. Though the comprehensive negotiations between AEG and GE were interrupted for some time, this information helped the two firms to settle on a smaller-scale agreement covering electric motors.[24]

After having tested each others' reliability for some months, AEG and GE agreed in 1923 to renew their pre-war contract concerning the exchange of patents and the allocation of markets.[25] AEG's newly established connections with GE worked very well. For instance, it was AEG which in 1924 got the first big credit received by a German enterprise from the USA after the period of German inflation was over. In 1924 Siemens signed an agreement with Westinghouse covering the exchange of patents and the allocation of markets.

Though Siemens did not have an agreement with GE, the relations between the two companies remained friendly. When in 1921 Siemens was going to resume its exports to the USA, Swope intimated to Frank that GE had no objection as long as Siemens respected GE's price-level.[26] In autumn 1921 C. F. von Siemens met Owen D. Young, Vice-President of GE. At the same time Swope again expressed his hope of a mutual understanding in the future and he made the gesture of inviting C. F. von Siemens to pay GE a visit in Schenectady.[27]

There was yet another important area for agreements: the production of light bulbs. Before the First World War, light bulbs and their technical development were one of the most important items of electric enterprises. After a big fight, mainly between AEG and GE but involving more than 30 enterprises, the matter was settled by agreements.[28] Again the US and the German industry with their foreign subsidiaries were the main suppliers of light bulbs to the world market. After the war, in 1919, the leading German enterprises merged their light bulb production and founded Osram GmbH. Westinghouse was interested in an agreement with Osram,[29] but again GE acted more quickly. In August 1920 A. W. Burchard, President of International GE, and E. A. Carolan, Vice-president, met W. Meinhardt, Generaldirektor of Osram, in Basle, Switzerland. Though this meeting was purely 'accidental',[30] Burchard handed over a draft agreement for a renewal of the world-wide light bulb cartel and the three started talks. Meinhardt stressed that the Germans 'during the war conducted their business in such a way that we are prepared to abide by the old treaties to their full extent'.[31] During the subsequent negotiations Herr Jensen of Osram emphasized that the pre-war agreements were still in force. This was of course denied by GE, which was acting on behalf of the US light bulb producers.[32] Circumstances had indeed changed in several ways. GE had taken a substantial interest in the Dutch Philips company, Europe's second-biggest light bulb producer. Furthermore GE had already signed a variety of agreements covering the main light bulb producing countries and companies.[33] The agreement with Osram was meant to be the key-stone in that world-wide building. The

German aim in the negotiation was to acquire as much weight as possible in the cartel, especially in Europe, but this conflicted with the other agreements GE had already signed. When asked on this point Swope assured Meinhardt that he would support Osram against the other members of the cartel.[34]

Differences had already arisen between Osram and the French Thomson-Houston company. On the basis of Article 310 of the Versailles Peace Treaty this enterprise had taken over for its own country important patents which had been German-owned before 1914. At his very first contact with Swope and Burchard, Meinhardt stressed that GE could not enforce an 'understanding' with France: 'We are not used to paying for licences, especially not for those rights which were ours before. We would rather take up a fight and see what will come out of it before paying for licences.'[35] This was a surprising stance to be taken by the losers of the First World War. Indeed Osram had little fear of GE and its light bulb interests. First of all, being the biggest light bulb producer in Europe meant that it could rely on its own weight. Secondly, the European light bulb patents were mainly in the hands not of GE but of AEG, a fact which strengthened the German position considerably.[36] This applied even to GE's share in Philips, because Philips had to renegotiate an extension of its licences from Germany only six months later.[37] Last not least, since it was the key-stone in the new world-wide light bulb cartel Osram was fully entitled to ask for more than the other members and the company was willing to exploit this position.[38] During the negotiations Jensen (Osram) told Burchard (GE) that GE 'underestimates our strength very much' and to him the proposals seemed to be 'rather an imperialist document'.[39] Burchard gave a plain reply: 'Yes, I admit, the document does read like that, but not intentionally so. You have to know that all questions, especially about prices are to be settled only with your consent. But after all we have to control the light bulb business in the world.'[40]

The cartel was founded, but because of several differences[41] it was not before the well-known Phoebus agreement was signed in 1924 that the world light bulb industry was again organized in an efficient and smooth-running cartel, which existed until 1939.

After the Phoebus agreement was signed Swope again added to his reputation as a 'trust builder'. He was busy in building the International Notification and Compensation Agreement (INCA), signed on 13 December 1930. This cartel included most of the leading enterprises of all countries.[42] For Swope this was, however, merely a first step. His policy was to acquire for GE a stake in every electrical enterprise of importance in the world.[43] In some cases GE was invited to take an interest. With the approval of the shareholders it acquired, for example, 16% of the Osram stock in 1929.[44] To Osram this meant not only better finances but – much more important – greater security in its international market relations. In Great Britain GE was offered the chance of reorganizing substantial parts of the electrical industry of that country by taking over several enterprises. In France GE added to its interests in Thomson-Houston and Alssthom a substantial minority share of the Cie. Générale d'Électricité in 1931. In other countries the practice of buying up shares, using a 'man of straw' at the stock exchange, was vigorously repulsed by the old shareholders and indigenous banks.[45]

The German enterprises AEG and Siemens reacted differently to GE's policy. AEG revised its agreement with GE dating from 1923 and GE took over a substantial part of AEG shares (15%).[46] Later this share was augmented to 25%. Though GE, being the only big shareholder in AEG, had gained considerable influence by this means, its policy was not to interfere in the management of the enterprises. This basic line of GE's strategy, which was also stressed in negotiations with other companies, was designed to sustain the feeling of independence of the respective firms.[47] Siemens reacted with greater reluctance: in general, it was in favour of understandings between enterprises, but only when it could expect to derive adequate advantage from them. In 1925 Siemens thought that the time was not yet ripe for large-scale international agreements because of the after-effects of the First World War.[48]

During the negotiations with Dillon Read & Co. for a substantial credit, Mr Dillon privately told Siemens that Owen D. Young was interested in obtaining for GE a minority share of 25% in Siemens. This idea was strongly repudiated by the Siemens Board ('... under no circumstances... '[49]). The official reply was diplomatic but firm ('... not possible... '[50]). Nevertheless, the relations between the two companies did not cool off. On the contrary, when Siemens drew a $14 m. gold debentures credit from Dillon Read & Co., the bulk of this sum was immediately bought by GE. As the money was to be paid back in 999(!) years it was in fact a lost credit from the start with which GE strengthened Siemens.[51] During the following years up to 1932 the companies remained in close contact by an exchange of letters between the presidents themselves. Both sides kept in mind that a world-wide understanding in the electrical industry was likely to be achieved. In 1930 Siemens signed a secret agreement with AEG about export prices.[52] In 1931 the Swiss-based Brown Boveri & Cie signed a patent agreement with Siemens.[53] At the same time Siemens and AEG negotiated about a merger of Siemens-Schuckert-Werke and AEG. This plan was finally dropped, but GE had been kept informed by both sides. Thus Siemens was neither strictly against a world-wide understanding nor was it inactive. It was the consistent strategy of Siemens first to obtain substantial weight in the international field of electrical enterprises and afterwards to make this position secure by international agreements.[54] Siemens's international policy in the interwar period was to obtain a fair share of the export market based on an excellent technical standard. In contrast to and in consequence of the pre-war period Siemens avoided foreign investments whenever possible. This was due not only to the lack of capital but also to considerations of political stability;[55] the same policy was pursued by AEG.[56] Siemens's heavy investments in foreign telephone concessions were merely an implement for holding its ground against ITT.[57] When the world-wide telephone fight (1929–32) was over,[58] Siemens made no further big foreign investments but pursued its old policy of cartelization. AEG on the other hand was so much shaken by the world economic crisis that new foreign investments were out of the question.

GE, too, had problems in 1932 and postponed most of its widespread plans. But its stepping stone, the INCA, was kept intact. It was organized in 1933, and in 1936 the International Electric Association, Zurich, was founded to handle the administration. The membership of INCA grew rapidly, only very few major enterprises (such as ASEA) remaining outside. After the Second World War it was revived as a European agreement. Inspite of all these understandings INCA, the International Cable Development Corporation (ICDC) and so on did not suppress a certain amount of competition. For instance the 'community of interests'[59] of Siemens and Westinghouse did not prevent the latter from buying up a Norwegian enterprise – in a territory dominated by German electrotechnical firms – just before Siemens could acquire the shares. However, these agreements avoided cut-throat competition.

On the whole the German electrotechnical industry expanded its international activities in a way which did not differ much from that followed by the electrotechnical firms of other countries: there was no specifically German aggressivness or reluctance. Most of the deviations from the patterns followed by foreign enterprises derived from the Versailles Treaty. Before the First World War the American and German industry followed similar patterns in international business, though the US industry was always more extensively based on its vast home market than was the German. After the loss of German foreign investments resulting from the Versailles Treaty, the US industry dominated the world market. One of the most vital questions for the German industry was therefore that of its relationship with its US counterparts on the world market. This was satisfactorily settled, but only after the German industry had managed to persuade the Americans that there was considerable strength left in AEG and especially in Siemens: 'For GE international accords and foreign direct investment continued to accompany one another.'[60] There is no great contrast here with the German industry, which also emphasized international agreements. Through these AEG and Siemens managed to avoid direct foreign investments whenever possible. Though this policy was largely due to relative lack of capital, it was to a great extent successful. Alice Teichova has pointed out that other branches of German industry pursued the same patterns of implementing international cartelization.[61] In the case of the electrical industry at any rate it was the main competitors – that is GE and Westinghouse – who made this German industrial policy possible by their agreements with AEG and Siemens. The multinational side of an enterprise cannot therefore be measured solely by the level of its foreign direct investments. It is rather the entirety of its foreign activities, which may to a certain extent complement each other, that should be considered in assessing the multinational character of a company. In the aftermath of the First World War AEG and Siemens had lost most of their foreign assets.[62] This backlash affecting their multinational character was compensated for to a great extent specifically by their cartel policy. They still operated in the world market, though they preferred to do so by exporting rather than by manufacture abroad.

NOTES

1 For a definition see J. H. Dunning, *International production and the multinational enterprise* (London, 1981); R. Caves, *Multinational enterprise and economic analysis* (Cambridge, 1982).

2 'Before World War I, it is necessary to consider the existence of cartels and their relation to corporate investment strategies. Indeed, I would suggest that the time has come to relook at cartels in the light of the on-going work on multinational business investment strategies' (M. Wilkins, 'Multinational enterprises', in *The rise of managerial capitalism*, ed. H. Daems and H. van der Wee (Louvain, 1974), pp. 213–35; p. 221).

3 In this paper all enterprises are named by their parent company: 'Siemens' includes 'Siemens & Halske AG' as well as 'Siemens-Schuckert-Werke AG'; 'GE' includes 'General Electric Company' as well as 'International General Electric Company' and so on.

4 V. Schröter, *Die deutsche Industrie auf dem Weltmarkt 1929–1933: Außenwirtschaftliche Strategien unter dem Druck der Weltwirtschaftskrise* (Frankfurt, 1984).

5 'The proud French idea of taking over Germany's position as an industrial power, for which the material conditions – iron and steel – were laid down in the Versailles Peace Treaty, seems to be frustrated even now' (internal memorandum of the Swedish Foreign Office, dated 8.2.1921; Utrikes Depatementets Arkiv, HP 64 CT IV).

6 CP. Czada, *Die Berliner Elektroindustrie in der Weimarer Zeit* (Berlin, 1969), p. 317.

7 SAA (Siemens Archiv Akte) 4/Lk 77; G. Siemens, *Carl Friedrich von Siemens: Ein großer Unternehmer* (München 1960), p. 57.

8 Draft version in SAA 21/La 826.

9 Letter from C. F. von Siemens to G. Swope, 15.9.1920, SAA 27/La 877.

10 See P. Hertner, *Von Wandel einer Unternehmensstrategie: Die deutsche Elektroindustrie in Italien vor dem Ersten Weltkrieg und in der Zwischenkriegszeit*, forthcoming, p. 5; F. Blaich, 'Absatzstrategien deutscher Unternehmen im 19. und in der 1. Hälfte des 20. Jahrhunderts', in *Absatzstrategien deutscher Unternehmen Gestern-Heute-Morgen*, 23. Beiheft zur *Tradition*, pp. 5–46; p. 18.

11 H. G. Schröter, *Außenpolitik un Wirtschaftsinteresse: Skandinavien im außen-*

wirtschaftlichen Kalkül Deutschlands und Großbritanniens 1918–1939 (Frankfurt, 1983), p. 330.
12 H. G. Schröter, 'Siemens and central and south-east Europe, between the two world wars', in A. Teichova and P. L. Cottrell, (eds.), *International business and central Europe 1918–1939* (Leicester, 1983), pp. 173–92.
13 E.g. Frank's reports to Siemens in: SAA 27/La 877.
14 Words of G. Swope, then President of International GE to Frank (Frank's letter to C. F. von Siemens, 11.6.1920, SAA 27/La 877).
15 *Ibid.*
16 Frank's letter to Siemens, 25.6.1920 (SAA 27/La 877).
17 Letter of instruction to Frank from Direktor Henrich, 15.7.1920 (SAA/La 877).
18 *Ibid.*
19 Blaich, 'Absatzstrategien'.
20 In a conversation with Frank, Mr Terry, Vice-President of Westinghouse, said that he was very interested in rebuilding the international light bulb cartel (Frank's letter to Siemens, 2.7.1920, SAA 27/La 877).
21 Mr Kahn of Kuhn, Loeb & Co. was the brother-in-law of Felix Deutsch, a senior representative of AEG, who after the assassination of Rathenau became president of the enterprise.
22 'I have to assume that you are not well informed about the historical proceedings of relations concerning understandings between your and my enterprise' (letter of 15.9.1920, SAA 27/La 877).
23 *Ibid.*
24 Swope informed Siemens of this in a talk with Frank (Frank's letter to Siemens, 16.11.1921, SAA 27/La 877).
25 In this well-known agreement the USA and Canada were allotted to GE while central, north, east and south-east Europe were reserved for AEG (SAA 4/Lf 973).
26 Talk between Swope and Frank on 16.9.1921 (Frank's letter of the same day to Siemens, SAA 27/La 877).
27 Frank's letter to C. F. von Siemens, 16.11.1921 (SAA 27/La 877).
28 W. Meinhardt, *Entwicklung und Aufbau der Glühlampenindustrie* (Berlin, 1932), pp. 11–15.
29 Talk between Vice-President Terry and Frank (Frank's letter of 2.7.1920. SAA 27/La 877).
30 Meinhardt's notes of the talk, dated 2.9.1920, p. 1 (SAA 27/La 877).
31 *Ibid.*, p. 2.
32 Jensen's notes of the negotiations on 24.9.1920 between Burchard, Carolan, Swope (all International GE) and Meinhardt, Schlüpmann, Sydow, Jensen (all Osram), p. 9 (SAA 27/La 877).
33 Great Britain (Thomson-Houston), France (Thomson-Houston), Belgium, Holland (Philips), Italy, USA (Westinghouse), Japan, China, Brazil and even Russia – for AEG – were incorporated in this list (*Ibid.*, p. 8).
34 GE had to respect the signed agreements, therefore 'they [GE] had to restrict themselves to assisting us in our negotiations with other companies in so far as our interests are clashing with theirs' (Meinhardt's letter to Schlüpmann (Osram) about his conversation with Burchard and Swope, 2.9.1920, SAA 27/La 877).
35 Meinhardt's notes, 2.9.1920, p. 7 (SAA 271/La 877).
36 Jensen's notes, 24.9.1920, *ibid.*
37 'Our already strong position vis-à-vis the Americans is further improved by their share in Philips. Philips's entire production of gas-filled-lamps in Holland depends on our patents', *ibid.*, p. 11.

38 *Ibid.*, p. 11.

39 *Ibid.*, p. 5.

40 *Ibid.*, p. 5. Osram should know 'that the Americans will supervise and control the whole light bulb business with some kind of paternal interest, helping and advising every partner. But finally there must be an agreement about the right of decision-making, and this right could only be with the Americans because of their position' (*ibid.*, p. 6).

41 E.g. Osram felt dissatisfied, especially as France was not willing to give way. In 1924 both the political and the economic scenes were sufficiently settled for realistic estimates to be made of the strength of the cartel members concerned.

42 GE, Westinghouse (by means of a Webb-Pomerence-Association), Siemens, AEG, British Thomson-Houston, British Electric Co., The General Electric Co. Ltd., Metropolitan Vickers, Brown Boveri & Cie.

43 M. Wilkins, *The maturing of multinational enterprise: American business abroad from 1914 to 1970* (Cambridge, Mass., 1974, p. 68). For GE's pre-1914 attitude see M. Wilkins, *The emergence of multinational enterprise: American business abroad from the colonial era to 1914* (Cambridge, Mass., 1970, pp. 57–9, 93–6).

44 Meinhardt, *Entwicklung*, p. 17.

45 See e.g., the case of the Swedish ASEA (J. Glete, *ASEA under hundra år, 1883–1983* (Västerås), 1983, p. 100).

46 Nominal value: 30 m. reichsmark (RM) out of 200 m. RM (Spezial-Archiv der deutschen Wirtachaft, Die AEG 1931).

47 Glete, p. 99.

48 Internal protocol, 18.7.1925, SAA 4/Lf 529.

49 Note of Direktor Haller, 11.11.1929, p. 2, SAA 4/Lt 398, vol. III.

50 Protocol of 14.11.1929, p. 5, SAA 4/Lt 398, vol. III.

51 The interests were low too: only 6%!

52 Because of the close connection between AEG and GE we can assume that GE was informed by AEG about this. Siemens in turn regularly sent summaries of the negotiations and their progress to GE – not to Westinghouse (SAA 4/Lf 529); see Czada, p. 277.

53 SAA 54/Li 91.

54 Note of Herr von Buol, 22.9.1931, SAA 4/Lf 793.

55 H. Lindgren is right in calling for more political awareness in economic history research ('Om internationella företag och behovet av ett historisk angreppsätt', in *Historisk Tidskrift* I (1984), 45–65).

56 *Zum 70. Geburtstag Felix Deutsch* (1928) p. 34.

57 V. Schröter, pp. 331–41.

58 H. G. Schröter, 'Siemens and central and southeast Europe', p. 184.

59 S. von Weiher and H. Götzeler, *Weg und Wirken der Siemens-Werke im Fortschritt der Elektrotechnik 1847–1972* (München, 1972), 8. Beiheft der *Tradition*, p. 170.

60 Wilkins, *The maturing*, p. 69.

61 A. Teichova, *An economic background to Munich* (Cambridge, 1974), p. 56.

62 See P. Hertner's contribution in this volume.

12 Participation in market control through foreign investment: IG Farbenindustrie AG in the United States: 1920–38

VERENA SCHRÖTER

Since it was the largest industrial enterprise and by far the largest chemical concern in interwar Germany, IG Farbenindustrie AG, founded through merger in 1925, provides a representative and interesting case study for German industrial expansion abroad.

As were many other German firms, IG Farben was engaged in a worldwide network of economic activities, some of them dating back to the decades before the First World War. Despite this, the concern did not favour foreign investments. Products were to be manufactured in Germany as far as possible. Only if a market was in danger of being lost due to import restrictions, tariffs, or competition was manufacture abroad accepted reluctantly as the remaining means of maintaining sales. In this respect, IG Farben had still adopted national rather than multinational concern strategies.[1]

This policy can be demonstrated clearly in the dyestuffs field, IG Farben's most important export sector, where between 64% (1936–7) and 77% (1926–8) of the output was sold abroad. Most of IG Farben's major foreign producing companies also manufactured dyestuffs. But whereas in 1931, for example, 74.3% of the overall dyestuffs products of the concern were sold abroad, only 12% were manufactured outside Germany (values).[2]

An important exception to this policy was the extensive involvement of IG Farben in the United States. During the First World War, the German industries, among them IG Farben's predecessors, had lost their US subsidiaries and participations, which were seized by the Alien Property Custodian of the United States Government. For a number of prominent German firms – such as Deutz, Degussa, and Zeiss – this meant a clear dividing line in their foreign investment policy. After the war they did not regain capital participations in their former subsidiaries, which were now fully American-owned. They renewed the old ties to a certain extent during the 1920s by concluding licence and market agreements which secured income for them as well as protecting world markets outside the USA. But on the whole, the American firms remained independent.[3]

171

By contrast, the IG firms, especially the Farbenfabriken vorm. Friedr. Bayer & Co., Leverkusen, began immediately after the war to reconstruct their influence in the US dyestuffs and pharmaceuticals business, one of their most important prewar markets.

In 1918, Sterling Products Inc., New York, had purchased the seized Bayer factories together with the trade-marks and patents covering the USA, Latin America, and Great Britain. The American company merged the pharmaceuticals business into its concern whereas the dyestuffs factories and patents were resold to Grasselli Chemical Co., Cleveland.[4] Grasselli, an important producer of heavy chemicals, had started with the manufacture of dyestuffs during the war.

As to the efficient evaluation of the former Bayer patents and production facilities, both American companies suffered from a certain lack of know-how. They were also interested in the access to further technical innovations in the field but wanted to avoid costly research investments. Thus they were not unwilling to cooperate when Bayer approached Sterling and Grasselli in turn shortly after the war in order to conclude agreements regulating the further relations between the parties.[5]

As Bayer was in a difficult legal position after the war, the German enterprise considered negotiations with Sterling as the appropriate way to come to terms with a competitor who used the same patents and trade-marks and had started a fierce competition against the German concern in the American pharmaceuticals market. Already in October 1920 the profitable Latin American aspirin business was regulated in a mutual agreement.[6]

In 1923, Bayer entered into several additional contracts with Sterling, dealing with the sales of pharmaceuticals in the USA, Canada, and Cuba, as well as in Great Britain and the British Commonwealth. Sterling's US pharmaceuticals business had been transferred to a newly founded subsidiary, the Winthrop Chemical Corp., Inc., New York. According to the agreement of 1923, Winthrop took over from the German concern exclusive licences on all patents and trade-marks as far as they were registered in the USA. Bayer also offered its technical expertise and new inventions in the pharmaceuticals field to the American company for exploitation in the United States, and agreed to retreat from the US market. Bayer, in return, received 50% of the net profits gained in the Winthrop business. Furthermore, the American firm restricted its business to the contract territory – i.e. the USA, Canada, and Cuba – and left the world market to Bayer.[7] The production and sale of pharmaceuticals in the USA and all management decisions in general remained completely in the hands of Sterling and Winthrop respectively. In view of the experience of the First World War, both parties were very much concerned to state that 'this agreement shall not be construed as in any way creating a partnership or joint venture'.[8] For the time being, Bayer was contented to share profits in a big and prosperous market.

With regard to dyestuffs, Bayer wanted to regain hold of production facilities in the USA from the outset. The United States was the biggest dyestuffs market of the interwar period – about one-quarter of the world consumption was sold here – and the most important export outlet for the export-orientated German dyestuffs industry. Though the German industry had lost its dominant prewar position in the market, it regained the leadership in imports. After 1924, more than half of the US dyestuffs imports (by volume) were supplied continuously by Germany,[9] that is IG Farben and, before 1925, mainly Bayer. Compared to the development of other markets in the 1920s, however, the German dyestuffs sales in the United States suffered considerably, because of the growing output of the national dyestuffs industry and the existence of high protective tariffs.[10] For these reasons, Bayer was afraid that the manufacture of dyes in the USA might become inevitable.

In the early twenties, American dyestuffs factories were analysed by the German concern regarding their suitability to fit in with Bayer's reconstruction plans. Grasselli, who had purchased the former Bayer factories and trade names from Sterling in 1919, was found to be 'most suitable'. Besides this, Bayer wanted to prevent Grasselli from using the acquired Bayer know-how to become a serious competitor on the world market.[11]

Both firms entered into negotiations. In June 1924, an agreement was signed.[12] The parties founded a new company, the Grasselli Dyestuff Corp., Delaware (GDC), which was to manufacture organic dyestuffs, chemical intermediates, and auxiliaries. Grasselli, merging all its production facilities in the dyestuffs field and the former Bayer patents and trade-marks into the joint venture, received a 51% participation and a payment of $3.25 m. from GDC Bayer got the remaining 49% of the joint-stock. The German company, in return, transferred its patents, trade-marks, technical know-how, and inventions in the dyestuffs sector to GDC for exploitation in the USA and Canada, and paid $1.1 m., half of which was delivered as commodities. Bayer and Grasselli received 50% of the GDC profits each, those deriving from the GDC production as well as those from Bayer sales via GDC. The activities of the American company were restricted to the USA and Canada, leaving the world market to Bayer. Even future technical inventions and know-how which might be developed by GDC were to be exploited on the world market exclusively by Bayer, though in this case profits would be transferred to GDC. Bayer had succeeded in shielding the world market from a potential competitor. But even so, the German firm was interested in the prosperity of its US participation as regards the growing national competition. The agreement left open the possibility that GDC might expand its exports in the future in order to keep its competitive position towards the other American dyestuffs producers. Until the Second World War, however, this option was never realised; GDC even agreed to leave the Canadian market to IG Farben.[13]

After the merger of IG Farbenindustrie, the German involvement in the US chemical industry became more direct. IG Farben entered into the agreements with Sterling and Grasselli, which were somewhat modified. From 1926 onwards, the German concern held a 50% participation in Winthrop Chemical Co., and IG Farben's US pharmaceuticals interests were merged into Winthrop, which acted as a holding company.[14] Formally, Winthrop remained an independent American firm. According to the IG Farben-Winthrop agreement of 1926, the latter should control sales management and organization in the United States and Canada.[15] Nevertheless, Winthrop had to pass on all kinds of business information to IG Farben and to discuss all questions of importance concerning management, sales, prices, and public relations with IG Farben representatives. The close relationship with the German mother company was also underlined by the presence of an IG Farben trustee on the Winthrop management board.[16]

At the same time, the German IG Farben enterprises merged their American dyestuffs investments into GDC. They took over 65% of the capital stock and a leading position in its management board. IG Farben paid a $2 m. increase of capital to GDC and 65% of the money to Grasselli which GDC still owed to this company according to the agreement of 1923. The profit share of 50% which Grasselli had received from the IG Farben dyestuffs sales in the USA and Canada since 1923 was reduced to 10%.[17]

In 1928, DuPont, the biggest dyestuffs producer in the United States, took over the Grasselli Chemical Co. In order to comply with the antitrust laws, Grasselli sold its GDC participation to a trustee of IG Farben and terminated the agreement of 1925. IG Farben changed the name of its now fully owned subsidiary into General Aniline Works, Inc., New York (GAW).[18]

Bayer merged with IG Farben in 1925, and the cooperation hence refers to Bayer up to 1925 and to IG Farben afterwards. Many former Bayer chemists were employed by Grasselli after the war to continue with their work in the dyestuffs factories, and prominent IG Farben managers belonged to the board of directors of GDC. The IG Farben technical commission, where the top decision-making concerning technical and investment questions took place, used to discuss GDC – and Winthrop – balance sheets and annual reports.[19] As an internal IG Farben memorandum stated in the late 1920s, there had always been a good relationship between the German concern and Grasselli, and no problems at all had occurred between them concerning the management of the GDC.[20]

Having established its interests in the pharmaceuticals and dyestuffs markets, IG Farben started to expand into further sectors of the US chemical industry by the end of the 1920s.

IG Farben sales of films and photographical materials were too severely hampered by the tariff situation and technical difficulties to guarantee high-quality deliveries through exports from Germany. One further factor which prompted the idea of taking up production in this field was the heavy competition between IG Farben and Eastman Kodak Co., Rochester, on the world market and even in Germany, where the latter had established a subsidiary. In return for Kodak's step towards manufacture in the United States, IG Farben intended to exert pressure upon Kodak on its home market.[21]

In 1928, IG Farben merged its US 'Agfa' sales agencies with an old-established American firm, Ansco Photo Products, Inc., Binghamton. A new company, Agfa Ansco Corp., Binghamton, was founded with a capital stock of $5.35 m.[22] Agfa Ansco was supplied by IG Farben with the assets of the former 'Agfa' sales agencies, all US patents, trade-marks, know-how, manufacturing and sales rights in the photographical field for the territory of the United States, and an additional $1.8 m. in cash. The German company, in return, received a 56% majority of the capital stock. The Agfa Ansco business was restricted to the USA. As was the case with GDC, new technical inventions developed by Agfa Ansco were to be exploited by IG Farben on the world market alone, against financial compensation payable to the American subsidiary. From Ansco Photo Products, the new enterprise could take over not only some production facilities, but also the firm's good reputation and its traditional trade names. As with Sterling and Grasselli immediately after the war, Ansco Photo Products agreed to merge with the IG Farben affiliates in order to gain access to the research potential of the German concern, and to save high investment and research costs.[23]

During the first years, the technical and scientific cooperation between IG Farben and Agfa Ansco does not seem to have been very intense. Only in July 1930 an IG Farben representative in the United States, W. Greif, did suggest in a meeting of the Arbeits-Ausschuß, the management board of IG Farben, that a permanent and close contact should be created between Filmfabrik Wolfen (a subsidiary fully owned by IG Farben) and Agfa, Berlin, on the one side, and the American subsidiary on the other. A German Agfa representative was to exercise continuous control in the Agfa Ansco factories.[24]

Heavy chemicals were another sector of chemical production in which manufacture abroad became more interesting to IG Farben during the 1930s, as export conditions grew more and more adverse. This applied especially to far away markets such as the USA. Beside tariffs, transport and production costs, sales figures, market conditions, and competition were analysed by the IG Farben chemicals department in various internal papers. In the years 1930 and 1933, the enterprise examined the possibilities of producing chlorate in the United States. Because of high transport costs and tariffs, chlorate exports from Germany to the USA were not profitable any more. Besides, the German concern wanted to prevent any competitor from establishing itself on the US market. Moreover, if IG Farben started with a chlorate works of its own, the argument ran, it might also succeed in reserving a respectable percentage of the market for its exports from Germany, which might be lost completely to the national competitors otherwise. The two main customers of IG Farben chlorate in the USA were to take part in the capital stock of the prospective producing company in order to minimize capital costs for the German enterprise. IG Farben wanted to contribute mainly its licences and expertise to the new company; potential payment in cash would have to be raised by IG Farben's US American holding company, the AIG (see below). This project was not realized, as the potential market was found to be too small and costs for raw materials too high.[25]

Another project, which was eventually carried out in 1933, was the manufacture of Perchloron. In 1931 IG Farben, together with the Pennsylvania Salt Manufacturing Co., Philadelphia, had founded a sales agency, Penchlor Inc. The company was to handle the sale of this chemical, and possibly also of other heavy chemicals, in the United States. It started with a capital stock of $50,000, with IG Farben and Pennsylvania paying in 50% each. IG Farben paid only half of its share in cash; the other half was transferred in the form of patents, trade-marks, and expertise. Pennsylvania possessed a slight majority of votes and took over the management, but important questions needed a two-thirds majority, i.e. mutual consent of the partners.

At first, the chemicals were produced by IG Farben in Germany and exported to the United States. Only in 1933, when the demand had grown and Pennsylvania favoured such a step, did Penchlor start manufacturing Perchloron. The company was supplied with raw materials and energy by Pennsylvania on a cost price basis plus 10%. IG Farben had to pay a share of another $55,000 for the new factory.[26]

The production of magnesium in the USA was another sector which IG Farben would have liked to occupy in the early 1930s in order to intensify its control of the market. Since 1928, IG Farben had possessed the know-how to produce magnesium alloys, namely Elektronmetall and Hydronalium, which could compete technically and on production costs with aluminium.[27] Being in a leading technological position in this field, the German concern pursued the strategy of granting licences to finishing industries all over the world which were engaged in the processing of magnesium and its alloys, including the motor car and aircraft industries. It did so firstly because it wanted to cover at least part of its very high research and development expenditure by way of licence earnings;[28] and secondly because the licence agreements used to include a paragraph which obliged each firm to buy its raw materials, i.e. magnesium or its alloys, and chemical auxiliaries, from IG Farben.[29] The German concern had a very large interest in these sales, for it was by far the biggest magnesium producer in the world.[30] Consequently,

IG Farben tried to postpone national magnesium productions in its main export markets, e.g. Great Britain.[31]

The situation in the US market was different in so far as the transport costs factor was more considerable, and there existed a potential national competitor. In 1927, the Aluminum Corp. of America (Alcoa) on behalf of its subsidiary, the American Magnesium Corp. (AMC), and the Dow Chemical Corp. had divided the US American magnesium market among themselves. Dow concentrated on the production of magnesium and delivered the metal at preferential rates to AMC, which processed it. One year later, Alcoa approached IG Farben in order to avoid price competition in the light metal sector and to get access to IG Farben's technology in the field.[32]

In October 1931, an agreement was signed.[33] IG Farben and Alcoa founded a research and licensing company, the Magnesium Development Co. (MDC), on equal terms, paying in $50,000 each. MDC was to hold the US patents and know-how of both parties in the magnesium field. Profits would be shared, but IG Farben was to receive an additional payment of $1 m. from the future profits of MDC as a special compensation. The agreement also included an option to start with the production of magnesium in the USA. In this case, the productive capacity of the new joint venture could be restricted by IG Farben, and should not exceed 4,000 tons p.a. In view of the falling demand during the world economic crisis, the still narrow market for the new light metal, the low world production figures (2,600 tons in 1929[34]) Alcoa's considerable aluminium interests, and the agreement between Alcoa and Dow, this restriction was desirable from the point of view of both parties. Incentives to establish a new magnesium producing company were very low in 1931. Only when the IG-Alcoa agreement was renegotiated one year later did the German concern press the point of a manufacturing basis for magnesium. Because of the economic crisis and patent difficulties, IG Farben's hopes of earning considerable profits from its participation in MDC had not been realized. Looking for profitable alternatives, IG Farben representatives argued that it would be necessary for MDC to gain a completely free hand in the US magnesium market by way of an involvement not only in the processing but also in the manufacture of magnesium metal.[35] As this would have meant a break of the Alcoa-Dow agreement of 1927 and, consequently, fierce competition on the market, Alcoa did not consent. The American concern was fundamentally interested in stable price conditions on the US American light metals market and in further good relations with Dow. Moreover, in view of the economic crisis, Alcoa was ready to invest in production facilities only if there developed a growing demand for magnesium in the USA, and if the IG Farben manufacturing process resulted in production costs considerably lower than the prices charged by Dow for the deliveries of the metal.[36] As these preconditions were not fulfilled in early 1933 and Alcoa remained adamant, the parties did not engage in the production of magnesium. The negotiations with Dow, which had been taking place for some time, were continued instead, and in June 1933 deliveries for another five years at reasonably low prices were arranged.

How was IG Farben compensated? Firstly, all agreements restricted Alcoa, AMC, and Dow to the US market and left the European market to the German concern.[37] Secondly, the new agreement between Alcoa and IG Farben which was signed in February 1933 gave the latter a 50% participation in AMC. This subsidiary of Alcoa processed more than 50% of the US magnesium production.[38] IG Farben, however, had to renounce its claim on the sum of $1 m. which had been part of the first agreement, and paid $125,000 to AMC.[39] In this way, it could participate in the profits of the biggest magnesium processing company of the USA, and thus in a developing and, in the long run, presumably prosperous market.

On the whole, it is difficult to assess how much and in what ways IG Farben gained by its subsidiaries and participations in the United States. Some sectors turned out to be quite profitable. The pharmaceuticals business in the USA and Latin America yielded profits amounting to a total of $21.5 m. from 1919 to 1937. In 1930, for example, a still comparatively prosperous year, the IG Farben mother company earned RM 14.65 m. with its national and worldwide sales of pharmaceuticals. Another RM 9.6 m. was transferred to IG Farben – directly or indirectly – by the American Sterling companies in the same year, RM 4 m. of which was the profit share of the Latin American aspirin sales, RM 5.6 m. that of the Winthrop business in the United States. So the American business contributed an important part of IG Farben's capital returns in the pharmaceuticals sector. This share dropped considerably, however, in the 1930s, when the Winthrop profit shares – expressed in dollars – shrank to less than one-quarter of their pre-crisis level. As the German pharmaceuticals sales recovered quickly in the 1930s and exceeded their pre-crisis level, the relative importance of IG Farben's American ventures sank considerably.[40]

Whereas the Winthrop participation had been based exclusively on the transfer of expertise, licences, and trade-marks, IG Farben had to raise substantial sums on behalf of Agfa Ansco and GAW. Beside the capital shares which had to be paid in cash, both companies needed extensive modernization investments from the start.

Agfa Ansco built a new factory which started production early in 1929 and was able to substitute the imports from Germany qualitatively and quantitatively within a few months. After 1929, no more films were exported to the USA from the German IG enterprises. The second largest film and photographical materials producer in the USA after Kodak, the new company held a strong market position. Its productive capacity, which was still fully employed in 1929, was able to supply 30 to 40% of the US raw film market.[41]

The new factory, however, had required a $3.25 m. investment. According to calculations of the IG Farben technical commission, the capital needs of the company amounted to a total of $9 m. Of these, $5 m. was raised through the share capital. AIG, IG Farben's US American holding company and main share-holder of Agfa Ansco, granted another $4 m. as a credit.[42] When the world economic crisis hit the business, Agfa Ansco got into financial difficulties. In 1932, losses – including writing off, interest payments, etc. – amounted to an estimated $1 m. and the credit could not be paid. Early in 1932, prominent IG Farben directors were sent to the USA to investigate the situation. The IG Farben management board discussed the remaining alternatives, either to reorganize, or to close down the company. Though the management board favoured the latter solution strongly in order to avoid further losses and capital expenditure, Agfa Ansco was eventually re-organized. AIG granted another credit, and IG Farben and a Swiss bank closely affiliated to the German concern, Ed. Greutert & Cie, acquired minor capital shares directly. The most convincing argument in favour of a reorganization had been that the bankruptcy of Agfa Ansco would have meant an immense loss of prestige for its share-holder AIG and, indirectly, for IG Farben.[43]

Though the financial situation of the new Agfa Ansco remained tough for some years yet,[44] the company recovered slowly. From 1935 onwards, it showed small but growing profits and could meet its financial obligations. In 1937 the highest sales figures were reached since the foundation of the company, and Agfa Ansco paid its first dividend. There were even plans to extend its production facilities.[45]

In the dyestuffs sector, the old GAW factories which had been built by Bayer before the war needed complete modernization. From 1926 to 1932 IG Farben invested a total of $12 m. The sum was raised by successive increases of the capital stock – from $5 m. in 1924 to $13 m. from 1929 onwards – and by a capital reduction in 1928 which compensated for the losses of the previous years. After 1928, the GAW balance sheets showed profits, though the investments were written off regularly. In 1933, the company even reported a 'satisfactory' capital return of 12.5%.[46]

These figures reflected the favourable business situation of GAW, which remained virtually unaffected by the crisis. Between 1926 and 1933, the production values of the company were almost quadrupled. But even so, GAW could not meet the demand for its products in the following years. In the 1930s, it supplied about one-quarter of the US American dyestuffs market, thus belonging to the three biggest dyestuffs producers.[47]

This successful development had taken place within comparatively few years, though IG Farben still preferred its exports to the manufacture of dyestuffs in the USA.[48]

Consequently, GAW were to produce only such dyestuffs which the German concern could not import into the United States on a profitable basis any more due to import restrictions and tariffs.[49] A comparison of GAW and IG Farben sales in the USA shows how these factors influenced the development in the 1920s and 1930s. Both were handled by a common sales agency, the General Dyestuffs Co., New York. The turnover of General Dyestuffs showed high growth rates which were influenced only very slightly by the crisis.[50] Until 1929, IG Farben imports and the GDC – GAW production shared in this development. Only from 1930 onwards did the share of the GAW products as a percentage of the total sales of General Dyestuffs grow considerably. In 1933, GAW supplied more than half of the turnover of the sales agency, whereas the IG Farben share had dropped to one-third. In 1929, precisely the inverse ratio had held. This development had been caused by the tariff law of 1930, the price-cut on the American dyestuffs market, and the devaluation of the dollar in 1933. From 1929 to 1934, dyestuffs imports into the United States dropped to one-quarter of the pre-crisis values.[51]

Nevertheless, the switch-over from imports to US production of dyestuffs had to be decided from case to case. Even the high US tariffs of 45% were not principally prohibitive. Despite these tariffs, many special dyestuffs of high quality yielded higher profits for IG Farben when they were manufactured in Germany, because the German company calculated production costs in the GAW factories as about two to three times as high as in the German IG Farben enterprises. By contrast, most bulk dyestuffs could be manufactured much more favourably in the USA.[52]

After the modernization of its factories, however, GAW manufactured a growing number of high-quality dyestuffs too. In 1931, the company had taken up, on the basis of IG Farben patents, the production of 27 dyestuffs which had been imported from Germany before.[53] These new production lines were most important for GAW's business success in the 1930s, as it suffered considerable setbacks with the sales of its traditional products.[54] On the whole, GAW manufactured a wide range of different dyestuffs, though it remained dependent on management decisions, deliveries of intermediates, and technology transfer from IG Farben.[55] The latter relationship, however, was not one-way. As the IG Farben director von Knieriem stated in 1939, there had been a number of valuable improvements of products and technical equipment deriving from the technical cooperation with GAW.[56]

As one of the most important US dyestuffs producers in the 1930s, GAW also became an important link between IG Farben on the one side, and leading American chemical concerns, especially the E.I. Du Pont de Nemours Co., on the other. Despite the existing antitrust laws, the US American dyestuffs market was regulated by a number of informal agreements, exchange of information, and a 'common interest to keep or improve the price level'.[57] After a period of competition, a 'very good cooperation' had been reached between the big enterprises in the early 1930s, in the USA as well as in third markets, e.g. China.[58] GAW and Du Pont were closely connected 'by a friendly regulation of all patent difficulties, a common sales policy, and bulk purchases of GAW from Du Pont of heavy chemicals and intermediates'.[59]

On the other side, through GAW IG Farben kept an important percentage of the US American dyestuffs market which otherwise would have been lost to the national producers. According to von Knieriem, this was a welcome opportunity for IG Farben 'to cut back the possibilities of expansion and the competitive position in the international dyestuffs business' of these firms.[60]

On the whole, IG Farben had succeeded within comparatively few years after the First World War in regaining a strong foothold in the American chemical industry and market. One reason for this success lay in the technological advantage which the concern still possessed in several crucial chemical fields and which was an important trump card in all cooperation agreements with American firms and subsidiaries. In return, IG Farben participated directly or indirectly in market shares and profits, and could usually reserve the world market outside the US territory for itself.

Moreover, licences and expertise provided an opportunity of acquiring some capital shares and influence and so of minimizing direct capital investment. But, unlike the German industry and capital market in general, IG Farben did not suffer from any lack of capital in the interwar years. The company satisfied its capital needs via the international capital markets. Not least for this reason, two formally independent Swiss and American holding companies, the Internationale Gesellschaft für Chemische Unternehmungen AG, Basle (IG Chemie), and the American IG Chemical Corp., New York (AIG), had been founded in 1928 and 1929 respectively. They held IG Farben's foreign subsidiaries and participations, raised capital funds, financed investments and granted credits, and administered the profits of the foreign IG companies.[61]

In view of IG Farben's cautious international investment strategies in general, it is remarkable that the German enterprise did not hesitate to finance large-scale investments in US manufacturing subsidiaries in order to replace exports. Long-term considerations to keep the most important US market and to meet the US concerns as strong potential competitors on their home market as well as on the world market were decisive motives in this context. They resulted in business strategies which might be called multinational for the first time in the history of the concern.

NOTES

1 Cf. in detail V. Schröter, *Die deutsche Industrie auf dem Weltmarkt 1929 bis 1933*: *Außenwirtschaftliche Strategien unter dem Druck der Weltwirtschaftskrise* (Frankfurt am Main, 1984).
2 *Ibid.*, p. 540, table 26.
3 *Ibid.*, p. 386, ch. 3.4.1.
4 If not noted otherwise, the following paragraphs are based on: Bayer Works Archives (BWA) 9/A.1, Confidential memorandum von Knieriem, 9 May 1939, Werdegang und heutiger Stand der USA-Zusammenhänge auf dem Gebiet der Farbstoffe, Photographika und Pharmazeutika. For further details see Schröter, pp. 404–14 and 471–8.
5 BWA 19/Pharmazeutische Produkte 4, Aktennotiz über eine Besprechung mit Herrn Dr. W. H. Duisberg in New York am 18. März 1955 über: Die Entstehung der Weiss-Verträge und ihre Entwicklung (Weiss was General Manager of Sterling Products Co.).
6 For details, see Schröter, p. 405.
7 BWA 19/Pharmazeutische Produkte 4, letter Sterling Products Co. Inc. (Weiss) to Farbenfabriken Bayer & Co., 9 April 1923; *ibid.*, Bayer Verträge New York; *ibid.*, letter Solicitors Arnold, Fortas & Porter, Washington DC, to the Patent Dept., Farbenfabriken Bayer AG, Leverkusen, 27 March 1956, including a statement given by Sterling Products on 23 March 1956 on 'cartel agreements between the parties'; Hoechst Works Archives (henceforth Hö), without file no., Activities of the former 'Bayer' IG Farbenindustrie AG in the Pharmaceuticals Industry, ed. the Economics Division, Decartelization Branch, Control Office, IG Farbenindustrie AG, US Zone, 1946, vol. B, Agreements.
8 BWA 19/Pharmazeutische Produkte 4, Agreement between Bayer Leverkusen and Winthrop Chemical Corp. Inc., New York, 9 April 1923, § 19.
9 Hö 1293, Bericht U.S.A., 1933, p. 1; Hö 2274, Import-Statistik (USA); BWA 81, USA 1.1, Reports 'Über das Farbengeschäft in den Vereinigten Staaten von Amerika', 1933 and 1934; H. Wagemann, *Die Einfuhrzollpolitik der Vereinigten Staaten von Amerika seit Beginn des 20. Jahrhunderts und die deutsche Farbstoffindustrie* (Mainz, 1967), p. 35, table 3.
10 Wagemann, pp. 14, 22f., 42 (table 5), 75, 86, 113; Hö, Activities Dyestuffs, p. 27.
11 BWA 9/A.1, von Knieriem, 9 May 1939, pp. 1–5; BWA 19/Farbstoffe 17, Rückblick über die historische Entwicklung unseres Geschäftes in den U.S.A., undated, p. 3.
12 BWA 19/Farbstoffe 17, contract between Bayer Leverkusen, Grasselli Chemical Co. and Grasselli Dyestuff Co., 17 June 1924; Hö, Activities Dyestuffs, Contract no. 22, pp. 100–2.
13 BWA 9/A.1, von Knieriem, p. 4; Hö, Activities Dyestuffs pp. 12 and 100f.
14 BWA 9/A.1, von Knieriem, 9 May 1939; BWA 19/Farbstoffe 17, Rückblick; Hö, Activities Pharma, vol. B, p. 60.
15 BWA 19/Pharmazeutische Produkte, Agreement between IG Farbenindustrie AG and Winthrop Chemical Co., 15 November 1926.
16 BWA 19/Pharmazeutische Produkte 4, letter Winthrop Chemical Comp. Inc., New York, to IG Frankfurt am Main, 15 November 1926; BWA 13/12, Meeting of the Arbeits-Ausschuß, 12 December 1932, pp. 4f.
17 BWA 19/Farbstoffe 17, Rückblick, pp. 7,10; *ibid.*, contract of 31 July 1925; BWA 9/A.1, von Knieriem, 9 May 1939, pp. 4f.; Hö, Activities Dyestuffs, p. 11.

18 BWA 9/A.1, von Knieriem, 9 May 1939, pp. 4f., 13f.; Hö, Activities Dyestuffs, pp. 12, 100f.

19 BWA 19/Farbstoffe 17, Rückblick, p. 6; Hö 260–1, Auslandslizenzen; Hö, Activities Dyestuffs, p. 101; Hö 43, e.g. meeting of the technical commission, 29 October 1926, p. 3.

20 BWA 19/Farbstoffe 17, Rückblick, p. 10.

21 BWA 9/A.1, von Knieriem, 9 May 1939, pp. 5–9.

22 *Ibid.*; BWA 6/14, Agreement between Agfa Ansco Corp., IG Farbenindustrie AG and Ansco Photo Products, Inc., 19 March 1928; 'Die großen Chemiekonzerne Deutschlands 1931', Das Spezial-Archiv (Berlin 1931), 37.

23 BWA 6/14, letter H. W. Davis, President Ansco Photo Products, Inc., to Agfa Ansco Corp., 19 March 1928, p. 3.

24 BWA 13/12, meeting of the Arbeits-Ausschuß 24 July 1930, p. 2.

25 BWA 13/9, meeting of the Commercial Commission 26 February 1930, p. 3; *ibid.*, Bemerkungen zur Kaufmännischen Ausschuß-Sitzung am heutigen Tage (26 February 1930), Betr.: Gründung einer Chloratfabrik USA; Hö 108a, meeting of the Chemicals Commission 28 November 1933, p. 2.

26 BWA 13/15, meetings of the Technical Commission 27 March 1931, pp. 5–7 and 10 November 1933, p. 5.

27 F. ter Meer, *Die I.G. Farbenindustrie Aktiengesellschaft: Ihre Entstehung, Entwicklung und Bedeutung* (Düsseldorf, 1953), p. 99; Schröter, pp. 241ff. (also relevant to the following paragraphs of this paper).

28 ter Meer, p. 83.

29 Hö 260–2, Lizenzen.

30 German magnesium production (IG Farben was the only German producer) in % of world production (scrap processing excluded) was:
   1919:   94.8
   1929:   76.9
   1934:   78.8
   1938:   56.9 (ter Meer, p. 100).

31 Cf. in detail Schröter, pp. 242f.

32 See G. W. Stocking and M. W. Watkins, *Cartels in action: case studies in international business diplomacy*, 2nd edn (New York, 1947), pp. 276ff.

33 BWA 19/Magnesium 1, 'Alig' agreement between IG Farbenindustrie and Aluminium Corp. of America, 23 October 1931; Hö 259, Auslandslizenzen, Kurze Wiedergabe der vertraglichen Abmachungen betr. Magnesium/USA, 11 March 1938; Stocking and Watkins, pp. 289f.

34 ter Meer, p. 100.

35 Hö 2367, letter from Duisberg and Hochschwender, 14 January 1933, p. 6; Hö 2271, letter W. Duisberg, 3 May 1932, p. 2.

36 Hö 2367, letter from Duisberg to Hochschwender, 14 January 1933, p. 5; BWA 13/15, meeting of the Technical Commission 3 March 1933, p. 2.

37 See Schröter, pp. 246, 277 (n. 101).

38 BWA 19/Magnesium 1 and Hö 2367, Magnesium Agreement between IG Farbenindustrie and Aluminium Corp. of America, 8 February 1933; Hö 259, Auslandslizenzen, Aktennotiz Magnesium/USA, 11 March 1938.

39 *Ibid.*

40 BWA 9/A.1, letter from I. G. Leverkusen to GAW, New York, 25 February 1939; BWA 9/A.3, Aufstellungen über an I.G. und GAW ausgeschüttete Gewinne 1919–1937; Nö 1031, Pharma-Gewinnberechnungen.

184   Verena Schröter

41 BWA 6/14, issue of $30 m. debentures for American IG Chemical Corp., New York, 1 May 1929, p. 3; Annual Report of IG Farbenindustrie AG 1928; BWA 13/15, meetings of the Technical Commission, 20 June 1929 and 9 January 1930, p. 4; A. Friedrich, 'Amerika-Interessen der I.G. Farben', *Wirtschaftsdienst*, XVIII (1929), pp. 756f.; 'Agfa Ansco Corporation', *Berliner Börsen-Zeitung*, 162, 6 April 1939.

42 BWA 9/A.1, von Knieriem, 9 May 1939, p. 18.

43 *Ibid.*, BWA 6/14, telegram from von Schnitzler and ter Meer, New York, to IG Berlin, 15 March 1932; BWA 13/12, meeting of the Arbeits-Ausschuß, 17 February 1932, p. 3.

44 Hö 2271, letter from W. H. Duisberg to ter Meer, 22 March 1933.

45 *Berliner Börsen-Zeitung*, 6 April 1938.

46 See also regarding the following paragraphs Schröter, pp. 411ff. and n. (with figures in detail); Hö 1293, Bericht U.S.A.; Hö 2261, annual report GAW, 1932; BWA 13/15, meeting of the Technical Commission, 14 April 1932, p. 5; Hö 260–1, Auslandslizenzen, GAW; Hö 2508, Vortrag Dr. Loehr, Allgemeines Farbengeschäft in USA 1926–1930 und Anteil der I.G. daran, undated (1931); Hö 2478, H. W. Grimmel, Kurze tabellarische Studie über den Anteil der Albanier [i.e. GAW, Albany works] Farbstoffproduktion am U.S.A. Markt, 3 October 1936.

47 Hö 2261, Bericht von Schnitzler über die neueste Entwicklung in Amerika, 6 June 1933, p. 9; *ibid.*, Bericht des Tea-Büros (Loehr) für Direktor Walther, 13 December 1933, Betr. Farbengeschäft der I.G. in U.S.A., p. 1.

48 Hö 2661, Dr O. Jordan, Erfahrungen und Eindrücke in Amerika: Abschlußbericht über meine Amerikareise, February 1931, p. 71; Hö 2299, letter from ter Meer to von Schnitzler, 15 September 1931.

49 BWA 9/A.1, von Knieriem, 9 May 1939, p. 3; Hö, Activities Dyestuffs, p. 101.

50 Figures in detail in Schröter, p. 475 (n. 200).

51 'Chemieeinfuhr USA', *Wirtschaftsnachrichten der IG*, 9 May 1935, pp. 1,5, tables; Hö 2274, Aufzeichnung Loehr für Dir. Walther, 29 December 1933; Hö 1293, Bericht U.S.A., p. 2.

52 Hö 2299, letter from ter Meer to von Schnitzler, 15 September 1931; Hö 2508, Vortrag Loehr 1931, pp. 4–6.

53 'Die großen Chemiekonzerne Deutschlands 1931', 36.

54 Hö 2261, annual report GAW, 1932, p. 2.

55 BWA 9/A.1, von Knieriem, 9 May 1939, p. 4.

56 *Ibid.*

57 Hö 2261, von Schnitzler, über die neueste Entwicklung in Amerika, 6 May 1933, pp. 9f.

58 Hö 2283, letter GAW to Dir. ter Meer, 22 July 1931; Hö 2261, von Schnitzler, 6 May 1933.

59 Hö 1495, talks between IG Farbenindustrie and Du Pont in Wilmington, 22 October 1935, pp. 1f.

60 BWA 9/A.1, von Knieriem, 9 May 1939, p. 4.

61 Cf. in detail Schröter, pp. 395, 398–401, 407, 474 (n. 194).

Banks and capital markets

13 Multinational banking in the Danube basin: the business strategy of the Viennese banks after the collapse of the Habsburg monarchy

HANS KERNBAUER and FRITZ WEBER

The field of action of the Viennese joint stock banks was, in a certain sense, multinational since their foundation in the third quarter of the nineteenth century. Most of their subsidiaries were situated in Hungary, Czechoslovakia and Upper Italy before the turn of the century. In 1913 the 10 largest Viennese banks ran 149 branches outside the capital, of which 114 were located in towns later on belonging to the successor states.[1]

During the decade before the First World War the Austrian banks strengthened their business relations with commercial and industrial firms throughout the monarchy. The banks started to finance long-term investment projects and floated the shares of newly founded joint stock companies of which they retained a controlling majority, at least in their portfolio.[2] Since the banks concentrated their activities in the backward fringelands of the Empire some authors[3] accused them of an imperialistic attitude (*Binnenimperialismus*, 'inland imperialism').

After the collapse of the Habsburg monarchy at the end of the First World War, the Austrian banks had to choose between two alternatives. On the one hand they could opt for a genuine *multinationalization* of their business strategy and thus stick to their traditional line of policy, hoping that political borders were not economic ones – as an often-cited contemporary phrase had it. The second alternative may be called *Austrification*, the consequence of which would have been the selling of shares of and claims on firms now located in the so-called successor states and the restriction of their field of action to the Austrian Republic.

The bank managers generally decided in favour of the first alternative a few months after the armistice.[4] But contrary to their expectations business along traditional lines was no longer possible in the face of the changing political and economic structure of the Danube basin. What at first sight seemed to be a mere continuation of pre-war activities soon turned out to

185

be banking within a complicated transnational framework. The Austrian banks had to learn their bitter lesson that banking within a multinational empire was fundamentally different from *transnational* banking. The multinationalization of the business operations of the Viennese banks therefore has to be seen as a special and unique case in the general process of internationalization.

This paper deals with the business strategy of the great Viennese banks during the first half of the 1920s. In the first part the economic position of the banks at the end of the War is sketched briefly. There follows a description of the banks' efforts to preserve their sphere of influence outside the Austrian Republic. The third part outlines the relationship between the Viennese banks and banks in western Europe and the United States which during the inflation period could gain a strong foothold in the Austrian banking community. The fourth part deals with the credit policy of the large banks in Vienna during the last stage of the inflationary process, and the final paragraph will sketch the re-establishment of 'normal' financial relations with their clients in the Danube basin.

The Viennese banks prior to 1918

The outbreak of the First World War brought the period of economic growth which had started in the late nineteenth century to a definite end.[5] During the two decades before the War an intimate relationship between industry and banks had developed. Vienna remained by far the most important financial center of the Empire, although the Prague banks expanded their business very rapidly after the turn of the century.[6] The financing of long-term investment projects and the floating of shares had become the main activity of the Viennese banks since the 1890s. As an Austrian historian reports,[7] the number of firms in which the banks had a controlling influence increased substantially in the years immediately before the World War. Two-thirds of the share capital issued in the years 1907 to 1913 by newly founded joint stock companies were taken over by the Viennese banks. During the war years the financing of the budget deficit caused by the steadily increasing expenditure of the state became the main business of the banks in Vienna. They took over more than 15% of the total sum of war loans.[8]

An overall evaluation of the economic position of the Viennese banks at the end of the War is almost impossible. The balance sheets drawn up for the year 1918 reflected the precarious situation in east central Europe: the reliability of the published figures must generally be questioned because the uncertainty surrounding the future development of companies with factories in two or more of the successor states made the assessment of the true value of shares a mere guess. The same was true in respect of the credits the Viennese banks had granted to their non-Austrian clients and of the debts the banks owed to their creditors in western Europe.[9] Not until 1925, when the so-called 'gold balance sheets' were drawn up, could the status of the banks be estimated accurately.[10] It seems somewhat surprising from the perspective of today that the Austrian banks decided for the continuation of their traditional lines of business in 1919: at that time they must have been aware of the widespread nationalistic sentiment and the eagerness of the governments of the new states to get rid of the Viennese influence on their economy.

The Viennese banks' attempt to preserve their sphere of interest in the successor states

After the liberation from 'Habsburg's yoke' the successor states wanted to gain economic independence from 'Austria' too. To this end the currency union was dissolved by overstamping the notes of the Austro-Hungarian Bank, the bank of issue of the Empire.[11] Of even greater importance was the nostrification ('nationalization') of the banking system and of the most important industrial undertakings. The Viennese banks had to transform their subsidiaries in the successor states into independent 'national' institutions, in which capital groups of the respective states generally had a controlling influence. In some cases the subsidiaries of Austrian banks had to be merged with existing local banking establishments. As a result, the number of branches of the 10 largest Viennese banks situated outside the territory of the Austrian Republic was reduced from 143 in 1918 to nine in 1923. Of these only the branches of the Wiener Bankverein in Budapest and Zagreb were of greater economic significance.[12]

The Czechoslovak government exercised the strongest pressure on the Viennese banks to give up their holdings in its territory. From the end of the War to August 1919 44 joint stock companies had already transferred or decided to transfer their headquarters from Austria to Czechoslovakia.[13] Moreover, Czechoslovak citizens purchased, at the Vienna stock exchange, large amounts of shares of industrial firms operating in Czechoslovakia. In order to be able to nationalize big industrial undertakings such as the Škoda works or the Mining and Metallurgic Company the Czechoslovak government sought financial support of west European capital groups. Thus the French Schneider Le Creusot group could gain a considerable influence on Czechoslovak heavy industry.[14]

As already mentioned, the Austrian banks were reluctant to give up their assets in the successor states. The founding of holding companies in the Netherlands and in Switzerland was one counter-move to avoid the sale of shares of foreign firms.[15] However, the Austrian banks lost their most prosperous clients during the years immediately after the breakdown of the monarchy. First of all the holdings in Czechoslovak and Upper Italian heavy industry had to be given up, whereas in Yugoslavia and Poland, where the local banking system was in a less developed state, the Viennese banks could preserve their influence almost entirely.[16]

The various Austrian banks were hit by the process of nostrification to different degrees. The Bodencreditanstalt (BCA), which did not run any branches, had to transfer its current business in Czechoslovakia to the Živnostenská banka in the summer of 1919. The BCA also concluded an agreement of cooperation with the Bank Malopolski in Krakow and tried to intensify its business relations with Hungarian and Yugoslav banks.

The Creditanstalt (CA) and the Niederösterreichische Escomptegesellschaft (NEG) also lost their influence on banks and heavy industry in Czechoslovakia. Moreover, the CA had to give up the financing of the Czech sugar industry, whereas it preserved its relations with the textile industry and with various distilleries.[17] The Wiener Bankverein (WBV) seems to have been most successful in maintaining the economic ties with its subsidiaries in Czechoslovakia. Together with its Belgian partners it founded the Allgemeiner Böhmischer Bankverein, which took over the 18 branches of the WBV in Czechoslovakia. The Mährische Agrar- und Industriebank held a minority share in the new bank without, however, any substantial influence on the managerial decisions. The reorganization of the WBV's business interests in Poland and at a later date in Yugoslavia too turned out to be favourable.[18]

The strengthening of the financial relations between the Viennese and 'western' banks

Vienna, the financial center of the Habsburg monarchy, had attracted in one form or another the savings of more than 50 million inhabitants. The funds deposited at the banks formed the basis for the financing of investment projects within the whole monarchy. After the dissolution of the Empire the Viennese banks were cut off from a considerable proportion of their former depositors. When the managers of the banks decided to continue their traditional credit policy, they had to look out for alternative sources of funds. In the following years the business relations with 'western' financial institutions were strengthened: foreigners participated in Viennese banks and granted them credits on an ever increasing scale.

Various financial ties between the banks in Vienna and the dominant financial centers of western Europe had existed since the foundation of joint stock banks in Austria in the middle of the nineteenth century. Suffice it to mention the close alliance of the CA and the Rothschild group in Paris and London, and the foundation of the Anglobank by British and the Länderbank by French capitalists.[19]

In contrast to the past, however, after the First World War the Viennese banks were so to say 'addicted' to the financial support of banks in western Europe (and the USA) in order to be able to meet the financial needs of their

Table 13.1 *Percentage of share capital of the largest Viennese banks held by foreigners*

	1913	1923
Creditanstalt	3.9	20.2
Bodencreditanstalt	17.8	c.46.0
Niederöster Escomptegesellschaft	0.7	36.0
Länderbank	31.4	c.70.0*
Anglobank	3.0	55.6†
Wiener Bankverein	18.3	38.4
Unionbank	1.5	c.10.0
Verkehrsbank	?	37.6
Depostitenbank	?	16.3
Average of total share capital‡	10.4	30.5

* French company
† British company
‡ 1923 without Anglo- and Länderbank.

clients outside Austria. On the other hand, the Western banks were readily prepared to enlarge their sphere of influence, the more so since the participation in a Viennese bank implied – and we quote – the 'access to the most important industrial undertakings in central Europe'.[20] Moreover, the financial risks involved were not very high in view of the rapid depreciation of the Austrian crown in the post-war years. Calculated at the current exchange rates the total value of shares of the CA amounted to about $61 million at the end of 1913 but to $1.5 million only in mid 1922.[21] Between these dates the share capital of the CA had been increased several times. In winter 1922 Morgan and Schroeder could acquire 500,000 shares or 21% of the share capital of the BCA for a sum of £70,000. Table 13.1 shows the proportion of the capital of the Viennese banks held by foreigners in 1913 and 1923.

There are no data available concerning the amount of capital which the Viennese banks received by selling their own shares abroad. In the case of the Anglobank and the Länderbank the increase of the proportion of shares held by foreigners was due to the change of pre-war foreign debts into shares. In 1922 the Länderbank and the Anglobank were transformed into foreign-based companies.[22] The BCA, too, had to hand over 120,000 shares to its French creditors which held mortgage bonds issued by the BCA before the First World War.[23]

During the post-war inflation period the Viennese banks increased their indebtedness in foreign currencies since western banks resumed their granting of credits, initially on a small scale. Two of the largest banks in Vienna, the CA and the BCA, acquired affiliates abroad in order to gain access to the money markets of western Europe and the USA: in 1920, the CA, in cooperation with the Viennese Rothschild, founded the Amstelbank in Holland.[24] In the same year the CA took a minority interest in the International Acceptance Bank in New York, which was designated to finance the central European foreign trade. Two years later the CA, the Böhmische Escomptebank und Kreditanstalt (BEBKA) and the Živnostenská banka acquired the Bank für Handel und Industrie in Berlin.[25] The BCA together with the Amsterdam'sche Bank took a controlling interest in the Nederland 'sche Reconstructebank in 1924. This establishment failed to meet the expectations of the BCA management and was therefore transformed into a holding company in the late 1920s.[26]

Financing of firms in the successor states during the period of inflation in Austria (1919–22)

The foreign business operations of the Viennese banks did not achieve a 'normal' shape during the first few years after the War. The efforts to continue business as usual were checked by both the introduction of strict exchange controls in all Danubian states and the depreciation of the Austrian currency. Until the crown was stabilized in September 1922, the banks had – to quote a contemporary commentator – 'ceased to play a role as creditors in the successor states at all'.[27] But even in those years the Austrian banks proceeded to purchase systematically shares of their client firms in east central Europe. No doubt, this strategy was part of the transnational orientation of the banks. But it should also be interpreted as a symptom of the common *flight into real assets* accompanying every inflationary process. The banks chose a similar course in domestic matters, trying to convert credits on current account into new share capital, in order to prevent losses due to devaluation, and to accumulate assets of an allegedly stable value. The banks, one could argue, were 'hoarding' shares of domestic and foreign companies.

With regard to foreign loans, the course differed distinctly between the banks.[28] The strictly centralized structure of the Bodencreditanstalt did not allow the granting of credits to clients abroad prior to the second half of 1923.[29] The Bankverein and the Creditanstalt succeeded in maintaining ties with some of their customers in Poland, Hungary and Yugoslavia. Financing Czechoslovak firms proved to be more difficult, since the Czech crown was of a more stable value than the other currencies.

The Bankverein remained one of the most important creditors of the biggest Hungarian steel producer, the Rimamurany works, even in the crucial period of inflation in Austria. With regard to the Czechoslovakian parts of the Rima concern the Bankverein had to cooperate with the Mährische Agrar- und Industriebank, which was to be a large shareholder in the newly founded Allgemeiner Böhmischer Bankverein in 1921.[30] In general, the lending was done by the respective branches of the WBV; in some cases, however, the bank succeeded in financing foreign parts of its conglomerate via the Prague branch office.[31] Foreign advances by the Viennese headquarters did not start before mid 1923.

The Creditanstalt, too, provided with credit several undertakings in Poland, Hungary and Yugoslavia. In Hungary it continued financing several textile firms related to Swiss holding companies founded by the bank itself. In cooperation with S. M. v. Rothschild, advances were given to the Petroleum Refinery Budapest, which was part of the widespread Photogen trust, the administrative center of which was based in the Netherlands. The Polish works of the Photogen, too, and other Petroleum firms like Dabrowa, were bound into the credit operations of the Creditanstalt during the inflation period in Austria. Other prominent debtors in Poland were the Lemberg Brewery, Polski Głob, two important cement firms (the Szczakowa Company and the Golleschau works), and Zieleniewski, the largest Polish engineering works.

By far the greatest foreign credit transaction of the Creditanstalt during the inflation period was undoubtedly an investment loan granted to Zieleniewski in cooperation with several Polish banks in spring 1921. It amounted to 450 m. Polish Marks, of which 63 m., i.e. 14%, were supplied by the Austrian bank.[32] In contrast to this lively activity, there was only one important credit operation in Czechoslovakia until 1923: the co-financing (as the junior partner of the Živnostenská banka) of the Helios Company, the biggest domestic producer of matches.[33]

In some cases it is not clear whether credits provided by the Creditanstalt to Austrian undertakings were used for domestic or exterior aims. Often the headquarters of a company was situated in Vienna, whereas considerable parts of the enterprise were located in the successor states: examples are the Iron Works Rothau-Neudeck, the Schodnica Petroleum Company, and some textile firms.

In general, during the inflation period the Viennese banks could provide only a minimum of credit to their customers abroad. Substantial increases of loans usually occurred only after the stabilization of the Austrian currency. The Creditanstalt, however, could afford more venturous policies than other banks. It participated in capital increases and in the founding of more than 30 important undertakings outside Austria in the years 1919–22.[34] In addition, the Creditanstalt was able to grant loans to foreign clients in a more liberal way. Its favored status arose because of its close ties with the house of Rothschild, which had resulted in the foundation of the Amstelbank in 1920.

It is impossible to assess in money terms the importance of the Amstelbank as an intermediary between western capital markets and eastern European borrowers related to both the Creditanstalt and S. M. v. Rothschild. The archives of the Creditanstalt-Bankverein do not contain detailed information about the Dutch bank: the Creditanstalt board was engaged with Amstelbank matters only twice throughout the twenties, on 30 March 1926 and 15 June 1928, when guarantee credits were eventually agreed to.[35] However, despite the general lack of information, it is known that the guarantees of the Creditanstalt to Amstelbank amounted to about 50 m. Austrian Schillings (1 AS = 10,000 crowns) in 1925, i.e. 10% of CA's own liabilities.[36] Of course, one has to add this sum to the credits granted to clients abroad by the Viennese bank itself.

Resuming traditional credit operations abroad. The Viennese banks and the Danubian basin after 1922

Prior to the stabilization of the Austrian currency the Viennese banks had been able to maintain credit relations with enterprises abroad, especially in Poland, Hungary and Yugoslavia. The ties with Upper Italian and Czechoslovak companies had been cut almost completely. In 1923, however, an attentive spectator could have seen various auguries of change: at the beginning of the year, the Bodencreditanstalt, which had been condemned to inactivity, obtained a new arrangement with the Živnostenská banka providing for a 50% share in future loans to the Mautner Textile Works, a large and renowned textile trust in the Danubian area.[37]

Another clear symptom was the agreement concerning the participation of the Creditanstalt in the Romanian Credit Bank, a former affiliate of the Anglobank, in summer 1923. This venture also included the placing of a $0.5 m. credit at the disposal of the Romanian bank.[38] Finally, a $1 m. advance granted by the CA to the Timber Holding Company, Zurich, at the end of the year signalled the onset of a more expansive stage in foreign lending.[39]

The prerequisite of extended lending, however, was an increase in the funds procured on western capital markets. In 1923, therefore, only the Creditanstalt could afford more aggressive credit operations abroad, because it was able to make use of the almost unlimited international credit provided by its chairman, Louis Rothschild. The other Viennese banks had to take into consideration withdrawals of foreign credits on short notice, and remained reluctant to increase their liabilities vis-à-vis the West, at least until 1925. This is true especially for the Bankverein, which was administered in an outspokenly conservative manner.[40] But even the usually expansion-oriented management of the Bodencreditanstalt called little on foreign short-term deposits prior to mid 1925.[41]

Although the attraction of foreign funds was an essential part of the strategy of the Austrian banks, one could argue that they were 'pulled' to heavy foreign borrowing, at least in its actual short-term form. In mid 1924, when smaller Austrian banks were affected by the withdrawal of capital after

Table 13.2 *Foreign short-term borrowing by three Viennese banks, 1924–31* (m. AS)

	Bankverein	Bodencreditanstalt	Creditanstalt
December 1924	16	?	?
February 1927	35	105	?
October 1929	73	296	197 (?)
April 1931	120	—	536

Sources: Minutes of the management board of the WBV (henceforth MMB-WBV), 2 January 1925, 2 February 1927, 16 October 1929, 5 May 1931; *MMB-BCA*, 7 February 1927; *County Court Vienna*, 23 d VR 6373/31, no. 9; Kurt W. Rothschild, 'Wurzeln und Triebkräfte der Entwicklung der österreichischen Wirtschaftsstruktur', in W. Weber (ed.), *Österreichs Wirtschaftsstruktur gestern – heute – morgen* (2 vols., Berlin, Duncker & Humblot, 1961), I, p. 57.

the stock exchange crash, the management of the Wiener Bankverein discussed – and we quote – 'ample credit offers in foreign currency'.[42] The excess supply in foreign short-term credits, as a consequence of the international drift in interest rates, was not to change in the following years,[43] provoking blame on – we quote again – the 'obtrusiveness' of the western banks.[44].

The Austrian bank managers were fully aware of the fact that the east central European economies in particular required *long-term investment credits*, but the raising of such western loans on a sufficient scale proved to be impossible. Moreover, experience soon showed that the foreign short-term deposits were not recalled but used to be renewed. Before long, the Viennese banks therefore entered upon the adventurous course of borrowing short and lending long. A great part of the foreign capital was invested in Austria, and a smaller proportion used for lending abroad.

At the end of 1924, the total foreign indebtedness of the large Viennese banks can be estimated at about 370 m. AS, i.e. *c.* 30% of bank deposits.[45] At year-end 1930 the foreign liabilities had been increased to 980 m. AS, not including 135 m. AS of guarantee credits of the Creditanstalt to the Amstelbank. The ratio of foreign to total deposits had remained stable at 30%.[46] The records do not supply information about the intermediate years, but there are good reasons to assume a faster growth of foreign deposits only after 1925, as can be seen from Table 13.2.

It is even more difficult to calculate the credits granted to undertakings abroad, since the banks were eager not to publish any information concerning operations in the successor states.[47] All we can do is to try to estimate the general trend, using compilations worked out by Hugo Zienert, a civil servant

194   Hans Kernbauer and Fritz Weber

Table 13.3 *Total advances and amount of non-Austrian loans, 1923–8* (index: 1923 = 100)

Year	Total*	Non-Austrian*
1923	100	100
1924	137	112
1925	158	152
1926	186	175
1927	212	217
1928	223	239

* Without Länderbank and Anglo-Austrian Bank
Sources: *Monatsberichte des Österreichischen Institutes für Konjunkturforschung*, XII (1938), p. 138; H. Zienert, 'Die Zahlungsbilanz Österreichs', in W. Exner (ed.), *10 Jahre Wiederaufbau* (Wien, Wirtschaftszeitungs-Verlag, 1928), p. 301; *Statistische Nachrichten*, VIII (1930) 48.

Table 13.4 *Non-Austrian deposits and loans, 1923–8* (m. AS)

Year	Deposits	Loans
1923	377	305
1924	594	341
1925	480	465
1926	685	535
1927	836	662
1928	649	728

Sources: Exner, *10 Jahre Wiederaufbau*, p. 301. *Statistische Nachrichten* (1930), 48.

at the time, and by the Ministry of Finance, although the figures are not reliable in every respect (see Table 13.3).

The conclusions suggested by Table 13.3 seem to be of great accuracy. They coincide with various contemporary statements which report that capital export to the successor states was resumed to a greater extent only in the second half of the twenties. The table also supports the contemporary view of 1928 as 'a year of capital export'.[48] Table 13.4 shows another important phenomenon: advances to foreign clients were growing continually independent of the changing rhythm of borrowing in the West.

There is no satisfactory explanation of the sharp fluctuations in foreign deposits as presented by Zienert. However, the real development is better thought of as a rather steady one; at least, that is the impression one gets reading the minutes of the Wiener Bankverein, which contain regular reports on liabilities in foreign currency.

Obviously the Viennese banks began financing industries abroad on a large scale only after the onset of the short upswing in central Europe in 1927. However, if we take the Zienert figures at their face value, the ratio of foreign to total loans remained almost stable, amounting to 30% in 1923 and 32% in 1928. This would suggest that the Viennese efforts to regain a pivotal financial position within the east central European economies had stuck fast – despite the evident signs of a more aggressive foreign credit policy from the Austrian banks since 1925 – the new interpretation of the 1919 agreement concerning Czechoslovakia by the Bodencreditanstalt managers[49] and a greater agility abroad even on the part of the Wiener Bankverein.[50] The capital increase of the latter bank, carried out in 1927 with the participation of the Deutsche Bank and American partners, was clearly made with expansion in mind,[51] and the transformation of the Yugoslav branch offices into the Allgemeiner Jugoslawischer Bankverein, initiated by the Belgian correspondent banks of the Bankverein, aimed at business expansion beyond the Yugoslav frontiers to Romania and Turkey.[52]

Outlook

After the First World War the Viennese banks never regained their traditional financial predominance in the Danube basin. The main factor behind the failure of the expansion strategy of multinationalization was the weakening of the banks by both domestic inflation and the depreciation of the Austrian currency until autumn 1922. It was during this early period that the Austrian banks failed to reconstruct stable foundations for their foreign business on the assets side.

Only one area of Viennese banking strategy proved to be successful in the years immediately after the War: the attraction of western banks as shareholders – a fact which did not result in any kind of *Überfremdung*, i.e. rigorous control by the respective foreign investors, except in case of the Länderbank and the Anglo-Austrian bank. From 1923 onwards, the Viennese banks were more able to acquire foreign credits.

But business in eastern Europe was not to fulfill the great expectations of the Viennese bank managers who, in 1925, were still hoarding employees, counting on a future spectacular boom in foreign credit operations.[53] Left to the Austrian banks were, in the somewhat exaggerated judgement of a contemporary, 'only long-term credits to non-prosperous enterprises' abroad.[54] This statement, made in 1931, reflects the immense losses from foreign textile and petroleum firms suffered by both the Creditanstalt and the Bodencreditanstalt.[55]

In an *aide-mémoire* written in the 1930s, the Dutch general manager of the Creditanstalt, van Hengel, stated retrospectively that the dissolution of the Habsburg monarchy had set the bank 'the impossible task of maintaining a multinational bank in Vienna'.[56] However, this was not realized in the years immediately after the War. In 1921, even the Governor of the Bank of England felt sure that Vienna would remain the financial center of central Europe.[57] He therefore favored the take-over of the Anglo-Austrian Bank.[58] In view of the growing economic problems in the Danube basin, the British owners of the bank soon decided to liquidate their foothold in Austria: in 1926, the Viennese branch of the Anglo-Austrian Bank was amalgamated with the Österreichische Creditanstalt.[59] This merger was the first clear symptom of the structural crisis of the Austrian banking system which culminated in the financial crash of 1931.

In May 1931, the largest Austrian bank, the Creditanstalt, had to announce heavy losses and to call on state support. In order to cover the claims of the foreign creditors, the Creditanstalt had to sell off almost all its foreign assets (loans and equities). In other words, the bank was compelled, under rather unfavourable conditions, to enter the path of *Austrification* which its management had refused to follow voluntarily in 1919.[60] The adjustment via the shrinking of the Austrian banking system was completed by the great amalgamation of 1934 which left only one big bank, the Österreichische Creditanstalt-Wiener Bankverein.[61]

Although the new bank succeeded in maintaining – to some extent – some of the interests of the Bankverein abroad, especially its banking affiliates in Yugoslavia and Poland, it had ceased to play an important role as creditor and owner of enterprises in the Danubian area. It is doubtful, however, whether the Viennese bank managers had learnt their lesson and were fully aware of the irreversibility of the development: in 1937, an official of the Austrian Ministry of Finance summarized the lecture given by the new general manager of the Creditanstalt-Bankverein, Josef Joham, in Berlin thus: 'The banks are only waiting for the withdrawal of the international trade and payment barriers in order to be able to resume their transnational business'.[62]

NOTES

1 *Compass* (1915), I.
2 E. März, *Österreichische Industrie- und Bankpolitik in der Zeit Franz Josephs I. Am Beispiel der k.k. priv. Österreichischen Credit-Anstalt für Handel und Gewerbe* (Wien, Europaverlag, 1968).
3 See J. Křížek, *Die wirtschaftlichen Grundzüge des österreichisch-ungarischen Imperialismus in der Vorkriegszeit (1900–1914)* (Prag, 1963).
4 E. März, *Österreichische Bankpolitik in der Zeit der großen Wende 1913–1923: Am Beispiel der Creditanstalt für Handel und Gewerbe* (Wien, Verlag für Geschichte und Politik, 1981).
5 H. Kernbauer and E. März, 'Das Wirtschaftswachstum in Deutschland und Österreich von der Mitte des 19. Jahrhunderts bis zum Ersten Weltkrieg – eine vergleichende Darstellung', in W. H. Schröder and R. Spree (eds.), *Historische Konjunkturforschung* (Stuttgart, 1980), p. 281.

6 F. Baltzarek, 'Finanzplatz Wien – Die innerstaatliche und internationale Stellung in historischer Perspektive', *Quartalshefte*, IV (1980), 56.
7 W. Reik, *Die Beziehungen der österreichischen Großbanken zur Industrie* (Wien, 1932), p. 14.
8 M. Sokal, *Die Tätigkeit der Banken* (Wien, Verlag der Kammer für Handel Gewerbe und Industrie, 1920), p. 5.
9 März, *Bankpolitik*, p. 373–7.
10 H. Kernbauer and F. Weber, 'Die Wiener Großbanken in der Zeit der Kriegs- und Nachkriegsinflation (1914–1922)' in G. Feldman et al. (eds.), *Die Erfahrungen der Inflation im internationalen Zusammenhang und Vergleich* (Berlin, Walter de Gruyter, 1984), pp. 178–80.
11 S. Pressburger, *Oesterreichische Notenbank 1816–1916* (Wien, Eigenverlag der Oesterreichischen Nationalbank, 1966), pp. 230–5.
12 *Compass* (1919), I and (1925), I.
13 *Der österreichische Volkswirt* (henceforth *ÖVW*) (23 August 1919), 893.
14 A. Teichova, *An economic background to Munich: international business and Czechoslovakia 1918–1938* (Cambridge University Press, 1974), pp. 92–107, 195–9.
15 Kernbauer and Weber, Die Wiener Großbanken, pp. 156–7.
16 See the minutes of the board of directors of the BA and the WBV and the regional distribution of the industrial holdings of these banks.
17 *Finanzarchiv Vienna*, 57.606/1919.
18 *Minutes of the board of directors [henceforth MBD] of the WBV*, 15 December 1921; Report of the management concerning 1922, enclosed to *MBD-WBV*, 25 April 1923.
19 März, *Österreichische Industrie- und Bankpolitik*, pp. 8–22; P. L. Cottrell, 'London financiers and Austria: the Anglo-Austrian Bank, 1863 to 1875', *Business history* (1969); A. Piberger, *100 Jahre Länderbank* (Wien, 1980).
20 M. L. Recker, *England und der Donauraum 1919–1929* (Stuttgart, 1976), p. 72, n. 137.
21 *Compass* (1915), I and (1925) I.
22 A. Teichova, 'Versailles and the expansion of the Bank of England into central Europe', in N. Horn and J. Kocka (eds.), *Recht und Entwicklung der Großunternehmen im 19. und frühen 20. Jahrhundert* (Göttingen, 1979), pp. 368–80.
23 *MBD-BCA*, 4 October 1921; 20 December 1922.
24 März, *Bankpolitik*, pp. 449–50.
25 *ÖVW*, 11 November 1922, 144.
26 *MBD-BCA*, 28 February 1925.
27 W. Federn, 'Der Zusammenbruch der Österreichischen Kreditanstalt', *Archiv für Sozialwissenschaft und Sozialpolitik*, LXVI (1932), 410.
28 The archives of the Creditanstalt-Bankverein in Vienna contain only the minutes of the boards of BCA, WBV and CA. No records are available concerning NEG. Thus our article concentrates only on the first three banks.
29 The minutes of the BCA do not provide detailed information about credit operations at all. The first substantial loan to a foreign firm is mentioned in *MBD-BCA*, 24 September 1923. For further figures and explanations supporting our view see also: Report of the management for the first half-year 1923, enclosed with *MBD-BCA*, 9 November 1923.
30 See *MBD-WBV*, 16 June and 27 October 1919; and, reviewing the situation, 25 April 1923. On the foundation of the Böhmischer Bankverein, see: Report of the management for 1922, enclosed with *MBD-WBV*, 25 April 1923, and *MBD-WBV*, 15 December 1921.

31 *MBD-WBV*, 4 May 1923, which mentions that a loan originally granted by the Prague subsidiary to the Sarajevo Brewery had been transferred from Allgemeiner Böhmischer Bankverein to the Viennese headquarters of the Bankverein.

32 *MBD-CA*, 27 May 1921.

33 *MBD-CA*, 30 March and 27 May 1921.

34 März, *Bankpolitik*, p. 534.

35 The relationship with the Bank für Handel und Industrie in Berlin was similar. Originally this bank had been taken over by CA, BEBKA and Živnostenská banka to elude exchange controls in central Europe. Later on, one of the main activities of the Berlin bank was granting credits to undertakings in Germany as well as in the Danubian states. See *County Court Vienna*, 26 d Vr 6373/31, no. 9, hearing of witness Otto Deutsch, former manager of the Creditanstalt, and no. 503, Expertise Sedlak/Neumann/Letz, 16 May 1935, concerning Amstelbank and Bank für Handel und Industrie, Berlin.

36 *County Court Vienna*, 26 d Vr 6373/31, no. 503.

37 *MBD-BCA*, 16 February 1923. The share of participation in capital increases of the Mautner works should also amount to 50%. See *MBD-BCA*, 24 May 1924.

38 *MBD-CA*, 17 July and 5 September 1923.

39 *MBD-CA*, 12 December 1923. The Timber company had been founded by the Unionbank, a Viennese medium-sized bank which was to be merged with the Bodencreditanstalt in 1927.

40 In 1924, for instance, the Bankverein management repeatedly refused money claims of the Zagreb branch in order to prevent expansive credit operations in Yugoslavia. See *MMB-WBV*, 18 August and 3 September 1924. On the other hand, the management intentionally slowed down the acquisition of foreign short term deposits in 1924. See *MMB-WBV*, 10 June 1924; further, Report of the management for the first half-year 1924, enclosed with *MBD-WBV*, 7 October 1924.

41 Speech of chairman Sieghart, *MBD-BCA*, 20 May 1925. Report of the management for the first half-year 1925, enclosed with *MBD-BCA*, 4 November 1925.

42 *MMB-WBV*, 22 August 1924. For examples of offers see 27 August and 22 September 1924.

43 See M. Sokal, *Die Tätigkeit der Banken im Jahre 1925* (Wien, Verlag der Kammer für Handel, Gewerbe und Industrie, 1926), p. 15. Same author, *Die Tätigkeit der Banken im Jahre 1926* (Wien, Verlag der Kammer für Handel, Gewerbe und Industrie, 1927), p.10.

44 Bank of England Archive, O.V. 28/30, Zimmermann to Norman, 16 April 1925.

45 Sources for the estimate: *Finanzarchiv Vienna*, 78.843/1926, which contains a secret compilation of the Austrian Bankers' Union (Verband Österreicheischer Banken und Bankiers); *MMB-WBV*, 2 January 1925, which gives detailed figures about deposits of non-Austrians in crowns.

46 Sources: G. Wärmer, 'Die Auslandsverschuldung Österreichs', *Mitteilungen des Verbandes österreichischer Banken und Bankiers*, xvi (1934), 282; *County Court Vienna*, 26 d Vr 6373/31, no. 503.

47 In 1927, a symptomatic conflict arose between the Austrian National Bank and the private banks which refused to provide detailed quarterly balance sheets, especially concerning their foreign business operations. See *MMB-BCA*, 8 June 1927.

48 Kammer für Arbeiter und Angestellte in Wien (ed.), *Wirtschaftsstatistisches Jahrbuch 1928*, (Wien, Verlag der Kammer für Arbeiter und Angestellte, 1929), p. 393.

49 *MMB-BCA*, 10 July 1925.
50 Report of the management for the first half-year 1926, enclosed to *MBD-WBV*, 19 October 1926; Report of the management for 1926, enclosed with *MBD-WBV*, 2 May 1927. Particular mention should be made of the participation of the Bankverein in two noteworthy syndicate investment credits to Upper Italian shipping companies in 1926/7, the syndicates led by the Basler Handelsbank, the Swiss shareholder of the Bankverein. See *MBD-WBV*, 19 October 1926 and 2 May 1927.
51 Report of the management for 1926, *MBD-WBV*, 2 May 1927.
52 *MBD-WBV*, 3 October 1927.
53 *Finanzarchiv Vienna*, 76.843/1926.
54 Federn, 'Der Zusammenbruch', 411.
55 Mautner and Fanto in the case of the Bodencreditanstalt; Gallia and Photogen in that of the Creditanstalt.
56 *County Court Vienna*, 26 d Vr 6373/31, no. 233, *aide-mémoire* Adrianus van Hengel.
57 Cited by P. L. Cottrell, 'Aspects of western equity investment in the banking systems of east-central Europe', in Alice Teichova and P. L. Cottrell (eds.), *International business and central Europe 1918–1939* (Leicester, 1983), p. 309.
58 See *ibid.*, pp. 316–21, Teichova, 'Versailles and the expansion of the Bank of England', pp. 366–87. Teichova's article also contains an analysis of the British deliberations about giving up the Anglobank branch in Vienna in 1926.
59 See Public Record Office, London, FO 371/11213/149: Anglo-Austrian Bank Ltd, *Monthly review of central Europe*, no. 21, mid-September 1926. The review contains an analysis of the causes which forced the bank to give up its Austrian foothold.
60 See Hans Rutkowski, *Der Zusammenbruch der Österreichischen Credit-Anstalt für Handel und Gewerbe und ihre Rekonstruktion* (Bottrop, 1934), pp. 101–2.
61 Cf. Max Sokal, 'Neugestaltung und Zusammenfassung im österreichischen Bankwesen', *Mitteilungen des Verbandes österreichischer Banken und Bankiers*, 1/2 (1935), 10–15.
62 *Finanzarchiv Vienna*, 16.289/1937.

14 Banks and early Swedish multinationals

RAGNHILD LUNDSTRÖM

Introduction

Almost until the First World War there was a fear in Sweden of foreign influence in industry; it was reflected in recurrent parliamentary debates even since the 1870s. Until 1910 Sweden was a net importer of capital. Although foreign capital markets were relied upon mainly for state and city loans and bonds issued by larger institutions, there was also a sizeable amount of foreign investment in Swedish firms, particularly after industrialization in Sweden had grown rapidly in the 1870s and there were high profits to be gained. There was a relative shortage of capital in Sweden and its credit market was slow to develop.

Things changed, and changed dramatically from the beginning of the 1890s. Bank deposits more than doubled for every decade, and the importance of banks for industrial development increased. The absence of a well-functioning stock exchange until the early 1900s was one reason for the latter development. Later, banks took part in and eventually themselves became part of a – sometimes speculative – merger development.

Around 1910, when Sweden turned into a net exporter of capital, the larger Swedish banks in practice functioned as did the German banks. Basing their activity mainly on deposits, they actively participated in the founding, reconstruction and merger of Swedish firms. Banks themselves were not allowed to own shares in other companies. In the first decade of the 1900s, this ruling was evaded by the owners of the banks founding investment and holding companies. These companies borrowed heavily from the banks with shares in their portfolio as security.

Embryos of Swedish multinational enterprise appear from the early 1870s. Around the turn of the century, their development was marked. Swedish foreign direct investments increased. From the point of view of Swedish firms, starting production abroad can be seen mainly as a substitute for exporting. Because of the nature of their business, Swedish industrialists in this period of fierce competition grew nationalistic;[1] and through the increased share of

200

interest between industry and banks, the larger banks – which had hitherto by the nature of their business had a more international outlook on capital – gradually became more nationalistic also.

The paper deals with this period of transition, 1900–30, on the one hand, Swedish industry needed the international expertise and connections of the Swedish banks for starting business abroad and for financing such business and, on the other hand, the relationship between banks and Swedish industry became closer. During this period a great number of the large Swedish multinationals of to-day began manufacturing abroad – the telephone companies, the electroengineering companies, the separator companies, the match trust and so on. Since their investments in production abroad were a substitute for exports, they were first directed towards the great markets of Great Britain, Russia, France, and North and South America. The implications for the growth of Swedish multinationals of this relationship between industry and banks is the main issue of the paper.

The question of the importance of banks

Very little attempt has been made on the aggregate level to measure the importance of banks for industrial development in Sweden. This is scarcely surprising, since it is an immense undertaking. In what is still the standard work on the financing of Swedish industry from 1830 to 1914, various sources of finance are assessed from a sample of company accounts.[2] According to this study, banks proper increased their share in the financing but slowly, from around 20% at the end of the 1850s to slightly above 30% at the beginning of the 1900s. Bonds which first acquired importance in the 1860s increased their share to a little above 30% in the early 1900s and to 40% around 1910. Other sources naturally decreased, from more than 80% in the 1850s to around 30% 1910.

The role of banks as suppliers of credit for industry is most likely more extensive than it appears from the books of the companies. Unless one turns to the banks' records, it is impossible to assess the amount of bonds and debentures that the banks had been unable to sell and for that and perhaps some other reason had themselves kept. Neither are the bank loans or other forms of credit given to the private individuals who make up part of 'other sources' visible in the accounts of the companies whose shares they held.[3]

From other sources relevant to the banks we know that shares formed the collateral for 30% of the loans of all Swedish commercial banks around 1910.[4] In certain larger banks, like Stockholms Handelsbank and Stockholms Enskilda Bank, with an alleged closer link to industry, this percentage in some years was as high as 75%, and often between 50 and 60.[5] Not only in these two banks, but also in several of the more provincial banks, loans to board members and their business affiliates took a large part of the banks' outstanding credit.[6] In Stockholms Handelsbank around 1910, the board members and the corporations within their sphere of influence accounted for 25% of the bank's credit given, and another group of people or businesses with close connections with its managing director for another 15%.[7] In Stockholms Enskilda Bank, the figure for credit to companies within the sphere of interest of the board members was usually even larger.[8]

As early as 1901, Stockholms Enskilda Bank owned a holding company, the purpose of which in the beginning seems to have been to consolidate the bank's business by letting the holding company build up reserves. Soon, however, it was in fact used as an investment institute. When the bank inspector remarked that it was against the law for banks to own shares, the holding company was eventually reorganized into a separate company and the owners of the bank's shares given preference to buy shares in the new investment company proportionately to their holdings.[9]

Other banks followed suit. In 1907, Stockholms Handelsbank together with Skandinaviska Kredit AB founded 'their' investment company, formally owned in the same manner as that of Stockholms Enskilda Bank. The name of the company, Svenska Emissions AB, implies that it was intended to be an issuing house as well.

There was a lively debate in Sweden at the time as to the disadvantages versus the advantages of investment banks of the German type. Among the advantages was stressed the fact that it would be better to have this sort of business done within the formal realms of the banks, where it could be controlled through the rather rigid Swedish bank inspection. Therefore, and also of course because a basic need for such institutes was felt, a law permitting investment/issuing banks was enacted in 1909. The law stipulated, however, that it took four banks to form an investment bank, no one bank being allowed to own more than one-third of the shares.[10]

No such investment bank was ever founded in Sweden: the Swedish banks evidently did not want to cooperate with three other banks in this. In view of the fierce competition between the larger banks in particular, this is not surprising. Legislation was far behind actual development.

In 1911, the law against the owning of shares by banks was eased. It now became possible for banks to own shares in proportion to a ratio between the banks' reserves and their share capital.[11] This was practised by most of the banks that fulfilled the requirement, 19 out of the 76 commercial banks then in existence.[12] Since the sum total allowed for such shareholding was fairly low, several banks founded holding companies with a very small share capital. The turnover and assets of these companies were sizeable, since they could borrow from the banks with the shares they held as collateral.

In its turn, this became the subject of lengthy parliamentary debates and committee investigations and in 1921 it was enacted that banks were not allowed to own shares in companies the main purpose of which was the purchase and sale of shares. In 1933, a new bank law was enacted, again altogether forbidding banks to own shares in other companies except when taken against forfeited debts, and then only temporarily.[13] The formal situation in this respect was then the same as it had been in the first decade of the 1900s.

The banks reacted to this legislation as did Stockholms Enskilda Bank when it sold its first holding company to its shareholders and later bought it back when the law was modified. Holding and issuing companies that were founded passed in and out of the ownership of banks according to the changes in the law.

In 1911, there were at least 40 finance companies, in 1918 about 100, and in 1925 there remained 55.[14] 'Working in close cooperation with banks' were the daughter companies, holding companies and side-companies;[15] the others were classified as 'independent of banks'. However, after 1910, most of the independent companies worked in rather close cooperation with the banks, underwriting part of an issue of shares of which one or several of the banks' companies had underwritten the larger portion. The independent companies had then been guaranteed to borrow from the banks and in their turn lent money to the buyers of the shares.[16] This was of course nothing special for Sweden, but it has been alleged that Swedes were in those days perhaps more accustomed to borrowing against shares than were people in other countries.

From their very start, most Swedish firms, including family firms, were organized as joint-stock companies. In 1908, there were 4,937 joint-stock companies in Sweden, or 909 per one million inhabitants, whereas in Germany there were 5,222, or 81 per one million inhabitants – if the GmbHs are included, 344 per million.[17] There was therefore no great need for Swedish banks to participate in the transformation of family firms into joint-stock companies, but rather in the founding of new companies and in the expansion – and mergers – of older ones. During the first decade of the 1900s speculation was in evidence, and the Swedish share market became used to rising quotations. This continued after 1910, and during the war years the speculation was obvious. In 1918, turnover on the stock exchange was five times larger than it had been in 1912, while total turnover of stocks and bonds on the entire Swedish market was three times larger.[18]

The issuing of new share capital increased at a hitherto unknown speed; in 1917, new issues were five times, and in 1918, eight times larger than during the pre-war years. When the depression reached Sweden in 1920 with decreasing exports and prices, the crash was so much worse. The depression in the early 1920s was more severe in Sweden than the one in the early 1930s. In 1922, five fairly large banks had to go into liquidation and were reconstructed. Sweden's largest bank, Svenska Handelsbanken, had to

Table 14.1. *Percentage share of external financing of industry in Sweden*

Branch	1911–13	1923–5
Mines:		
northern Sweden	11.9	31.2
central Sweden	22.4	44.1
Ironworks	51.7	53.5
Separator factories	12.6	24.3
Ball-bearing factories	18.0	8.4
Engineering industry with		
specialized production	42.7	42.9
Electrical engineering industry	40.3	33.1
Saw mills	55.8	64.7
Paper pulp industry	46.3	57.4
Match factories	35.1	20.5

Table extracted from Svenska aktiebolags balansräkningar åren 1911–1925. Undersökning utgiven av socialiseringsnämden SOU 1929:4 (Stockholm, 1929), p. 59.

consolidate and write off a sizeable amount of its reserves. Swedish industry now became more directly dependent on the banks for their survival through the lean years.

There are two studies of the growing dependency on banks by Swedish industry in the early 1920s. One, made by the Bank Committee of 1924, estimates that the percentage share of companies that were in practice controlled by banks increased from around 3% in 1913 to 26% in 1924. The share of the companies that were considered independent of banks decreased from 91% in 1913 to 66% in 1924.[19] Another committee, appointed by the social democrats when forming a minority government during a short period in 1920 and called the Socialization Committee (Socialiseringsnämnden), investigated the financing in all branches of industry on the basis of company balance sheets.[20] The percentage share of 'exterior sources' – the remainder being equity – in certain branches is shown in Table 14.1

Both the studies referred to above look at firms' borrowing. Naturally, neither of them includes the financing of the share capital. From 1912, the statistics on banks make it more difficult to arrive at accurate figures for loans and other credit *used* against the collateral of shares, since they now show credit *granted* on cheque accounts (overdrafts granted) plus actual loans and the share of such credit against the collateral of shares. The figures in Table 14.2 may still give some idea of the development.[21]

After the large merger movement in the first decade of the 1900s and especially after the accelerated merger movement during the First World War, it became more common for companies to borrow also with shares of merged companies as collateral. Holding companies in general mostly borrowed

Table 14.2. *Overdrafts granted and actual loans against the collateral of shares*

	as % of all bank lending (incl. of bills of exchange, acceptances)	as % of bank lending (excl. of bills of exchange etc.)
1913	36	40
1917	46	53
1921	36	36
1924	33	45

Table 14.3. *Distribution of credits granted by Stockholms Enskilda Bank*

Total lending incl. of bills of exchange and acceptances (bank statistics)	194 m. SK
Overdraft allowed *plus* actual loans given (This is the figure reported in the bank statistics. It comprises 'loans' plus all credit limits on various cheque accounts)	170
Whereof against the collateral of shares	92
Overdrafts allowed on accounts	98
Overdrafts used, or actual credit given on these accounts	61
Actual lending (loans, overdraft etc.) against all kinds of collateral to board members and companies in which these had a controlling interest	103
Whereof against the collateral of shares	38

against shares. The example in Table 14.3 from the lending of Stockholms Enskilda Bank in September 1916 shows some of the components.[22]

Banks and the growth of Swedish multinationals

In the 1890s, the Swedish engineering industry had its breakthrough. It was now that the more specialized manufacturing of engineering products became more preponderant.[23] Older companies started specializing and new companies were founded which specialized from the very beginning. By the very nature of their type of production, and by the introduction of more specialized machinery, these industries were capital-intensive. Several companies were founded on the basis of new inventions or – which was perhaps even more common – on some patented improvement of other inventions.

The new, more specialized engineering industry immediately had to look to foreign markets, since the Swedish market was too small to absorb the mass production of engineering products. Exports of engineering products grew faster than any other kind of exports. It is within this branch of industry that most early Swedish multinationals, as well as those of to-day, are to be found.[24]

There are no studies of the financing of the growth of Swedish multinationals on the aggregate level, nor of the role of banks in this financing. This essay certainly does not pretend to be such a study. For the reasons discussed above, great difficulties are encountered when one tries to assess the sources of finance of Swedish industry as such. At this stage of research it is only possible to give an impressionistic view and some circumstantial evidence of the role of banks, which, one must say, is usually played down in such histories of the various multinationals as exist.

The first Swedish multinationals, those that started manufacturing abroad in the 1870s and 1880s as separate companies and were later merged with the original companies, did so on a very modest scale. Thus, retained profits and trade credit from the mother company, sometimes in combination with only modest bank loans, were sufficient to cover the rather minor costs involved. Both when these companies wanted to expand on a larger scale and when the new engineering companies of the 1890s and early 1900s founded subsidiaries in other countries, they had to obtain financial assistance from exterior sources.

If the financing of Swedish multinationals is looked at from the point of view of the banks, even the very short period from 1900 to 1930 can be divided into three sub-periods. One ends around 1911, while the second comprises the boom period and the buoyant 'gründerperiode' and ends in 1917. The third lasts for the rest of the period and in fact all through the Second World War.

Around the turn of the century, not even the larger Swedish banks were prepared to undertake too much unassisted. On the international capital market therefore, they cooperated with banks and merchant bankers in other European countries. This was the case when in 1900 a consortium headed by Stockholms Enskilda Bank managed to attain the concessions for telephone operation in Moscow and Warsaw.[25] Stockholms Allmänna Telefon AB took 40% of the shares in the Swedish-Danish-Russian Telephone Co., which was founded in that year. The Stockholm Telephone Co. had until then only been a small customer of Stockholms Enskilda Bank, and the initiative to the Russian affair came from the bank's managing director. The bank subscribed for $32\frac{1}{2}\%$, the Danish Landsmansbanken for $12\frac{1}{2}\%$, the Banque de Paris for 10%, and Behrens & Söhne for 5% of the shares. A loan against bonds, in sum much larger than the share issue, was granted by the Banque de Paris. Stockholms Enskilda Bank became the company's main bank connection, and eventually had to take over the rather sizeable acceptance which they had guaranteed.

A similar consortium, consisting of the Banque de Paris and some of its board members and Stockholms Enskilda Bank and a group of people connected with it, was formed in 1905 for the development of an at the time rather sensational Norwegian patent for extracting nitrogen out of air. The fact that the method was energy-consuming would imply that the abundance of Norwegian waterpower could be exploited. Norsk Hydro was founded, the Swedish bank and its group subscribing to the majority of ordinary shares. These were taken over by the bank's holding company and by individual members of the group, these members in their turn borrowing from the bank. When the German combine Badische, which was at that time developing a similar patent, showed an interest, a new agreement was reached a year later. Two companies were now founded, one for the development of the water-power and one for the nitrogen factory. In the waterpower company each group, the French-Scandinavian on the one side and the German on the other, received shares according to its holding of rights to waterfalls. In the nitrogen company, the French-Scandinavian group and the German chemical group each received half the shares. Since this was a much larger enterprise with much more capital involved than in the original Norsk Hydro, the share of Stockholms Enskilda Bank and its group diminished considerably.[26]

Stockholms Enskilda Bank had entered, or started, the negotiations mainly to obtain orders for ASEA, the General Electric or AEG of Sweden, which at the time was almost totally owned by the bank and its group and which was doing poorly because of the heavy competition from the German electro-engineering companies in particular. Apparently, some members of the French group had similar aspirations for the companies within their sphere of interest. The Rothschilds insisted on the possibility of Westing-house delivering part of the generators.[27]

The banks entered the agreement for the French and Swedish groups; for the German group this was done by the large chemical combine, although it was in its turn backed up by the Diskonto Gesellschaft. It was not only a matter of difference in size between the German chemical company and the Swedish engineering company. There was also some difference in attitude as to the function of banks vis-à-vis industry. Stockholms Enskilda Bank still acted foremost as a merchant banker, and the policy of its directors was still to sell out the shares as soon as considered feasible. Most of the shares in the Swedish-Danish-Russian Telephone Co. that the bank's holding company held were sold out around 1910. The shares in Norsk Hydro were also eventually sold.[28]

The directors of the bank, above all the two brothers Wallenberg, who together held 30% of the shares in Stockholms Enskilda Bank, also did business without formally involving the bank. In the early days of the Diesel patent, they managed to acquire the option of the patent for Scandinavia and Russia. In Russia a company was founded with Emanuel Nobel as the main shareholder and with Diesel himself, his associate Bing and the Wallenberg brothers taking, or receiving, minority parts. The same group also founded the Swedish Diesel company, but with the Wallenberg group in majority.

In 1912, a syndicate headed by M. Wallenberg and consisting also of the group around National City Bank and Brown Brothers of New York founded a company in the United States for the production of reversible diesel engines, based upon a patent held by an engineer at the Swedish Diesel Co., the Swedish group acquiring approximately 60% of the shares. In the way already described, some of the shares belonging to the Swedish group were acquired by the holding company of Stockholms Enskilda Bank, some by private members of the group and some by the Swedish Diesel company.[29] The American corporation was formally a free-standing firm[30] in relation to the Swedish company. However, since the Wallenberg group held the majority of shares in both, McIntosh & Seymour – the American company – and the Swedish Diesel company were considered as a joint enterprise. Swedish technicians were sent to the United States to give advice about production matters.[31]

Similar assistance was naturally supplied also by the other major banks in Sweden. Stockholms Handelsbank, at the time perhaps regarded as the most fierce competitor of Stockholms Enskilda Bank, helped in financing the international expansion of the Ericsson telephone company, which manufactured telephone equipment. The director of the bank at the time had connections in the European financial circles that were equally as good and, in certain aspects perhaps even better than, those of the directors of Stockholms Enskilda Bank. They helped in financing the establishment of Ericsson's manufacturing subsidiary in France, Vienna and Budapest. As for the company's subsidiaries in England and the United States, it seems as if loans from and drawings on Stockholms Handelsbank were the main financial sources.[32]

The interest behind SKF, the ball-bearing company, was to be found within the group around the Gothenburg division of Skandinaviska Banken, the then largest Swedish bank. The bank assisted in financing the company's first subsidiaries abroad, those in Great Britain and in Russia. When manufacturing was to be started in France and the United States as well, Stockholms Enskilda Bank, with its apparently better contacts on the capital markets of those countries, arranged for the shares to be issued in Paris and New York. The shares of the American Ball Bearing Co. were bought by a rather small group, including the Swedish owned McIntosh & Seymour, the managing director of the company and M. Wallenberg.[33]

The expansion of SKF belongs to the second of the sub-periods mentioned above, which began around 1911. Sweden had now become self-supporting with regard to capital and turned into a net exporter of capital. The liquidity of the Swedish economy had increased considerably. This, of course, made it easier for Swedish companies to finance their expansion by issuing new shares with the country. Naturally, the change was not as abrupt as it is made to appear here. There was only a relative shortage of capital before, and there were periods, e.g. in the 1890s, when Sweden was a net exporter of capital.[34] It had also been easy to raise capital for shares in the first decade of the 1900s, particularly before the depression of 1907.

Yet, it can be argued that a change did occur in the 1910s. On the one hand, there was no longer any need to make use of foreign capital markets for Swedish issues. On the other hand, the markets that had been used the most for state and city bonds at the end of the borrowing period, viz. the German and French capital markets, had turned their interest more markedly towards east central Europe and Russia. When this very close and necessary cooperation with foreign capital markets and their bankers diminished somewhat, Swedish bankers devoted more time to Swedish business. Earlier, the banks had received a larger part of their profits from their intermediating Swedish bond loans abroad, and in addition always received sizeable amounts of short-term deposits. They now generally became more dependent on deposits from Swedish firms and Swedish individuals. During the war it was definitely increasing deposits that headed the expansion of Swedish banks. The founding of so many issuing companies working in close cooperation with banks has sometimes been explained in terms of banks having difficulty in lending when deposits increased so much.

Swedish industry did well, especially during the first years of the war. Swedish exports increased, and so did profits. In 1916, 42% of the Swedish production of iron, metal and engineering products was exported. Before the war Russia was developing into the most promising market for Swedish engineering products, and now took almost 30% of the exports.[35] Several Swedish corporations had already founded manufacturing subsidiaries in Russia, mainly in those branches of industry in which customs tariffs were an obstacle to exports or state authorities were the main buyers. With the outbreak of the war, German competition naturally decreased. Swedish businessmen now used the opportunity to try to fill the place of their German competitors. ASEA and SKF, which were already manufacturing in other countries, now invested in factories in Russia, as did numerous smaller engineering firms. A company which manufactured a special type of steel wire and aerial rope-ways opened two factories in Russia; and a company producing diamond rock-drills began manufacturing there, only to mention two of the firms which were more successful in the long run – i.e. those which eventually regained their multinational status. Innumerable firms in other branches of industry also founded production subsidiaries in Russia: examples are a small company manufacturing emery plates, a soap factory, and a

Table 14.4. *Quotations on the Stockholm stock exchange*

	1917	1918	1919	1920	1921	1922
ASEA	375	194	126	75	36	35
Separator AB	305	220	169	117	70	77
SKF	625	304	195	116	82	76

(par value for all = 100 SK)

furniture factory. Even the new department store of Stockholm opened branches in St Petersburg, Moscow, and Buenos Aires.[36]

Good credit facilities were essential in exporting to Russia. Companies that sold agricultural machinery were expected to give around two years' credit, and firms which sold to state authorities almost as long. In Swedish discussions at the time, the great success of International Harvester on the Russian market was ascribed to its excellent means of financing long credits.[37] Closer cooperation between Russian and Swedish banks for credit guarantees was started a couple of years before the war. Until then no such cooperation had existed.[38]

In several other countries there were manufacturing subsidiaries founded by Swedish firms during this period.[39] Rising profits, however nominal, and rising share quotations were a stimulus. There appeared to be good grounds for mergers and for the expansion of business. Although the issuing of new shares was the main source of financing this expansion, it was carried out in close cooperation with the banks and mostly administered with their help or through one of their daughter or associated companies.[40] ASEA raised its share capital from 3 million SK to 75 million SK in 1919. SKF, which had been founded in 1907 with a share capital of 110,000 SK, was already the largest Swedish multinational, with, for instance, three factories in the United States; during the war its share capital was raised from 12 to 98 million SK.[41]

By 1917 the boom was over. Difficulties had arisen, especially for the Swedish engineering industry, in early 1918 and these became more profound during the year. They were aggravated by the conditions in Russia at the time and difficulties within Sweden with regard to both production, because of a shortage of raw materials, and exports. Share quotations had already started to fall in the early part of the year, and the decrease continued despite the somewhat better conditions in 1919, as Table 14.4 shows.[42]

In the summer of 1920, the Swedish economy was also affected by the Depression; the Depression deepened, and in 1922 35% of organized labour were unemployed. In the engineering industry, the figure was 42%.[43]

Shares and property changed hands on a scale hitherto unparalleled in Swedish economy. The influence of banks increased. According to one estimate, the 'ownership margin' vis-à-vis the banks decreased from 50% in 1918 to 36% in 1921.[44] Industry itself became more directly dependent on banks, and indeed loans were necessary if business were to continue. On the other hand, it can be said also that banks were now equally dependent on industry. Because of the large percentage of outstanding debts for which shares formed the collateral, it lay in the interest of the banks to see to it that business could be continued in the companies whose shares they held as collateral. Besides, of course, it was in the banks' own interest to protect direct lending to industry. (Some banks did not succeed and defaulted or were reconstructed, as already mentioned on p. 203 above.)

There were several ways in which this was done. There were also several means of doing it without damaging the formal solvency of the firms. As for the multinationals, they had practically all integrated both vertically and horizontally during the preceding period. Mortgaging of fixed assets of the smaller companies in the group became common; this did not usually become visible in the accounts of the mother- or holding-company.[45]

For banks which had difficulty with their own solvency and liquidity, it was sometimes preferable to arrange credit through bills of exchange; if these were considered safe enough – and this was usually the case as regards large and now well-known companies – such bills could immediately be rediscounted with the Swedish central bank.[46]

Naturally ordinary credit was given also to the larger companies. However, even in cases in which new debts became visible on the balance sheets of the mother companies, their share capital was still usually so large that formal solvency was only slightly affected. (The largest increases in share capital had been made during the inflationary years, but new debts were needed in deflated money.) Finally, shares were taken over by banks when debts of individual owners were forfeited.

Thus – it is argued here – Swedish multinationals became more dependent on banks than may appear from their own accounts. ASEA is one such example. In 1921, it turned to its bank requesting credit for the purpose of giving a dividend for 1920. In 1922 it presented the bank with a plan for all its companies with cost-cutting and letting some companies hibernate. It was assumed that no interest would be paid on its loans from the bank.[47] In those two years, despite great losses amounting to nearly 10% of the balance-sheet total, ASEA's formal solvency (solidity) was 79% and 82% respectively.[48]

Other examples can be given from the separator industry and the match industry, which both showed lower than average figures for external financing (see p. 204 above). In the early 1920s, when Sweden accounted for half the world production of separators,[49] there were three Swedish multinationals within this branch. The largest of the three, Separator AB, had already established itself as a multinational in the 1890s, when it founded a manufacturing subsidiary in the United States. Towards the end of the decade its relationship with its bank, Stockholms Diskontobank, grew closer, mainly through ownership in the company by owners of the bank. It apparently became the policy of Separator to publish high profits and give large dividends, thereby making it possible to issue bonds and new shares. The shares of Separator were considered as 'speculation papers' in the early 1900s.[50] Thus, it has been said, the gross profits of the American subsidiary were reported and sometimes delivered to the Swedish firm, which then supplied the American subsidiary with working capital.[51] During the war, Separator was apparently consolidated. Its share capital was only raised from 28 to 63 million SK, which was a moderate rise for those days. When difficulties arose for Separator as for most other Swedish firms at the beginning of the 1920s, it could raise the value of some of its subsidiaries. Its bank helped in issuing a bond loan and in buying preference shares that were issued.[52]

The second separator company, Baltic, founded in 1908, became a multinational by acquiring the Empire Cream Separator Co. in the United States, which was owned and founded by two Swedes. During the war, Baltic expanded tremendously, and diversified into various other types of production geared towards the agricultural sector. For a time, it was considered the future Swedish counterpart of International Harvester, since it was able to supply all kinds of farming equipment. Its amalgamation with various firms in Sweden for that purpose was organized through one of the independent issuing houses, backed by share loans from no fewer than six banks. In 1920 it had to be reconstructed with the help of the banks supplying new credit. When it had to go into bankruptcy in 1923, one reason was evidently that it had so many bank connections that no one bank felt a responsibility to avoid it.[53]

The third multinational separator company, Pumpseparator, was the only one of these three that was considered as controlled by a bank by the 1924 Bank Committee. The bank had helped in financing its international business, mostly by credit guarantees to banks in other countries. From 1918, direct lending had increased.[54]

In the 1920s, when all three separator companies were facing great difficulties besides competing strongly with each other, Pumpseparator and Separator bought the new Baltic and later merged. Both the purchase and the merger were administered by the banks.

The Swedish match industry was completely controlled by Ivar Kreuger from 1917 to his death in 1932. The monopolizing of the Swedish match industry in 1917 was made possible entirely through the large bank loans given to Kreuger. An additional and for its time exceptionally large loan, also with shares as collateral, which was given by the two largest banks in Sweden, Svenska Handelsbanken and Skandinaviska Banken, and their associated companies made possible the purchase of a large number of match factories in several countries. Around the middle of the 1920s, when Kreuger started to offer large loans against match monopolies, the British and in particular the American capital market were relied upon as well.[55] However, this situation only lasted for a couple of years. Towards the end of the 1920s, most loans were guaranteed, and finally had to be taken over by Swedish banks. Although Kreuger was certainly dependent on Swedish banks and had Skandinaviska Banken in particular to thank for his introduction on the international capital market – and for adding to his prestige – Kreuger's personality made it appear to contemporary Swedes to be the other way around. In a sense Skandinaviska Banken became as dependent during the 1920s on the well-being of Kreuger and his business as Kreuger was on the bank. When Kreuger died in 1932, the bank had to write off great losses and needed assistance in consolidating. It was because of the banks that Swedish Match could develop into a large multinational so quickly. It was also thanks to the Swedish banks that the control of both the Ericsson telephone company and Swedish Match was to remain in Swedish hands after Kreuger's death.

When depression hit Sweden in the early 1920s, the interdependence of banks and industry became obvious. Admitted that evidence is rather weak, it still seems as if it were the intention of the banks to rid themselves of the strong dependence on industry brought about by conditions and to regain a somewhat larger field of action. Firms were to be carried through the lean years, eventually reconstructed, and their shares sold with profits as soon as it was deemed possible. There is no evidence to the contrary. The portfolios of the banks and their associated companies consisted mainly of shares either taken over against forfeited debts or belonging to new issues which it had been impossible to place on the market.

What no one foresaw was that this situation was to last until the Second World War was over. Although conditions for Swedish industry improved during the latter part of the 1920s, the market for shares was negligible. The great losses which followed the speculative boom were all too easily remembered. In the early 1930s the situation on the Swedish share market was again aggravated by the Kreuger crash. In Sweden as elsewhere, the economy of the 1930s was characterized by autarky. The importance of the home market for Swedish industry, and particularly for the Swedish engineering industry, increased.

Thus, Swedish banks and Swedish industry were to have almost 25 years of getting used to relying mainly on each other. It was in the interest of the banks to see to it that the companies whose shares they had had to take over grew and prospered, and the larger banks were all active in finding good managers of 'their' industries, in helping them to integrate and to expand. There was no difference between the banks in this respect.

Differences did exist, however, between Stockholms Enskilda Bank and the other larger Swedish banks, and new differences developed which were to affect the relationship between industry and banks. The difference which did exist, and which had done so even since the end of the 1800s, had to do with the fact that ownership was so much more concentrated in Stockholms Enskilda Bank than in other banks. The control by the Wallenberg family of both Stockholms Enskilda Bank and the various holding companies associated with it was perpetuated when the largest shareholder, Knut Wallenberg, turned his shareholding in 1917 into a foundation to be administered by the head of the bank. Ownership was much more dispersed in the other large banks and there was no homogeneous group of owners in control.

This may not have meant much in practice had it not been for the fact that one of the new generation of Wallenberg brothers who took over developed a special interest in industry – to the extent that he has been considered perhaps more of an industrialist than a banker. When Marcus Wallenberg Jr became head of Stockholms Enskilda Bank after the Second World War, the holding companies associated with the bank kept and further developed a controlling interest in several of the largest Swedish enterprises, at this time almost synonymous with the largest Swedish multinationals. The embryo of this industrial empire consisted of shares that had been unplaceable on the Swedish share market in the 1910s and 1920s. Marcus Wallenberg and Stockholms Enskilda Bank took a very active part in the further multi-nationalization of Swedish industry.

On the whole, the Wallenbergs took an active part also in the management of the companies in which their group held a controlling ownership. The other large banks were themselves run by employed managers and it is probably correct to say also that the managers of the corporations in which the holding companies associated with these banks owned a large amount of shares were more independent vis-à-vis their shareholders than were managers in companies within the sphere of influence of Stockholms Enskilda Bank.

Concluding remarks

Only one aspect of the growth of Swedish multinational enterprise has been dealt with above – the role of banks. It has been argued implicitly that it was vital for the founding, growth and in particular the life-saving and life-keeping of Swedish multinationals during this period, when most of the largest Swedish multinationals (as they are still to-day) started production abroad.

Elsewhere I have argued that the immediate causes of foreign direct investments in this period had to do with rising nationalism.[56] The home market was too small for the new, more specialized Swedish engineering firms. Because of scale economies, most Swedish multinationals would have preferred to export, but because of obstacles to their exporting, they had started manufacturing abroad. During the period dealt with here, the obstacles increased through rising nationalism. In very few cases, one of which was the telephone operating company, was the acting of Swedish banks the main reason for Swedish firms making foreign direct investments. On the other hand, the financing of such investments was of course vital. In almost all Swedish cases, the banks either provided or assisted in providing the means of finance when production was started in foreign countries.

For the further growth of multinationals, financing is of course only one of the conditions, competitive products and entrepreneurial and managerial capacities being others.[57] Although, in the long run, growth is self-financed, in the short run, lack of external financial means may put a definite stop to any further growth. In view of the rather extraordinary circumstances of this period and the comparatively small size of Swedish firms, the importance of the banks for the further growth of the nascent Swedish multinationals was particularly great. On the other hand, with the banks' growing commitment in Swedish multinationals during the period, the sustained growth of these multinationals became of vital importance for the banks.

NOTES

1 R. Lundström, 'Swedish multinational growth before 1930', in P. Hertner and G. Jones (eds.), *Multinationals: theory and history* (London, forthcoming). A multinational enterprise is here defined as a firm having made foreign direct investments, viz. in production.

2 T. Gårdlund, *Svensk industrifinansiering under genombrottsskedet 1830–1913* (Stockholm, 1947).

3 K.-G. Hildebrand, *I omvandlingens tjänst Svenska Handelsbanken 1871–1955* (Stockholm, 1971), p. 5, where the grouping of Gårdlund's figures, referred to in the preceding paragraph, has been made. Another reason why Gårdlund's figures probably underestimated the role of banks is that he follows a cohort of firms. Because of the long period that his study encompasses, most of the firms are old; only two of the 33 firms investigated were started after 1870.

4 *Ibid.*, p. 39; also BiSOS, Uppgifter om bankerna, 1910.

5 *Ibid.*

6 Bankinspektionens undersökningsberättelser, Riksarkivets 1909, 1910.

7 Hildebrand, p. 30.

8 O. Gasslander, *Bank och industriellt genombrott, Stockholms Enskilda Bank kring sekelskiftet 1900*, II (Stockholm, 1959), p. 299: cf. BiSOS, Uppgifter om bankerna, 1909–11.

9 Gasslander, pp. 293ff.

10 1917 års bankkommitté, Betänkande 30 Nov. 1918, p. 11.

11 The value of shares that the banks were allowed to own was limited to half the amount by which funded reserves exceeded half the share capital: see n. 10.

12 E. Söderlund, *Skandinaviska Banken i det svenska bankväsendets historia 1914–1939* (Uppsala, 1978), p. 19.

13 Söderlund, pp. 23f.

14 These figures are minimum figures, though comprising the main companies: Svenska aktiebolags balansräkningar åren 1911–1925. Undersökning utgiven av socialiseringsnämden, SOU 1929:4 (Stockholm, 1929), p. 521.

15 1917 års bankkommitté, Betänkande 30 Nov. 1918, pp. 23–9.
16 A. Östlind, *Svensk samhällsekonomi 1914–1922* (Stockholm, 1945), pp. 266f.
17 E. Heckscher, 'Aktiebolagsformen och dess svagheter', pp. 2–3, in *Ekonomiska studier tillägnade Marcus Wallenberg* (Stockholm, 1914).
18 The Stockholm Stock Exchange increased its share of the total turnover of stocks and bonds on the Swedish market from 21% in 1912 to 35% in 1918: Östlind, p. 259 (table), p. 563.
19 1924 års bankkommitté, Betänkande; Östlind, pp. 674–5; see also J. Glete, *Kreugerkoncernen och krisen på svensk aktiemarknad* (Stockholm, 1981), p. 51
20 Socialiseringsnämnden was a parliamentary committee consisting of only seven members, four of whom were social democrats. Its directives were soft and pointed more towards a mixed economy. It never resulted in any government bill for socialization or nationalization, either partial or general. See L. Waara, *Den statliga företagssektorns expansion* (Stockholm, 1980), pp. 144f.; SOU 1929:4.
21 BiSOS, Uppgifter om bankerna, 1913; SOS, Uppgifter om bankerna, 1917, 1921, 1924. The year 1917 was the peak year for loans, etc. against the collateral of shares, and 1921 the trough year.
22 SOS, Uppgifter om bankerna 1916; Stockholms Enskilda Bank (SEB) Archive.
23 See *inter alia* L. Jörberg, *Growth and fluctuations of Swedish industry 1869–1912* (Lund, 1961), *passim.*
24 See n. 1 above.
25 Gasslander, pp. 227f.
26 *Ibid.*, pp. 172ff. The House of Rothschild joined in the second agreement as did two other German chemical companies.
27 SEB Archive, correspondence.
28 The largest sales were not made until the 1920s: SEB Archive.
29 SEB Archive; *Affärsvärlden*, årg. 11, no. 23, p. 651.
30 The expression is Mira Wilkins's. See further M. Wilkins, 'Defining a firm', in Hertner and Jones (eds.), *Multinationals.*
31 SEB Archive.
32 Hildebrand, p. 71.
33 SEB Archive.
34 E. E. Fleetwood, *Sweden's capital imports and exports* (Geneva, 1947), p. 18.
35 Östlind, p. 234.
36 SEB Archive; *Svenska Aktiebolag och enskilda banker*, 1916, 1917, 1918 (Stockholm, 1916, 1917, 1918), *passim*; K. Sågvall-Ullenhag, *AB Åtvidabergs förenade industrier med föregångare* (Uppsala, 1970), p. 47.
37 I. Bäckman, *Sveriges handelsintressen i ryska riket* (Stockholm, 1912), pp. 82f.
38 It was Stockholms Enskilda Bank and the Azov-Don Bank that started this: SEB Archive; Bäckman, *op. cit.* p. 11.
39 See n. 1 above.
40 1924 års bankkommitté, Betänkande, SOU 1927:11 (Stockholm, 1927), pp. 55f, pp. 95f.
41 J. Glete, *ASEA under hundra år* (Västerås, 1983), p. 77; B. Steckzén, *Svenska Kullagerfabriken* (Göteborg, 1957), p. 298; *Svenska Aktiebolag och Enskilda Banker*, 1919 (Stockholm, 1919), p. 577.
42 Östlind, p. 544.
43 *Ibid.*, pp. 416ff.
44 *Ibid.*, pp. 706ff. From the value of fixed assets and stocks Östlind has subtracted all debts including shareholders' debts, viz. bank credit against the collateral of shares (table, p. 709).

45 Several examples in SEB Archive; and also in the investigations made by 1924 års bankkommitté (Riksarkivet).
46 Söderlund, pp. 344ff.
47 SEB Archive.
48 Glete, *ASEA under hundra år*, pp. 80ff. Solvency or solidity is there estimated as share capital and reserves plus profits or minus losses as a percentage of total assets.
49 M. Fritz, *Ett världsföretag växer fram Alfra-Laval 100 år* (Stockholm, 1983), p. 85.
50 Gasslander, I, pp. 176ff.
51 Memo by one of the owners of Empire Cream Separator Co., 1912, SEB Archive. When looking at the balance sheets of both the Swedish mother company and the American subsidiary (Fritz, pp. 474, 497) of which the latter were never presented in Sweden, one notices in fact that the amount for dividends from the American company as presented in the balance sheets of the mother company is larger than even gross profits as reported in the United States by the subsidiary.
52 Fritz, pp. 66ff.
53 *Ibid.*, pp. 69ff., p. 77.
54 SEB Archive.
55 L. Hassbring, *The international development of the Swedish Match Co.* (Stockholm, 1979); U. Wikander, *Kreuger's match monopolies* (Stockholm, 1980), *passim*; Glete, *Kreugerkoncernen, passim*.
56 See note 1.
57 This implies that I find that E. Penrose's dynamic theory of the growth of the firm best covers the Swedish development. Here the resources of the firm are stressed (E. Penrose, *The theory of the growth of the firm* (Oxford, 1959). If one accepts Penrose's point of view, there is no need for a general theory on multinationals; multinationals arise in much the same way as does trade. The picture of Swedish multinationals seems to confirm such a view.

15 British overseas banks in the Middle East 1920–70: a study in multinational middle age*

GEOFFREY JONES

1 The problem

In the period after the First World War foreign-owned institutions dominated the modern banking sector of the Middle East. In areas of British political influence, British overseas banks virtually monopolised banking. They had pioneered modern banking in the region, replacing or rather supplementing indigenous money-lenders. In Persia, the Imperial Bank of Persia faced no competition except from a moribund Russian institution. Iraq had two British banks and an Anglo-French one. The Arabian Gulf was devoid of modern banking facilities until 1920, when a British bank established a branch in Bahrain. When the first modern banks were established elsewhere in the Gulf after 1940 – in Kuwait (1942), Dubai (1946), Oman (1948) and Qatar (1950) – they were branches of British overseas banks. It was a similar picture in areas of French influence. The Banque de Syrie et du Grand Liban, established in 1924 and managed from Paris, dominated interwar Lebanese and Syrian banking.

By the early 1970s the role of British overseas banks had been much diminished. Some countries, notably Egypt, Syria and Iraq, had nationalised foreign banks during the 1950s and 1960s or, as in the case of Kuwait in 1970, obliged them to discontinue their business. Almost everywhere locally owned banks had overtaken the old overseas banks as market-leaders. In so far as foreign institutions were still powerful in the region, as for example in the recycling of petro-dollars, it was American banks that seemed to be dominant.

This paper examines the comparative decline of the British overseas banks in the Middle East over this period. It is in part a contribution to the debate on the historical performance of British multinational enterprise, which has hitherto focused on the manufacturing sector.[1] It is also a case study in multinational – host country relationships. However, given the sparseness of the existing literature on banking in the twentieth-century Middle East,[2] and the considerable differences between individual countries in the region, this

218

essay must be regarded as an exploratory survey which will be qualified by later research.

Section 2 looks at the characteristics and policies of British overseas banks in the Middle East. Section 3 examines some factors behind their comparative decline between 1920 and 1970.

2 The roles of British overseas banks

The definition of a multinational or international bank remains elusive. C. P. Kindleberger doubts their existence even by 1983, finding it hard to distinguish between local, regional, money-market and international functions.[3] More prosaic writers have argued that a bank must have branches in a minimum number of different countries – often three or five – to qualify as 'transnational' or 'multinational'.[4] By such criteria, the British overseas banks in the Middle East can be safely described as multinational.

The Appendix to this paper lists the British-registered overseas banks with branches in the Middle East in 1922, 1952 and 1970. In 1922, these six banks fell into two groups. They were either regional specialists, such as the Imperial Bank of Persia which largely operated in Persia, or multi-regional banks with some representation in the Middle East, such as the Bank of British West Africa. By 1952 a third category had appeared, in the shape of Barclays (Dominion, Colonial, Overseas), a subsidiary of the major British domestic bank. Barclays (DCO) had been formed in 1925 by the acquisition and merger of three formerly independent British overseas banks, including the Anglo-Egyptian Bank with a considerable Egyptian branch network, and it also possessed a large number of branches in Africa and the West Indies.[5] By 1970 there had been substantial consolidation. Apart from Barclays (DCO), the three remaining British overseas banks in the Middle East formed part of larger multi-regional groups, although the British Bank of the Middle East (BBME, descendant of the old Imperial Bank of Persia) retained autonomy within the Hongkong Bank Group. This analysis includes one oddity but excludes another. Included is the Imperial Ottoman Bank (the 'Imperial' was dropped from the title in 1925). This bank had British, French and Turkish shareholders, and possessed a wide Middle Eastern branch network before 1969, when it sold its branches in the region to National and Grindlays. Excluded is the National Bank of Egypt, an Egyptian-registered institution formed in 1898 with its Board in Cairo, but with half of its capital subscribed in Britain and special rights granted to its London Directors. This bank's London Committee was abolished in 1940, after which date the staff and Board were largely Egyptian.[6]

The British overseas banks were run from London, although occasionally the chief executive would reside abroad. The Chief Manager of the Imperial Bank of Persia before 1952, for example, lived in Tehran, although he was subject to decisions of a London-based Board. Senior staff of branch manager and higher level were overwhelmingly of British nationality in all banks, supported only rarely by Continentals and practically never by 'locals'. The major exception seems to have been the Imperial Ottoman Bank, which employed Arab and other local staff at manager level much earlier than the 'purely' British banks.

What did these banks do? They are often described as 'exchange banks': that is, primarily concerned with the foreign exchange requirements and the finance of foreign trade of the countries in which they operated.[7] But this term is misleading, especially in the early twentieth century, for one of the most noticeable features of British overseas banks was the range of banking activities they undertook. These activities fall into three groups.

First, some of the overseas banks in the Middle East regularly undertook the functions of a central or state bank, including handling government accounts, the issue of currency, and serving as the bankers' bank and lender of last resort. The Imperial Bank of Persia, for example, held the accounts of the Persian government until 1928, and issued the paper currency until 1932. The National Bank of Egypt performed similar functions in Egypt. In Iraq, the Eastern Bank had a somewhat more limited role as the banker to both the British Mandate administration and, after 1932, the independent Iraqi state. The Banque de Syrie et du Grand Liban performed all the functions of a central bank in interwar Lebanon and Syria.

From the late 1920s governments began to limit the role of foreign banks in this respect by replacing them by new, state-owned banks, such as the Bank Melli formed in Persia in 1928. Yet in the Arabian Gulf the tradition of British overseas banks acting as de facto central banks lasted until the 1970s. In Oman, for example, the British Bank of the Middle East held a monopoly banking concession between 1948 and 1968. In addition to holding and servicing the government accounts, the Bank took responsibility for currency matters. In 1959 BBME undertook the replacement of the Indian rupee – which had been the universal currency in the Gulf – by the special Gulf rupee. And in 1970 – after the expiry of its banking monopoly – BBME introduced a new national currency, a particularly difficult operation given the largely illiterate Omani population at that time, and then managed the Currency Board. In Dubai, where BBME was the sole bank between 1946 and 1963, it took over the Customs administration in 1955. Its managers acted as advisers to the Ruler on many issues, helping – for example – to form an electricity company on behalf of the government. The Bank, one BBME Director noted in December 1962, was 'a sort of unofficial department of the administration'.[8]

Secondly, the overseas banks undertook various merchant banking functions, and in particular the issue of loans. Before the First World War the British overseas banks had challenged the dominance of the City of London-based merchant banks in this field.[9] The Imperial Bank of Persia, for example, issued Persia's two pre-war foreign loans floated in London, in 1892 and 1911. In the interwar years this kind of business almost disappeared because of depressed economic conditions, changed political circumstances and official restrictions on British overseas lending. After 1945 Middle Eastern countries tended to be either too wealthy, because of oil discoveries, or else too poor to offer scope for such merchant banking activities. It was not until the oil price rises of the early 1970s that a demand appeared, especially in the Gulf, for consortium finance for large public works schemes, medium-term loans, leasing of equipment and investment management services. But the British overseas banks lacked experience in such fields, and the initiative fell to others.

Thirdly, the British overseas banks in the Middle East performed all the functions of a retail, commercial bank. Large branch networks were constructed, and deposits were collected. Interest was often paid to attract deposits: hostility to the concept of interest on Islamic grounds is a product of more recent years in most countries, although in Saudi Arabia banks always refrained from interest payments. In 1964 BBME paid interest on around 70% of its Middle Eastern deposits: in contrast, the English clearing banks paid interest on only 30% of their deposits at the same period.

The collection of deposits was important for British overseas banks, for the conventional wisdom between 1920 and 1970 was that business in a country should be financed from local resources. The banks disliked trans-ferring funds from Britain to finance their operations and, of course, the option of buying funds on a wholesale banking market did not exist. Reliance on local resources was seen as essential to a bank's security. 'The local arrangement', the General Manager of BBME wrote in 1953, 'would be for all Branches to be able to finance themselves out of their own resources, requiring an overdraft in London only to cover sterling bills en route. In this way exchange and political risks are eliminated.'[10] However, Middle Eastern governments, especially those with large populations and limited resources, found such policies rather less than ideal. They were not helpful, for instance, to countries whose growth was hampered by a trade constraint. The reluctance of the overseas banks to invest 'capital' in the countries in which they operated became a major criticism against them. Legislation in Iraq in 1938, Iran in 1949 and Kuwait in 1968 obliged foreign banks to import a minimum amount of 'capital' into their host countries.

The funds of the overseas banks were used, in the tradition of British banking, for self-liquidating commercial transactions. British overseas banks in the Middle East saw their role as the provision of short-term trade finance, either by bill discounting, advances or credits. In August 1959, for example, 70% of BBME's total lending of £32 million was to finance imports. Long-term investment in industry or agriculture was, except in special circum-stances, avoided by British banks, and property finance, loans to small industry and personal loans were also discouraged. In August 1959 agricultural loans formed less than 1% of BBME's total lending, and that was largely in bad debts in Syria.

Although these lending policies have been widely criticised as 'conservative', aspects of them were radical by British banking standards. In particular, many loans were unsecured, in a western sense, because it was traditional practice in Middle Eastern countries to lend solely on the basis of a customer's standing. In addition, merchants had little collateral to offer a bank, especially as many countries prohibited foreigners from acquiring property. It can be estimated that at least 60% of BBME's loans during the 1950s were unsecured. The Middle East also lacked any equivalent to the Chinese *comprador*, or local intermediary, who would guarantee the loans made by British banks on his recommendation.

3. Pressures on the overseas banks

3.1 Governments

It was not surprising that it was interwar Persia (or Iran as it became known in 1935) where governmental pressures against British overseas banks first mounted. Under Reza Khan, who became Shah in 1925, a programme of social, cultural and economic reforms was launched, designed to modernise the Persian economy using the power of the state. The new nationalist regime soon clashed with the British-owned company which ran the country's oil industry, the Anglo-Persian Oil Company (later called BP).[11] The creation of a national bank was inevitable in such a context. The Imperial Bank of Persia's role as state bank had always been qualified by its status as a British institution, subject to influence by the British Foreign Office. During the First World War and early 1920s the Bank was forbidden on occasion to advance funds to Persian governments considered undesirable by the British government. It was not a situation that the new nationalist order would countenance.

Following its formation in 1928, the Bank Melli took over the government accounts from the Imperial Bank of Persia, and that bank was subjected to curbs on its commercial business. In 1930 a foreign exchange law forced the Imperial Bank to hand over 50% of its foreign exchange purchases to the Bank Melli. The Bank subsequently gave up its note issue as a quid pro quo for the relaxation of this decree, but in 1936 an even tougher Foreign Exchange Law established an Exchange Commission, and obliged the Bank to deal in foreign exchange only on behalf of the Commission. The result of these measures, plus the general thrust of autarkic policies, was that throughout the 1930s the Imperial Bank's Persian business made very meagre profits (and actual losses between 1932 and 1936), and that the Bank only paid dividends through virtue of its investment income in London. This period was a low point for the Imperial Bank, and perhaps for the other British overseas banks. Unfamiliar economic nationalism, economic depression and an all-pervading sense of 'conservatism', compared to the 'pioneering' days before 1914, were not a recipe for dynamism. 'Between the two wars our Bank was remarkable for its inactivity', the General Manager of BBME remembered in 1953; 'We feared all new things and an ultra conservative policy, which we grew accustomed to when we had a complete monopoly of the banking business... dominated all we did.'[12]

The British and Soviet occupation of Iran during the Second World War brought the relaxation of banking restrictions, but after 1945 they were reasserted. The Governor of the Bank Melli between 1942 and 1950, Abul Hassan Ebtehaj, had been a Persian employee in the Imperial Bank, but had left in 1936 because of the blocked promotion prospects for local nationals in that Bank. After 1945 he worked systematically to curb the Imperial Bank's role in Iran. He argued that the Bank Melli, as the central bank, had to take a leading part in regulating the economy for the purposes of development, and that it had to provide money and the resources needed for Iranian industrialisation, a feeling reinforced as prospects of substantial American development aid dwindled.[13] He considered it inappropriate that a foreign bank should hold a large amount of Iranian deposits – the Imperial Bank still held nearly 30% of total bank deposits in 1946. 'You take our deposits and don't use them', he told the Bank's Chairman in 1946. 'You must recognise our right to require you to use them when we need them. We need them now.'[14] Unlike many subsequent critics of foreign banks, he believed that the Imperial Bank had a role in Iran, but not in retail banking. A foreign bank, he argued, should finance foreign trade and – given the centralisation of exchange controls in Tehran – a single branch in that city was all that was required. Moreover, in return for the privilege of operating in Iran he argued that foreign banks must bring capital into the country.

Between 1945 and 1950 Ebtehaj attempted to put his policies into effect. In 1946 banks were obliged to deposit 15% of their demand, and 6% of their term deposits with the Bank Melli, and to hold an equal amount of the government's Treasury Bonds. The Bank Melli deprived the Imperial Bank of access to foreign exchange. In 1949 the Imperial Bank had to agree to import £1 million capital into the country and to close three branches.

The Imperial Bank never understood why Iranians wanted to limit the powers of foreign banks. Like most British politicians and diplomats, the bankers were locked into a view of the country as it had been in the 1900s, seeing only irrational emotions and demagogic personalities rather than a legitimate nationalism.[15] The Imperial Bank blamed everything on a personal vendetta of Ebtehaj, whom they regarded as having a 'grudge' against the Bank, and of being 'jealous' of its success. The fallacy of the argument was shown after July 1950, when Ebtehaj was dismissed following an internal shift in Persian politics, but pressure against the Bank was not relaxed. In September 1951 the Bank's permission to deal in foreign exchange was withdrawn, a by-product of the crisis following the Iranian nationalisation of the Anglo-Iranian Oil Company.[16] The Bank ceased operations in Iran in July 1952.

The Iranian experience led the BBME to reconsider its strategies in the Arab Middle East, where it had been opening branches since the early 1940s. 'We must', its Chairman wrote, 'accommodate ourselves to local sentiment... Jealousy of foreign institutions is only beginning, and... it will grow.'[17] Local staff had their status raised within the Bank and – alongside other British overseas banks – joint ventures with local interests were made when it seemed politically appropriate.

However, such attempts to 'accommodate' local sentiment proved an irrelevancy to the new nationalist, Baathist or socialist governments which developed in the Arab Middle East from the 1950s. Foreign banks were disliked because of their Western ownership, and sometimes attacked because of wider political issues. Barclays (DCO) was nationalised in Egypt following the Suez Crisis in 1956.[18] In Syria foreign banks were required to import capital after 1955, and in 1961 they were nationalised. Iraq had regulated the banking sector since the 1930s, obliging banks for example to maintain a certain percentage of deposits with the Central Bank, but after the 1958 Revolution pressure on foreign banks mounted with exchange controls, maximum interest rates, and restrictions on expatriate staff. In 1964 all banks in Iraq were nationalised as part of a wide-ranging socialisation decree designed to transform the Iraqi foreign economic system along the lines of that of Egypt. In 1969 banks were nationalised in the Republic of South Yemen (the former British colony of Aden) and in the following year in Libya as part of an extensive process of removing 'imperialist' influence over these economies.

Undoubtedly the decline of British political influence in the Middle East after the Second World War was a factor in the problems of the overseas banks. It is important to bear this macro-political picture in mind in this context. The British overseas banks in the Middle East had developed when British diplomatic influence was powerful, and they had usually worked closely – if not always harmoniously – with the Foreign Office. The subsequent withering of British power in the Middle East from the 1950s helps to explain the declining fortunes of the overseas banks. British Ambassadors could no longer 'influence' governments as they had before 1914, especially after the Suez débâcle.

The experience of the British overseas banks in these countries reinforces a general point that needs to be made, that in most cases governments hold the upper hand in power relationships with multinationals. Banks have no alternative but to obey the restrictions placed on their activities, while after

1945 they were often nationalised because of general political developments or even – as in the case of the withdrawal of foreign exchange authorisation in Iran in 1951 – because a government was in dispute with another British company.

Moreover, banks found it hard to cease operating in a country when danger signals appeared. It proved difficult to recover advances if a bank ceased operations in a territory, especially as local staff normally resented their loss of employment. Prestige considerations acted to reinforce banks' unwillingness to pull out of territories even when conditions became hostile. 'The closing down of a branch', the General Manager of BBME observed in 1958, 'has repercussions in the Bank's business as a whole in other countries.'[19] In these senses the barriers to exit faced by the banks were high, even if they did not have the large-scale capital investments of an industrial company.

3.2 Local banks

In countries which did not see outright nationalisation before 1970, the most serious threat to the British overseas banks came from local banks. The demand for the creation of locally owned national banks had arisen in both Egypt and Iran in 1907 and 1908, but no progress was made until the creation of the Bank Misr in Egypt in 1920. The Bank was established in 1920 by large landowning interests (who produced 92% of the original share capital), seeking to free themselves from the control of foreign banks and diversify from cotton into industrial enterprise. It developed into a major industrial group before nearly collapsing in 1939.[20] The second powerful private-sector bank of the interwar years was the Arab Bank, founded by Palestinians in Jerusalem in 1929, which by the time of the Second World War had a wide branch network in Palestine, Egypt, Lebanon and Syria.[21] In addition, in 1938 Saudi Arabian merchants founded the National Commercial Bank.

Other countries opted for state-created local banks. The Bank Melli in Persia made a disastrous start under corrupt German advisers, but by 1939 it had overtaken the Imperial Bank of Persia in terms of advances and deposits. In Iraq in 1941 the nationalist government of Rashid Ali, shortly before its overthrow by the British Army, established the Rafidain Bank, which within ten years had replaced the three British overseas banks in Iraq as the leading bank.

In the small Gulf sheikhdoms, after oil revenues began to flow in the 1940s, it was the private-sector model which was followed. In 1952 the National Bank of Kuwait, owned by Kuwaiti merchants, opened for business, despite the fact that the British Bank of the Middle East officially held a banking monopoly in Kuwait until 1971. By 1960 its deposits and advances in Kuwait exceeded the BBME's. Three more Kuwaiti banks were set up in the 1960s. In Bahrain the duopoly of the Eastern Bank and BBME was broken in 1956 by the formation of the National Bank of Bahrain, owned by local merchants. In 1963 the National Bank of Dubai was formed – again despite BBME's having an official banking monopoly until 1974.

The creation of the local banks in the Gulf was not opposed by the British overseas banks. In an oil-rich state such as Kuwait there was business for all and, perhaps more importantly, no practical alternative to obeying a Ruler's wishes. Moreover, the British banks were unenthusiastic about banking monopolies, which often obliged them to undertake unwelcome tasks. 'We as monopolists have corralled the bulk of the capital in Kuwait', one of BBME's Directors observed in 1950, and that fact placed the bank 'under an obligation'.[22] Monopolies also, as the same Bank's Chairman wrote, 'attract hostility and detraction... and excite suspicion in the minds of authorities and customers'.[23]

The moves to establish local Gulf banks did not, as a whole, rest on criticism of the policies of the British overseas banks. Merchants sometimes resented being asked for any 'security' other than their honour and good name, but there was no demand or requirement for banks to finance long-term industrial or agricultural development. The new Gulf banks followed the same principles of 'conservative' banking as their British predecessors. They had low advances/deposits ratios – 19% for BBME and 22% for the National Bank in Kuwait in 1960 – and invested surplus funds in London. The primary motive of the merchants who established the new Gulf banks was not to introduce new banking methods, but to get a share of an increasingly prosperous cake.[24]

The success of the post-1945 local banks in the Gulf rested on a number of factors. Primarily, the fact that leading merchants were also shareholders in local banks usually meant that much of their business was transferred to those banks. Local Boards of Directors responded quickly and with flexibility to requests for large loans, while the branch managers of British banks often had to refer such requests to London. Moreover, the new banks were often established with the help of British banks, and usually initially run by experienced British staff. Thus the Midland Bank, one of the 'Big Five' British clearing banks of the time, sent staff to help organise the National Bank of Kuwait, and the Jordan National Bank in 1956, while the Ottoman Bank helped to establish the National Bank of Bahrain. Similarly, the chief executives of the new banks were almost always British overseas bankers. The National Bank of Kuwait recruited such a man from the National Bank of Egypt, while the National Bank of Dubai recruited from National and Grindlays.

3.3 Foreign competitors

By the end of the period under review, a new source of competition had arisen for the British overseas banks in the Middle East, especially the Gulf. By the early 1970s the leading American multinational banks – Citibank, Chase Manhattan and Bank of America – had built up within a few years a substantial presence in the region, as had to a lesser extent the British clearing banks, especially Lloyds, Midland and National Westminster. It was these banks, rather than the British overseas banks with long experience in the region, which did the bulk of the recycling of petro-currency earnings following the oil price rises after 1973.[25] Their success demonstrated that the difficulties of the British overseas banks were by no means entirely due to nationalistic pressures in the region.

The British overseas banks were undoubtedly handicapped by the weakness of sterling. Until 1967 the majority of Kuwaiti and other Gulf funds had been kept in sterling and employed in London, a policy apparently supported by British governments in an attempt to protect sterling's increasingly weak position as a reserve currency. The devaluation of sterling in November 1967, however, caused large losses, and subsequently the Gulf states and merchants began to diversify their currency holdings, especially into Euro-dollars. This trend was reinforced because the oil exporting states invariably received payments in dollars. American banks were a natural channel for dollar funds. The problems of sterling as a reserve currency are as important as the decline of British political influence in understanding the difficulties faced by the overseas banks in the Middle East.

Nevertheless, the comparative by-passing of the British overseas banks had endogenous causes. Part of the problem was that they were too small, and could not offer the facilities or security of the American banks. The Bank of England had recognised this as a general problem in British overseas banking in the 1950s, and had sponsored or encouraged a series of mergers designed to keep the banks out of the hands of British 'asset strippers' or American banks. Yet the new banks, despite further mergers in the 1960s, remained small by American standards.

The overseas banks also remained wedded to the mentality of retail banking. Banks such as BBME and Eastern had pioneered modern banking in, say, the Arabian Gulf after 1940, and this was what they felt themselves good at doing. In the late 1960s and early 1970s the British overseas banks could have offered greater facilities for depositors in other currencies, including the dollar, but their experience of the Euro-markets was minimal. They had effectively lost their pre-1914 roles when they had combined wide-ranging banking roles, and saw themselves as regional specialists offering retail and trade finance facilities. It was perhaps a case, as in the manufacturing sector, of the British being more willing to make multinational investments than to develop appropriate multinational structures to run them.[26] On the other hand, official British government policy towards British banking must be taken into account. Between the 1920s and the 1960s official policy strove to keep British banking in separate compartments: domestic banking; overseas banking; discount houses; merchant banks. Competition was discouraged between sectors.

The result was that in a few crucial years at the turn of the 1960s British overseas banks in the Middle East seemed to stand still. While local banks used their advantages to capture business in retail markets, Middle Eastern governments and entrepreneurs in search of merchant or wholesale banking services had to turn elsewhere. This trend was visible even in Oman, where the BBME had been the only bank between 1948 and 1968 and continued to enjoy a close relationship with the government. Yet when the National Bank of Oman was formed in 1972 the Bank of America was given the management contract, and when Oman negotiated its first external loan in 1973 it was raised by Morgan Grenfell. It was not until the mid 1970s that the British overseas banks in the Middle East began matching the large American multinational banks in organisation, knowledge of world financial markets, and wholesale expertise.

4 Conclusion

This paper has been a brief study in multinational middle age. The British overseas banks had been established before 1914, and had pioneered banking in the Middle East. They survived the following 50 years, which was a considerable feat given the political and economic upheavals in the region, but seemed fated to follow in one country after another a cycle of pioneering, growth, local competition, restriction and nationalisation.

The banks had both endogenous and exogenous difficulties. Their adherence to British commercial banking practice caused resentment in countries such as Iran which wanted banks to make a more positive development contribution. And they retained a regional and retail perspective when the oil producing countries of the Middle East needed a wider range of banking services. The banks also, especially before 1950, seem to have made little effort to come to terms with national aspirations. As so often in Britain, the legacy of the past was a heavy one.

Yet many of the problems of the overseas banks were exogenous. On the one hand, British economic decline and the waning of British diplomatic power in the Middle East had an inevitable impact on their activities. On the other hand, they faced difficulties from the growth of nationalism, or the reluctance of Middle Easterners to have their banking controlled by foreigners. This is, of course, a recurring feature in the general history of multinational – host country relations after 1920. Where governments expressed this nationalism, banks were effectively obliged to follow their dictates. The power of the banks was further circumscribed because government policies were not dictated, in the last resort, by their economies' 'need' for the banks, but by wider nationalistic and political considerations. 'Only a fit of madness could drive these people to throw us over in such a way', the Imperial Bank's Chief Manager in Persia remarked in 1928 on hearing of the projected formation of the Bank Melli.[27] It was a contagious 'madness'.

NOTES

* I would like to thank the Hongkong Bank for permission to cite the archives of the British Bank of the Middle East in this paper. I am completing a history of that Bank, due for publication by Cambridge University Press in 1986. Fuller documentation for arguments advanced here will be found in that history. Mrs F. Bostock, Dr P. L. Cottrell and Professor L. S. Pressnell made valuable comments on an earlier draft of this paper.

1 See Geoffrey Jones, 'The performance of British multinational enterprise', in Peter Hertner and Geoffrey Jones (eds.), *Multinationals: theory and history* (London, forthcoming).

2 There is a survey by R. Wilson, *Banking and finance in the Arab Middle East* (London, 1983). Also useful are Abdul-Amir Badrud-Din, *The Bank of Lebanon* (London, 1984) and E. Davis, *Challenging colonialism: Bank Misr and Egyptian industrialisation 1920 – 1941* (Princeton, 1983).

3 Charles P. Kindleberger, *Multinational Excursions* (Cambridge, Mass., 1984), pp. 167–8.

4 For example, G. N. Yannapoulos, 'The growth of transnational banking', in M. Casson (ed.), *The growth of international business* (London, 1983), p. 237.

5 J. Crossley and J. Blandford, *The DCO story* (London, 1975).

6 *National Bank of Egypt 1898–1948* (printed for private circulation, 1948). The bank's main inspiration in Britain was Sir Ernest Cassel. See P. Thane, 'Sir Ernest Joseph Cassel', in D. J. Jeremy (ed.), *Dictionary of business biography* (London, 1984), volume I. Cassel was also behind the less successful National Bank of Turkey, launched in 1909.

7 The best general accounts of British overseas banks remain A. S. J. Baster, *The imperial banks* (London, 1929) and *The international banks* (London, 1935). Alaine M. Low, *British commercial banking and commonwealth development* (London, forthcoming) promises to be a pioneer account of British overseas banking in the English-speaking regions of Africa and the Caribbean.

8 Notes for Directors, 4 December 1962, BBME (Archives).

9 S. Chapman, *The rise of merchant banking* (London, 1984), pp. 89, 172.

10 Notes for Directors, 24 December 1953, BBME.

11 R. W. Ferrier, *The history of the British Petroleum Company* (Cambridge, 1982), chapter 13.

12 H. Musker to G. Eley, 18 September 1953, BBME.

13 R. K. Ramazani, *Iran's foreign policy 1941 – 1973* (Charlottesville, 1975), pp. 154–7.

14 Notes on the visit to Iran and Iraq, 26 November 1946, BBME.

15 W. R. Louis, *The British Empire in the Middle East 1945–1951* (Oxford, 1984), pp. 638–40.

16 Ramazani, pp. 181–218.
17 Memorandum by Lord Kennet, 15 September 1952, BBME.
18 Crossley and Blandford, *The DCO story*, pp. 187–9.
19 Notes for Directors, 31 July 1958, BBME.
20 Davis, *Challenging colonialism*.
21 Wilson, *Banking and finance in the Arab Middle East*, pp. 43–9.
22 G. Prior to Lord Kennet, 8 July 1950.
23 *Ibid.*, Lord Kennet to G. Prior, 23 March 1950.
24 Interviews in the Arabian Gulf. There is a good account of the Gulf merchants in M. Field, *The merchants* (London, 1984).
25 Wilson, *Banking and finance in the Arab Middle East*, p. 125.
26 Geoffrey Jones, 'The performance of British multinational enterprise', in Hertner and Jones (eds.), *Multinationals: theory and history*.
27 E. Wilkinson to S. F. Rogers, 29 April 1928, BBME.

APPENDIX: Branches of British overseas banks in the Middle East, 1922, 1952, 1970

1922

Bank	Egypt	Iran	Levant*	Arabian† Gulf	Other Middle East	Non-Middle East
Anglo-Egyptian Bank	12	—	—	—	5	1
Bank of British West Africa (BBIWA)	2	—	—	—	5	36
Eastern Bank	—	—	3	1	—	5
Imperial Bank of Persia	—	19	2	—	—	1
Imperial Ottoman	5	1	17	—	—	84
Ionian Bank	2	—	—	—	—	22
National Bank of India (NBI)	—	—	—	—	2	28

* Levant = Present-day Iraq, Syria, Lebanon, Palestine/Israel
† Includes Saudi Arabia

1952

Bank	Egypt	Iran	Levant	Arabian Gulf	Other Middle East	Non-Middle East
BBIWA*	—	—	—	—	1	35
Barclays DCO	35	—	2	—	9	605
British Bank of Iran and Middle East†	—	7	7	6	—	1
Eastern Bank	—	—	5	2	1	10
Ionian Bank	9	—	—	—	—	28
Ottoman Bank	11	—	14	—	3	40
NBI	—	—	—	—	2	41

* Lloyds Bank acquired BBIWA's Egyptian branches in 1925, and sold them in 1927.
† Imperial Bank of Persia was renamed Imperial Bank of Iran in 1935, BBIME in 1949, and British Bank of the Middle East (BBME) in July 1952.

1970

Bank	Iran	Levant	Arabian Gulf	Other Middle East	Non-Middle East
Barclays DCO	—	44	—	43	1,420
BBME*	†	7	23	2	3
Chartered‡	†	1	10	5	121
National and Grindlays§	—	7	5	17	300

* BBME was acquired by the Hongkong Bank in 1960, but remained autonomous until 1980 with its own Board in London.
† Joint venture banks with Iranian interests.
‡ Chartered Bank acquired Eastern Bank in 1957.
§ National Bank of India and Grindlays Bank merged in 1957 to form National and Grindlays. In 1969 it acquired the Middle Eastern branches of the Ottoman Bank.

16 The multinationalisation of British and American banks

OLIVIER PASTRÉ and ANTHONY ROWLEY

It is generally agreed today that the British banks initiated the process of internationalisation of financial capital, and that competition/rivalry between the British and the Americans underlay the progress of bank multinationalisation until the middle of the 1960s. It would therefore be vain and superfluous to try to present within these few pages a complete historical survey of the development of the British and American multinational banks (MNB). Our purpose is deliberately macro-economic, which implies that many exceptions and specific cases have been cast aside. On the other hand, questions concerning the reality, pace and chronological variations of the formation and subsequent extension of these financial groups deserve to be raised. The aim of our paper is, therefore, to find preliminary answers to the three following questions: What has been the process of the internationalisation of the banks? Where have they become implanted and how has the international hierarchy of financial capital been organised? And finally, what was the relationship between the MNB and governments at the most decisive moments of Anglo-American rivalry?

By placing the emphasis upon the questions raised, we wish to show that our aim is not to produce new statistics; nor is it to dwell upon the various controversies concerning the definition of the MNB. Despite its somewhat arbitrary character, we have chosen to abide by the institutional criteria, without concerning ourselves, unlike C. P. Kindleberger,[1] with the number of installations established abroad. In our view, an MNB satisfies three conditions: international activities, a network of foreign subsidiaries and a true involvement in foreign industrial operations be they public or private.[2] This definition implies that a stage beyond internationalisation has been reached: here lies all the difference between foreign operations developed from London by houses like Rothschild, Seligman or Hambros at the end of the nineteenth century and the multinationalisation interests and locations of Lazard, Morgan or Barclay.[3] In fact, only the clearing or commercial banks are relevant to our analysis because their internationalisation involves a strategy and, in more general terms, a mode of behaviour which it is important to identify.

The two stages of multinationalisation

Upon first sight, an obvious asymmetry appears to exist between the distribution of British and American capital. In the first case, the internationalisation of the banks preceded that of the industrial firms: in 1914, there were 2,091 branches of British MNBs in the world, controlled by 36 banking companies; if the 3,538 colonial banks are added to the list, it becomes clear that Great Britain was the only country to have a world-wide network at its disposal. This network was much more extensive than its industrial counterpart: in 1914 there were only 60 subsidiaries of British Multinational Firms (MNF) in the world. Conversely, while there existed only 26 branches of MNBs of American origin and not a single colonial bank, the MNF subsidiaries already numbered 122. The conclusion is apparently quite simple: because of the importance of commercial capital, the internationalisation of British banks *preceded* industrialisation while *American industrial capital* was the most internationalised. In reality, this conclusion under-estimates both the brittleness of such a situation and the movements of internationalisation: British banking imperialism in 1914 appears to have been the result of the colonial and industrial expansion between the years 1850–1906, whereas American implantation was dispersed but increasing in intensity as companies set out to conquer the 'free competition zones', most notably in Latin America. In this respect, our figures tend to distort reality by emphasising the number of overseas links per country rather than the size of financial movements. Proof of this can be seen in the success of American investments in Mexico and Argentina between 1910 and 1913.

In addition, the fact that the modest expansion of the American MNB can also be attributed to institutional factors and to the privileged links that were inherited from dealings with the British Empire contributes to the conclusion that the asymmetry in development was caused rather by a difference in timing than by the adoption of divergent strategies. It is for this reason that the international investment zones that received large amounts of British and American capital did not necessarily coincide with those chosen by the MNF. Even in Latin America, the only region where both countries were well established, banking capital and industrial capital were rarely invested in the same place: in Mexico and Argentina, financial confrontations were, to all external appearances, quite independent of the industrial 'preserves' of oil, agriculture and foods.

This unusual situation, which differed considerably from the behaviour of the French and the Germans, was radically altered as the Americans strengthened their position between 1913 and 1920. This must be considered as the period in which the national legislation was modified to allow for the possibilities of internationalisation. Only after 1913 was American banking capitalism legally in a position to compete with British capitalism. The Federal Reserve Act gave authorisation to any bank whose capital and reserves exceeded one million dollars to 'open branches in foreign countries in order to develop American foreign trade'. The Agreement Corporation, set up in 1916, and the Edge Act Corporation, set up in 1919, acted as vectors for the internationalisation of American banking capital until 1929. At that time, within the context of the reconstruction of financial circuits at the end of the First World War, a veritable 'American banking industry' was born, sustained notably by the issue of international loans to Europe. In this respect, the years 1921–9 can be considered as the climacteric of the first wave of bank multinationalisation, but equally as the beginning of Anglo-American confrontation.[4] The discord between M. Norman and B. Strong over the reformation of the London and River Plate Bank[5] bears witness to this fact. The British had the advantage of being familiar with the Argentinian market, but the overvaluation of sterling, the lack of available capital and the limited size of the MNB all favoured the penetration of the American rivals. The practices and structures handed down from the nineteenth century were seemingly no longer adequate to meet the demands of local governments.

In this respect, the depression years were less a cut-off point than an opportunity for reorganisation in the race for supremacy in the banking world. New legislation, a wave of concentrations and international re-spreading out were the main features. Voted in 1933, the Glass Steagall Act established a strict separation between 'investment banks' and 'commercial banks' which compelled the American MNB to grant autonomy to a number of their subsidiaries.[6] The J. P. Morgan Commercial Bank had thus to break off its privileged relations with the Morgan Stanley Investment Bank. It was not until the end of the 1960s that the MNB started to press forward once more: in 1966, 12 American Banks controlled 244 foreign branches; in 1974, 106 banks had opened 475 new branches. Does this mean, as certain American authors would have it, that the internationalisation of American banking capital progresses spasmodically? In our view, this internationalisation is the result of the growing internationalisation of the industrialised countries: the boom in American MNB was a direct consequence of the successful reconstruction of Europe. It is understandable, therefore, that such dominance should coincide with the disappearance of the British MNB which for the years 1965–8 onwards fell victim both to the weakness of sterling and the obsolescence of industrial products. The equilibrium of the banking world in the years 1910–29 has been replaced by a new international order characterised by three geographical factors: the implantation of American MNB in the Far Eastern and Middle Eastern markets as a result of the oil boom and the decline of British hegemony; the strengthening of their penetration in Europe and Latin America; and finally, the co-ordination of industrial and banking investment.[7] On the whole one may ask if those changes were not the result of a strong dollar and a weakening pound, the multi-currency situation favouring the United States.

Strategies and multinationalisation

Up to the present recession, the British MNB still possessed more than 300 operating bases throughout the world. They maintained 'preserves' in Africa and the Middle East, and in eight countries they established as many branches and subsidiaries as the American MNBs. But these 'preserves' were quickly whittled away, leaving only fragments of the old Empire, from Ghana to Zambia. In the Far East, the British withdrawal was accelerated further by the advance of the Americans and later the Japanese. In fact, only the overseas banks such as the English Scottish and Australian Bank were able to stand up to competition from the American MNB by virtue of their numerous regional branches.[8] What explanation can be given for the fact that Britain lost this second multinationalisation battle? There appear to be three decisive reasons. Firstly, the internationalisation of capital led to the multiplication of 'free competition zones' – countries in which five foreign countries possess more than four bank operating bases, but in which no one country controls more than one-third of the market. Hence, between 1960 and 1973, Great Britain lost exclusive control over its favoured investment sites: Iran, Argentina, Canada, and Australia. Secondly, the development of the American industrial base resulted in a demand for banking capital which led to a switch from joint internationalisation of the two forms of capital in favour of an increasingly independent internationalisation of financial capital: this financial strength made it possible to consolidate the traditional American MNB operations and to conquer new zones at the expense of the British. Finally, it is worth considering to what extent the permeability of the major financial markets, such as those of France, the Federal Republic of Germany and Great Britain itself, has led, through mobilisation of capital, to a movement in favour of the Americans. In a certain sense, the international financial timing mechanism worked out by the British before 1914 seems to have smoothed the path for American progress.

These conclusions remain somewhat unsatisfactory because of their very general nature. They might even be compared to observations of simple common sense such as those made by W. Moore concerning his experience as president of First National City Bank:

Historically, there has always been a close relation between trade and investment on the one hand, and international activities of American banks on the other. During the 1920's, when trade and industry were developing, American banks established themselves abroad. During the 1930s when the world depression and attempts at self-sufficiency caused cut-backs in trade and international investment, the American banks also underwent a similar contraction. The same correlation exists today.[9]

These comments do not explain in what way the increased share of banking investments in the total of American investments provides evidence of an accentuation of the purely banking aspect of internationalisation. Maybe this phenomenon is linked with the withdrawal of British banks from the Commonwealth area.[10] Similarly, can American expansion be attributed to strategy, to favourable economic conditions – such as the creation of a Euro-currency market as a low cost means of mobilising international capital – or, indeed, to the diminishing possibilities for internal expansion?

In fact, all these questions come down to the problem of understanding the process by which the strategies of MNBs and governments are conceived. The attitude of the British in the aftermath of the First World War bears witness to this. Firstly, the exigencies of war – in this case the issue of Treasury Bills – had reduced the capacity of the MNB to contribute to the provision of short-term international credit; secondly, the banks and public authorities were obliged to take into account the fact that because of war debts, they were in a situation of financial dependence on the United States.

On the other hand, the international situation provided an ideal pretext for implementing deflationist policies and accelerating the formation of banking cartels as a defensive measure. In other words, between 1921 and 1925, the economic aims of the British MNB and of the government coincided: they were playing for time. But this strategy, while safeguarding some British 'preserves', accentuated the imbalance between the United States and Great Britain, to the extent that one wonders whether the confirmation of American supremacy was not accelerated by the acceptance of these economic policies. Such a return to financial orthodoxy seems to have brought about the international decline of the City for the very reason that this strategy did not correspond to the true position of the MNB. A somewhat comparable example might be found when studying American policy during the 1960s: the run for Euro-currency coincided both with the government's needs to finance the balance of payments deficit and the banks' search for new markets. But the epilogue was the reverse to the British one.

On a theoretical level, this observation implies that the principal indicators of international activity, the assets of the branches, the amount received in deposits and the size of the loans granted, were of greater importance than the form of the loans or the services offered by the banks, be they financial, commercial or industrial. But from 1919 onwards, the City and the British MNB exported their know-how to a greater extent than their capital. True, orthodox economic policies which favoured the outflow of capital, but not its investment in industry, were designed to combat the decrease in international opportunities. But the initial mobilisation of the British MNB was insufficient to cope with the growing might of the Americans, and at the end of the 1960s, they were unable to take advantage of the transformation in the financial circuits that had resulted from new American monetary policies.

Two conclusions and two questions can therefore be put forward, subject to confirmation from further statistical evidence. The success of economic policy is directly correlated to the financial strength of the MNB; this strength is linked to industrial power and, in all events, there can never be equilibrium between multinational banks. So we may try and answer the first question: is there an explanation for the shift from a British domination to an American one? If we consider the four main parameters, military, industrial, monetary and banking, we can notice that the industrial one does not have a secondary role (see the US example) and that the monetary function is probably different from the banking one (see the Japanese or the British examples). From this point of view, the banking factor looks like the link between industrial and monetary parameters. Hence, because of the reciprocal character of these relations, the key role is played by banks, whereas their initial position is secondary. The second question deals with the specificity of the present crisis. Until 1978, attitudes were rather erratic and policies mixed up new legislation and deregulation (see President J. Carter's policy). But, from 1979 onwards, we may wonder if policies are not on the same path as those of the 1930s. The 'nationalisation' of Continental Illinois, new legislation on equities and the switch in monetary policy since the Mexico affair are indicating a strengthening of American banking policy at home. Is that reorganisation a prelude to a third American MNB boom, or to a new order? But are the American and the world situations still compatible?

NOTES

1 On this subject, see C. P. Kindleberger, *Multinational excursions* (Cambridge, Mass., 1984) and J. F. Hennart, *A theory of multinational enterprise* (Ann Arbor, 1982).
2 This implies favouring branches and subsidiaries, given that correspondents or agencies are not in a position to ensure sustained bank intervention in local industry.
3 Notice that British banks are either internationalised or multinationalised and that the American banks are only multinationalised.
4 Even the experience of City Corp. in the 1920s appears as a partial withdrawal. See for instance the competition between British and American banks in central Europe. The case of City Corp. illustrates rather the flexibility of financial capital and its geographical stability compared with the industrial one.
5 Cf. A. Rowley, *La Politique économique du Gouvernement Britannique 1919–1924* Ph.D. thesis, Paris, 1981, pp. 156ff.
6 See W. Andreff and O. Pastré, 'La Genèse des banques multinationales et l'expansion du capital financier international', CEREM Seminar (Paris, CNRS, 1981).

7 Between 1960 and 1972, direct American investment grew from 3.8 to 15.4 billion dollars.
8 See D. F. Channon, *British banking strategy and the international challenge* (Macmillan, 1977).
9 W. Moore, 'International growth: challenge to U.S. banks', *The national banking review* (September 1936).
10 Today American and Japanese MNBs are the only ones with a world-wide network.

Part II

Government and multinationals

17 The hierarchical division of labour and the growth of British manufacturing multinationals: 1870–1939

STEPHEN NICHOLAS

Efficiency and the transaction cost model

Research into the historical development of the multinational enterprise (MNE) has focused almost exclusively on transactional cost approaches as the theoretical construct for studying the MNE. Historians of international business have borrowed extensively and uncritically from the new micro-institutional economists[1] who analysed the firm as a hierarchical alternative to market transacting. The foundation of the transaction cost approach was Coase's insight in 1937 that vertical integration (internalisation) attenuated transaction costs until the cost of organising an extra transaction within the firm became equal to the costs of carrying out the same transaction through exchange in the market. At the heart of the Coasean market-hierarchy choice is economic efficiency. However, the tendency has been to justify the efficiency of the hierarchical firm by the simple expedient of hypothesising high enough transaction costs in the market place and low enough costs of internal firm administration.[2] Making a similar criticism, Oliver Williamson[3] admitted that the Coasean model tended to be tautological and that the transaction costs of markets and firms had not been operationalised, nor was it obvious how they could be. Economists have been forced to argue that if a market or firm exists, it must be optimal, and if it does not exist, that is because it would have been too costly. Efficiency is assumed and the validity of the assumption is not amenable to analytical proof.[4] Further, the Coasean market-hierarchy paradigm is static. It fails to explain the transition from one mode (internal or external) to the other.[5] At the same time the dichotomy between firm and market is too narrow; firms are not islands of planned co-ordination in a sea of market relations but co-operate through contracts with other firms.[6]

In response to these shortcomings, economists[7] have developed an alternative institutional approach focusing on a range of discrete contractual forms, including markets, intermediate modes (long-term supply contracts, franchises, licences and agents) and the hierarchical firm, which attenuate transaction costs. Intermediate modes are clearly differentiated from both allocation by the price-market system and allocation by fiat in the hierarchical firm. Market contracting through the price system does not involve the promise of future conduct and is subject to potential risks of price changes, supply availability, demand shortfall and depreciated quality of service. The firm is a mode of transacting in which an employment relation binds employees to follow the directions of management within limits. Intermediate modes are contracts between independent firms involving assurances of future conduct relating to price, quality and quantity of intermediate or final goods and services.

By a differentiation between the *reasons* firms transact from the *form* (market, intermediate mode or hierarchy) of transacting the alternative institutional approach was shown to be dynamic.[8] MNEs transact abroad to transfer property rights in goods and services and to gain quasi-rent from firm-specific assets, most importantly knowledge related to technology. The form of transacting depends on the relative cost of each alternative mode. Within the firm, Williamson[9] has emphasised the costs of bounded rationality and opportunism. Given uncertainty, bounded rationality is human behaviour that is 'intendedly rational but only limitedly so', that is, bounded rationality recognises the cost of human knowledge, information storage and language limits inside the hierarchical firm. When choosing the market there are costs of search and negotiation and the costs of contract preparation and enforcement. Most importantly, there are costs due to the loss of any potential quasi-rent on firm-specific knowledge not appropriated in a pure price-market exchange. Intermediate modes involve costs dependent on the frequency of transactions, the nature of transactions and opportunism.[10]

Alternative institutions, including exporting, agents, franchises and sales branches, have always formed part of the historian's description of the growth stages in international involvement by American and European firms.[11] It was hoped, that through an analysis of the contracts for agents within the transaction cost framework, the transition between agents and the hierarchical firm could be explained and not simply described.[12] After the detailed study of contracts between British MNEs and independent agents[13] the transaction cost functions could not be specified in a fashion which allowed the determination of the *actual* costs of alternative institutional arrangements to be compared.[14] Opportunism and bounded rationality in the presence of frequent transacting and idiosyncratic investments were common to all non-market modes including agents and the firm. The choice (existence) of one mode required the assumption that all other modes were less efficient in attenuating transaction costs. Mode choice was not explained but assumed away. At best, the very detailed work on agency contracts identified unmeasurable transaction cost factors important in the choice of the most efficient form of international involvement by British MNEs.

This paper suggests an alternative approach to the transaction cost-efficiency explanation for British MNE growth after 1870. The MNE is defined as a mode of transacting characterised by an employment–authority relation between labour and capital. The employment–authority relation is a form of relational contracting in which capital and labour have unequal bargaining power. Given unequal power, capital extracts work from labour through the hierarchical division of labour. Relational contracting recognises that social as well as economic factors contribute to the hierarchical division of labour and that the division of labour has a distributive as well as an efficiency rationale.

The division of labour and relational contracting

While nurtured in the same Coasean tradition, Marxist historians of the MNE offer an alternative perspective on the growth of the international firm. Stephen Hymer's[15] early work forged the basis of mainline MNE theory, emphasising the costs of transacting in firm-specific assets through imperfect markets. Implicitly, the Marxist approach draws the same sharp distinction between the reasons firms transact abroad and the mode of transacting. Hymer's departure from mainline theory turned on the international division of labour.[16] Radically adapting Chandler's concept of internal firm administrative centralisation, Hymer distinguished a hierarchical division of labour between labour in developed central economies and labour in the world's peripheral, underdeveloped nations. According to Hymer, the MNEs caused the international division of labour by accumulating surplus capital in the central core at the expense of the developing periphery. The Marxist emphasis on the division of labour pointed to the omission by mainline business historians of the role of labour as an input into production. However, the Marxist concern with the division of labour between countries begs the prior question of the division of labour within the firm. Both Marxist and traditional business historians fail to analyse the essential nature of the MNE: the MNE is a transactional mode in which labour enters an employment contract with capital. The growth of the MNE involves the international hierarchical division of labour within the firm.

Defining an MNE in terms of the employment contract is consistent, but more general than the 'standard' definition of the MNE as a firm with production or sales facilities in two or more countries.[17] The employment contract definition of the MNE is the economic definition of a firm.[18] The sale or production facility definition proxies the employment definition since control or ownership of sales and production facilities is assumed to involve control over labour. Further, the sales or production facility definition facilitates the simple counting and size measurement of the MNE. Through the use of the economist's definition of 'the firm', the business historian's analysis of MNEs is directed in a new direction towards the employment contract.

Like all contracts, employment contracts are sets of promises by labour (employees) to follow, within limits, the instructions of capital (employers) for a wage payment. The employment contract not only formally delivers labour power but by implying the right of capital to extract labour (work) from labour power is the basis of the authority relation between capital and labour. Labour contracts are relational: they are dynamic, continuing economic and social relationships, modified for unforeseen events according to the relative bargaining power of the parties to the contract.[19] Relational contracting contrasts with neoclassical contract theory, according to which contracts are discrete, specifying behaviour for each independent firm for all known contingencies. Such contracts are presentiated: they attempt to bring all future behaviour into the present.[20] Since the breaking of contractual promises threatens the discrete contract, each firm seeks enforcement of the presentiated promises through the market[21] or in law. Neoclassical contract theory obscures the relational aspects of inter- and intra-firm contracting. Discreteness and presentiation ignore the day-to-day adjustments built into contractual relations between labour and capital to harmonise and preserve the agreement. Applying relational contracting to all institutional arrangements presents a contractual spectrum from relational contracting between independent firms, corresponding to intermediate modes, to the employment–authority relationship within the hierarchical MNE.

Ownership, control of labour and the firm

The agency system has been analysed as an institutional arrangement for transacting internationally between independent firms. The agency system involved both agents who worked exclusively for one firm and agents who sold non-competing products of several firms. Although this paper deals only with the former, an agent handling the non-competing products of several firms might be viewed as a part-time employee making much of the analysis for exclusive agents applicable to agents working for two or more principals. The transition from agency to sales branch attracted attention because the transition marked the dividing line between an intermediate mode and the hierarchical firm.[22] Such a view is misleading. For example, Marshall, the British agricultural machinery firm, signed a standard sole agency contract with Grarpel Hugo, Hungary, specifying stock levels, payment systems, termination conditions and commission (15% plus $2\frac{1}{2}\%$ for cash sales).[23] Marshall's contract was an employment relation: Hugo agreed to follow Marshall's instructions for selling machinery in return for a wage payment. Unlike some agency contracts, Marshall's agreement with Hugo specified that Marshall paid for the depot, the stock of goods, insurance and part of the show expenses. Gust Levin's 'agency' contract took the standard form, except that Gourock Rope, the British principal, paid the rent and insurance on a 'suitable' store.[24] Linen Thread paid the rent and other expenses of Robert Malcolm, their New Zealand 'agent', and the rent and all expenses of their Canadian agent and his travellers.[25] Fowler's contract to sell agricultural machinery with Gustov Toepffer included rent for an office and depot, payment of a Fowler-appointed bookkeeper and storekeeper, travelling expenses and wages for mechanics and engine drivers and all current expenses.[26]

Using the definition of ownership or control of sales and production facilities, each of these 'agencies' is a branch of the parent British firm. What appears to be a contract between two independent firms is the control by a British firm of a firm in another country. But ownership or control of physical assets is at best a simple proxy for identifying an MNE. For example, a firm which owns a sales office in a foreign country but rents it to a third party should not be classed as an MNE. Only when ownership or control of physical assets involves capital's control over labour and other inputs in production does a firm qualify as an MNE. Business historians have sought a sharp distinction between branch and agency by using a legal definition to describe an economic relationship. By searching behind the legal contract to exchange, one can analyse the economic and social control capital exercises over labour. When capital and labour enter into an employment–authority relation, economically, a single multinational firm exists, whether the legal arrangement is an agency or a branch.

An employment–authority relation differs from relational contracting between two independent firms as marriage differs from a casual encounter; but as does the formal marriage contract, the employment contract itself provides only limited information on the relationship between labour and capital. Basically, the employment contract makes labour power available for a wage and recognises the right of capital to control labour, within limits. Since the right to control an individual appears as power, the essence of the labour contract is the continuing power relationship between labour and capital. The power to extract work is the power to make another person do something he would not otherwise do.[27] Power of capital over labour in continuous relational contracting (bargaining) is the unique feature of the employment–authority relationship. Relational bargaining searches for joint policies and offers at least one party higher welfare without reducing the other party's welfare.[28] Joint policies can be forced on labour by capital. Of course, joint policies offering higher welfare are also obtained by co-operation between labour and capital, making co-operation a major ingredient in relational contracting. But conflict and force are more dominant elements in the bargaining process. For example, different expectations concerning the bargain or different reactions to external changes which impact on the original bargain turn co-operation into conflict. More importantly, the relative power between labour and capital in relational bargaining determines distributional shares, where gains for one party come at the expense of the other party. Since gains to one party are losses to the other party, conflict is the essential characteristic of distributional struggles. Capital is likely to have more complete information (although not perfect information) than labour, giving employers greater tactical power in bargaining over distributional gains. The fact that the employment contracts give capital the general right to control labour is the best indication of capital's power over labour.

Since continuing bargaining is based largely on power, relational contracting may involve no or absolute control of capital over labour. When capital controls labour, workers are the firm's employees, subject to an employment–authority relation. When there is no control over labour, there is relational contracting between economically independent firms. Relational bargaining which defines an employment–authority relation is reflected in the firm's letter books, directors' minutes and reports, not simply in the formal legal contract between agent and principal.

Control, power and bureaucratic work processes

The employment contract involved implicitly (and sometimes explicitly) the promise by the agent to devote energy to working a sales area, including the direction of his own employees. Since the performance of a labour service like selling is more difficult to monitor than the physical output of labour, a more detailed than usual employment contract was drawn. The contract involved a complex incentive payment scheme of discounts, salary and commission. Like the conflict over time versus piece payments in British and American domestic mining, building, iron, steel and engineering firms,[29] the payment scheme for British MNEs was an area of conflict between labour and capital. Conflict did not take a collective form because of the difficulties in organising collective action over shared grievances by spatially separated workers. As a result the agent's bargaining power over pay, discounts and commissions was greatly limited. Further, agents accepted the incentive payment scheme principle, limiting wage conflicts to the level rather than the type of payment. Discounts, commissions and salaries were the subject of relational contracting, with changes reflecting the need to clear stock and open new agencies as well as complaints about the level of payments with 'troublesome' employees.[30] Conflict also arose over the promptness of payments from sales. Principals encouraged prompt payments by offering a discount – usually $2\frac{1}{2}$–3% – for each payment and charging interest on unpaid debts. Employers discouraged their employees from taking orders from uncreditworthy customers by forcing agents to share the loss from customers' bad debts.[31] These procedures, either written as rules into the employment contract or the outcome of relational contracting, made the work process bureaucratic.

Bureaucratic work processes necessarily involve hierarchy, with some people giving orders to others.[32] The development of bureaucratic procedures including information on sales, standardised bookkeeping practices, and regular written reports were methods for assessing worker performance.[33] They correspond to many of the bureaucratic work rules introduced into British and American industry during the period of 'scientific management'.[34] Rules reduced the probabilities of disputes over the timing of payment or the working of a sales area. When disputes did arise they were first tackled, and frequently settled, by bargaining through the regular correspondence between the employer and his agent.[35] While these formal indirect monitoring procedures economise on the cost of extracting work from labour, all employment–authority relations required the direct monitoring and supervision of work. Capitalists visited their employees, or deputised travellers from home to do so, to solve specific problems. For example, in 1905 Osborn, a specialised finished steel producer, corresponded with B. M. Jones, their American employees, to reduce their outstanding debt of £23,000. When the next six months witnessed the dispatch of goods valued at £11,000, but payments of only £9,600, a director's investigation resulted.[36] While visits to solve specific problems were not uncommon, most firms employed home travellers or a director to visit agents regularly in order to supervise and monitor the work intensity of their employees.[37] Supervision and monitoring were methods of extracting work from labour and the intensity of working the sales area became the major area of conflict between labour and capital.

Employers exhorted their employees to sell more through working harder, but agents argued that competitors had better products, lower prices and faster delivery.[38] Cowan,[39] the paper maker, rejected such excuses, insisting that a renewed effort by their Dublin employee was the 'only means of continuing the Agency in your hands'! Threat of employment termination was frequently used but rarely carried out, since the breakdown of the employment relation marks the failure of relational contracting. Rather than relying on the explicit threat of employment termination, employers used their power to limit the independence of their employees. For example, principals insisted that their agents carried stock, usually on consignment but sometimes on a sale basis. The employer controlled stock levels, although contract-prescribed stock levels were frequently altered through relational contracting.[40] In most cases the employee was forced to pay some of the costs related to stock carrying, such as rent on showrooms and insurance. Many agents were required to hire warehousemen, stockmen and specialised mechanics either in the formal contract or through relational contracting. These specialised investments by the employee have been viewed as 'credible commitments' to exchange, bonding employee to employer to reduce opportunism.[41] Valueless outside the specific transaction, such investments are also 'hostages' forced upon the employee by the principal's reducing the employee's bargaining power with his employer. An agent who had invested in mechanics trained in the repair of one employer's machines or signs and advertising material for a specific product presented fewer contract renewal problems for the employer than an agent without similar investments. Even if all specialised investments furthered exchange, they simultaneously reduced the employee's bargaining power with his employer.

While most agency agreements were renewed, contract renewal time offered capital an opportunity for changes in the employment contract. For example, contract renewal allowed Marshall[42] to increase the stock level and move consignment stock after 12 months to a sales account for their Swedish agent, Johannes Dancelson. New conditions unfavourable to agents were more easily negotiated during contract renewal after agents had made transaction-specific investments. Although contracts were sometimes terminated mid-stream,[43] contract renewal was also the time when employment relations were usually terminated.[44]

While control and power over labour in agencies have been ignored, the employer's control over the branch has been seen as absolute. While economists have only recently turned to the study of administrative control mechanisms between branch and home office,[45] subsidiary-independent behaviour has been recognised for some time.[46] Before 1939 many British sales branches exercised a high degree of autonomy, partly in default of any effective internal administrative, financial and policy structure for exercising control centrally.[47] For example, Rowntree-Mackintosh and Crosse and Blackwell branches were given a long and loose rein, delivering an annual report and only subject to an occasional visit from home.[48] The engineering firm Harvey experienced problems over stock and payments with their South African manager, reminiscent of the most troublesome agents.[49] After months of correspondence including the charge that 'remittances have gone out of fashion', and that 'our engineering department is replying to your usual batch of denunciations', Harvey ordered their manager home in July 1892 only to have him delay his visit until December. Fowler[50] complained that their Indian branch organised insufficient canvassing and travelling, treated 'the natives' badly and kept poor records. Although the firm were well aware of these problems, things were 'let go at present' because of a prospective visit to India by a Fowler director in 1911. Gourock[51] found J. C. McCall, their Sydney manager, a 'man who wants his own way' and 'difficult to guide'. Therefore, control over sales branches could be strictly limited or absolute depending on capital's control over labour. Many agencies were more tightly controlled than sales branches and should be analysed as part of the MNE.

The hierarchical division of labour and the growth of the MNE

Although some contracts specified wages and tasks for specialised labour within the agency, most formal employment contracts were arrangements between the employer and the agency head. All contracts to sell the principal's goods treated the agent as a subcontractor, directing and supervising other workers. Subcontracting is not inconsistent with 'the firm' or an employment–authority relationship. Subcontracting, for example, was widespread in domestic firms. In Britain, the little-butty men in mining,[52] the minder-piecer system in textiles[53] and the piece system in engineering, iron and steel were organised along subcontract lines before 1900. So were most American iron and steel, small arms and engineering firms, where the subcontractor hired, paid and discharged his own men, kept track of the hours they worked, and determined their work, rates of pay and training.[54] Singer, the Whitin Machine Works and Winchester were all 'firms', although all three had a subcontract labour system before 1890.[55]

The agent as a subcontractor of labour was a central factor in the MNE choice of agent. When considering an agency in Australia, Linen Thread[56] required the agent to operate staff, travellers, depot, stock and showrooms in Sydney, Melbourne, Brisbane and Wellington and showrooms in Adelaide. The agent was expected to supervise labour for the capitalist, even when the labour was paid by the MNE. For example, mechanics and technicians appointed by the principal were nominally under the control of the MNE but in practice were controlled and directed by the agent. Bookkeepers, stockmen and warehousemen hired by the MNE were explicitly under the control of the agent. Agents were non-commissioned officers for the capitalist, extracting work from other workers. But agents were also workers. The agents' supervisory role did not make them equal partners with capital.[57] For example, Gourock[58] explicitly required their Sydney manager to be a salesman. Agents occupied a social position inferior to their employer, reflecting the agent's inferior power relative to his employer. Agents were privileged workers who sold their employer's products. There was a class dimension to the agency system with social factors broadening the mere economic relations. The class dimension spread upwards and downwards from the agent since he held a social position both as employer and employee. Some MNEs exercised control through social criteria for hiring agents, including marriage, religion and family background.[59] Sometimes agents formed close social relationships with their employers, as did Joseph Leete with Sir Walter Palmer. While Leete's[60] two-volume typescript history of Huntley and Palmers catalogued the regular social visits between Leete and Palmer, Leete travelled to Europe six months in every year selling biscuits, and after his death in 1913 it was Huntley and Palmers who wound up Leete Ltd.[61] The distribution of goods involved a social hierarchy ruled by social norms, which explains much of the smooth informal adjustments at the heart of relational contracting. The agent was a worker, although his supervisory functions meant he was a privileged worker.

When payment through-the-office ended subcontracting in domestic firms, the foreman retained control over hiring and work routines before 1914.[62] Similarly, the formation of the branch by the MNE brought payment through-the-office, but frequently involved little more than a change in name from agent to branch manager. Rather than the agent hiring, paying, allocating work, training, supervising and disciplining labour the branch manager now carried out these tasks. In many cases where the agency was 'taken-over' to form a branch, the agent became the branch manager. The agent, now designated branch manager, continued to supervise labour and to travel and sell the firm's products.[63] Further, branch managers' employment contracts were similar to those for agents, specifying a salary plus commission or percentage of net profit.[64]

The agency system divided labour into specialised tasks, creating a hierarchical economic organisation. For example, Cowan's 'agency' in Brisbane involved 16 staff, including a manager/agent, three town and two country travellers, motormen, warehousemen and storemen, office boys, clerks and typists.[65] Cowan's 'legal' sales branches in Sydney and Melbourne had an identical hierarchical structure to their Brisbane agents. The hiring of specialised mechanics and technicians for repair, servicing and demonstration of machinery and the employment of bookkeepers and warehousemen by the principal are examples of the MNE's ability to subdivide labour within an agency agreement. The provision of skilled mechanics did not always form part of the formal contract. Through relational contracting, the Glasgow engineering firm A. W. Smith[66] agreed to provide technicians for their Indian agents. The hierarchical organisational structures within the agency system were reflected in the salary structure. In South Africa, Gourock's[67] managers received £35.45 per month, travellers £28–33, storemen, £20–6, juniors, £10 and lady assistants, £7–11. Similar pay structures for managers, travellers, storemen, juniors and women applied to Linen Thread,[68] Gourock,[69] Blackie,[70] and Morton Sundour.[71] The hierarchical division of labour involved sex discrimination with women occupying the less skilled jobs of typist and clerk and receiving the least pay.

The growth of MNEs involved an increasing hierarchical division of labour internationally. Growth occurs by initiating hierarchical employment relations with labour in different countries and the further hierarchical division of labour within one country. When the further hierarchical division of labour takes the form of a production branch, the economic explanation can largely be understood in terms of a multiplant investment decision.[72] When MNE growth has taken the form of agency-sales branches, labour's subdivision occurs whenever capitalists organise separate labour tasks allowing workers to develop differential skills. The motivation for hierarchically subdividing labour is a mix of efficiency and power considerations. Employment–authority relations require a different concept of efficiency than simple technical efficiency. Unlike other inputs, labour inputs impose limits or a zone of acceptance on the orders and instructions of capital.[73] The relative bargaining power of labour and capital determines the limits of capital's orders and instructions. For example, employees' investment in transaction-specific investments, stock, and specialised staff widens the zone of acceptance by reducing labour's relative bargaining position. What might be an efficient employment relation for an employee without transaction-specific investments need not be an efficient arrangement for employees with such investments. Even if all institutional relations were arranged exclusively around efficiency criteria, power would determine the context for the efficacy of any arrangement.[74]

Second, the relative bargaining power which allows capital to subdivide labour determines the allocation of distributional shares. Depending on the zone of acceptance there are a range of possible wage rates for labour implying wage indeterminacy. Since only one of these rates can be equal to labour's marginal product, any rate within the zone of acceptance below labour's marginal revenue product 'exploits' labour. Unfortunately empirical obstacles to measuring the marginal product of labour prevent any standard being constructed with which to compare labour's actual wage. Rather than searching for an absolute measure of exploitation, exploitation is used here in a relative sense. Supervision, monitoring, bureaucratic work processes forcing labour to work harder for a constant wage, unchanging piece rate or fixed commission imply a relative deterioration in labour's distributional share. Labour was exploited in a relative sense when capitalists' work processes extracted more work with an unchanging wage reward. Increased work intensity at a fixed wage reflected the power of capital to make labour work harder than labour wanted. The parameters of labour exploitation await detailed case study analysis of work effort, capital's control of the work process and the payment system. What is clear is that the neoclassical price-auction model of labour markets is inconsistent with the historical evidence of relational contracting, power and distributional struggle between labour and capital.

Third, there were efficiency factors accounting for the employment–authority relation where capital hierarchically divided labour. For example, authority relations reduce opportunism if only as a side benefit from intensifying work through monitoring.

Conclusion

The legal definition of branch and agency disguises the true nature of the MNE – a firm with an international hierarchical division of labour. Gourock[75] in Chile and Fowler[76] in Germany did not 'register' branches because of legal constraints, but their agencies in both countries operated as branches. Of course, not all agencies involved employment–authority relations, and consequently agency and MNE were not identical. But a significant proportion of agents were employees of British capitalists. Economically these agencies have not been recognised as part of the British MNE, seriously underestimating British foreign direct investment before 1939. The identification of employment–authority relations requires archival research into the nature of relational contracting. If we use a database of 20 British MNEs, 15 sales or production branches had been formed by 1914, but so had 72 agencies with authority-based employment contracts. In 1939, the 20 firms had converted 30 agencies with employment–authority relations, either by take-over or replacement, into sales or production branches. Based on the 30 new branches formed from agencies after 1914, legal definitions of MNEs underestimated British overseas foreign direct investment before 1914 by two-thirds. If the figure of 72 agencies is taken, the reliance of legal branches underestimates British multinational activity by a factor of 6.

Besides underestimating the spread and growth of British pre-1939 MNE activity, the use of a legal definition of agency and branch has obscured the authority relation and the distributional issues which arise when capital has power over labour. In the determination of the mode of contracting, distributional factors have been ignored while the choice of contractual modes has been analysed exclusively in economising terms. But the economising approach is seriously flawed by the failure to specify the actual transaction-cost functions between modes requiring the efficacy of a particular mode to be assumed. Distributional struggles between labour and capital within British MNEs await detailed study, but the explicit introduction of power through employment–authority relations suggests that distributional struggles between labour and capital is a neglected issue in the choice of contractual mode. Power and distributional struggles are additional factors in mode choice and do not replace efficiency factors. For example, when capital extends the zone of acceptance through direct supervision or forcing employees to invest in idiosyncratic capital, supervision and idiosyncratic investments also increase efficiency by reducing opportunism. Therefore, the choice of mode is more complex than the transaction-cost approach allows. Economic and social power in labour–capital relations promises new perspectives on the historical growth of British multinational enterprise before 1939.

NOTES

1 O. Williamson, *Markets and hierarchies: analysis and antitrust implications* (New York, 1975); the same, 'Transaction-cost economics: the governance of contractual relations', *Journal of law and economics*, XXII (1979), 233–61; the same, 'The organisation of work', *Journal of economic behaviour and organisation*, I (1980), 5–38; the same, 'The modern corporation: origins, evolution, attributes', *Journal of economic literature*, XIX (1981), 1537–58; M. Casson, *Alternatives to the multinational enterprise* (London, 1979).

2 R. H. Coase, 'The nature of the firm', *Economica*, IV (1937); S. Cheung, 'The fable of the bees: an economic investigation', *Journal of law and economics*, XVIII (1973), 11–34; A. Alchian and H. Demsetz, 'Production information and economic organisation', *American economic review* LXII (1972), 777–95; C. J. Dahlman, 'The problem of externality', *Journal of law and economics*, XXII (1979), 141–62.

3 Williamson, 'The modern corporation', 1546.

4 See Dahlman.

5 A. K. Calvet, 'A synthesis of foreign direct investment theories and theories of the multinational firm', *Journal of international business studies*, XII (spring/summer 1981), 43–57.

6 G. B. Richardson, 'The organisation of industry', *Economic journal*, LXXXII (1972), 883–96.

7 Williamson, 'Transaction-cost economics'; the same, 'Credible commitments: using hostage to support exchange', *American economic review* (1983), 519–40; P. Buckley and M. Casson, 'The optimal timing on foreign direct investment', *Economic journal*, XCI (1981), 75–87; M. Casson, 'Transaction costs and the theory of the multinational enterprise', in A. Rugman (ed.), *New theories of the multinational enterprise* (London, 1982), pp. 24–43.

8 See Calvet.

9 Williamson, *Markets and hierarchies*, p. 137.

10 Williamson, 'Transaction-cost economics'; the same, 'Credible commitments'; B. Klein, 'Transaction cost determinants of "unfair" contractual arrangements', *American economic review*, XX (1980); M. C. Jensen and W. H. Meckling, 'The theory of the firm: managerial behaviour agency costs and ownership structure', *Journal of financial economics* (1976), 305–57; B. Klein and K. Leffler, 'The role of market forces in assuring contractual performance', *Journal of political economy* LXXXIX (1981); P. Rubin, 'The theory of the firm and the structure of the franchise contract', *Journal of law and economics*, XXI (1978), 223–33; B. Klein, R. Crawford and A. Alchian, 'Vertical integration, appropriable rents and the competitive contracting process', *Journal of law and economics*, XXI (1978); S. Nicholas, 'Agency contracts, institutional modes and the transition to foreign direct investment in British manufacturing before 1939', *Journal of economic history*, XLIII (1983); the same, 'Theory of the multinational enterprise as a transactional mode: pre-1939 British overseas investment', in P. Hettner and G. Jones (eds.), *Multinationals: theory and history* (London, forthcoming).

11 M. Wilkins, *The emergence of multinational enterprise* (Cambridge, Mass., 1970); the same, *The maturing of multinational enterprise* (Cambridge, Mass., 1974); I. Johansen and Jan-Eric Vahlne, 'The internationalisation process of the firm: a model of knowledge development and increasing foreign market commitments', *Journal of international business studies*, VIII (1977); S. Nicholas, 'British multinational investment before 1939', *Journal of European economic history*, XI (1982),

606–30; Peter Buckley and B. Roberts, *European direct investment in the U.S.A. before World War I* (London, 1982).

12 Nicholas, 'Agency contracts'; the same, 'Theory of the multinational enterprise'.

13 *Ibid.*

14 Williamson, 'Transaction-cost economics', 254; M. Casson, in Hertner and Jones (eds.), *Multinationals: theory and history*.

15 Stephen Hymer, *The international operations of national firms: a study of direct foreign investment* (Farnborough, 1976).

16 Stephen Hymer, 'The efficiency (contradictions) of multinational corporations', *American economic review* (1970), 441–8; the same, 'The multinational corporation and the law of uneven development', in H. Radice (ed.), *International firms and modern imperialism* (Harmondsworth, 1975), 37–62.

17 United Nations, *The impact of multinational corporations on development and on international relations*, E.74 II A5 (New York, 1974), p. 255; United Nations, *Transnational corporations in world development: a re-examination*, E.78 II A5 (New York, 1978); John Dunning, *International production and the multinational enterprise* (London, 1981).

18 Coase, 'The nature of the firm'; Williamson, *Markets and hierarchies*, p. 4; the same, 'Transaction-cost economics', p. 250; Rubin, p. 223; S. Cheung, 'The contractual nature of the firm', *Journal of law and economics*, XXVI (1983); H. Malmgren, 'Information, expectations, and the theory of the firm', *Quarterly journal of economics*, LXXV (1961), 399–421.

19 I. R. MacNeil, 'The many features of contracts', *Southern California law review*, XLVII (1974), 691–816; the same, 'Contracts: adjustment of long term economic relations under classical, neoclassical and relational contract law', *Northwestern University law review*, LXXII (1978), 854–905.

20 MacNeil, 'The many features of contracts', p. 197.

21 See Klein and Leffler.

22 Nicholas, 'Agency contracts'.

23 Marshall, *Agency term book no. 1* (1884), pp. 235–7, Institute of Agricultural History, University of Reading.

24 Gourock, *Agency agreements*, 1/8/1914.UGD42/103/3, University of Glasgow Archives.

25 Linen Thread, *Minute Book* (1898), pp. 366–7, 380–5, UGD143/7/1, University of Glasgow Archives.

26 Fowler, *Toepffer agreement*, Col/9. Institute of Agricultural History, University of Reading.

27 M. Casson, *The entrepreneur* (Oxford, 1982), p. 248.

28 *Ibid.*, pp. 272–5.

29 D. F. Schloss, *The methods of industrial remuneration* (London, 1892), pp. 11–120; J. Jefferys, *The story of the engineers 1800–1945* (London, 1945), pp. 63–210; D. Clawson, *Bureaucracy and the labour process*, (New York, 1980), pp. 167–250.

30 Nicholas, 'Agency contracts', 680; Marshall, *Agency term book no. 1*, pp. 183–4; Cowan, *Private letter book*, 12/1902.UGD311/2/17, University of Glasgow Archives; Ransomes, *Agency term book no.* 1881/7, Institute of Agricultural History, Reading University.

31 Nicholas, 'Agency Contracts', 682–3.

32 Clawson, p. 16.

33 Nicholas, 'Agency Contracts'.

34 C. R. Littler, *The development of the labour process in capitalist societies* (London, 1983); H. Braverman, *Labour and monopoly capital* (New York, 1974).

35 Cowan, *Report: India, 1936* (October 1936), UGD311/7/34, University of Glasgow Archives.
36 Osborn, *Letter book*, Osb.17, pp. 222–30, 357, 421, Sheffield Public Library Archives.
37 Nicholas, 'Agency Contracts', 682.
38 Ransomes, *Agency book*, 14/3/84, 26/6/84.
39 Cowan, *Private letter book*, 23/8/1903.
40 Marshall, *Agency term book no.* 1, pp. 165–8, 283.
41 Nicholas, 'Agency Contracts'; Williamson, 'Credible commitments'; Klein, 'Transaction cost determinants'.
42 Marshall, *Agency term book no.* 2 (1880–1900), pp. 165–280.
43 *Ibid.* (1883), p. 31.
44 Nicholas, 'Agency Contracts', 683.
45 Yves Doz, 'Strategic management in multinational companies', *Sloan management review*, XXII (Winter 1980), 27–45; Yves Doz and C. K. Prahalad, 'Headquarters influence and strategic control in MNCs', *Sloan management review*, XXIII (fall 1981), 15–29.
46 J. Stopford and L. T. Wells, *Managing the multinational enterprise: organisation of the firm and ownership of the subsidiaries* (London, 1972); T. Parry, 'Internalisation as a general theory of foreign direct investment: a critique' (mimeo, Australian National University (1984), pp. 10–11.
47 Nicholas, 'Theory of multinational enterprise'.
48 D. Barron, 'The development and organisation of Rowntree Mackintosh Ltd.', *LSE seminar on the problems in industrial administration* no. 449 (1972/3), p. 2.
49 Harvey, *Letter/Book*, pp. 121–685, DD14/2/191, Cornwall County Record Office.
50 Fowler, *Branch reports*, AD6/9, October 1910, Institute of Agricultural History, Reading University.
51 Gourock, *Australia branch*, 11/7/31.
52 C. Fisher, *Custom work and market capitalism* (London, 1981).
53 W. Lazonick, 'Industrial relations and technical change: the case of the self-acting mule', *Cambridge journal of economics*, III (1979); the same, 'Production relations, labour productivity and choice of technique: British and U.S. cotton spinning', *Journal of economic history*, XLI (1981).
54 Clawson, pp. 71–2.
55 *Ibid.*, pp. 71–110.
56 Linen Thread, *Minute book* (1898), p. 226.
57 J. Foster, *Class struggle in the Industrial Revolution* (London, 1974), p. 237; K. Stone, 'The origin of job structure in the steel industry', *Review of radical political economics*, VI (1974), 116–18; D. Montgomery, 'The new unionism and the transformation of workers' consciousness in America, 1909–1922', *Journal of social history* (1974), 4.
58 Gourock, *Australia*, 11/7/1938.
59 Peek Frean, *Agency agreements*, PF26/1, University of Reading Library Archives.
60 J. Leete, *The history of Huntley and Palmers' trade upon the continent of Europe* (unpublished manuscript, 1912).
61 T. A. B. Corley, *Quaker enterprise in biscuits: Huntley and Palmers of Reading 1822–1912* (London, 1972), p. 217.
62 Clawson, pp. 125–40.
63 Nicholas, 'Agency Contracts', p. 685.
64 Morton, *USA*, 7/11/1938, UGD326/303/2, University of Glasgow Archives.

65 Cowan, *Australia, 1936*, UGD311/7/34, University of Glasgow Archives.
66 Smith, *Minute book*, 29/1/09, 23/4/09, UGD118/13/1, University of Glasgow Archives.
67 Gourock, *Report: South Africa*, 1918, UG42/102/2, University of Glasgow Archives.
68 Linen Thread, *Minute book* (1898), p. 265.
69 Gourock, *Australia*.
70 Blackie, *Bombay branch*, UGD61/37/2, University of Glasgow Archives.
71 Morton Sundour, *U.S. and Canada*, UGD326/303/2, 326/321/1, University of Glasgow Archives.
72 Nicholas, 'Theory of the multinational enterprise'.
73 J. March and H. Simon, *Organisations* (New York, 1958), pp. 89–91; Williamson, 'The organisation of work', p. 17.
74 V. Goldberg, 'Bridges over contested terrain', *Journal of economic behaviour and organisation*, I (1980), p. 268.
75 Gourock, *Letter book*, 10/12/03, D42/103/3, University of Glasgow Archives.
76 Fowler, *Agency records* (1892).

18 Foreign oil companies, oil workers, and the Mexican Revolutionary State in the 1920s

JONATHAN C. BROWN*

The social impact of multinational investment in the Third World is a neglected area of research. A labor history of the Mexican oil industry between 1901 and 1938 would be especially instructive, given the role that oil workers played in the nationalization of the foreign petroleum companies. Based upon the author's research in company files, diplomatic records, and Mexican government documents, this paper seeks to explain the internal dynamic of labor militancy over a period of three decades. The world marketplace, the presence of privileged foreigners, the revolutionary ethos, and domestic politics all played a role in the lives of oil workers.

The relationship between the oil worker and his foreign employer centered upon their conflicting expectations. The laborer sought the security of working for a powerful patron, while foreign oilmen, beset by the vagaries of markets and competition, desired a strictly economic relationship with labor. Despite having its own disagreements with the foreign companies, the Mexican government does not appear to have been the motive force in the organization of the petroleum workers. Revolutionary ideology did indeed stimulate the petroleum workers' movement, which politicians eagerly assisted, but the state neither controlled the formation of unions nor did it 'coopt' them.[1]

Nonetheless, the scholar must distinguish between labor leaders and the workers themselves. This paper proposes that the leaders of the Mexican oil workers, playing out the competitive process of unionization, sought a class alliance with the governing elites and in 1938 literally forced the Revolutionary State to expropriate the oil companies. It appears that labor leaders intended that their unions guarantee the security of their members and be the great patron that the foreign employers had refused to become.

The conflict of expectations

At the turn of the century, Mexico attracted the interest of American and British oil producers because of the growing importance of Mexico's internal

257

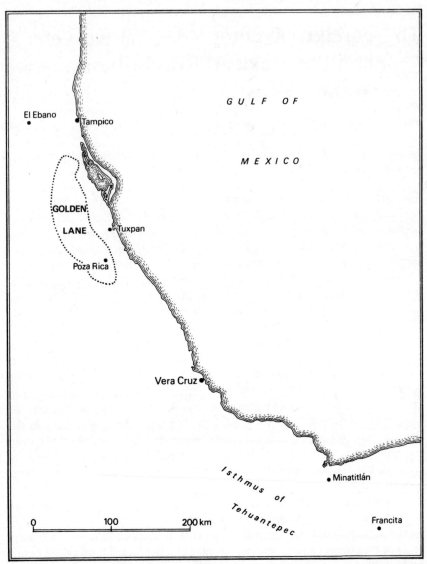

Figure 18.1 The Mexican oil zone in the 1930s (one inch equals approximately 70 miles)

market for petroleum products and because of its proximity as an exporter to markets in the United States. Two independent producers, Edward L. Doheny of Los Angeles and Sir Weetman Pearson (in 1911, Lord Cowdray) of London, brought in the first Mexican production, mainly in the Gulf state of Vera Cruz.[2] Doheny's Huasteca company worked the fields west of the port of Tampico, and Sir Weetman's El Aguila (the Eagle) explored the Isthmus of Tehuantepec. Between 1910 and 1919, these two companies led numerous other foreign interests into the famed Golden Lane near Tuxpan (see Figure 18.1). By the end of the First World War, Mexico was second only to the United States as the world's largest producer of crude oil.

Those foreign concerns operating in the Mexican oil industry were among the most technologically innovative industrial institutions in the world. The very survival of companies like El Aguila and Huasteca depended upon markets for their production and consequently upon volatile international prices. Rising oil prices throughout the First World War promoted rapid growth of these pioneer companies in Mexico and attracted powerful competitors such as Standard Oil New Jersey, Gulf, the Texas Company, and Royal Dutch Shell. But collapse of the prices after 1920 squeezed those companies without market outlets in the United States and Europe. The lack of sales assets abroad soon led Lord Cowdray to sell El Aguila to Shell. Doheny's Huasteca was absorbed by Indiana Standard, which subsequently sold the company to Jersey Standard.[3]

If the world of the foreign oil companies was competitive and industrially advanced, their Mexican workers had strong agrarian traditions. The oil zone itself was located in tropical regions of relatively scant settlement. Foreign oil pioneers therefore resorted to the traditional system of *enganche* in which Mexican labor contractors traveled to the populous highlands to entice workers with cash advances. Agricultural peons, accustomed to making 25 to 50 centavos a day, received promises of one to three pesos working for foreign oil companies.[4] Those who served as carpenters, boiler and metal workers, and mechanics undoubtedly had prior experience in foreign-owned railways and mining and smelting operations. Both skilled and unskilled laborers were available during the growth period of the oil industry because the Revolution from 1911 to 1920 had dislocated other economic sectors in Mexico.[5] All new workers in the expanding oil industry labored at the pleasure of the employers under individual and verbal contracts.

The differential nature of work and workers within the industry in part explains the subsequent labor history of the oil zone. The refinery town of Tampico and surrounding oil districts drew so many migrants that refinery operators early dispensed with *enganche*. Workers came to Tampico from the highland states to the east and west of Mexico City and from the northern states.[6] Because four large refineries dominated the industry here, wages and living conditions in Tampico tended to be superior to those found elsewhere in the oil zone. On the Isthmus of Tehuantepec, *enganche* made up for the scarcity of resident workers in the isolated, tropical environment. El Aguila established a refinery at Minatitlán, although the low productivity of the surrounding oilfields prevented the growth of refining experienced at Tampico. Wages tended to be lower on the Isthmus, and living conditions, particularly in the field camps, were primitive. Cities of migrants and skilled refinery workers, both Tampico and Minatitlán became hotbeds of labor militancy.

In the Golden Lane near Tuxpan, one found more resident laborers, be they agriculturalists, cattlemen, or peons on large haciendas. The agrarian social order endured, and labor militants were unwelcome. Here the armed watchmen of the oil camps became known as *guardias blancas* (white guards) for their arrogance and bullying tactics.[7] During the Revolution, the Tuxpan area spawned a reactionary movement led by General Manuel Peláez, on whose land El Aguila had drilling leases. Peláez was something of a mixed blessing for the oil companies. While the General said he defended their rights, he also extorted money from the companies to support his troops and yet proved unable to prevent opposing revolutionary forces from entering the oil camps.[8] Subsequent labor organization in the Tuxpan area came late and largely at the instigation of stronger Tampico unions.

In addition, a secondary industry developed in the oil zone to provide drilling and construction services. North American and Mexican contractors built pipelines, pump houses, oil camps, storage tanks, and provided American drillers and well riggers. For the Mexicans, work in the contracting industry was temporary, lasting until completion of specific projects.[9] Nevertheless, the metal workers and carpenters succeeded in organizing the contractors at about the same time that their skilled brethren were unionizing the refineries.

Initially, Mexican laborers in the petroleum industry may have enjoyed benefits not available elsewhere in the labor market. At the height of the industry in 1921, foreign oilmen employed more than 44,000 Mexicans (exclusive of Mexican clerks) and an additional 1,300 foreign workers.[10] Together with clerks and those Mexicans depending upon employment with contractors, the native work force in the industry may have approached 55,000. Wages tended to increase during the growth period of the industry, roughly from an average of one peso per day in 1910 to three pesos in 1920. Mobility also was possible, as in the case of one Rafael Guzmán, who in 1918 went to work for El Aguila as a tool guard at $96 (pesos) monthly and in 1925 was appointed foreman of 400 men loading barges at $400 per month.[11] Even so, the migrant labor force showed a more rapid turnover than oilmen desired. 'Of course, when we get [labour], it must be made comfortable', wrote the superintendent of Sir Weetman's nascent oil interests. 'The mere fact of getting it and not looking after it when it is got is, I fear, what we are suffering from to some extent.'[12]

Without doubt, early labor relations were such as to create much loyalty among the workers. Mexicans assumed control and operation of all the oil installations when American managers and workers abandoned the oil zone in 1914 because of the US invasion of the port of Vera Cruz and again in 1916 because of the intervention of Gen. John J. Pershing in northern Mexico.

Upon returning to the oil zone in 1914 one astonished foreign manager wrote: 'I believe... that full reports on the situation will indicate conclusively that the unexpected loyalty and initiative of the Mexicans left in charge was a very material factor in preventing what we all feared and dreaded, serious overflows, resulting in fire.'[13] Obviously, the Mexicans took seriously the customary obligations contained in the agrarian-based patron–client relationship: the worker traded dependence and loyalty for the security of working in the employ of a powerful and wealthy patron.

The paternalistic nature of capital–labor relations, such as they were, could withstand neither the extraordinary political turmoil of the Mexican Revolution nor economic retrenchment in the oil industry. Both events exacerbated the differences in expectations between workers who wanted security and oilmen who desired to be economically competitive.

Crises and decline of Mexican oil

The dynamic of labor organization in Mexico's oil industry owes much to the condition of work itself and to the decline of the industry after 1921. Workers encountered an environment of insecurity. In addition to individual and verbal contracts, oil workers contended with the danger of accident and sickness, with the differences in living conditions between the fields and the refineries, with revolutionary turmoil and cost-of-living rises, and with their problematic relationship with foreigners.

Work in the oil industry could be dangerous. Tropical diseases were endemic to oil camps, particularly in the early days, as malaria, dysentery, and even bubonic plague afflicted the worker and his family. The oil companies established hospitals in the larger camps and refinery towns, but those who worked in isolated oilfields or for contractors had little access to such facilities. Accidents around the heavy equipment were common, and explosions and fires proved to be ever-present hazards.[14] Through government and union pressure, safety and medical conditions improved over time. Yet no worker was completely secure in his job and livelihood, and families of incapacitated workers very soon had to vacate company houses.

Housing also seemed to be a problem even for healthy workers. In Tampico, the refinery compounds had well-constructed dwellings, electricity, sanitary facilities, recreational sites, and schools. Transportation and rental housing was at hand for those without company facilities, and commissaries and dining halls were hygienic and affordable.[15] Material conditions in the oilfields suffered by comparison. The worker *barrio* in the oldest oilfield, El Ebano, was congested and unserviced by electricity and potable water. The lack of 'servicio de excusados' necessitated that workers and families excused themselves at the outskirts of the camp.[16] Conditions in the relatively unproductive fields in the Isthmus of Tehuantepec were much the same.

Bigger and more productive fields had superior facilities, as did the new camp at Poza Rica which, after opening in 1932, still grew beyond the capacity of El Aguila to furnish adequate housing and school facilities.[17]

That the material conditions even in the most isolated and unproductive oilfields may have been better than those available in other industries soon was forgotten by Mexican workers who every day confronted the privileges of foreign workers. Foreign managers, drillers, foremen, and skilled workers were usually paid twice as much as the Mexican. Natives who served as *empleados* (clerks) received only $250 pesos per month, while North American and British clerks received $400 to $500.[18] Companies maintained that foreign workers were more skilled and had greater responsibilities; yet as time passed, such arguments held less currency with Mexican workers. Most evident were the living quarters of foreign workers. In one of the worst camps, at the Francita oilfield on the Isthmus, workers built their own thatched-roof huts on a lowland. Meanwhile, foreign workers inhabited company-constructed, hillside dwellings with corrugated roofing, timber floors, screened windows and doors, and covered porches. Francita camp became known to El Aguila managers for its 'communist' organizers.[19] Undoubtedly, the Mexican oil industry needed foreign technicians; El Aguila managers wrote that technology changed so rapidly that the endless adjustments to equipment retarded the training of native staff.[20] Nonetheless, the Mexicans soon felt embittered at the prejudices inherent in their treatment by foreigners. As one worker noted, 'all the Americans, principally the contractors and also the employees of all the petroleum companies, exercise an enemy-making pressure [*presión enemistosa*] over us Mexicans; while the companies give us no security, [the foreigners] have all the security from the companies and they control the best jobs and the best salaries...'.[21]

Mexican salaries for a time may have been high, but the revolutionary deterioration of the domestic economy eroded this advantage, marking the first crisis in the material conditions of the Mexican worker. Beginning in 1914, the depredations of armed bands unsettled both farmers and oil workers. The British consul at Tampico, upon riding through the previously productive fields west of Tuxpan in 1916, noted the absence of agriculturalists and the abundance of overgrowth. As banditry and looting became widespread in the oil zone, prices of foodstuffs rose sharply at the same time that the value of the paper peso deteriorated.[22] Labor unrest forced the companies to pay workers in American dollars and Mexican silver and to increase commissary and mess hall services – but with reluctance, for oilmen did not want to appear to give in to workers' pay demands. 'Even with these facilities and selling [commissary goods] at cost', wrote El Aguila's superintendent, 'a 10% increase will hardly be sufficient to bring wages into line with the increased cost of living.'[23] The conditions of insecurity were to become even more apparent to native workers.

Table 18.1 *Production, prices, employment, and nominal wages in the foreign-owned petroleum industry of Mexico, 1913–37*

Production in thousands of barrels	US price per barrel	Year	No. of Mexican workers	Ave. nominal wages in pesos
25,696	$0.81	1913	5,000	1.25
87,073	$1.56	1917	10,000	n.a.
157,069	$3.08	1920	n.a.	n.a.
193,398	$1.73	1921	50,000	n.a.
44,688	$1.27	1929	n.a.	n.a.
38,172	$1.00	1934	n.a.	4.73
40,141	$0.97	1935	15,255	n.a.
46,401	$1.18	1937	n.a.	7.66

Sources: Production from American Petroleum Institute, *Petroleum: Facts and Figures*, 9th edn (New York, 1950), p. 444; average price of crude oil in the US from *ibid.*, p. 121; and work force and average wage from Archivo Histórico de Hacienda at the Archivo General de la Nación, México, Legajo 1866–157, fols. 47, 50, 1937, and Legajo 1859–133, fols. 653, 1937

A second major crisis, the combined result of geological, political, and market conditions, struck the Mexican oil industry in 1921. Company after company began to report its wells going to salt water, particularly in the Golden Lane. There began a downturn in Mexican production that was not reversed until El Aguila opened up Poza Rica in the thirties. Meanwhile, international prices also plummeted. Finally, President Obregón, having just come to power over an impoverished Mexican economy (and treasury), sought to increase taxes on the oil industry, an action that oil executives considered as a violation of their private contracts and their concessions with previous governments. In protest, the companies temporarily shut down in the summer of 1921 and laid off thousands of oil workers, most of whom were fortunate if they had received a week's severance pay. Unemployed workers poured into Tampico, requesting Federal officials to provide them with free transport back to the highlands. Some companies attempted to impose wage reductions on those workers who remained, and all expanded the use of contract labor.[24] Foreign oilmen continued to prune their permanent work force throughout the 1920s.

A third crisis afflicted the Mexican oil industry in the 1930s, when world depression dampened international petroleum markets. Once again, foreign companies showed losses on their books and resorted to lay-offs and reductions in pay. El Aguila's expansion into Poza Rica was facilitated only by an expansion of Mexico's domestic market, as the company constructed a pipeline to a new refinery in Mexico City.[25] Yet by 1935, only 15,255 workers and employees remained in the Mexican oil industry, one-third of the work force of 1921. The companies responded to falling prices and a production by laying off employees, even though the workers organized to resist and successfully to demand higher compensation (see Table 18.1).

Labor organization and strikes

Mexican oil workers, encouraged by the ideology of the Revolution, responded to insecurity within the industry by engaging in a two-decade cycle of organization. The three crises ultimately impelled workers to divert their clientelistic loyalties from company to union patrons. Their protests concerned issues of security, unequal material conditions throughout the oil zone, and the privileges of foreign employees. Workers began organizing at the trade level during the first crisis, at the refinery and company level following the 1921 crisis, and at the industry-wide level during the Depression until nearly all the unions in the industry had formed into one confederation. The competitive nature of this process, however, lent significance to the labor strike, that necessary political weapon of survival and consolidation. Those unions defeated in strikes were replaced, and their loyalist followers lost their jobs. Consequently, labor leaders sought political allies and government assistance not only against the companies but also against rival unions. The Mexican Revolutionary State mediated the competition between autonomous union groups, while competing politicians likewise sought alliances among rival labor leaders.

The first crisis in the Mexican oil industry, that of revolutionary upheaval and cost-of-living rises after 1914, resulted in a period of incipient class conflict. Skilled workers such as carpenters, mechanics, boiler workers, and boat crewmen formed trade unions within the oil industry. Few unskilled workers as yet seem to be involved in the organizations, nor was there much cooperation between politicians and unions. Labor agitators of this period subscribed to anarchist and syndicalist ideologies, called 'Bolshevism' by the companies, and they found assistance only from the more established railway, stevedore, and merchant marine unions.[26] A number of strikes broke out between 1916 and 1921 in which workers sought wage increases, union recognition, and an end to individual work contracts. The early strikes largely failed, because the companies responded, often with the blessing of local authorities, by increasing wages and firing the agitators.[27] At least the companies understood that paternalism in Mexico involved both reward and punishment.

The oil crisis of the 1920s as well as the political rise of Generals Obregón and Calles encouraged oil workers to perfect their organizations first at the installation and then at the company level. Refinery laborers at Tampico and Minatitlán amalgamated their existing trade groups and gradually incorporated the budding unions in the oilfields. The assistance of the Revolutionary State was helpful. Union leaders found that their demands had been embodied in the Constitution of 1917 and in numerous state laws, which recognized the rights of Labor to organize and to bargain collectively. These laws also codified the responsibilities of Capital to provide for the security and welfare of Labor.[28] In addition, the Revolutionary State expanded its labor bureaucracy in Tampico and Minatitlán and established numerous Federal Boards of Conciliation and Arbitration. Thereafter, Union leaders appealed directly to federal bureaucrats, to local and state officials, to supporting union organizations within the oil industry and in other industries, to governors, and inevitably to the President of Mexico. During the second crisis, the element of alliance between organized labor and the governing elites seems to have replaced class conflict.

Two national labor movements meanwhile were vying for influence among the nascent oil unions. The Regional Confederation of Mexican Laborers (CROM) reached a national hegemony in the mid twenties under the leadership of Luis Morones, political ally and cabinet secretary of President Calles. Its rise was attended by a plethora of strikes in the oil and other industries as CROM-affiliated unions struggled for worker loyalty and for political patronage.[29] CROM assisted in the organization of the Huasteca and El Aguila refineries, but many oil workers soon became alienated by CROM's corrupt tactics and broke with the national leadership. Rival unions affiliated to what became known as the Confederation of Mexican Workers (CTM), began to displace CROM unions during the return of former President Obregón in 1927 and 1928 (when he was assassinated) and during the political flux of the early depression years.[30] Strikes were as much a result of political and union rivalries as of genuine grievances against the companies.

By 1925, nevertheless, the unions had made important gains in the refineries and oilfields of the larger companies. Oilmen had recognized unions and signed collective contracts that guaranteed pay increases, fringe benefits, and indemnities for lay-offs, death, and disabilities. One union contract tended to be a copy of those previously gained by other unions.[31] The private contract had become a thing of the past – except on those occasions when a union lost a strike and disintegrated.

The role of the strike in the dynamic of organization is best illustrated by the case of the Huasteca union. Led by the refinery group at Tampico, the Huasteca union in 1925 had succeeded in incorporating most of the company's oilfields around Tuxpan into one company-wide organization. Concluding the strike, the Huasteca union signed a collective contract with the company that began the process of equalizing the pay, benefits, and material conditions at all the company's installations. The union did not consolidate its power without using strong-arm methods on its rivals. When competing workers killed a member of the majority union, the latter declared another strike, demanding that the company fired fourteen members of the rival group. Many workers did not support the second strike, and the government was unsympathetic. Both the strike and the union disintegrated after several months. The Huasteca company took advantage of the situation in order to economize, hiring non-union workers as permanent replacements and offering to rehire only one-third of the strikers.[32] While strikes were essential to the consolidation of a union's control over workers and to the mainten- ance of political alliances, a broken strike spelled doom to union patrons and their client workers.

The road to expropriation

Passage to the Federal Labor Law in 1934 and consolidation of political power by Lázaro Cárdenas made possible the final unification of various petroleum unions under the auspices of the CTM. A coalition led by the most powerful petroleum union, El Aguila's Tampico group, which had just organized the new Poza Rica field, eclipsed the CROM-affiliated groups in the oil zone. Decay of CROM's national leadership caused several refinery leaders at Minatitlán to switch their allegiance. Even Vicente Lombardo Toledano, the national leader of CTM, had once served as a CROM official.[33] In Mexico City, meanwhile, a number of strikes racked El Aguila's new refinery as rival unions struggled for supremacy. At first, the CROM unit won labor-department sponsored elections, but in 1934, the CTM union succeeded in mobilizing El Aguila's Mexican office workers and defeated its opponent in a successful strike.[34] By the mid 1930s CTM-affiliated oil unions had taken over most of the collective contracts in the industry.

Control of the labor marketplace had always been the underlying goal of union leaders. Competing leaders had strived unsuccessfully to exclude the clients of rival groups, while affiliated unions struggled even against each other to expand their *radio de acción* (area of control).[35] Both the Presidential Accord that settled the 1934 Minatitlán refinery strike and the Federal Labor Law of the same year recognized an 'exclusionary clause' that prevented companies from hiring workers without first considering the members of the majority union.[36] Exclusionary clauses provided the 'verticality' of control that some felt compelled to protest – for union leaders banned from jobs those workers who did not 'conform to their ideas'. Unions also attempted to force the companies to dismiss workers not favored by the leadership.[37] Now that labor leaders had the legal tools to control labor competition and to ensure their own longevity, foreign oilmen found that union consolidation had undermined company control of personnel.

The logical conclusion of some two decades of labor organization came in 1935, when the CTM unions amalgamated into the industry-wide Sindicato de Trabajadores Petroleros de la República Mexicana (STPRM). STPRM was composed of some 20 sections, each one a pre-existing union representing specific refineries, oilfields, companies, and contractors. Tampico's El Aguila group served as a catalyst of the amalgamation, reserving for itself the appellation of Section 1. In order to consolidate its power with a new collective contract, STPRM sections launched several strikes within the next two years, seeking to equalize pay and benefits throughout the industry. A problem arose. STPRM had to gain an industry-wide pact superior to any existing contract, meaning that smaller companies would have had to concede pay increases and fringe benefits in excess of those earned by the most privileged workers of Huasteca and El Aguila. These demands represented a financial burden that few of the companies could afford and still remain competitive. The government intervened, and STPRM leaders conferred with representatives of the foreign oilmen and of the labor department. Labor officials emphasized grievances likely to win popular support against the foreign companies. They demanded parity between Mexican and foreign workers, security for oil workers, union control of most personnel matters, and large pay rises. The minutes of the labor talks reveal that these veterans of labor organization, having learned the cost of failure, were moved to reject a number of company concessions as insufficient – an act that threw the conflict into the political arena.[38] Mexican politicians were understandably hesitant to support the foreign companies, so STPRM could afford to be as intransigent as the companies. The government's nationalization of the oil industry resolved the labor-induced conflict. When the companies in 1938 rejected even the Mexican Supreme Court's decision favoring the oil workers, President Cárdenas had little choice but to nationalize the industry.[39]

Consistently with the internal logic of its own formation, STPRM had to exploit its alliance with the state and win the industry-wide strike in order to assure its seigniorial survival. The petroleum union may have been prepared even to assume managerial control of the industry so that its client workers would be guaranteed the security that they had expected from a powerful patron. Working conditions peculiar to a foreign-owned industry in decline, the developing ideology of revolution, and domestic political competition all stimulated labor militancy in the petroleum companies. Labor leaders bargained amongst themselves as well as with the ruling elites in order to organize successfully. The strike decided the victors in the union movement. Far from being coopted by the Revolutionary State, the oil unions exercised an autonomous agenda and indeed forced the state ultimately to take control of the foreign companies. In this, the oil workers seemed to have responded to Mexican precepts of social organization – especially to the patron–client relationship – rather than to imported working-class ideologies. There is evidence to suggest that the labor leadership even imposed the patron–client relationship upon those who wished to continue working in the industry. Finally, the history of the native workers in the petroleum industry of Mexico

268   Jonathan C. Brown

illustrates that the presence of technologically advanced foreign companies
may create a situation of class alliance between labor leaders and the national
political elites.

NOTES

* Generous summer grants from the National Endowment for the Humanities and
  from the Graduate Research Institute of the University of Texas supported my
  research in Mexico. I wish to thank Lynore Brown and Ricardo Salvatore for their
  comments on earlier drafts of this article.
1 On the state's cooptation of organized labor, see N. Hamilton, *The limits of state
  autonomy: post-revolutionary Mexico* (Princeton, 1982), pp. 38, 95.
2 See G. Philip, *Oil and politics in Latin America: nationalist movements and state
  companies* (Cambridge, 1982), ch. 1; P. Calvert, *The Mexican Revolution,
  1910–1914: the diplomacy of Anglo-American conflict* (Cambridge, 1969); and
  L. Meyer, *Mexico and the United States in the oil controversy, 1916–1942* (Austin,
  1977).
3 J. C. Brown, 'Foreign oil companies and the shift from Mexico to Venezuela',
  American historical review, vol. XC, no. 2 (April 1985); and M. Wilkins, *The
  maturing of multinational enterprise: American business abroad from 1914 to 1970*
  (Cambridge, Mass., 1974).
4 J. Silva Herzog, *El petróleo de México* (México, 1940), p. 5.
5 See J. Womack, jr., 'The Mexican economy during the Revolution, 1910–1920',
  Marxist perspectives, I, no. 4 (winter 1978).
6 Departamento de Trabajo at the Archivo General de la Nación, México, Caja 326,
  Expediente 4 (hereafter cited as DT, C. 326, E. 4), Araujo to Chief, 17 March 1922.
7 *Ibid.*, C. 220, E. 6, fol. 91, 18 September 1920; and Papeles Presidentiales, Fondo
  Presidentes Obregón y Calles at the Archivo General de la Nación, México
  (hereafter cited as Fondo Obregón-Calles), 104–P1–C, 26 May 1984, 8 August
  1923.
8 See H. Fowler Salamini, 'Caciquismo and the Mexican Revolution: the case of
  Manuel Peláez', unp. MS (September 1981).
9 DT, C. 36, E. 15, fol. 8, 23 March 1925, and C. 728, E. 3, fols. 39–40, 89, 127,
  135, 286, 406, 1925.
10 Foreign Office Records at the Public Record Office, London (hereafter cited as
  FO), 371–2702, fol. 142126, 13 June 1916; and DT, C. 329, E. 30, fol. 36, 21 July
  1921.
11 Doheny testified that wages ranged from $1.50 (pesos) to $9 per day in 1915 and
  from $2.50 to $16 in 1919. US Senate, Subcommittee of the Committee on Foreign
  Relations, *Investigation of Mexican affairs*, 66th Congress, 1st Session (3 vols.),
  Washington, DC, 1919), I, pp. 220, 235. Also Historical Records, S. Pearson &
  Son, Ltd, at the British Science Museum, London (hereafter cited as Pearson
  Papers), C45, file 1, 'Schedule C–6' (1916), p. 16; and Junta Federal de
  Conciliación y Arbitraje at the Archivo General de la Nación, México (hereafter
  cited as JFCA), C. 70, E. 13, 10 February 1932.
12 US Senate, *Investigation of Mexican affairs*, I, p. 225; and Pearson Papers, A–4,
  Body to Pearson, 25 July 1902.
13 Department of State Records at the National Archives, Washington DC (hereafter
  cited as DS), Record Group 812.6363/85, 29 May 1914.

14 DT, C. 224, E. 24, fols. 15–19, 9 January 1920, C. 688, E. 11, 1923, and C. 447, E. 3, 1922; and Shell Group history: Country Series, Mexico management at the Shell International Petroleum Co., London (hereafter cited as GHC/MEX), file D29/1/1, fols. 1–2, 20 September 1921.
15 DT, C. 224, E. 24, Enrique S. Cerdán, 'Informe', 9 January 1920.
16 *Ibid.*, C. 724, E. 3, fol. 412, 5 December 1925.
17 Departamento Autónomo de Trabajo at the Archivo General de la Nación, México (hereafter cited as DAT), C. 134, E. 1, Fernando Iriarte de la Pez, Memorandum, 22 January 1938.
18 Pearson Papers, C45, file 4, 'Tampico and Minatitlán refinery estimates', 1916; and Archivo Histórico de Hacienda at the Archivo General de la Nación, México (hereafter cited as AHH), Legajo 1857–117, fol. 390, 11 July 1937.
19 DT, C. 1411, photos nos. 21, 29, 1928.
20 GHC/MEX/D29/1/1, fol. 8, 27 October 1924.
21 DT, C. 1209, E. 5, Zamora to Secretary, 19 May 1927.
22 FO 371–3241, fol. 5107, 14 November 1917; and DS 812.6363/389, 17 February 1918.
23 Pearson Papers A–4, Body to Cowdray, 22 December 1916, and Vaughn to Anglo-Mexican, 4 December 1916.
24 Fondo Obregón-Calles, 104–H–10, Legajo 1, 1921; and DT, C. 489, E. 10, 1922.
25 JFCA, C. 53, E. 20, 7 September 1931, and C. 75, E. 9, 30 July 1932; DAT, C. 9, E. 13, 27 May 1933; and AHH 1866–157, fol. 44, 1937.
26 FO 371–3830, fol. 83812, 20 May 191; and J. M. Hart, *Anarchism and the Mexican working class, 1860–1931* (Austin, 1978).
27 DS 812.504/121, 26 July 1926, and 812.504/46, 6 April 1916; Pearson Papers, A–4, Davies to Reed, 11 June 1917; and DT, C. 118, E. 7, fol. 19, 7 December 1918.
28 GHC/MEX/D29/1/1, fol. 12, 27 October 1924, and fol. 156, 3 August 1925.
29 J. W. F. Dulles, *Yesterday in Mexico: a chronicle of the Revolution, 1919–1936* (Austin, 1972), pp. 293, 631; and M. R. Clark, *Organized labor in Mexico* (Chapel Hill, 1934).
30 DT, C. 772, E. 5, fols. 277–284, 11 June 1924, and C. 977, E. 1, fols. 690–705, 15–16 July 1926; GHC/MEX/D29/2/2, fols. 16–17, 23 August 1927; and S. Lief Adleson, 'Coyuntura y conciencia: factores convergentes en la fundación de los sindicatos petroleros de Tampico durante la década de 1920', in Elsa Cecilia Frost, *et al.* (eds.), *El trabajo y los trabajadores en la historia de México* (México y Tucson, 1979), pp. 632–60.
31 GHC/MEX/D29/1/1, fol. 8, 27 August 1924.
32 DT, C. 1140, E. 14, 1925, and C. 725, E. 2, 1926.
33 GHC/MEX/D29/4, fols. 22–3, 10 September 1930.
34 DAT, C. 26, E. 14, 1934; and JFCA, C. 51, E. 5, fols. 105–6, 23 October 1937.
35 *Ibid.*, C. 16, E. 6, 25 May 1929.
36 See the *Laudo* of President Abelardo Rodríguez in Papeles Presidentiales, Fondo Presidente Lázaro Cárdenas at the Archivo General de la Nación, México, 432.2/2, 1934, and 4321.2/8, E. 1, 15 December 1934.
37 *Ibid.*, 432.3/170, 8 January 1936; and DAT, C. 28, E. 1, fol. 322, 27 June 1934.
38 AHH 1843–1, 6 July 1937, and 1866–163, fols. 1–6, 7 June 1939. Transcripts of the 1936–7 labor–management talks are found in *ibid.*, 1866–163, 1857–117, and 1858–119.
39 For recent works on the expropriation, see Meyer, *Mexico and the United States*; Philip, *Oil and politics in Latin America*; and George W. Grayson, *Politics of Mexican oil* (Pittsburgh, 1980).

19 Foreign policy and international business in Poland: 1918–39

ZBIGNIEW LANDAU and
JERZY TOMASZEWSKI

The situation of the reborn Polish Republic after 1918 was in many respects different from that of other countries which emerged or were transformed after the peace treaties.[1] She was the only country which came into being as a result of the unification of three regions entirely different from the socio-economic point of view: the three separate economic and political entities of Austria-Hungary, Germany and Russia. The First World War and revolution deepened economic distinctions between the territories which went to the making of the reborn Poland. All this seriously influenced the conditions of foreign business activity in Poland and the attitude of foreign capital to the new Polish statehood.

It was and still is a rule that decisions concerning foreign activities, either direct investments or credits, are subject to expected benefits. In the Polish Second Republic two different kinds of foreign business activities may be distinguished after her frontiers were finally settled in 1922. Firstly, there were shares or credits of firms which had engaged in the Russian or Austrian sector enterprises before 1914 and had headquarters outside Austria-Hungary or Russia. In Austrian Poland this refers mainly to the oil industry, while in the Russian partition it refers to textiles, heavy industry and some other branches. Thus foreign capital was flowing into Poland as a result of decisions made by company managements. In another kind of foreign involvement in Poland decisions were made outside, beyond the control of company managements, because of changes in the map of Europe. This was the case above all with Upper Silesia and, to a lesser degree, with Great Poland and Pomerania, which had belonged to Germany before 1918 or 1922. Some of their companies had central headquarters in other parts of the German Reich. After Poland regained independence they became foreign enterprises in a new state. These firms included mining and metallurgical concerns like the Vereinigte Königs- und Laurahütten AG, the Hohenlohe Werke AG, the Kattowitzer AG für Bergbau und Eisenhüttenbetrieb and others. In some cases their plants were divided by the Polish–German frontier. This state of affairs made it necessary to reorganize enterprises, divide assets and establish separate companies in both countries. Legally independent enterprises situated in Poland were still subject to parent firms in Germany. On a lesser scale this phenomenon was also recorded in Galicia, where some companies had been controlled by Vienna or Prague capital before 1914. In the former Russian sector it was not so, since all private enterprises in Russia were nationalized after the Bolshevik revolution.

The situation and objectives of foreign firms belonging to these two groups differed in many respects. They were also treated differently by the Polish authorities, who had to take into account tense relations between Poland and Germany.

The Polish government was usually friendly to foreign capital investment in Poland, though not unconditionally. This attitude was also changing in the course of time. German capital was an exception: Polish politicians feared negative political effects of the predominant position of Upper Silesian companies controlled by German financial centres. The question of the attitude of German business circles to independent Poland still requires further study. Some memoirs seem to indicate that the idea previously prevailing in the historiography of exclusively hostile attitudes is a simplification.[2]

The Versailles Treaty of June 1919 gave the Polish state the right of compulsory purchase of German companies, but neither the government nor Polish capitalists had sufficient means to take advantage of this. The Upper Silesian concerns were therefore pressed to turn over part of their shares to French companies, being given a possible Polish participation in return for the waiving of Polish rights resulting from the Versailles Treaty.[3] Although in some cases, e.g. the Hohenlohe Werke AG, the French did take a proportion of the shares, the desired results were not achieved by the Polish side. Former shareholders maintained a predominant position, while new ones agreed to co-operate with them. French businessmen instead became partners of German owners vis-à-vis the Polish government and not, as was expected, allies of the Poles.

Besides this, in the course of disputes over the Silesian problem the Polish government tried to gain the support of Entente business circles for a division of the controversial area which would be favourable for Poland. The French, the British and the Italians were offered long-term leases of state-owned enterprises and mining areas in Upper Silesia which would naturally follow in case Poland were given this area. The offer was of interest only to French businessmen, since France was eager to weaken Germany. Under these circumstances two companies were established: the Polskie Kopalnie Skarbowe na Górnym Slasku SA/Société fermière des mines fiscales de l'état polonais en Haute Silésie and the Polska Huta Skarbowa Ołowiu i Srebra w Strzybnicy SA.[4]

In the late 1920s the Polish authorities were still mistrustful of German capital and aimed at polonization of Silesian enterprises, at least superficially. This made German businessmen co-operate with entrepreneurs from the Entente countries – France, Great Britain and most of all the United States – who were welcome in Poland. For instance W. A. Harriman was thus encouraged to enter Upper Silesian business (this will be examined later).

The Polish government regarded the inflow of Allied capital as economically and politically favourable for Poland[5] and hence foreign investments were encouraged. The damage suffered in the First World War, lack of native capital and the financial troubles of the Polish state made the inflow of foreign capital one of the basic conditions of Poland's recovery and development in the eyes of ruling circles, no matter what their opinion was in other matters. This idea was strengthened by inflation, which developed after the war and which reached its peak in Poland in 1923. Examples of other countries, like Germany or Austria, showed that the situation could be mastered only with foreign credit aid.

It was not until the policy of Władysław Grabski, the prime minister who came to office in December 1923, that the idea of currency stabilization based on foreign aid was given up.[6] This was rather making a virtue out of necessity. Grabski did not oppose government loans or foreign participation in the Polish economy but refused all political implications involved as he feared a gradual direct or indirect subordination to German interests.

Grabski was successful with his primary objective: in 1924 he stabilized Polish currency. But soon he was politically defeated since a temporary weakening of the currency in late 1925 led to his resignation. After the short-lived cabinet of Aleksander Skrzyński the major political benefits were gained by Józef Piłsudski, who staged a coup d'état in May 1926, at the initial stages of economic recovery.

The cabinets which followed under Piłsudski's control tried to make use of the improving world market situation to attract foreign investments to Poland.[7] This policy remained unchanged even during the Great Depression.[8] The Polish government consequently maintained the convertibility of the Polish złoty and freedom of international payments, hoping to create an image of stable policy and secure investments of foreign business. Poland was one of the few debtor countries which took such a course.

As late as April 1936, when the negative effects of this policy became apparent and foreign firms were still hesitating to invest in Poland, the government decided to introduce foreign exchange restrictions, temporarily stopped discharge of debts and converted them on more favourable terms.

At the same time the government's attitude towards foreign firms was slightly modified. Financial difficulties of some foreign concerns, e.g. Banca Commerciale Italiana, meant a threat of bankruptcy for dependent Polish enterprises. The Polish government therefore undertook readjustment of the most important of them, took over some of their foreign commitments, or even bought their shares. Prominent among the firms whose shares were taken over were the German Upper Silesian firms, e.g. the Wspólnota Interesów. Though efforts were made to pass these shares to Polish private capital circles, in most cases the private capitalists proved too weak. The take-over of Silesian business was only partially due to economic reasons: the Polish government also wanted to get rid of the subordination to foreign centres whose attitude towards Poland was unfavourable.

Disputes over French participation in the Żyrardów textile industry and the Warsaw power plant were also of a political nature. Though they started because of excessive exploitation by foreign firms, the government's determination was connected with the worsening of Franco-Polish political relations in the early 1930s. Improvement of these relations led to a compromise solution of the Żyrardów affair, quite favourable for the French.[9]

At the same time, however, Polish authorities backed those foreign firms which were treated as favourable or neutral for Polish political interests. Such was the case for example with the British Overseas Bank, involved in financing the Polish sugar industry and banking.

While the attitude of the Polish government towards foreign business activity was generally positive, foreign firms were usually more aloof.[10] Soon after the First World War this was natural in view of uncertainty as to the future of a new country, threatened by revolution and lacking stable frontiers. Though many firms were established in Poland with British, French or Belgian participation, they were of very little significance. They were small and the capital engaged was quite inconsiderable. Commercial or shipping companies frequently kept their major assets such as vessels outside Poland to minimize probable loss in the event of the collapse of the Polish state. There were cases of foreign business interests entering Polish enterprises. The shares involved were, however, only insignificant and probably treated as a stepping-stone to further decisions. These operations were sometimes of a speculative nature under diplomatic pressure, e.g. purchase of the Żyrardów factory by a French Boussac group, while direct engagement of capital was minimized.

This reserve lasted during the period of inflation. It seemed probable that the 1924 stabilization of the Polish currency and introduction of the złoty would break it. Negotiations were started to attract some foreign financial groups to Poland, but a repeated depreciation of the currency in the second half of 1925 and a trade war with Germany led to suspension of these talks and only after 1926 did the situation change.[11] In the years 1926–9 several foreign firms granted Poland credits and invested their capital in the country. The Harriman group and the Banca Commerciale Italiana were perhaps the best-known examples.

The Great Depression changed this trend. Though at first foreign firms took advantage of the critical situation of Polish enterprises and tended to strengthen their position with minimum engagement of new means, later the growing financial difficulties led many of them to withdraw from Poland. Capital withdrawn from Poland was only partially replaced by other foreign firms. That was for example the case with the Banca Commerciale Italiana, whose shares were taken over by the British Overseas Bank. Shortly before 1939 the latter found itself in trouble and had to decrease credits granted to Polish enterprises.[12] International companies like Schicht[13] or Philips maintained their positions or even extended their networks of subsidiaries.

The point should be made that the caution of foreign businesses over investment in Poland in the 1930s was also due to political reasons. The growing tension in east central Europe and the worsening position of Poland in relation to Germany effectively checked financial engagement in this part of Europe.

The changing evaluation of Poland's political and economic prospects was influencing forms of foreign capital inflow to industry and banking. From three basic forms – buying shares or granting long-term or short-term credits – foreign firms preferred to gain maximum profits given the highest possible safety of invested capital. During prosperity and political stability they chose to buy shares. Foreign firms rarely undertook construction of new plants or considerable extension of factories already in existence. Since the Polish home market was rather limited, construction of new factories was a risky business. It was safer to invest in an enterprise with established customers and a ready sale. Hence the inflow of foreign capital meant a change in the decision making centre, but hardly any increase in productive capacity. On the other hand the Polish government usually made tax or tariff reductions subject to extension of enterprises by new shareholders, as the case with, for instance, the Harriman group's entrance to the zinc industry.

Given such uncertainty, foreign firms preferred to grant long-term credits, since this form of engagement facilitated the withdrawal of investments. The sale of shares could lead to losses due to a decline of stock quotations; but credits gave a creditor the possibility of controlling indebted enterprises to an extent which sometimes equalled that of direct participation.

When the economic and political situation deteriorated foreign business groups resorted to short-term credits, systematically prolonged. Their withdrawal was also relatively easy and debtors' fears of such an eventuality strengthened their dependence on creditors. There were cases in which large Polish industrial plants could not pay back foreign short-term credits because of depression difficulties and had to give up a considerable part of their shares to the creditors. That was the case of the S. A. Wyrobów Bawełnianych I. K. Poznański, a textile factory indebted to the Banca Commerciale Italiana.[14]

The dependence of foreign capital inflow on the economic and political situation of Poland may be confirmed by statistical evidence. In the years 1927–9 direct investments prevailed in the shape of the buying of shares. As a result the share of foreign capital in Polish joint-stock companies increased from 21.1% in 1927 to 41.0% in 1930 (see Table 19.1). Even if we treat these data as approximate estimates, the growing trend can hardly be doubted.

Information concerning credits based on debentures or mortgage bonds is available from 1928, but these credits were never very large. The maximum amount was recorded in 1931 at 96.4 million złoty, that is 10.8 million pre-1934 US dollars.[15] In the following years this form of investment declined.

Short-term credits were of greater significance. It is, however, hard to state what part of these credits were purely commercial, (probably a great majority) and to what extent they covered capital investments. Even initial hypotheses can be formulated only after examining the finances of a representative group of Polish enterprises. The growing political tension in Europe in the late 1930s caused even this form of foreign investments in Poland to decline. It should be stressed that after 1931 discharge of short-term credits granted to Polish enterprises by foreign creditors exceeded new loans.

It is clear that short-term credits seemed most secure from the point of view of foreign investors. Capital invested in shares was much more difficult to withdraw. From the point of view of Polish enterprises the form of investment was not crucial for the degree of dependence on foreign business. This is why foreign direct participation in Polish stock capital decreased after 1930 (see Table 19.1). Fluctuations in the direct participation of foreign firms in the stock capital of Polish enterprises were rather small. Slight increases did not result from buying new shares, but from the take-over of firms in return for unpaid debts.[16]

On these grounds it may be presumed that the international connections of Polish enterprises can only partially be explained by direct investments and participation in joint-stock companies. In the 1930s this form was gradually replaced by credits. As a rule foreign business groups were interested in large enterprises, and so all the highly concentrated industries had a relatively high share of foreign capital. On the other hand foreign participation in industries in which small factories prevailed (food-processing, leather or clothing) was much lower. Dependence of Polish enterprises on foreign business centres because of the Polish firms' participation in international cartel agreements is a separate question.

With the above reservations we include data concerning direct foreign participation in Polish joint-stock companies (Table 19.1). The statistics cover the years 1927–37; they may contain certain inaccuracies, about which it is difficult to be certain, since they were based on information given to the Central Statistical Bureau by the companies themselves. It is known that a precise determination of all shareholders is not possible even when shares are presented to the general meeting. The possibility cannot be excluded that some

Table 19.1 *Foreign capital in industrial joint-stock companies registered in Poland, 1927–37 (% of total stock capital)*

Branches of industry	1927	1928	1929	1930	1931	1932	1933	1934	1935	1936	1937
Petroleum (wells and refineries)	60.0	76.4	76.5	83.2	87.3	84.0	87.6	93.3	86.7	85.0	87.5
Mining and metallurgy	32.0	—	—	74.7	75.5	77.1	—	—	71.0	48.3	52.1
Mining	—	38.1	38.8	—	58.6	61.7	64.2	67.4	—	—	—
Metallurgy	—	65.0	65.4	—	82.9	89.8	84.4	82.5	—	—	—
Engineering (with electrical equipment)	—	19.8	24.3	—	29.7	31.5	—	—	—	—	—
Electrical equipment	35.0	—	—	48.2	61.5	47.4	—	30.5	55.1	57.5	66.1
Chemical	18.7	38.7	40.6	45.1	38.7	41.6	57.7	70.1	60.0	59.5	59.9
Metal	9.2	10.6	11.3	28.1	25.8	28.8	25.2	32.4	31.5	27.3	15.7
Textile	10.6	15.1	15.9	23.1	23.8	28.1	21.9	23.0	22.2	23.7	22.1
Timber	15.0	12.8	16.7	15.9	21.7	25.9	27.6	37.6	44.5	42.7	52.1
Paper	14.7	23.2	28.0	34.9	27.9	25.8	32.2	33.7	25.6	22.2	22.8
Leather	—	—	—	8.7	20.2	24.6	—	—	—	—	27.1
Mineral	12.0	19.9	20.8	20.5	22.1	21.5	19.3	24.5	17.1	24.0	26.9
Building	—	10.8	14.5	12.1	19.6	19.2	29.9	32.5	31.1	32.1	25.0
Food	3.9	8.7	9.6	12.0	12.7	—	14.5	9.8	9.7	8.4	8.4
Confectionery	—	2.1	3.3	—	—	—	12.6	14.4	—	—	—
Electricity, gas, water supply	44.6	72.5	75.6	74.0	76.2	75.4	77.2	82.4	80.8	85.3	81.3
Total	21.1	31.7	33.3	41.0	39.8	43.2	45.4	47.1	44.2	38.4	40.1

Sources: *Mały Rocznik Statystyczny*, 1933, 28; 1934, 39; 1935, 52; 1937, 94; 1938, 98; 1939, 108; Z. Landau and J. Tomaszewski, *Gospodarka Polski międzywojennej 1918–1939*, II, *Od Grabskiego do Piłsudskiego. Okres kryzysu poinflacyjnego i ożywienia koniunktury 1924–1929* (Warszawa, 1971), p. 78; M. Smerek, *Bilans płatniczy Polski za rok 1929* (Warszawa, 1931), p. 89; J. Tuszyńska, 'Kapitały zagraniczne w spółkach akcyjnych w Polsce', *Polska Gospodarcza* (1933), 400.

companies gave inaccurate data, but perhaps that happened only on occasion. The data at least give a general picture of direct foreign participation in Polish enterprises and its general trends.

The statistics show that foreign participation in Polish joint-stock companies almost doubled over the years 1927–30. Further changes were not significant; it cannot be ruled out that they were due to the changing accuracy of statistical evidence. The decrease of shares in 1936 was probably connected with the government's take-over of some major enterprises.

Table 19.2 *Foreign capital in Polish joint-stock companies according to the country of origin, 1929–38 (at 1 January every year, in % of the total amount of foreign capital in joint-stock companies)*

Country of origin	1929	1930	1931	1932	1933	1934	1935	1936	1937	1938
France	30.4	26.7	25.8	24.6	24.4	24.9	25.6	24.4	26.1	26.2
USA	12.1	15.9	21.3	20.4	21.9	21.8	21.9	21.9	18.5	18.6
Germany	24.1	21.9	25.0	23.7	23.4	21.5	19.8	19.3	13.2	13.3
Belgium	14.8	11.6	9.4	11.0	10.0	9.7	10.5	11.0	13.3	13.3
Switzerland	4.2	8.5	2.8	2.1	2.8	3.9	4.8	4.5	8.5	8.5
Great Britain	5.3	4.9	4.8	4.7	4.9	5.2	4.7	5.1	5.4	5.4
Netherlands	1.7	2.3	1.8	2.5	2.8	3.0	2.9	3.1	3.9	3.9
Austria	3.3	2.8	3.9	4.4	3.5	4.1	3.4	3.4	2.9	2.9
Sweden	1.1	1.4	2.0	2.8	2.3	2.3	2.3	2.4	2.6	2.6
Czecho-slovakia	2.6	2.3	1.1	1.3	1.3	1.3	1.4	1.4	1.7	1.7
Other	0.4	1.7	2.1	2.5	2.7	2.3	2.7	3.5	3.9	3.6

Source: T. Małecka, 'Udział kaptału amerykańskiego w kapitałach akcyjnych przemysłu polskiego w latach 1918–1939, in *Materiały do seminariów z najnowszej historii gospodarczej Polski*, pod redakcją. J. Kalińskiego i Z. Landaua (Warszawa, 1974), p. 48.

The highest participation of foreign capital was recorded in oil wells, power plants, gas and water supply systems, the electrotechnical industry, the chemical industry, mining and metallurgy. These branches of industry were characterized by the highest concentration of production.

In the textile industry some major factories were subordinated to foreign centres by means of short-term credits whereas direct participation was relatively small. This was probably due to a difficult situation in the industry all through the interwar period. Similar forms of foreign capital influence were recorded in sugar refining.

The 'nationality' of capital active in Poland is also a grave methodological problem.[17] Firstly, because of anonymity of shares it was frequently hard to state who owned them. Secondly, in many cases it was hard to judge what country a financial group was connected with: its headquarters could be situated in a country for formal reasons, e.g. taxation. Thirdly, the Germans frequently preferred their capital not to appear under their national banner but hidden behind the signboard of neutral or Entente countries. We know that this role was played by some firms situated in the USA, France and other countries. The data concerning the nationality of capital included in Table 19.2 should therefore be treated as approximate only. They show that the major role was played by French, German, American and Belgian capital.

The French were interested in investing in the Polish economy only at the beginning of the 1920s, which probably had something to do with their desire to connect Poland with their sphere of interest. The Treaty of Locarno and a cool policy towards France followed by Piłsudski decreased French interest in Poland and this led to a decrease of French participation in Polish enterprises.

A gradual decline in German participation in Polish joint-stock companies – the data seem to be an underestimation – resulted from Polish pressure and a take-over of some enterprises by the Polish government. German capital was also replaced by investments from other countries, although this was frequently only a pretence.

A considerable increase of US capital in the years 1929–31 was mainly due to the entrance of the Harriman group to some Upper Silesian enterprises. Polish historians have usually thought that this was to preserve the strengthening of the position of German capital in Poland.[18] However, this hypothesis needs to be verified.

Other business groups played only a minor role. It should be mentioned that a neglect of Poland among British business circles was due to the marginal role which east central Europe played in British diplomacy and especially to political aversion to Poland – a country connected with France. Interconnections between individual capital groups in Poland can be illustrated by the history of Upper Silesian companies.[19]

Upper Silesia was the major Polish industrial region in the interwar period. Its division between Poland and Germany was followed by a division of enterprises possessing factories and mining areas on both sides of the frontier. Shares of new companies situated in Poland and subject to Polish law were mainly in German hands (usually special holdings) and only a small proportion belonged to other owners.

Thus some percentage of shares in the Hohenlohe Werke went to the French (7.5%) and to the Polish government (7.5%). The latter had also shares in the Upper Silesian United Steel Mills Królewska and Laura SA (17.5%), the majority of whose shares were in the hands of the Berlin holding Vereinigte Königs- und Laurahütten AG, which soon became part of the Friedrich Flick empire. Flick also took over shares of other Upper Silesian companies and established a so-called Wspólnota Interesów (community of interests or *Interessengemeinschaft*), including the United Steel Mills Królewska and Laura and the Katowicka SA dla Górniotwa i Hutnictwa. The new concern included US capital from the Harriman group.[20]

Harriman established the Silesian-American Company (SACO), which took over 51% of the largest zinc mining and processing plant in Poland – the Giesche SA. The rest of the shares of this firm were in the hands of Georg von Giesche's Erben AG in Breslau (now Wrocław).

Companies changing hands and the investment in them of US capital caused the Polish government anxiety about the negative effects of German capital domination in political life. When, therefore, during the Great Depression bankruptcy threatened the Huta Pokój SA (1931) and the Wspólnota Interesów (1934), which could have led to closure of factories and mass unemployment, the Polish government took over the majority of their shares and readjusted their finances at enormous cost.[21] This resulted in a substantial decrease of the role of German capital in Poland.

The story of the engagement of the Milan Banca Commerciale Italiana in Poland was different.[22] Shortly before the First World War the majority of its shares went to a group of Italian businessmen headed by Giuseppe Toeplitz, son of a Warsaw banker, who had family and marriage ties with Poland (his brothers lived there and both his wives came from Poland).

Banca Commerciale Italiana started their Balkan expansion in the years preceding the First World War.[23] After the war they were associated with a powerful group, Assicurazioni Generali di Trieste (with Toeplitz, this company disposed of the majority of the BCI shares), which provided a sound financial foundation for extensive activity in many European and some overseas countries.

In 1931 the BCI already controlled a group of international banks such as Banca Commerciale Italiana (France), Banca Commerciale per l'Egitto, Banca Commerciale Italiana Trust Company (USA), Banque commerciale italienne et roumaine, Banque commerciale italienne et bulgare and Banca Commerciale Italiana e Greca. Besides these the bank's reports specified nine 'allied' banks: Banca della Svizzera Italiana, Banca Ungaro-Italiana, Banco Italiano Guayaquil et Manta (Equador), Banco Italiano (Peru), Banque française et italienne pour l'Amérique du Sud (France), Česká Banka Union, Hrvatska Banka, Societá Italiana di Credito (Austria) and Bank Handlowy w Warszawie SA.[24]

The BCI interest in Poland was natural because of the family links of Giuseppe Toeplitz, who considered investments in Poland soon after she regained independence.[25] After the war the Italian bank took over some shares in the Bank Zjednoczonych Ziem Polskich SA in Lublin, but the latter was of minor importance. In 1924 the BCI approached the largest Polish private bank – the Bank Handlowy w Warszawie SA, with which Giuseppe's father Henryk Toeplitz had connections before 1914.

After the final stabilization of the Polish złoty in 1927 the BCI took over a great part of the Bank Handlowy shares, leading a group of foreign shareholders (W. A. Harriman and Co., Banque de Bruxelles, Niederöster-reichische Escompte Gesellschaft and, after 1928, Hambros Bank and Pesti Magyar Kereskedelmi Bank). This transaction was approved of and aided by the Polish government. In 1924 the BCI granted the Polish government a small credit in lieu of the tobacco monopoly. They were also interested in other aspects of the Polish economy. The BCI financed certain large textile companies of Łódź, such as Zjednoczone Zakłady Przemysłowe (United Industries), K. Scheibler and L. Grohman SA, and the cotton mills Ludwik Geyer SA or I. K. Poznański's SA Wyrobów Bawełnianych. In 1930 the BCI took over half of the latter's shares, while Zygmunt Toeplitz (Giuseppe's brother) became chairman of the board.

The BCI had an interest also in the Tomaszów silk factory (Zygmunt Toeplitz was on its board), which belonged to the SNIA Viscoza concern, as well as some other firms including SIPMER – a Polish-Italian mining company and an insurance company, Polonia SA. This influence was extended thanks to the Toeplitz family and financial contacts in Poland. Among people closely co-operating with the Italian bank Jerzy Meyer and Stanisław Lubomirski at least should be mentioned. This background helped the BCI practically to control the Bank Handlowy w Warszawie though formally they owned only about 10% of its shares.

Control of the Warsaw bank made it possible for the BCI to influence companies financed by or otherwise dependent on the Bank Handlowy. These included certain engineering works, commercial firms, and an insurance company Warszawskie Towarzystwo Ubezpieczeniowe SA, through which the Assicurazioni Generali di Trieste strengthened their position on the Polish insurance market. One should also mention the BCI connections with Polish enterprises participating in the international concern Solvay.[26]

The Great Depression put an end to the BCI activities in Poland. Though at first the BCI managed to extend its interests, its industrial involvement proved to be too extensive. In 1931 the bank faced financial troubles and in 1933 was forced to ask the Italian government for help.[27] The BCI was nationalized and Giuseppe Toeplitz gave up business. In Poland the collapse of the BCI brought about liquidation of its activity. The Polish government helped in the readjustment of the Bank Handlowy finances and took over commitments of many industrial companies from the BCI, which was given state bonds.[28] At the same time the Bank Handlowy w Warszawie was merged with the Bank Angielsko-Polski SA, controlled by the British Overseas Bank.

Expansion of the Swedish concern of Ivar Kreuger in Poland was somewhat different.[29] In the 1920s the company aimed at creating a world match monopoly granting countries which faced financial troubles credits in return for leases of match monopolies. Poland was one of the first countries to obtain such a loan in 1924. It was worth six million US dollars, for which Kreuger leased the Polish match monopoly and was given privileges safeguarding high profits. For instance the agreement made the price of matches subject to increasing costs of production without any other reservation. Kreuger rapidly subordinated suppliers of raw materials and could thus control costs of production and gain increasing profits.

Apart from his credit to the Polish government Kreuger promised to invest a further five million złotys in the stock capital of a company exploiting the match monopoly in Poland and five and a half million złotys in its other assets. The mean annual engagement of Kreuger was estimated at less than 34 million złotys, and his yearly profits at about 11 million złotys, that is about 30% of the invested capital.

Kreuger tried to control not only the production of matches in Poland but also the supply of materials and the investments and financing of the industry. He therefore established a number of separate companies connected with his international dealings by means of persons who managed these companies and through exchange of shares. Aspen supplies – essential for match production – were, together with its exports, in the hands of SA Trak Eksploatacja i Handel Drzewny, established in 1924. Matchsticks were produced by SA Przemysł Osikowy, established in 1924, while potassium chlorate was supplied by SA Fabryk Chemicznych Radocha (a monopoly in Poland), taken over by Kreuger. Technical and chemical supplies were concentrated in Towarzystwo Handlowe Inwestyoja SA, established in 1927, whereas construction works were carried out by Origo Ltd. All this was controlled by the Bank Amerykański w Polsce SA, founded in 1925 for financing the Kreuger activities in Poland.[30] The system of interconnected enterprises prevented any perception of the financial operations and foreign transactions of the Polish branch of the international match concern and ensured that actual profits were hidden.

In 1931 the match agreement with Kreuger was modified because of another loan granted by his concern. He was given further privileges such as high taxation of lighters so that they could not compete with expensive matches. Retail prices of matches grew and their exports decreased. The time-limit of the lease was prolonged until 1965.[31]

Acceptance of such unfavourable conditions by the Polish government was due to the desire to attract politically neutral capital to Poland, even at the cost of less favourable economic terms. In 1931 it was also due to the financial difficulties of the Polish government during the Great Depression.

The Philips interest in Poland was for different reasons than that of Kreuger. Both treated their Polish activities as parts of their world empires, but while Kreuger wanted direct profits and control of potential rivals, Philips treated his Polish investments as a stepping-stone for expansion in the USSR. Along with the establishment of a company in Poland, on the Soviet western frontier, he also started a similar enterprise in the East – in China.[32]

The Warsaw enterprise was established in 1922 as the Polskie Zakłady Philips SA for the production of light bulbs and radio equipment. The concern's central management did not, however, initiate the entire production process, and so the Warsaw company was not self-sufficient, either financially or technically: the light bulb factory was unable to produce wolfram wire, while the glass works had to import tools for glass melting, whose technology was unknown in Poland. The production of radio sets also required the import of important components.

Polskie Zakłady Philips was therefore unable to go into production with the co-operation of the parent Dutch firm. The necessity to import some basic semi-finished products made it possible to export profits gained in Poland concealed in the prices of components brought from the Netherlands and to avoid Polish taxation or, after 1936, foreign exchange restrictions.

Profits gained in Poland were high. The Polish branch of Philips initiated a light bulb cartel in which two other major producers participated: Polska Żarówka Osram SA and the Tungsram company. The cartel controlled the light bulb market in Poland as other firms were rather small. An outsider, the Helios company, was even tolerated in order to feign competition.

In the production of the radio equipment, and especially tubes, Philips held a monopoly in Poland. This situation made it possible to maintain the retail prices of some tubes at a level ten times higher than the cost of production.

The high prices of radio equipment checked the development of radiophony and radio communication for military purposes in Poland. In the 1930s there was therefore a plan to start a government radio equipment factory. The plan was not realized. Philips launched a patent blockade, so that the projected government factory would have had to face enormous costs. As a result a compromise solution was achieved: the Polish government gave up their plan and Philips agreed to start the whole production process in his Warsaw branch factory, establish design offices and laboratories in Poland and to decrease prices. This agreement was reached just before the outbreak of the Second World War and so its effects could not be seen.

The above examples of various foreign business activities in interwar Poland cannot lead to more general conclusions. We should remember that we do not possess sufficient information about many other firms with foreign business connections. There are no more sources for historical analysis of the problem in Polish archives, and this is only partially due to the destruction which affected documents of companies situated in Warsaw. Basic documentation was kept outside Poland, in archives of foreign concerns, so it is there that further questions could be answered and initial hypotheses verified.

It is worth mentioning that in the cases discussed above (as well as in that of the French group Marcel Boussac) foreign business groups aimed above all at high and rapid profits. Only some of the concerns involved thought of more permanent foundations for further activities; capital investments were usually avoided. There are a number of known cases in which investments were made only under strong pressure from the Polish government and in return for special privileges given to foreign firms. An analysis of fragmentary information on foreign business activities and statistical evidence seems to show that foreign capital made possible the extension and modernization of certain enterprises, mainly in the years 1927–9. A common approach in early days was to wait and see, while later on the practice was rather to limit involvement and withdraw previous credits. This did not mean a general withdrawal of foreign firms from Poland, and in fact forced cases of this kind during the Great Depression seem to be exceptional. But the general attitude of international concerns towards Poland was not enthusiastic. She was treated as a country with a minor part to play and as rather risky for larger investments. It is possible that a change for the better was expected, which led to maintenance of the ground which had already been gained and to expansion on a limited scale.

Finally, the foreign business activities in Poland were a considerable burden on her balance of payments through outflowing profits, debt instalments and other payments due to foreign investments. Fragmentary statistical data show that the capital turnover balance of interwar Poland brought an overall deficit. In other words, the Polish economy was de-capitalized. It should be remembered that we have partial information only, as some sums outflowing to other countries were concealed in commercial or service transactions. According to the available statistics in the years 1924–37 the inflow of capital into Poland amounted to 3.2 billion złotys, while the outflow amounted to 5.6 billion złotys.[33]

Service of foreign debts due to foreign business activity in Poland necessitated various forms of export promotion after 1930 if the country were to achieve a surplus in the balance to trade. Thus the Polish economy was burdened with costs of dumping which – at least partially – should be added to the foreign business activity costs. In the early 1930s annual costs of dumping in Poland were estimated at 300–500 million złotys.[34]

It should be pointed out that the take-over of German shares in Upper Silesian enterprises in the 1930s further increased the pressures on the Polish balance of payments. Although Poland's growing economic independence in relation to Germany should be considered, especially after Hitler's accession to power, as a desired political objective, the direct effects of the polonization of Upper Silesian industry had to include increased exports to the Third Reich to cover these commitments. The present state of knowledge of the role of German capital in Poland does not allow us to decide whether the approaching collapse of Upper Silesian concerns was a result of a conscious policy of major shareholders. It may be presumed that the German businessmen who operated in Poland according to the provisions of the Versailles Treaty were not too eager to stabilize and develop their enterprises normally in Poland, which distinguished them from most businessmen from other countries.

Generally speaking, the foreign business activity in interwar Poland did not accelerate her economic development.[35] However, the dependence of Polish economy on foreign centres made it possible for them to exercise political pressure on the Polish government. This was for instance true of French diplomacy in the first years of Poland's regained independence. Germany took advantage of the situation and started a trade war with Poland in 1925. On the other hand it would be hard to find examples of the positive influence of foreign shareholders from the point of view of Polish foreign policy.

NOTES

1 For basic information concerning Poland's economic development see Z. Landau and J. Tomaszewski, *The Polish economy 1920 to 1980* (Beckenham, 1984); for more details, Z. Landau and J. Tomaszewski, *Gospodarka Polski międzywojennej 1918–1939*, vol. I, *W dobie inflacji 1918–1923* (Warszawa, 1967); vol. II, *Od Grabskiego do Piłsudskiego, okres kryzy su poinflacyjnego i ożywienia koniunktury 1924–1929* (Warszawa, 1971); vol. III, *Wielki kryzys 1930–1935* (Warszawa, 1982); vol. IV, *Lata interwencjonizmu państwowego 1936–1939* (forthcoming).
2 S. Wachowiak, *Czasy, które przeżyłem: Wspomnienia z lat 1890–1939* (Warszawa, 1983), pp. 192–3, 266–7.
3 For documents see Z. Landau and J. Tomaszewski, 'Misja profesora Artura Benisa', *Teki Archiwalne*, II (1959).
4 J. Jaros, 'Gospodarka koncernu 'Skarboferm', *Zaranie Śląskie*, (1957), nos. 1–2.
5 Z. Landau, 'Stosunek rządu polskiego do pożyczek zagranicznych w latach 1918–1920', *Biuletyn Instytutu Gospodarstwa Społecznego* (1959), no. 1; T. Małecka, *Kredyty i pożyczki Stanów Sjednoczonych Ameryki dla rządu polskiego w latach 1918–39* (Warszawa, 1982), pp. 64–91.
6 More details in J. Tomaszewski, *Stabilizacja waluty w Polsce: Z badań nad polityką gospodarczą rządu polskiego przed przewrotem majowym* (Warszawa, 1961).
7 Z. Landau, 'Stosunek rządów pomajowych do napływu kapitałów zagranicznych do Polski', *Śląski Kwartalnik Historyczny Sobótka* (1962), nos. 3–4.
8 An interesting proof of the continuation of the policy is the book L. Wellisz, *Foreign capital in Poland* (London, 1938).
9 Z. Landau and J. Tomaszewski, *Sprawa żyrardowska: Przyczynek do dziejów kapitałów obcych w Polsce międzywojennej* (Warszawa, 1983).
10 Z. Landau, 'The influence of foreign capital upon the Polish economy of 1918–1939', in *La Pologne au XIIe congrès international des sciences historiques à Vienna* (Warszawa, 1965); Z. Landau, 'Quelques problèmes économiques des relations polono-américaines en 1918–1920', *Studia historiae oeconomicae* III (1968). The lack of interest of the British banks in Polish economy is obvious from P. L. Cottrell, 'Aspects of western equity investment in the banking systems of east central Europe', in A. Teichova and P. L. Cottrell (eds.), *International business and central Europe 1918–1939* (Leicester, 1983).
11 Z. Landau, 'Stosunek kapitału zagranicznego do lokat w Polsce (1926)', *Przeglad Zachodni* (1962), no. 3.
12 The Commercial Counsellor of the Polish Embassy in London to the Ministry of Foreign Affairs in Warsaw, 30 January 1939. Archiwum Akt Nowych (Archives of Contemporary Records, Warsaw, later AAN), Ministry of Foreign Affairs 9507, pp. 20–2.
13 The history of the Schicht company in Poland has not yet been written. Some information is contained in A. Teichova, *An economic background to Munich*:

international business and Czechoslovakia, 1918–1939 (Cambridge, 1974), pp. 299–312.

14 S. Lauterbach, 'Kapitał zagraniczny w Łodzi', *Gazeta Polska*, 5 December 1935, reprinted in Z. Landau and J. Tomaszewski, *Kapitały obce w Polsce 1918–1939: Materiały i dokumenty* (Warszawa 1964), pp. 112–15.

15 *Statystyka Polski* seria C, vols. XXII and LI.

16 Landau and Tomaszewski, *Kapitały*, p. 15.

17 See J. Tomaszewski, 'Fremdes Kapital: Ein Versuch zur näheren Bestimmung', *Jahrbuch für Wirtschaftsgeschichte* (1978), no. 2.

18 L. Grosfeld, *Polska w latach kryzysu gospodarczego 1929–1933* (Warszawa, 1952); Z. Landau and J. Tomaszewski, *Anonimowi władcy: Z dziejów kapitału obcego w Polsce (1918–1939)* (Warszawa, 1968).

19 Basic documents in Landau and Tomaszewski, *Kapitały* pp. 243–334.

20 See documents in AAN, Polish Embassy in Berlin 1030.

21 See documents in AAN, Polish Embassy in Berlin 1034, 1035, 1037.

22 Z. Landau and J. Tomaszewski, *Bank Handlowy w Warszawie S.A. Historia i rozwój 1870–1970* (Warszawa, 1970), or the short edition in English, Z. Landau and J. Tomaszewski, *Bank Handlowy w Warszawie S.A.: history and development 1870–1970* (Warszawa, 1970).

23 S. Romano, *Giuseppe Volpi et l'Italie moderne: Finance, industries et État de l'ère giolittienne à la Deuxième Guerre mondiale* (Rome, 1982), pp. 24–7.

24 Banca Commerciale Italiana, Liste des correspondents en Europe.

25 L. Toeplitz, *Il banchiere: al tempo in cui nacque, crebbe, e fiori la Banca Commerciale Italiana* (Milano), p. 129.

26 *Nowe Wiadomości Ekonomiczne ye Uczone* (1939), no. 1, 21. Teichova, *An economic background*, pp. 279–94, does not mention this question.

27 Toeplitz, *Il banchiere*, pp. 130–4; P. Ciocca and G. Toniolo, 'Industry and finance in Italy, 1918–1940', *Journal of European economic history*, XIII (1984), no. 2, 130–4; *Die Bank* (1932), 443–5; 1993, 338–9.

28 Landau and Tomaszewski, *Kapitały*, pp. 357–84.

29 Z. Landau, 'Działalność koncernu Kreugera w Polsce', *Przegląd Historyczny* (1958), no. 1; U. Wikander, 'The Swedish match company in central Europe between the Two World Wars', in Teichova and Cottrell (eds.), *International business*.

30 *Rocznik informacyjny o spółkach akcyjnych w Polsce* (1930), entries, 436, 1004, 1022, 1355.

31 Umowa dzierżawna z 17 listopada 1930 r. (The contract of lease of 17 November 1930), Sejm Rzeczypospolitej Polskiej okres III, druk nr 5.

32 Landau and Tomaszewski, *Kapitały*, pp. 137–43.

33 R. Gradowski, *Polska 1918–1939: Niektóre zagadnienia kapitału monopolistycznego* (Warszawa, 1959), pp. 193–4.

34 K. Sokołowski, *Dumping* (Warszawa, 1932), p. 133; R. Battaglia, *Zagadnienie kartelizacji w Polsce: Ceny a kartele* (Warszawa, 1932), p. 145.

35 Z. Landau, 'Wpływ kapitałów obcych na gospodarkę polska 1918–1939', *Finanse* (1965), no. 1.

20 Foreign enterprises and nationalistic control: the case of Finland since the end of the nineteenth century

RIITTA HJERPPE and JORMA AHVENAINEN

In spite of the fact that foreign trade plays an important role in the Finnish economy, multinational capital in the form of direct investment has been relatively insignificant within the country. International investors have obviously not been interested in this small, remote market. Reasons for their reluctance have been the small population, scarce natural resources – timber excepted – and a pre-1870 standard of living, lower than the living standards of most European countries. Even factors like the cold climate or the strange language have been claimed to hamper operations in Finland. Additionally, during the early stages of industrialisation, legislation started to protect the most important natural resources for domestic use.

Although multinational subsidiaries have been rare in Finnish industry, new foreign products as well as technology have found their way into the country, even though they may have taken some time to appear. Foreign multinationals have typically established distributive firms and sales agents to perform these functions. Foreign insurance companies had a strong foothold during the nineteenth century, but they lost their significance with the development of Finnish insurance companies and because it was almost impossible to secure one's claims from abroad. With the development of cars came foreign sales agents of cars and oil.

In the following account, we concentrate on the economic activities of foreign industrial firms, because, in general, industrial production requires larger capital than distribution and other services. Industry has therefore been considered more important from the point of view of economic policy towards foreign enterprises. Both proper multinational subsidiaries and foreign-owned firms are treated. We shall try to shed light on the legislation prescribing the working conditions of foreigners and the ideas behind this legislation. The period of Russian autonomy (1809–1917), the first decades of independence (from 1917 up to the Second World War) and the time after that have their special characteristics and are therefore treated separately.

286

Protecting legislation during the period of autonomy

Foreign entrepreneurs did not seem to have any great desire to invest in Finland. On the other hand, the Finns did not encourage them particularly, even though they would have brought capital to the country. Their wish to reserve key areas of the economy for their own citizens was clear from the mid 1800s onward. As early as in 1832 a statute limited burghers' rights to Finnish citizens only. In 1851 it was prescribed that any foreigner, Russian nobles excepted, had to obtain permission from the tsar to own land.[1] The statute clearly showed the desire to keep the forests under Finnish ownership as their value was gradually rising, and there were fears about the sufficiency of timber reserves in the future.

When it was passed, the statute may not have had much practical significance, but it introduced the principle that foreigners needed special permission to own land in Finland. This principle is valid even today, and in general, governments have been very circumspect in allowing the permits. No obstacles have been raised about renting land.

Before the First World War, some other statutes were passed to limit the economic activities of foreigners, and these, too, have remained law. After 1883 mining by foreigners became subject to licence; in 1886 it became impossible for foreigners to engage in banking; and constructing and operating private railroads were limited to Finnish nationals only (1889). A vast part of the economy was involved when it was prescribed in 1895 that in limited liability companies the majority of members on boards of directors had to be Finnish.[2] All this led to a situation in which foreigners had to register their firms as limited liability companies with a majority of Finns on the board of directors. Sometimes entrepreneurs fulfilled the requirements by acquiring Finnish citizenship.

Foreign entrepreneurs during the period of autonomy

During Russian autonomy, 1809–1917, Russian entrepreneurs and the Russian government owned a number of iron works using lake ore in eastern Finland, which produced iron for metal works in St Petersburg. At its largest, at the beginning of the 1870s, their share was over a fourth of the pig iron production and an ample tenth of bar iron. Production became unprofitable and decreased from the latter half of the 1870s onwards when the Russians' own iron production expanded. At the same time, Finnish iron production lost markets in Russia, partly because of low quality, technical underdevelopment and high production costs, and partly because of stiffer Russian and British competition, tightened further by the increase of export duties from Finland to Russia (1885).[3]

In the 1840s merchants from St Petersburg expanded the Finlayson & Co.

cotton mill into the largest in Finland and the Nordic countries, its main markets being in Russia. Like some other foreign entrepreneurs, the management gradually took Finnish nationality. The founder of this first cotton mill in Finland was a Scots technician, James Finlayson. Coming from Russia, he arrived in Finland penniless, and acquired the money for the foundation of the cotton mill by a loan from the Finnish Senate (government) in 1920.[4] On the whole, the input of foreign experts, supervisors and skilled workers was significant at the early stages of industrialisation, and it was typical that these were men without means. Some were hired by Finnish firms, others were given loans by the Finnish Senate or the Bank of Finland at favourable terms in order to set up factories. In these cases we cannot, of course, speak about multinationals, as there were no parent companies in another country behind them.

Foreign entrepreneurs first became interested in Finnish forest resources at the beginning of the 1870s, in connection with the vigorous growth of demand in western Europe for sawn goods. There was plenty of wood in Finland while in some western European countries forests were becoming seriously depleted. Around 1860 the legislation which restricted the establishment of sawmills was repealed and it became possible to construct steam-operated sawmills. To some extent this change attracted foreign capital to Finland to produce sawn timber.

Sawn goods are standard products and could be considered as suitable targets for international trust activities. No such developments, however, have occurred. Sawn timber only requires simple production techniques, and its production can be started with relatively little capital. Furthermore the raw material is spread widely throughout the northern hemisphere, and it is almost impossible to gain monopolistic control in the industry. Except for the Soviet state-owned company, Exportles, there are no international large-scale producers and no multinationals in the field.

From 1870 some consortia with international capital settled in Finland. Most of the foreign entrepreneurs were Norwegian with experience of the earlier decades of the timber trade in Britain and on the continent. In Norway the wood resources were largely exhausted and Norwegian business interests were directed to the seemingly enormous forests in Finland. From their own country the Norwegians acquired only part of the necessary capital. They invested British, French, Belgian and German capital in Finland. With that they built sawmills and bought raw material, i.e. logs. Much more important than foreign entrepreneurs in the sawmill industry were foreign short-term loans to Finnish sawmills guaranteed by future deliveries.[5]

Only a few of the foreign businesses were successful in Finland. After two decades only four or five out of about twenty companies were still in operation, relying on foreign capital and ownership. In relative figures, the proportion of foreign-owned sawmills was about one-sixth of the total value of all the medium- and large-scale sawmills in the 1880s.[6] By this time the involvement of the foreigners was obviously not at its height any more. The reasons for the bad results were numerous. Timber markets experienced a severe depression after the middle of the 1870s, and instead of expected profits, the activities showed losses. Since foreign capital had come in lump sums and was not anchored to more stable capital resources, there were no reserves to fall back on when losses occurred. Operations in a foreign country were much more expensive than expected. Foreign firms tried to compensate for their lack of local knowledge by buying raw material and services at overvalued prices. In this way they did achieve temporary success, but when their funds and resources were not sufficient to beat competitors, the free use of money was found to be a waste.

Foreign sawmill enterprises started to go bankrupt at the beginning of the 1880s. This often meant the transferring of capital to Finnish ownership when domestic merchant houses bought these establishments at prices which had no relation to the costs of setting them up. Raw material contracts, too, were sold at reduced prices.

But there were exceptions: a few foreign sawmills such as Gutzeit & Co., Halla Ab and T. & J. Salvesen Ab prospered. They were all businesses which up to the First World War expanded their activities. Gutzeit and Halla were among the 10 largest Finnish industrial enterprises before the First World War.[7] What they had in common was that the ownership was foreign and they could continually import capital for their activities. All these firms were also big landowners. The Norwegian company, Gutzeit's, owned at its largest over half a million hectares of land, and with this amount it was the biggest private landowner in Finland.[8]

In a few cases foreign firms founded proper productive subsidiary units in Finland with the intention of taking advantage of Finnish customs duties. Finland had lower duties to Russia than other countries and in some cases exports were partly duty-free. The Swedish porcelain factory, Rörstrand, and the German metal works, Westfälischer Draht-Industrie-Verein, above all took advantage of these benefits. The increases in Russian duties, however, stopped such practices in 1885 and also halted the foundation of further subsidiary companies with avoidance of duties in mind. Both Rörstrand and Westfälischer Draht-Industrie-Verein operated only a short time in Finland and sold their properties to Finns after the duty increases.[9]

Restrictive legislation during independence

After independence in 1917, a strong nationalism was reflected in the new legislation, which took a cool attitude towards foreign entrepreneurs and capital. The statute of 1919 regulated business and industry, and prescribed that a foreigner had to obtain a permit to establish a business in Finland.

Further, he had to guarantee in advance the payment of taxes and other charges due to the state and the municipality.[10] In the statute on business and industry, foreigners were placed in an unfavourable position compared to Finnish citizens, who had freedom of trade.

At the beginning of the 1920s, there were efforts to limit foreign influence even further, as there were plans to restrict foreigners' rights to own shares in Finnish limited liability companies. Behind this law proposal was the aim of preventing foreign land ownership through limited liability companies. The proposal was, however, rejected as the majority of the parliament did not want to tighten the economic relations between the young nation and foreign countries. On the contrary, foreign capital was needed in the country.[11]

The Great Depression of the 1930s did not disrupt the Finnish economy as badly as it did many other countries, and Finland prospered during the second half of the 1930s. Debts to foreign countries, which had been on a fairly high level in the 1920s, became insignificant in the following decade. Domestic financial sources were sufficient even for relatively large capital formation. This created a favourable atmosphere for tighter regulation of foreign economic activities. The other factor here was the change in the political climate of Europe. By 1937 there were clear signs of growing foreign interest in Finnish natural resources (timber, copper, and nickel). To stop speculation, preparations for new legislation were made and new laws approved by the parliament in 1939. Restrictive ideas, which did not get sufficient support in the 1920s, were now accepted. The main thrust of these laws, which still prevail, is that no foreigner or foreign organisations can acquire real estate in Finland without permission from the government. The law does not restrict foreigners only but also Finnish joint-stock companies, in which according to the company's articles of association, a foreigner may own more than one-fifth of the shares. Companies without this limiting rule are designated 'dangerous companies'. Legislation also restricts the operations of foreigners by prohibiting mining claims and the purchase of mines without the government's permission. A foreigner cannot be a member of a board of directors or the general manager of a firm.[12]

Foreign firms between the world wars

During the First World War and immediately after it, foreign capital tended to be taken out of Finland. The political situation of the country was considered unstable, and when during the war trade relations were cut off, the willingness to release capital invested in Finland was even more understandable. The three large foreign sawmill companies sold their properties, some to private Finnish firms, some to the state. When a number of other foreign enterprises also became Finnish owned, the economy became strongly nationalistic.

Economic liberalism never gained complete power in Finland, and the state always had a significant share in financing the economy. Specifically, the government constructed and maintained railways and canals. Before the First World War, the government did not, however, own industry.

After the First World War, the Finnish government undertook to secure the economic independence of the country. This was manifested for example by the purchase of the shares of the Gutzeit Company. The operational rights of the only significant mine in Finland, the copper mine in Outokumpu, also belonged to foreigners, although the mine was not effectively exploited because of technological failures. These rights, too, were bought by the state. While foreign capital sharply decreased, the state became an industrial entrepreneur. The purchase of the foreign interests was, however, financed with foreign loans. The situation was peculiar when, at the beginning of the 1920s, Finnish foreign loans increased, while dependence on foreign fixed capital decreased.

The Norwegian Diesen Wood Company was the only noteable pre-war firm in the timber industry that remained in foreign hands after the First World War; it came into Finnish ownership in the 1930s. Very few new foreigners set up companies in Finland in the woodworking industry in the 1920s and the 1930s. Ones worth mentioning are the German Waldhof Company and the British Dixon family, both building cellulose factories.[13] They did not make Finnish industrial circles very happy by intruding into this very domestic area, although the Insulite Company from the USA got a warmer welcome because of its innovative technology.[14]

The overseas chemical industry acquired a footing in Finland in an exceptional way when on the initiative of the Finnish government a chlorine and chloride of lime factory was founded in 1937. The founders were the British Imperial Chemical Industries Ltd., the Belgian Solvay & Cie and the German Vereinigte Farbenfabriken, each owning a third of Finnish Chemicals Ltd. Chlorine was produced for the needs of Finnish industry, and chloride of lime for defensive purposes against possible mustard gas attacks in times of war. The government financed the construction of the chloride of lime department and the purchase of the stock of salt.[15] In the 1980s Finnish Chemicals became Finnish owned when the British and Belgian owners sold their shares to Nokia Oy. The Germans had relinquished their ownership in 1940, because of the Moscow peace treaty.[16]

In the 1920s the Swedish Kreuger trust bought a few firms in Finland and forced the remaining factories into a marketing agreement. The making of matches, however, belonged to a declining branch of industry, and in the 1930s, in the midst of great difficulties, the Kreuger trust gave up some of its markets and changed some lines of production.

The Dutch-British company Unilever bought Finnish factories initially to refine foreign raw material. Gradually, it has acquired a leading position in the production of margarine and techno-chemical products. Margarine production is, however, controlled by the government, and domestic fat products are protected by customs policy. In this particular case Unilever got round the customs barrier by establishing a subsidiary firm. It was cheaper to import raw material and semi-finished goods than finished goods, on which the duty would have been much higher.[17] For the same reason, some other firms also established subsidiaries in Finland. Typical areas were the assembling of electrical equipment and the production of medicines. Capital in these businesses was relatively small, but as labour-intensive branches of industry they were significant in creating jobs and in the importing and developing of new technology.

Between the two world wars only a few proper multinationals (Unilever, Waldhof, Kreuger, AGA, AEG) founded industrial subsidiary firms in Finland. The share of industry in foreign ownership was probably lower than before the First World War, and sometimes even these firms came into Finnish hands. During the period of Russian autonomy most foreign industrial companies had come to Finland in order to sell their products either to western markets (timber) or to Russia (other products). During the 1920s and 1930s, the multinational companies came to Finland to exploit the Finnish market.

Foreign enterprises after the Second World War

If the founding of foreign firms was insignificant during the first decades of independence, the situation did not change much after the Second World War. According to estimates, direct foreign investments were at the same level in 1958 as they were in 1938.[18] In the 1960s foreign entrepreneurs started to find their way to Finland and the establishment of international businesses began to accelerate. The number of foreign industrial firms grew almost five-fold between 1960 and 1983 and the number of non-industrial 12-fold (see Table 20.1).

It is believed that international companies considered the political situation unstable in Finland in the 1950s. This may have been why the establishment of new foreign firms developed slowly, while the rest of the world was going through a rapid internationalisation. On the other hand, strict exchange rationing, the system of blocked accounts and regulations of imports still made investment rather untempting if not impossible in the 1950s.[19]

As of late, Finland has become known as a relatively risk-free country for investment. During the 1970s 'risk premiums' on Finnish international loans dropped from 1–2 percentage points to 0.5–1 percentage points; these 'risk premiums' depend on the credit reputation and market situation of the borrower and the repayment time on the loan. At present, the interest rate difference has probably vanished.

Table 20.1. *Number of foreign firms in Finland, 1960–83 (foreign ownership over 20% of the shares)*

	1960	1967	1972	1977	1983
Industrial	45	53	105	144	207
Non-industrial	69	158	349	410	829
Total	114	211	454	554	1036

Sources: Reijo Luostarinen, *Ulkomaisten ja monikansallisten yritysten toimintavaihto-ehdoista Suomessa*, FIBO-julkaisuja, 14:16 (Helsinki, Vientikoulutussäätiö, 1981), p. 49; Suorat sijoitukset Suomesta ulkomaille ja ulkomailta Suomeen 1983, Notification, SS 1983 (Helsinki, Bank of Finland, 1983), table 5

The legal obstacles to foreign investments are almost identical to, for instance, those of Sweden and, on average, stricter than regulations prevailing in the other OECD countries. In addition, because of low tariff rates, foreign companies do not have the incentive to set up businesses in Finland. In 1967 the attitude towards foreign firms was officially made more favourable, and a government body was set up to facilitate the settling of foreign firms in Finland. Legislation was not changed. In principle, foreign firms do not have advantages over domestic ones, but in some instances they are placed on an equal basis with them. Benefits like regional industrialisation subsidies, which the government and municipalities give to new industrial firms, also accrue to foreign businesses.[20]

After the Second World War, large timber companies have been totally in Finnish hands. In fact, the government has used its power based on the law of 1939 to keep foreigners away from this resource-based industry. Mining is also totally under Finnish ownership. Lately, the most important branches of foreign industrial operations have been metal and electrotechnical industries (see Table 20.2). About one-third of the plants belonged to this group in the 1960s and the 1970s, and mainly carried out the assembly of products. Another steadily growing branch has been the chemical industry, with a share of about one-fifth of all foreign-owned production. By far the greatest part of foreign firms are now subsidiaries of multinational enterprises, contrary to earlier decades, when foreigners set up independent firms in Finland. In the subsidiaries, the share of foreign ownership is very high, or often 100 per cent.[21] With few exceptions, they have settled in Finland to compete in the Finnish market. They mostly use imported raw materials or semi-finished goods in their production.

In the late 1960s, after the change in government attitude, a number of Swedish textile and clothing firms established subsidiaries in Finland. They came to Finland because of the lower labour costs which prevailed in the 1960s

Table 20.2. *The distribution of foreign industrial firms in Finland in 1960 and 1979*

	1960 number	%	1979 number	%
Food, beverages and tobacco industries	11	24	7	5
Textiles, clothing and footwear industries	—	—	33	26
Chemical industry	8	18	24	19
Metal and electrotechnical industries	14	31	50	39
Other	12	27	14	11
Total	45	100	128	100

Sources: Göran Ehrnrooth, 'Utländskt kapital i Finland', *Finlands samhällsekonomi inför morgondagens Europa, Festskrift, Ekonomiska Samfundet i Finland 1894–1964* (Helsingfors, Ekonomisk Samfundet i Finland, 1964), p. 108; Luostarinen, p. 54.

and 1970s. The Swedish textile firms sold their products first mainly to Swedish but later on also to Finnish markets. In certain instances, unindustrialised municipalities attracted foreign firms by constructing factory buildings on favourable terms. The procedure provoked heated discussion both for and against: supporters were in favour of new jobs and increased economic activity, while opposers were afraid that in times of difficulties foreign firms would more easily leave their operations and show less social responsibility. There was also fear of foreign control, balance of payments problems etc.[22] Fifty Swedish textile firms were set up in Finland between 1965 and 1982. Fifteen of them ceased operations during this time, which seems a reasonable turnover of industrial plants.[23]

The share of foreign-owned industry has remained at a low level. It has produced only 5–6% of the value added in total industry in the 1970s and it provided employment for about 5% of the industrial labour force. However, there are sectors in which foreign ownership is very significant: oxygen and related production is, in fact, a monopoly of the Swedish AGA, whilst Unilever is also a dominant producer in its own area.[24]

The majority of foreign firms are relatively small. In 1976, 40% of them were plants with less than 100 employees and were small when measured by sales. On the other hand, seven foreign subsidiaries were in the top 100 largest industrial enterprises in 1982. The Swedish-Finnish car manufacturer Saab-Valmet (half Swedish-owned) was the largest, in 37th place, and next came the long-established Dutch-British Unilever Company, dealing in food and chemicals, in 55th place. The five remaining subsidiaries were, except for one, all Swedish by origin, and were engaged in various fields (L. M. Ericsson, Siemens, Finska Fläkt, AGA and Mölnlycke).[25]

Swedish enterprises have been the most important investor group in Finland after the Second World War. Over one-half of the foreign firms are Swedish. Swedish interest in doing business in Finland has greatly increased lately, since in 1960 only a quarter of the foreign shares were in Swedish hands. Other foreign firms come from western industrialised countries, with Denmark, the USA and Switzerland in the lead.[26]

The effects of foreign subsidiaries on the Finnish economy have been studied by considering the spread of imported technology, technical management and marketing know-how. Their significance is of course great for the subsidiaries themselves and in some cases for business clients. From the point of view of the whole economy, their direct innovative effects are estimated as rather insignificant; their greatest importance may be that they offer an example and an impulse to succeed.[27]

Since the Second World War Finland has been a net importer of capital, although the savings ratio has been internationally high. At the end of the 1950s, the share of the Finnish foreign net borrowing was under 2% of GDP at market prices. At the end of the 1970s, some years showed about 20%. Direct foreign investments have been and still are a small part of all foreign capital in Finland. On the other hand, except for a few years since the end of the 1950s, direct investments in Finland have been lower than Finnish direct investments abroad. Direct foreign investments grew quickly between 1966 and 1972, but subsequently decreased steeply.

The continual rise of the number of foreign subsidiaries in Finland at the end of the 1970s and in the early 1980s, in spite of the decrease of foreign direct investments, is based on the fact that foreign companies have been able to finance new establishments with Finnish capital. Recently, foreign banks have been allowed to found branch[28] offices in Finland, and discussions are in progress about raising the foreign ownership limit in firms to 40%.

Summary and conclusions

In Finland, along with the beginnings of industrialisation came nationalistic restrictive legislation against foreign economic influence. For a long time restrictions were rather insignificant, but gradually they increased. A development towards even stricter attitudes became visible at the beginning of independence (1917) and legislation became more prohibitive. In 1939 legislation defined so-called dangerous companies as companies having over 20% foreign ownership. These companies could not acquire real estate in Finland without the government's permission. Exploitation of natural resources, especially, was to be kept under Finnish control. These laws still prevail, although the atmosphere has become more permissive towards foreign firms since the 1960s. In discussions about foreign ownership, the contradiction between national self-determination on the one hand and need for foreign technology, entrepreneurship and capital on the other hand has been noticeable.

Despite the strict nationalistic legislation, it has been possible to obtain permits to found foreign companies. However, the list of foreign firms which have operated in Finland since the middle of the nineteenth century is rather short, and many of those who came left the country after a while. Companies either stopped operations or ended up in Finnish hands. The Long Depression of the 1870s and 1880s sent home many Russian iron producers and sawmill owners of other nationalities. Political unrest at the beginning of independence (for example the civil war) scared away a few. Between the two world wars, the share of foreign ownership was possibly even lower than during the period of autonomy. A few proper multinational subsidiaries did come to the country, and some older foreign firms returned to Finnish hands. Only after 1960 have Finnish markets attracted a larger number of foreign subsidiaries; the proportion of foreign-owned industry is 5–6% of the industrial value added.

During the period of Russian autonomy, the greater part of foreign enterprises were single firms without a parent company abroad. They often used Finnish natural resources, timber and iron-ore, and exported their products to western countries or to Russia. Some of the few multinational subsidiaries took advantage of the lower Finnish duties to Russia; some brought new technology to the country. This situation changed between the world wars and instead of foreign-owned single companies, more subsidiaries of multinational firms came to Finland. After the Second World War almost all foreign firms have been subsidiaries of multinationals. The use of natural resources has not been granted to foreigners, and foreign subsidiaries have instead come to compete in the Finnish markets.

It is difficult to ascertain the significance of the restrictive policies in the development of the country. However, they have not prevented very fast economic growth in Finland over the last 100 years. The growth of the GDP per capita has been approximately 2% annually, which by international standards is quite high.

NOTES

1 Jukka Mikkola, 'Venäjältä tulleet teollisuudenharjoittajat Suomessa 1808–1880', *Venäläiset Suomessa* 1809–1917. Historiallinen Arkisto, 83 (Helsinki, SHS, 1984), pp. 211–12; Markku Ahonen, 'Tukkimetsistä tehtaisiin–patruunasta puulaakiin: Ulkomaalaisten taloudellisen toiminnan oikeudellisen sääntelyn kehitys Suomessa 1850–1938' (mimeograph, University of Helsinki, 1984), p. 34.
2 Asetus pankkiliikkeestä, jota yhtiö harjoittaa 10.5.1886/13; Asetus yksityisistä

rautateistä yleistä keskuusliikettä varten 15.4.1889/16; Laki osakeyhtiöistä 2.5.1895/34.

3 Eevert Laine, *Suomen vuoritoimi 1809–1884, II, Ruukit*, Historiallisia Tutkimuksia XXXI, 2 (Helsinki, SHS, 1948); Erkki Pihkala, 'Finnish iron and the Russian market, 1880–1913', *The Scandinavian economic history review*, XII (1964), 121–38.

4 Gustav V. Lindfors, *Finlaysonin tehtaat Tampereella, I. 1820–1907* (Helsinki, Finlayson Oy, 1938), pp. 91–111.

5 Jorma Ahvenainen, *Suomen sahateollisuuden historia* (Porvoo, WSOY, 1984), pp. 219–28, 300–2.

6 Kai Hoffman, *Suomen sahateollisuuden kasvu, rakenne ja rahoitus 1800-luvun jälkipuoliskolla*, Bidrag till kännedom av Finlands natur och folk, 124 (Tammisaari, Finska Vetenskaps-Societeten, 1980), pp. 80–4.

7 Riitta Hjerppe, *Suurimmat yritykset Suomen teollisuudessa 1844–1975*, Bidrag till kännedom av Finlands natur och folk, 123 (Tammisaari, Finska Vetenskaps-Societeten, 1979), pp. 170–1.

8 Ahvenainen, p. 244.

9 Keijo Alho, *Suomen uudenaikaisen teollisuuden synty ja kehitys 1860–1914*, Suomen Pankin taloustieteellisen tutkimuslaitoksen julkaisuja, B:11 (Helsinki, Suomen Pankki, 1949), pp. 222–4.

10 Laki elinkeinonharjoittamisen oikeudesta 27.9.1919/122.

11 Ahonen, pp. 92–5.

12 Laki ulkomaalaisten sekä eräiden yhteisöjen oikeudesta omistaa ja hallita kiinteätä omaisuutta ja osakkeita 28.7.1939/219; Laki ulkomaalaisten oikeudesta ryhtyä-yhtiömieheksi kauppayhtiöön ja henkilökohtaisesti vastuunalaiseksi yhtiö-mieheksi kommandiittiyhtiöön 28.7.1939/220; Laki osakeyhtiöistä annetun lain muuttamisesta 28.7.1939/221; Laki osakkeita koskevista välikäsisuhteista 28.7.1939/224.

13 Ahvenainen, pp. 310–11, 338; Ahonen, p. 166; Vilho Annala, *Outokummun historia* (Helsinki, Outokumpu Oy, 1960), pp. 95–103.

14 Ahonen, p. 149.

15 *Valtiopäivät 1937, Asiakirjat I–II*, Edusk, vast. – Esitys 62 (Helsinki, 1937).

16 Viktor Hoving, *Enso-Gutzeit Osakeyhtiö. 1872–1958, I–II* (Helsinki, Enso Gutzeit Oy, 1961), pp. 667–8.

17 Charles Wilson, *The history of Unilever*, I (London, Cassell, 1954), pp. 288–9.

18 Göran Ehrnrooth, 'Utländskt kapital i Finland', *Finlands samhällsekonomi inför morgondagens Europa, Festskrift, Ekonomiska Samfundet i Finland 1894–1964* (Helsingfors, Ekonomiska Samfundet i Finland, 1964), p. 109.

19 Ehrnrooth, p. 111.

20 Heikki Aintila, *Ulkomaisessa omistuksessa oleva yritystoiminta Suomessa* (mimeograph, Helsinki, Taloudellinen suunnittelukeskus, 1975), pp. 5–9.

21 Kurt Kääriäinen *et al.*, *Utländska företag i Finland – en kartläggning*, Preliminära forskningsrapporter, Serie C (Helsingfors, Svenska Handelshögskolan, 1972), p. 34.

22 P. J. Boldt and Christian Sundgren, 'Finland och de multinationella företagen', *Työväen taloudellinen tutkimuslaitos: Katsaus*, IV (Helsinki, 1977), pp. 23–39; Pentti Viita, 'Kansainvälisten yritysten etuja ja haittoja', *Kansantaloudellinen aikakauskirja*, III (Helsinki, 1973), pp. 190–203.

23 Information from Markus Fogelholm, Bank of Finland.

24 Aintila, p. 13.

25 *Talouselämä*, 19 (Helsinki, 1983), pp. 36–44.

26 Suorat sijoitukset Suomeen ja Suomesta ulkomaille 1982, Notification, SS 1982 (Helsinki, Bank of Finland, 1982).
27 Sari Baldauf, *Ulkomaisten ja monikansallisten yritysten innovaatiovaikutukset Suomessa*, FIBO-julkaisuja, 14:12 (Helsinki, Vientikoulutussäätiö, 1979), pp. 201–5.
28 Suorat sijoitukset Suomeen, pp. 1–3.

21 German multinationals and the Nazi state in occupied Europe

RICHARD J. OVERY

During the Second World War the relationship between German industry and industry elsewhere in Europe was transformed. By 1941 Germany was master of large parts of the industrialised continent. German leaders sought to co-ordinate the industrial resources of the conquered and dependent areas with the long-term economic interests of the Reich. An important part of this strategy was direct investment by German firms in the industry of the occupied areas. The opportunities opened up by conquest to extend German multinationalism were substantial, though much of the new multinational activity was promoted through state ownership and was governed in the main by political considerations and the needs of war. The relationship between government and multinational development is therefore of central importance.

This fact raises some problems of definition. Much of the new multinational activity did not spring in the main from commercial motives. Indeed the state sought to suppress purely economic motives and to substitute some rough notion of 'racial political' priority when supervising industrial acquisitions or controlling existing German subsidiaries. The government, dominated by radical nationalist politicians, became the self-appointed guardians of the national interest. Firms that co-operated with these interests were given greater freedom of action than others, but all German firms were subject to a set of regulations and controls over investment policy, product policy and labour dictated by the state economic apparatus. The New Order raised other problems of definition as well. German businesses which owned shares in Austrian or Czech firms found their holdings converted into German businesses as Germany's frontiers expanded. The same was true in western Poland and eastern France, areas absorbed back into Greater Germany. Elsewhere in occupied Europe constitutional questions were left in abeyance, so that the exact national status of captured businesses remained unclear. In many cases German private firms acquired trusteeship over foreign firms, leaving the question of ownership open until the end of the war, particularly in the case of those taken over by the Commissioner for Enemy Property, which were

299

still legally owned by Germany's enemies. For the purpose of this paper multinational activity is taken to be all direct investment in industry, whether state or private capital, outside the frontiers of the pre-1938 Reich.

There is no doubt that the political context within which this German penetration of European industry took place is unique in the history of multinationalism. But it does nonetheless raise important questions about the relationship between government and industry at an important stage in the development of large-scale German business, and provides an extreme example of political power used to further industrial expansion along multinational lines.

I

Before the Second World War German multinationalism was less developed than that of other industrialised countries. There were a number of reasons for this. German firms lost a large proportion of their foreign assets after the war and had to start rebuilding from scratch. They concentrated on reconstruction and reorganisation inside Germany. German firms also faced both political barriers and economic constraints in extending activities outside Germany in the 1920s and 1930s. In the case of Poland, for example, German industry was gradually excluded by the Polish government and German businesses taken over by the state. In Czechoslovakia and France there was strong resistance to the penetration of German capital. German investment in Czech industry comprised only 7% of all foreign investment there in 1937.[1] Political uncertainty, fear of nationalisation and the poor state of German finances combined to limit German multinational expansion. German firms preferred to export direct from Germany, particularly to hard-currency areas which could provide foreign exchange to buy raw materials abroad. Only in cases where foreign governments made it difficult to export did German firms set up subsidiaries producing direct for foreign markets; or in cases where it was necessary to safeguard sources of raw material supply.[2] On balance German firms lacked the financial strength and opportunity of French, British or American industry, and, where they could, they arrived at marketing or sales agreements with foreign competitors rather than undertake direct capital penetration. By 1939 the proportion of German industrial activity conducted by subsidiaries abroad was relatively small.

This situation was encouraged after 1933 by the German government with its controls over trade and preference for domestic production. But after the announcement of the Second Four Year Plan in 1936 the domestic political context began to change. Firms were encouraged with state backing to push more forcefully into central and south-eastern Europe. At the same time the state extended more and more controls over the industrial economy and the domestic capital market in order to divert the necessary resources to war preparation and to assert strategic priorities. Greater state control over the economy was an important pre-requisite for the period of expansion which began with the *Anschluss* in March 1938. Nazi leaders hoped to build up a German-dominated economic bloc in central and eastern Europe which could be used to contribute some of the vast military and strategic resources needed to wage a major war. Through its foreign policy the Nazi state sought to ease the conditions of access to the economies of the region through direct occupation and incorporation or through diplomatic and military pressure. After 1938 multinationalism became a device to further the political aims of the German government in using the resources of other countries to make up for what was lacking inside the Reich; direct investment in the region was closely controlled by the state.

The industrial spoils acquired in the first wave of expansion before the war were largely taken over by the state holding company, the Reichswerke 'Hermann Goering', with the help of the Dresdner and Deutsche banks, which co-operated in shielding the Reichswerke from publicity in its share dealings while buying up the major Austrian and Czech business on its behalf. The vacuum created in central Europe by the flight of western and Jewish capital was filled not in the main by private German firms but by state holding companies. The Reichswerke had begun life as a state company set up by Goering in the summer of 1937 to exploit low-grade German iron ores in the framework of the Four Year Plan. Instead, as Goering came to acquire extensive controls over the economy, it was used as the foundation for building up a vast industrial conglomerate to secure the gains of occupied Europe for Germany's strategic needs. It was not in this sense a true multinational, seeking to set up profitable subsidiaries abroad to the benefit of the parent company, but was a political instrument of the Nazi state designed to defend the interests of 'national economy' and to secure for the party extensive control over its imperial gains. 'Profits' came in the form of arms and resources for the Reich. The development of the Reichswerke was closely bound up with the political ambitions of those who ran it, a mixture of nationalist bureaucrats and small businessmen generally hostile to German big business. It was not simply an instrument for incorporating the spoils of Europe quickly into the German war machine, but became a key institution in the post-war planning for a state-controlled economy dominated by bureaucratic managers, very different from the Reichswerke set up to cope with armaments contracts in the First World War.[3]

The role of the state was made explicit from the outset of German expansion. The Austrian economy, said Goering, must be kept 'firmly in the hand of the state'.[4] The German Economics Ministry issued a decree a week after the *Anschluss* preventing any unauthorised capital transfers in Austria, to be enforced retroactively. Authorisation was granted to Goering as head of the Four Year Plan. When the Sudetenland was occupied in October 1938 the Plan was immediately extended to cover the area, and the chief industries taken under the supervision of the Economics Ministry pending their distribution.[5] Major private firms got very little from the takeover of Austria and Czechoslovakia, with the important exception of IG Farben, and there were limits even in this case. The chemical industry had the advantage of already being closely integrated with the industrial programmes of the Four Year Plan, but IG Farben was particularly well placed because of the progressive Nazification of its leading managerial circles.

IG Farben was involved in the takeover of foreign assets from the start, after a decade of growing influence in the chemical industry of central Europe. In Austria it acquired ownership from the Rothschilds of the Skoda Werke Wetzler, after its general manager, Isador Pollack, had unsuccessfully tried to merge with other European firms to avoid German control. IG Farben was also able to use its Czech subsidiary, Dynamit AG Bratislava, to gain entry to the Austrian and Czech chemical industry. In July 1938 Dynamit took over two Austrian chemical works, Carbidwerke Deutsch-Matrei and Österreichische Dynamit Nobel AG. In early 1939, before the occupation of Czechoslovakia, IG Farben was finally successful in penetrating the largest Czech chemical producer by taking over the Aussig and Kalkenau plants in the Sudetenland jointly with Chemische Fabrik von Heyden, both of which held 50% of the shares. With the break-up of Czechoslovakia IG acquired the full control over its Slovakian subsidiary which the Czech government had previously obstructed, and enjoyed a dominant position from which to launch further expansion into south-eastern Europe.[6]

By comparison other private transactions in Austria were much less important. Krupp was allowed to increase participation in the Berndorfer Metallwarenfabrik, though on the condition laid down by Goering that Krupp 'will do everything possible to raise the Austrian economy to the level which is desirable not only in the interests of Austria but also in that of Germany'.[7] The Stahlverein increased its participation in Böhler AG from 39.5% to 67%.[8] But the bulk of non-German businesses were brought under the control of the state. When Flick expressed interest in further Petschek holdings which had fallen into German hands in the Sudetenland, Körner, Goering's state secretary, replied that the German Petschek mines, some of which Flick had already acquired, would be 'the last coalfields to be transferred to private ownership... any lignite coalfield which would become available in the course of further aryanisation would have to be taken over or come under direct control of the state'.[9] This was a disappointment for the private firms which had been given to understand by officials in the Finance Ministry, who were either unsympathetic towards or ignorant of Goering's economic plans, that the Sudeten lignite mines would be sold off to IG Farben or Flick. Instead the state took them all over, reorganised them into a single business and transferred them as a whole to the Reichswerke.[10]

The same pattern was followed in Czechoslovakia. When the Škoda works fell into German hands both Flick and Krupp expressed interest. But the works were instead taken over by the Reichswerke, which gradually built up a majority shareholding. The state went further and put pressure on private German firms that already had a multinational interest in Austria to transfer the interest to the state in order to produce a unified exploitation of the area. The Vereinigte Stahlwerke was compelled to sell its controlling interest in the Alpine Montangesellschaft to the Reichswerke, eventually losing even the 10% stake it had been given as compensation in a new steel complex set up by the Reichswerke at Linz. Mannesmann sold out its 50% interest in Kromag to the state controlled Steyr-Daimler-Puch, though it was able to keep its interest in the Prague Iron Company after the German occupation.[11] Foreign multinationals in the occupied areas were also brought under considerable pressure to sell their shares to the German state, though a great number of non-German firms had abandoned the area before the German occupation. Only with American firms were German negotiators more cautious, for there were strong indications that German holdings in the United States were vulnerable to expropriation if undue pressure were put on American shareholders in European firms.[12]

There were certainly elements in the German administration and in German industry who were hostile to these developments. The Finance Ministry remained strongly critical of the Reichswerke, with its demands for state subsidy and tendency to monopoly. When the Czech lignite mines fell into German hands the Ministry felt that the claims of the Reichswerke were 'quite out of the question' and 'cannot be complied with'.[13] IG Farben was distrustful of Reichswerke ambitions too, particularly after the Sudeten mines were acquired by Goering to provide the raw material for a large synthetic oil plant at Brüx under state control, paying a licence to IG Farben in respect of the process; and even more so when the Reichswerke began to trespass on IG interests in the production and distribution of domestic gas.[14] But as Goering's economic and political strategy began to crystallise during 1938 and early 1939 the claims of the state became more insistent and wide-ranging. In Austria the Reichswerke gradually acquired ownership of the major iron, steel and machinery sectors, including Steyr-Daimler-Puch and the Alpine Montangesellschaft. In Czechoslovakia it took over all the lignite mines of the Sudeten area, major iron and steel businesses, including Ferdinand Nordbahn and Poldihütte and Vítkovice, and the arms and machinery works of Škoda, Erste Brünner Maschinenfabrik and Brünner Waffenwerke, extending the share of German capital in total foreign investment in Czechoslovakia to 47% by 1940. Shares in these companies were collected over a period of time from Austrian and Czech banks and from private shareholders. Full Reichswerke control of Poldi and Škoda took longest to acquire; in both cases the German state issued new shares against capital invested by the Reichswerke which finally gave it a controlling interest.[15] Only in the case of Vítkovice was there any difficulty since the ownership had been hastily transferred to the London-based Alliance Insurance before the German occupation. The works were occupied and operated by the Reichswerke, which attempted to annul the London shares and gain full ownership on the grounds that the business was Jewish as defined in Reich law. The Reich Protector, von Neurath, refused to allow the London shares to be annulled and instead the Reichswerke had to be content with a special operating treaty signed in 1941 which gave it trustee status but left the question of ownership until the end of hostilities.[16]

The Reichswerke was not the only state-funded institution to share in these acquisitions, though it was by far the most important, assuming a controlling participation in almost two-thirds of the heavy industry of the two countries. The ease with which the transfers were made can be explained in part by the absence of any large private German shareholding in the region which might have forestalled the growth of state ownership. Private firms were given access to industry that was either too small or too specialised technically for the Reichswerke to cope with. The German state also enjoyed the advantage that significant shareholdings had been sold by private owners to the Austrian and Czech states in anticipation of German expansion, which were simply bought up on very favourable terms by the German state when Austria and Czechoslovakia ceased to exist as sovereign units. These circumstances made it possible to pursue a policy of direct state investment straight away, in order to bring the new businesses quickly into the production programmes of the Four Year Plan and the armed forces.

II

The expansion into Austria and Czechoslovakia set the pattern for the war years after 1939. The guidelines for the economies of the captured areas were laid down by the state. At the centre of German economic strategy was a policy of direct investment, as the best guarantee of securing a dominant position for Germany in the post-war European economy and in order to exclude as far as possible the other major investing countries from participation in European industry. The process of direct capital penetration was authorised by Goering in September and October 1939, when the Finance Ministry was instructed that foreign acquisitions were to be kept in state hands on the grounds that it was essential that the economic extension of 'Germandom' should be properly co-ordinated.[17] Goering expanded these arguments in his directives on the Polish economy: 'Any wild confiscations, and any profiteering of individuals will be prosecuted... The essential point is that Polish property liable to confiscation shall be utilised in the interests of the Reich, i.e. of the community, but not for the benefit of individuals.' The area under German occupation 'formed a *homogeneous economic area* with manifold, mutual obligations which makes necessary a co-ordinated supervision from Berlin' (italics in original).[18] Even in cases where the state would not acquire ownership, particularly of property already owned by German nationals, all industry held abroad was to be 'guided by the state' (*staatlich gelenkt*).

The same policy was authorised after victory over France in 1940. Occupation authorities throughout Europe were instructed before any final peace settlement to take every opportunity in questions of future shareholding 'to make it possible for the German economy to obtain access even during the war to material of interest in the occupied countries'.[19] 'One of the goals of the German economic policy', Goering announced in August, 'is the increase of German influence in foreign enterprises... I reserve for myself the granting of permission for the purchasing of enterprises, participations etc... situated in the occupied territories.'[20] The decrees on shareholding outlawed any attempt to sell shares in the conquered areas to a third party, whether they had been sold before the decree was published or not. Nor were the military or the occupation authorities allowed to make 'independent commitments of any kind to individual German interested parties'.[21] All enemy property was seized immediately and placed under the Commissioner for Enemy Property; all other acquisitions came directly under the supervision of the Four Year Plan.

The state's role in all this was explained by Goering's state secretary in the Four Year Plan journal at the end of 1940. 'In a national economy highly developed technically and politically, which should serve not the profit motive of the individual but the common good, there will always exist huge tasks which have outgrown the private sphere and will be soluble only through the forces of the community.'[22] Behind these functional arguments can be detected important political motives. The extension of German control over Europe's economy meant more permanent power for the party in economic affairs. The Nazi government did not want the balance of power within the economy to tilt back decisively in favour of the big German concerns by handing them European economic resources on a plate. Paul Pleiger believed that the private firms were only interested in buying foreign assets to set them off against high tax liabilities in the Reich.[23] Nor could the party afford to ignore radical nationalist opinion, whether in the party or the administration, by openly rewarding German big business with the spoils of a war fought ostensibly on behalf of the German community as a whole. Economic populism and Prussian statist traditions met on common ground in resisting purely commercial pressures. There was also the question of sheer power. Nazi leaders by 1941 had a degree of personal authority in conquered Europe inconceivable a decade before. It is not difficult to understand their hesitancy in sharing this power unconditionally with industrial circles outside the favoured party few.

The response of German industry to these circumstances was far from uniform. Victory in 1939 and 1940 presented German industry with the opportunity to reverse the situation it had faced between the wars, to roll back foreign capital, particularly British and French, and to gain revenge for the losses brought about through the Versailles settlement. There is no doubt that sectors of German heavy industry did feel strongly that they deserved some form of compensation for the economic losses forced through political changes after 1919: 'I could write novels about that', minuted Friedrich Flick in 1938.[24] There was strong support for this view in the Economics Ministry, which in response to Goering's decree ordering the acquisition of shares by German firms discussed whether or not 'the stocks should be bought for private economy or for the Reich'. The outcome of the discussion was a general agreement that the transfers should be made to private hands via the German banks and that Goering must bow to 'superior opinions' in 'undertaking to hand them over to private industry. Under all circumstances, a further extension of control by trust is to be avoided.'[25] Both Funk at the Ministry, and Schwerin von Krosigk, the Finance Minister, preferred this policy, the one because of his fears of backdoor 'bolshevisation', the latter because of his dislike of state subsidy and bureaucratised industry.[26]

But this view was by no means shared by German industry as a whole. The growth of state power in the economy backed by influential figures in the party made businessmen wary of undertaking initiatives abroad in competition with the Four Year Plan. They were also constrained from setting up multinational organisations by lack of capital or skilled managerial personnel which the state was not, or at least not until the conquest of western Russia. Krupp's reasons for not taking up fresh commitments in Poland were based partly on considerations of this kind.[27] For even the largest private businesses the economic cost of taking up ownership of foreign assets during wartime, with the political and military situation unclear and with no guarantee of long-term financial security (Ruhr leaders warned Goering in 1940 of the dangers of challenging both Russia and the United States), made the strategy of foreign expansion less inviting than the private industrial lobby realised.[28]

There was another political consideration too. The occupied areas were taken over by Nazi appointees whose view of their new territories was a very proprietary one. In Lithuania, for example, the newly installed Gauleiter, Lohse, prohibited German firms from entering captured businesses and rejected private claims in favour of some kind of state monopoly. AEG was expelled from an electricity works which it had occupied without permission; Flick's advice to his representatives in the area was to 'proceed with caution'.[29] In Poland the SS and Governor Frank between them tried to pursue an independent economic policy, restraining both IG Farben and the Reichswerke from buying up captured Polish plants. Even established affiliates were not immune. The Osram plant in Poland was taken over by a Reich commissioner for alleged inefficiency in 1942.[30]

This world of 'Intrigenspielen' ('games of intrigue'), as one exasperated accountant put it, was nowhere more evident than in the conflicts over the industry of Polish Silesia and eastern France.[31] The conquest of Poland brought back the Upper Silesian heavy industrial region into German hands. Here there were old German claims going back before 1914. The Four Year Plan hoped to pre-empt these claims by keeping the industry of the region under state control, and if possible directly in state hands, by transferring it wholesale to the Reichswerke. A special trustee office was set up under Hans Winkler, the Haupttreuhandstelle Ost, which took over all captured property on behalf of the Reich. As in Czechoslovakia this transfer was made easier by the fact that many of the coal mines and steel works were directly owned by the Polish state and could be expropriated as enemy property. Goering met some resistance from Winkler himself, who thought it wrong to place all industry under one owner and was backed up by the Economics Ministry.[32] Goering insisted on obtaining at the very least the coal mines of the region to serve Reichswerke needs at Salzgitter and Linz. Winkler agreed to this, though the coal gave Goering strong influence on the steel works as well, which were dependent on the Silesian coalfield. The mines were consolidated into a single company, the Bergwerksverwaltung Oberschlesien GmbH. Krupp and Röchling, who were both interested in buying up Silesian plants, urged Goering to restore the mines serving Katowice and the Bismarckhütte to private ownership, but Goering refused.[33] The outcome was that the iron and steel works on their own were a much less inviting prospect. Flick, who had owned the Bismarckhütte before 1914, lacked the financial resources to compete with the Reichswerke after acquiring new lignite assets from the state in 1939, and was, after June 1940, more interested in acquiring something in Lorraine. Krupp abandoned the contest for the Dubenskogrube on grounds of cost, but presumably from political caution as well, since Goering had personally intervened to acquire it for the Reichswerke.[34] The Vereinigte Stahlwerke succeeded in getting operating contracts at the Katowice steel plants but was denied ownership on the grounds that this would strengthen the position of the Ruhr in an area where 'in the future, as now during the time of war economy, the people's economic necessities would have to stand ahead of private contracts'.[35]

Indeed it was by no means clear at first that private industry would gain very much of the iron and steel capacity either. The Reichswerke took over control of Berg-und Hüttenwerke AG at Trzynietz, the largest steel works in the region, and then, with the fall of Paris, succeeded in getting the shares bought outright by the Dresdner and Deutsche banks from the Union

Européene Industrielle et Financière which held them on behalf of Schneider et Cie. Berg-und Hüttenwerke then took over the other steel works, Bismarckhütte and Königshütte, with a view to selling them to the Reichswerke. In the end the shares were sold to a group of private buyers and not to the Reichswerke at all, though they were sold in such a way as to avoid a dominant position for any of the big concerns. Most of the shares were sold to smaller German Silesian companies that had lost out in 1922 and 1937 with Polish nationalisation of German participations. These same circles were successful in winning back the Hohenlohe zinc works too, which Goering had taken over along with the coal mines, but which he was forced to relinquish to the other zinc producers after vigorous lobbying.[36] Nevertheless Reichswerke nominees still dominated the boards of directors of the privatised iron and steel works and through Otto Fitzner, the local head of administration, and Hans Winkler, the Four Year Plan representative, were able to control the activity of the private firms.[37]

The same conflict developed over the heavy industry of Lorraine, Luxemburg and north-eastern France. Here again there were well-established German claims and here again Goering's initial response was to claim all the industry of the region for the state. Paul Pleiger, the managing director of the Reichswerke, argued that this strategy was based on a fear of the Ruhr firms 'getting together' in the area to challenge the position of the Reichswerke in the rest of Europe.[38] It was his view that the Reichswerke should try to get as much as it could in Lorraine 'for the reason that the rest of the German iron industry, particularly the west German industry, still considers the Herman Goering Works to be superfluous'.[39] These arguments were put to Goering in June 1940. He ordered that 'the endeavour of German industry to take over enterprises in the recently occupied territory must be rejected in the sharpest manner. Travel of industrialists into the occupied territory must not be permitted for the present.'[40] Trustees and special commissioners were sent in to take temporary control over the iron ore mines and the steel works of the area. Funk wrote to the iron and steel industry that it should 'repress any desire for annexation'.[41] Four Year Plan officials made it clear that the decision on ownership of the captured plants was Goering's responsibility and that there could be no guarantees that private ownership on the basis of past claims would be re-established in the region.

Pleiger's fears were well founded. Industrialists met with von Hanneken, the Four Year Plan plenipotentiary for iron and steel, on 10 June. At this meeting they pressed their claims for 'repatriation'. Firms with historic claims were to get their plants back; other private firms should also be considered; the iron ore mines should be consolidated and the flow of ore controlled jointly by all the steel companies of the area and those of the Ruhr and Saarland. The industrialists also put pressure on von Hanneken to ask Pleiger to abandon building the Reichswerke at Salzgitter altogether, as the acquisition of Lorraine solved the problem of output and threatened to produce a large surplus of sheet steel capacity if Pleiger persisted with the original scheme. His reply was 'write to Goering yourself'. Even von Hanneken, whom they regarded as an ally, was surprised by the stampede to acquire the best plants: 'Everybody is scrambling after Rombach, Hayingen and Differdingen, and in a little while the other plants will be offered like sour beer!'[42] By 26 June the industry had produced a set of principles on which the distribution of captured plants should be based, giving preference to old claims, but also to those firms in the Reich, like Flick, which had a poor ratio of coal to steel output and needed more steel capacity. These included Flick, Hoesch and Mannesmann, but adversely affected the claims of Vereinigte Stahlwerke and Kloeckner where the ratio went the other way. There was general agreement that in the future French participation in the region was to be excluded completely. By mid August the claims had largely been filed. Lists of these were sent to the Economics Ministry and to Goering and to the local administrators in Lorraine.[43]

By this time, however, it was known that Goering had plans of his own. It is not clear exactly when or why he was made to reduce his claim to take over everything. Even by August it was rumoured that the Reichswerke was looking for five million tons of steel capacity in the region.[44] Goering was clearly influenced by Pleiger's advice. Since it was impossible to expect a takeover of all plants and mines, Pleiger's strategy was to divide the minette ore mines from the foundries, as the coal had been divided from steel production in Silesia, in order to reduce the economic influence of any of the successful German claimants. The ore mines were reorganised and placed under a Reich trustee, Karl Raabe of the Reichswerke, where they remained until recaptured by the Allies.[45]

The Reichswerke then laid claim to the largest slice of the available steel capacity, the huge Arbed trust in Luxemburg, the de Wendel concern, itself a multinational with business interests in Holland, Germany and Luxemburg, and to the former Thyssen holdings which were now forfeit to the state after Thyssen's flight from Germany; in all a total of 1.4 million tons steel capacity. Mannesmann, Krupp, Gutehoffnungshütte, Hoesch and the Stahlverein were all denied what they had asked for. The remaining French plants were allocated to German firms on a trustee basis. Flick, after pressing his claims forcefully on Goering as compensation for 'losses' in Silesia, was successful in acquiring trusteeship of the Rombacher Hüttenwerke. The remainder was distributed among a number of smaller Ruhr and Saar companies, Röchling, Kloeckner, and the Neunkircher Eisenwerke. There was to be no question of French participation.[46]

The question of ownership was sidestepped by introducing a system of trusteeship, though there was little alternative since the former French owners refused to sell their participations voluntarily.[47] Trusteeship was, however, unpopular with the Ruhr firms which, according to Ernst Poensgen, head of the Stahlverein, wanted 'a free hand in the companies. Any attempt to gain control over the statutes or the appointment of the board of directors would not be suitable.' Nor was the Ruhr satisfied with the scale of Reichswerke gains, 'the cherries in the cake', complained Poensgen.[48] No doubt the Ruhr was influenced by the widespread feeling that the war was effectively over with the defeat of France, and could not see why the state would not permit the immediate sale of the plants where this was feasible, rather than a trustee system. Though they were able to make qualified gains in both Poland and France, the state kept overall control of both regions, dictating prices, product policy and conditions of access to the captured plants, while local Nazi officials, Frank and Winkler in Poland, Bürckel in Lorraine, pursued ambitions of their own.

III

From the world of industrial 'games of intrigue' it is possible to disentangle four distinct types of multinational activity within the New Order economy of occupied Europe; direct state ownership, monopoly organisations with mixed participation, trusteeship and direct private ownership.

1 *Direct state ownership or participation*

The German state, via state holding companies (VIAG: Vereinigte Industrieunternehmungen AG; VEBA: Vereinigte Elektrizitäts und Bergwerke AG) or state-owned German industrial undertakings, was the largest direct beneficiary of the German strategy of direct investment outside the Reich. The foremost example was the Reichswerke, which took over ownership of a large part of Austrian, Czech and Polish industry and mining, setting up an enormous conglomerate with assets in excess of five billion marks. Reichswerke participation was also built up through the activity of the major subsidiaries that it took over. Rheinmetall-Borsig, for example, had substantial holdings in the Dutch armaments firms N.V. Nederlandsche Maschinenfabriek Artillerie Inrictungen and the ship engine company Werkspoor NV Amsterdam. In France Rheinmetall was given the management of the major armaments works, including Schneider et Cie, on a trustee basis.[49] In Slovakia the Reichswerke eventually acquired ownership of the subsidiary of the Brünner Waffenwerke, Podbrezova Berg-und Hütten AG, from the Slovakian government in 1941; and via Vítkovice it acquired the Ruda Bergbau und Hüttenbetriebe.[50] Reichswerke activities were also expanded through setting up new plants in occupied territories, the Linz iron and steel complex, the massive Eisenwerke Oberdonau (which was by the end of the war the major supplier of tank hulls and turrets), and the hydrogenation plant at Brüx. All of these new plants were supplied with resources of coal, iron ore or steel from other businesses taken over by the Reichswerke. In some cases the Reichswerke co-operated with private firms in buying up foreign assets, as in the case of Krupp in Yugoslavia, where the Reichswerke prevented exclusive control over raw materials from falling into private hands.[51]

The state was also able to use the state multinationals as a 'battering ram' for entering economies that were not occupied territory. Capital participation in Roumanian heavy industry, including oil, was made possible by acquiring assets in Austria and Czechoslovakia which held shares in Roumanian firms. Political pressure was put on the Roumanian government to accept German capital penetration through German state-owned firms. The Reichswerke by 1941 enjoyed a 50% stake in a joint German-Roumanian holding company, 'Rogifer', which managed the affairs of the bulk of Roumanian heavy industry.[52]

2 Monopoly organisations

Early in the war the Four Year Plan office arrived at the decision to set up in the New Order economy a number of continental monopoly organisations made up of a mixture of state-owned and private firms, regulated by the state, which would accept responsibility for investment policy, pricing and trade. The first of these organisations were in textiles and oil. The state also set up territorial monopoly organisations, of which the Berg-und Hüttengesellschaft Ost in Russia was the best example; it took over control of all the industry in a given region on behalf of the state. The object of the monopoly organisations was to vest control of important industries in state hands so that the final structure of the New Order economy could be determined in German interests and not simply through market forces.[53]

The oil monopoly, Kontinentale Öl, was set up for strategic purposes as well. Goering argued that a commodity so vital in wartime would have to be kept permanently in state hands after the war. Set up in March 1941, the oil monopoly was run by Funk on Goering's behalf. Its capital was fixed initially at 50 million marks, 30 million to be held by the Reichswerke subsidiary Borussia GmbH, the remaining 20 million to come from a mixture of state and private chemical and oil companies. The Borussia shares carried multiple voting rights so that control would always be vested in the state. The monopoly was not only responsible for all oil exploration and production within Germany, but took over the oil holdings of enemy powers as well. This included the Belgian Concordia company, of which 45% of the capital was in German hands; French Colombia; and Südost-Chemie, which was linked with the Roumanian Petrol-Block, of which the Reichswerke held its own participation. By 1941 Germany controlled 47% of Roumanian oil output.

Negotiations began in 1941 with Standard Oil for the transfer of their Hungarian oilfields, valued at $30 million, but were interrupted by the outbreak of war in December. It was also planned to take the whole of the Russian oil industry, once it was captured, under the monopoly's control.[54]

The general drift of state thinking on the post-war economy can be illustrated by the recommendations drawn up by Paul Rheinländer, a Reichswerke director, for the control of the European iron, steel and coal industries after the war. The long-term goal was to reorganise the industry on co-ordinated lines on a continental basis. The Ruhr would be restricted to its pre-war level of output and the large planned increases in iron and steel output would come in Austria, Czechoslovakia, Silesia and from the captured resources in Russia. The whole industry was to be subject to regulations on resource use and price determined by the state, which would also provide the investment to build up the eastern economy. In this way major economic resources – the coal and ore – would be utilised on the basis of national needs and not for quick economic returns.[55] The monopolies were designed to enable the state to plan economic policy on major industries in a large multinational empire in which the sheer scale of the operation precluded reliance on private initiative, though it did not exclude the survival of private ownership.

3 Trusteeship

In addition to direct ownership and monopoly organisations, the state also set up a trustee system in which private and state firms alike took over and operated captured businesses on behalf of the state. This did not imply ownership, as party and state officials were at pains to point out, but was dictated by the wartime necessity of getting captured industries working again as quickly as possible on war orders. Trusteeship involved the granting of a special operating contract to the firm involved on the understanding that most of the money and equipment necessary would be provided by the state, and that the trustee was responsible for operating the works as economically as possible. A number of different grounds were used for justifying trusteeship. It was used in cases where sheer confiscation or purchase was not possible, for example, enemy property whose future had to be decided after the war, or the property of foreign nationals whose identity or whereabouts could not be discovered. It was used most commonly by the armed forces when allocating foreign armaments capacity to German firms, an area where there was in general less direct German investment; or in those cases where the question of ownership had formal political implications and could not be dealt with adequately until after the war, for example, in Lorraine or the Soviet Union.[56]

For private German firms trusteeship was a rather mixed blessing. It left considerable control in the hands of the state and gave the trustee the difficult responsibility of fulfilling the state's requirements under wartime conditions. The state could also decide who the trustees should be, discriminating against firms on political grounds. This was certainly the explanation on a number of occasions for the exclusion of the Stahlverein from trustee arrangements.[57] Trusteeship also meant the loss of personnel and equipment from the German parent company which, in the case of the trustee system in Russia, they could ill afford to supply by the middle of the war, and which might have been more effectively utilised if they had stayed in Germany. Nor did they operate on equal terms with the state firms. The Reichswerke in Russia had better access to equipment and labour than the private firms, and when the area was evacuated in 1943, helped itself to large amounts of machinery from all the Russian plants while allocating almost nothing to the other trustees.[58] This was hardly surprising given that BHO was run by Reichswerke managers, who had only agreed to allow private firms access to Russian production on the grounds that the state simply could not manage to provide the resources quickly enough to get the area working again.

When the private firms did assume trusteeship, the agreement bound them closely to the state. Flick's agreement with the BHO was so one-sided that his advisers recommended that he demand a lease-hold instead: 'whoever signed this contract would be delivering himself body and soul to the BHO'.[59] But under pressure Flick accepted trusteeship. The contract spelt out that 'The sponsored plant is neither legally nor economically part of the home plant of the sponsor.' All objects produced became automatically the property of the Reich, prices were determined by the BHO and sales as well. The trustee was not allowed under any circumstances to negotiate for credit for operating the plant, and could use his own funds only with the approval of the BHO.[60] In Lorraine Flick found that his trusteeship of the Rombach plant did not even entitle him to tax concessions available in the Reich, which he argued would result (given the difficulties of starting up capacity in the region again) in an operating loss to the trustee. Nor did the contract contain any reference to trustees having preferential claims for direct ownership of the plants after the war.[61] Although some officials in the Economics Ministry and the Finance Ministry were in favour of selling the plants held in trust to private industry after the war, and said as much, it was by no means clear that this would have been the outcome. Nazi administrators were reluctant to make any firm commitments and kept their options open on the future of state control. While this did not exclude privatisation, trusteeship did not provide a full guarantee of future ownership by any particular trustee.

4 *Direct private ownership and participation*

Direct investment by private German firms was limited during the war by the claims of the state firms and the reluctance of the state to offer more than operating contracts in captured plants to meet war requirements. There were German firms with foreign affiliates, Mannesmann, AEG, IG Farben and the Stahlverein among the most prominent, but apart from the example of IG Farben these do not seem to have been used as stepping-stones to the substantial expansion of multinational activity during the war. Some businesses acquired by the state in the first instance were returned to private ownership during the war, particularly in Silesia. Where this did happen the state and party authorities appear to have given preference not to the big concerns but to smaller firms which could not become 'multinational' without state help. This may well have fitted with ideological preferences but it also had the effect of creating a number of smaller, less organised and more dependent multinationals which would relatively strengthen the influence of the state. It had the further result of strengthening the competitive position of the big state-backed multinationals against domestically based heavy industry by restricting its access to foreign assets necessary for post-war competition (which was almost certainly Pleiger's object).[62]

The most successful private firm to operate on multinational lines was IG Farben. There are a number of explanations for this. In the first place the firm was closely identified with the aims of the Nazi state from at least 1936 onwards, even to the extent of sharing personnel with the Four Year Plan. It was able to use state power quite unscrupulously in its pursuit of corporate strategy. Secondly, IG Farben was the largest pre-war German concern, in a very capital-intensive and technically advanced sector. It possessed as a result the personnel and organisational skills necessary to make the transition to multinationalism rapidly which other firms lacked. After the defeat of Poland IG Farben defended its claims in the Polish chemical industry on the grounds that 'Only the IG is in a position to make experts available.'[63]

IG Farben policy in Europe was conditioned not only by its commitment to the state's plans for building up a resource base for major war in central Europe, but also by its desire to develop a continent-wide organisation to serve its commercial interests as well. IG planned to set up chemical raw material plants in south-eastern Europe to meet the needs of local agriculture, but to keep more sophisticated processing in the hands of the parent company in Germany and its affiliates in Austria and Czechoslovakia which it acquired in 1938–9. During the war IG used its Dynamit AG plant in Slovakia as a stepping-stone to expansion into central Europe and the Balkans. It acquired shares in six other chemical companies as well as setting up seven new plants mainly to meet expanded demand for basic chemicals from the German armed forces. However, the main Czech chemical producer, the Prager Verein, remained independent of IG Farben during the war, and became its major competitor in south-eastern Europe. Nor was the IG successful in its efforts to take over any of the Belgian Solvay company holdings since ownership was vested in two Swiss holding companies.[64] In Poland IG Farben either bought chemical firms outright or operated as trustee through arrangement with Frank and the SS. In France IG Farben again used the power of the state in its negotiations with the French dyestuffs industry, which was forced to accept reorganisation into a single holding company, Francolor, in which IG would have a 51% interest, in return for transferring to French industrialists 1% of IG stock. The agreement was drawn up and signed in November 1941, and drafted in such a way that IG hoped to be able to retain its position in the French industry, even if Germany were to lose the war. This agreement gave IG Farben effective control over the European chemical industry of occupied Europe, and placed it in a strong position in negotiating marketing agreements with Italian and Swiss competitors.[65] The ability of IG to exercise considerable influence on Nazi officials in its efforts to acquire ownership of foreign businesses and in discussing the shape of the post-war European economy gave it a uniquely privileged position during the war years.

IV

The scope and character of multinationalism in occupied Europe was dependent in almost all cases on the role of the German state, either directly or indirectly. The same was true of the operation of multinational firms, which were conditioned by policies over which they had only limited control. Of course the war distorted this development, by placing priority on industrial strategies to help the German war effort; so much so that on occasion firms resisted or obstructed efforts by the state to promote what they regarded as costly or poorly planned projects, for example, aluminium production in Norway.[66] Though war production involved a notion of efficiency – the justification given by the state for the reorganisation of the Sudeten lignite mines, or the rationalisation of ore supply from Lorraine – purely financial considerations were never a decisive factor. Pleiger claimed, not altogether truthfully, that 'money plays no part'.[67] It was certainly the case that the war encouraged rising costs and large sectors of the Reichswerke organisation never made an operating profit during the war, despite the efforts of the Finance Ministry to restrict subsidy to those cases where a fixed contract for regular repayments of Reich loans could be established. Where operating profits were made in the occupied areas they were usually swallowed up through reinvestment, helped by generous tax allowances for depreciation which released more funds to be ploughed back. The effect of this financial policy was to reduce the flow of payments to the Reichswerke from its major subsidiaries, which inhibited profit growth and the repayment of state loans.[68]

Firms acting as trustees rather than owners had a better chance of securing a regular return because they depended for most of their capital on the state.

But the government also had long-term plans for the development of European industry that went well beyond military priorities. The large iron, steel and armaments complex at Linz, for example, not only met war needs but was to be the core of a new central European industrial region deliberately centred in Hitler's homeland. The same was true of the large new investments at Vítkovice which were designed to turn it into 'the Eastern industrial pillar of the Reich', supplying steel to the industries of the Protectorate, Poland and the Ukraine.[69] It is clear that at least some of the state's capital penetration strategy was based on the need to secure adequate supplies of industrial raw materials to feed the finishing plants of the captured region, and to rationalise the transfer of resources between them, or from the occupied areas to the Reich. Though how extensive these transfers were and how rationally multinational operations were conducted is difficult to tell from the available evidence.

It would be wrong to conclude from all this that the German government had a co-ordinated programme for its industrial policy abroad. Differences in the political and socio-economic conditions of the occupied areas produced different treatment from the German rulers, particularly in places like Belgium and northern France where the army kept control. Political conflicts and the pressures of war made it difficult to be consistent in dealing with cases in different parts of Europe, or to be able to see the situation clearly as a whole. By the end of the war industrial planning was simply improvised. The largest multinational, the Reichswerke, was a model of inorganic growth. Its policy of grabbing everything that came its way, while it guaranteed foreign resources for the war effort, did create considerable confusion, giving it what one manager called a 'Warenhauscharakter' ('character of a department store').[70] The reorganisation of 1941 and 1942, brought about through the complaints of its leading managers, highlighted the unsystematic growth of the concern. During 1941 the organisation was rationalised into product groups, smaller, less essential firms were weeded out and closed down, and a clearer demarcation of managerial roles worked out. In 1942 the Reichswerke abandoned its armaments production altogether, which was then brought into Speer's system of industrial committees, though it remained predominantly in state hands. Steyr and Rheinmetall were held by the Bank der deutschen Luftfahrt, and Škoda and the Brünner Waffenwerke were converted into a state-backed holding company, the Waffenunion. Efforts by Krupp and the Stahlverein to assume ownership were vetoed by Goering.[71]

On the whole Reichswerke managers in the remaining sectors displayed a good grasp of the problems facing a large multinational organisation and were eventually able to implement operational strategies to cope with them. The role of the central organisation was, according to Pleiger, 'setting up production programmes in co-ordination, sharing technical experience, joint support between companies, regulating the questions of markets, division of market areas among the companies, price freight questions etc.'.[72] Questions concerning the nature of corporate strategy and management were not ignored during the war and may well have provided important lessons for the post-war period. Pleiger, for one, was well aware that peace would bring a very different economic environment. So too was IG Farben, the other major multinational, whose main priority was to strengthen its market position through direct investment and trading agreements, while getting the government to share in the cost of capital growth and to alter the political conditions for its negotiations. In return IG co-ordinated its product and labour policy with military requirements.

The government did, however, play a central part in providing the investment funds needed to expand abroad, either through buying up shares, or setting up new plants or expanding existing ones. This was true not only for state firms, but for private firms and trustees as well. The government did so to help the war effort, but also because the current state of the private capital market in Germany might have made it difficult for the state to rely to any great extent on private funds for expansion. Shares abroad were acquired in the main through the major German banks, which were then paid a commission by the state in addition to the purchase price of the shares where the state itself acquired ownership. New investment abroad was met either directly from state funds, usually via the major state financial institutions, or from occupation levies or forced loans from blocked clearing accounts with other European countries.[73]

There were a number of motives for investment, though they were all closely related to the war, or to Goering's strategy on direct investment. The state also found it necessary to promote technology transfer in order to raise foreign plants to the same operating level as German ones, which involved considerable investment in new machinery and equipment. Rheinmetall calculated that its sales per head in 1941 were 50–100% higher than the machinery and arms plants taken over in Austria and Czechoslovakia.[74] The Finance Ministry report on the Brünner Maschinenfabrik in 1940 points out that its capacity had been poorly organised and underutilised, and that it required some 32 million crowns of new investment over three years to modernise it. During that period it was recommended that all profits should be ploughed back into the firm.[75] In other cases large investments were needed to repair war damage, as in the case of the BHO, which was set up with an initial capital of 100 million marks. In all areas where the state directly acquired ownership or exercised trusteeship very large funds were spent on investment, or authorised to be spent on future expansion. The details are set out in Table 21.1.

Table 21.1. *Selected statistics on German state investment in European industry*[76]

Austria		
Steyr-Daimler-Puch	328m. RM	1938–44
Alpine Montangesellschaft	140m. RM	1939–45
Steirische Gussstahl	7m. RM	1939–45
Czechoslovakia		
Sudetenländische Treibstoff	420m. RM	1939–42
Skoda	455m. kčs	1939–41
Erste Brünner Maschinenfabrik	32m. kčs	1939–42
Brünner Waffenwerke	300m. kčs	1939–41
Vitkovice	504m. kčs	1940–2
Poldi	235m. kčs	1940–4
Poland		
Bergwerksverwaltung Oberschlesien	120m. RM	1940–4
France		
Hüttenwerksverwaltung Westmark	55m. RM	1941–4
Russia		
Berg-und Hüttenwerksverwaltung Ost	100m. RM	1942

These were very large sums indeed, and gave the Reichswerke, which was granted Reich loans totalling 1,500m. RM during the war, considerable economic influence through sheer scale in the areas where it was active. By comparison, IG Farben only invested an additional 124m. kčs in its Slovakian subsidiary between 1938 and 1943, less than one-tenth of Reichswerke investments in Czechoslovakia.[77] The state's long-term plans were greater still. Investment at Vítkovice was to increase by a total of 995m. kčs in a programme planned to go into peacetime; at Sudetenländische Treibstoff by a total of 607m. RM, and in Silesia by a total of 803m. RM.[78]

The state also influenced other aspects of multinational decision-making. The Four Year Plan fixed prices for major commodities, and did so to fit as far as possible with the interests of the war economy. Russian iron ore and coal, for example, were sold at 50% of the price in the Reich to speed up the recovery of the iron and steel industry of the Donez basin. In Austria the Four Year Plan forced the Alpine Montangesellschaft to reduce its prices in line with Reich prices so that the new works at Linz could be guaranteed a cheap supply of ore.[79] It was also possible for the government to fix the exchange rate between Germany and the occupied areas in favour of Germany so that the transfer of resources between plants from abroad could be effected to the advantage of the German company. The Reichswerke at Salzgitter were supplied with coking coal from its coal resources in Poland at a price below that offered by the Ruhr coal syndicate. In the early stages of the war foreign acquisitions, particularly in Czechoslovakia, were used to provide exportable goods which could no longer be produced in Germany but which were essential to provide the foreign exchange to buy strategic imports. Much more research needs to be done on the transfer of resources from occupied Europe to industry in the Reich, or between subsidiaries of the same multinational, before anything more definite can be said about sales or costs. Though Reichswerke firms outside Germany, for example, provided some two-thirds of all sales of the concern by 1944, we do not yet know how much was sent back to Germany, or what proportion of sales was kept in the concern.[80]

The government's role was also important in labour policy. The management boards of the major state-owned multinationals were filled with state appointees, party members, civil servants, bankers, and local collaborators. The state was represented too on the boards of the major private firms, and also appointed the trustees responsible for administering captured businesses. There was a considerable degree of integration and overlap in managerial appointments, which made it easier to co-ordinate the activities of the major subsidiaries.[81] With manual labour there were great difficulties. The mobilisation of foreign labour reserves for work in the Reich made it difficult to exploit foreign acquisitions to the full, and forced many to operate below capacity throughout the war. It also increased demand for labour in the occupied territories and pushed up costs. The wages bill at Vítkovice increased from 588m. kčs in 1939 to 844m. kčs in 1940 with only a 9% increase in the workforce.[82] The transfer of foreign labour to the Reich forced foreign subsidiaries to use more semi-skilled and unskilled labour which was cheaper, or to use more machinery which improved productivity. Real wages and conditions of work deteriorated throughout occupied Europe as the war went on and the German authorities adopted more Draconian and exploitative labour policies.

The effect of the foreign labour programme was to make it difficult for foreign subsidiaries to supply what was required of them; and to make them more dependent on prisoners and slave labour, which was much less productive because of the appalling conditions under which forced labourers worked. In Russia the workers were paid only one-eighth of German wages, and produced less than half the amount of coal per head of German miners.[83] The poor co-ordination between the investment priorities of the state and its foreign labour policy, which saw a stream of capital flowing out of Germany and a stream of labour flowing in, considerably reduced the usefulness of captured industry, and compromised German war production plans. The exploitative and ill-thought out labour strategy showed that there could also be real limits to the usefulness of state help in running multinational organisations. Some of the large sums allocated for foreign investment might from the German point of view more usefully have been kept in the Reich to encourage rationalisation and productivity growth at home, which would in turn have reduced the frantic demand for foreign labour and have allowed the state real benefits in keeping an adequate supply of domestic labour in the occupied territories.

V

The Nazi occupation or conquest of most of Europe opened up for German industry the possibility of developing multinational organisation in areas where political and financial constraints had prevented expansion during the inter-war years. In practice the vacuum created by the expulsion of foreign capital was filled largely by the state in order to safeguard the region for war purposes and also to permit the Nazi government to decide what the shape of the post-war economy would be. German private capital, with the exception of IG Farben, had to be content with modest gains and a system of trusteeship. The Nazis' purpose was to prevent a scramble for the spoils of Europe by replacing the free market with a state-dominated and co-ordinated economic order embracing the whole continent. Pleiger deplored 'earlier organisations in the economy formed as pure interest groups to safeguard the interests of their members against competitors and even against the state'. The new economic order, he told Speer, was to replace the old liberal economy with the supervision of the Nazi state.[84] These political ambitions gave the policy of direct investment a highly political character. This fact, coupled with the growing risks as the war situation deteriorated, seems to have restrained most of private German industry from pressing its claims in Europe too forcefully, except in France and Silesia, where the risks seemed fewer and the gains much greater. The high point of private industrial ambitions was the summer of 1940, when many businessmen, and other Germans, assumed that the war was over and that Germany could return to the position she enjoyed in 1914.

For the duration of the war corporate strategy was determined primarily by the needs of war. Investment and labour programmes were both geared to German war demands, though often so poorly co-ordinated that less was extracted from the host countries than German leaders wanted. The relationship between Germany and the host countries was one of exploitation, in the sense that the state used its political power to ensure the most favourable terms for German foreign participation even in areas not actually occupied by German forces. There was, however, a transfer of resources from the Reich of considerable size, involving a certain amount of technology transfer (though in the case of Russia and France it was all transferred back again to the Reich as German forces retreated). Host countries gained benefits only in the sense that some domestic production and employment was maintained, and even expanded in selected sectors, though on unfavourable terms, particularly for labour. In all other respects the relationship was very one-sided, and there is every reason to suppose that had Germany won the war, this relationship would have been a permanent feature of the New Order.

NOTES

1 J. Tomaszewski, 'German capital in Silesian industry in Poland between the two world wars', in A. Teichova and P. Cottrell (eds.), *International business and central Europe 1918–1939* (Leicester, 1983), pp. 227–44: A. Teichova, R. Waller, 'Der tschechoslovakische Unternehmer am Vorabend und zu Beginn des Zweiten Weltkrieges', in W. Długoborski, (ed.), *Zweiter Weltkrieg und sozialer Wandel* (Göttingen, 1981, p. 292).

2 This was the exception. On preference for exports over investment see V. Schröter, 'The IG Farbenindustrie AG in central and south-eastern Europe 1926–38', in Teichova and Cottrell, pp. 139–62; H. Schröter, 'Siemens and central and south-east Europe between the two world wars', in *ibid.*, pp. 173–89.

3 For details on the Reichswerke see R. J. Overy, 'Göring's a "multinational" empire', in Teichova and Cottrell, pp. 269–93.

4 *Der Vierjahresplan*, vol. II (1938), pp. 602–3.

5 *Trials of the war criminals*, Case X, pp. 475–6, Economics Ministry decree, 19.3.1938.

6 H. Radandt, 'Die IG Farbenindustrie AG und Südosteuropa 1938 bis zum Ende des Zweiten Weltkrieges', *Jahrbuch für Wirtschaftsgeschichte*, 1967 part 1, 78–84, 97–9; J. Borkin, *The crime and punishment of IG Farben* (London, 1979), pp. 95–8.

7 TWC, Case X, p. 477, doc. NI-766, Keppler to von Wilmowsky, 2.4.1938. Krupp acquired a holding of 86.9%.

8 N. Schausberger, 'Die Auswirkungen der Rüstungs-und Kriegswirtschaft 1938–1945 auf die soziale und ökonomische Struktur Österreichs', in F. Forstmeier and H.-E. Volkmann, (eds.), *Kriegswirtschaft und Rüstung 1939–1945* (Düsseldorf, 1977), p. 259.

9 Imperial War Museum, Case V, background documents (hereafter Case V), Steinbrinck doc. book IV, p. 172, Final report on the liquidation of the Petschek transaction, 26.11.1938.

10 Case XI, background documents, Pleiger doc. book VIIB, 'The economic development of the Sudetenländische Bergbau AG during the years 1939–1945', pp. 30–2; Pros. doc. book 168, NID-15635, file note of Reich's Finance Ministry, 17.2.1939; NID-15636, RFM Memorandum, 25.2.1939, 'Transfer of Czech coal interests in the Sudetenland'.

11 Imperial War Museum, G.ED. 43/0/34, *German industrial complexes: the Hermann Göring complex*, June 1946, pp. 11–13.

12 Case V, Steinbrinck doc. book IV, pp. 152–3, Steinbrinck memorandum, 1.2.1938; pp. 157–8, 'Status of negotiations with the Petschek Group', n.d. The American negotiators representing the Petscheks threatened that the American government would expropriate German holdings in America if the Germans did not agree to buy the Petschek shares on reasonable terms.

13 Case XI, Pros. doc. book 168, NID-15636.

14 National Archives, Washington, Reichswerke collection, microcopy T83 Roll 74, frames 3445163-4, IG Farben report 'Konzernaufbau und Entwicklung der Reichswerke AG', 19.10.1939; *Hermann Göring complex*, p. 15.

15 Overy, pp. 272–7; Teichova and Waller, p. 293.

322   Richard J. Overy

16 Case XI, Pleiger doc. book VIIA, Dr Nowak, 'The legal position of the Witkowitz Gewerkschaft, 23.10.1939'; Minutes of the 14th meeting of the Aufsichtsrat, 17.2.1941; Resolution of the Aufsichtsrat, Witkowitz Gewerkschaft, 14.12.1942.

17 TWC, Case XII, p. 655, NID-15640.

18 Case V, Flick doc. book XIA, EC-410, Letter from Goering to all Reich authorities, 19.10.1939, pp. 1–3. Paragraph 4 reads: 'In order to exploit the territories, and especially those to be incorporated in the Reich in the best way for the achievement of the Führer's goal, the property in real estate, plants, mobile objects and all rights taken out of Polish hands must be safeguarded and administered in a co-ordinated way.'

19 'Letter from Goering to Reich commissioners, 2.8.1940', in Royal Institute of International Affairs, *Hitler's Europe* (Oxford, 1954), p. 194.

20 International Military Tribunal, *Nazi conspiracy and aggression* (Washington, 1946), VII, p. 310, Göring to Thomas, 9.8.1940.

21 *Ibid.*, EC485, Goering conference, 1.10.1940 'about the economic exploitation of the occupied territories'.

22 TWC, Case XII, pp. 536–8, NI-002.

23 TWC, Case XI transcripts, 14891.

24 Case V Flick doc. book XA, NI-3249, Flick file note, 19.1.1938.

25 *Nazi conspiracy and aggression*, VII, pp. 258–9, EC-43, RWM discussion, 16.8.1940.

26 Case XI, Pleiger doc. book VA, pp. 79–81, letter from von Krosigk to Funk, 11.12.1940.

27 NA Reichswerke files, T83, Roll 76, frames 3446876–7, letter from Pleiger to Körner, 10.4.1940; 3446884–6, Pleiger to Krupp, 8.4.1940.

28 Case X, background documents, Bülow doc. book 1, p. 102.

29 Case V, Flick doc. book XIIID, NI-3100, notes of a meeting on Phoenix AG, 17.10.1941: 'It was Gauleiter Lohse's aim for the present to consolidate the larger and medium enterprises into monopolistic companies', under the Gauleiter's own supervision.

30 NA Göring Stabsamt, T84 Roll 8, frames 7309–10, Goering decree, 31.10.1942.

31 *Ibid.*, Reichswerke files, T83 Roll 75, frame 3445814, Dr Müller, HGW Wirtschaftsabteilung, 'Bericht der Arbeitsgruppe für Verkaufsfragen'.

32 *Ibid.*, T83 Roll 76, frames 3446860–1, Pleiger to Körner, 13.3.1940; TWC, Case XIII, 744–5, Winkler affidavit, 7.5.1948.

33 *Ibid.*, p. 749, NI–598, Agreement between HTO and Reichswerke Hermann Göring, NA Göring Stabsamt, T84 Roll 7, frames 6704–6, Winkler memorandum, 21.4.1942; *Hermann Göring complex*, pp. 21–2; Case XI, Pros. doc. book 115, NG-044, RWM note 'incorporation of Upper Silesian coal in the mining administration of the Reichswerke Hermann Göring, 9.11.1941'.

34 On Flick see Case XI, Pros. doc. book 113, NI-3548, Flick to Goering, 1.11.1940; Case V, Flick doc. book XIB, NI-3529, notes of a conversation with von Hanneken, 27.8.1940; on Krupp, Case XI, Pleiger doc. book VIII, Winkler affidavit, 6.3.1948, p. 4: NA Reichswerke files, T83 Roll 76, frames 3446860–1, Pleiger to Körner, 13.3.1940; frames 3446876–86, letter from Pleiger to Körner, 10.4.1940 enclosing a letter from Krupp to Pleiger, 27.3.1940; 3446891–2, Aktenvermerk Pleiger 'Dubenskogrube'.

35 Case XI, pros. doc. book 115, NG-044, p. 4.

36 Hermann Göring complex, pp. 21–2.

37 R. Jeske, 'Zur Annexion der polnischen Wojewodschaft Schlesien durch Hitlerdeutschland im zweiten Weltkrieg', *Zeitschrift für Geschichtswissenschaft*, V (1957), 1073–5.

38 NA Reichswerke files, T83 Roll 74, frame 3445217, 'Gründung und Wachsen der HGW 1937–1942'; Case XI, Pleiger doc. book X pp. 1–2, Gritzbach affidavit; TWC, Case XI transcripts, vol. CCXXXI, p. 14890.
39 Case XI, Pleiger doc. book VB, 51, Minutes of meeting of the Aufsichtsrat of the Reichswerke, 15.11.1944.
40 Case V, Flick doc. book XIA, 1155–PS, Notice of Goering conference, 19.6.1940, p. 1.
41 TWC, Case X, p. 484, NI-048, letter from Poensgen to Reichert, 10.6.1940, reporting meeting of the Kleiner Kreis, 7 June. Funk told the industrialists present that any attempt to push the interests of big business would arouse political hostility.
42 Case V, Flick doc. book XIB, NI-3516, note of discussion with von Hanneken, 10.6.1940, pp. 1–2; NI-3529, consultation with von Hanneken, 27.8.1940, p. 2.
43 Case V, Flick doc. book XIB, NI-048, Poensgen to Funk, 10.6.1940, NI-3518, Proposals made by the Reich Office Iron and Steel for the distribution of the iron industry in Lux. and French Lorraine, 26.7.1940; on French claims see NI-3533, Weiss memorandum for Burkart, 6.8.1940. It is clear from these documents that W. Długoborski's claim (Teichova and Cottrell, p. 301) that the Germans wanted to co-operate with the French industrialists 'to win friends rather than to seize by force' was not the case. When Flick took over the Rombach plant all the French managers were sacked and sent back to France.
44 Case V, Flick doc. book XIB, NI-3539, Flick conference, 16.8.1940.
45 Case XI, Pleiger doc. book X, pp. 3–9, Beckenbauer affidavit, 8.6.1948, who claims that Pleiger too had wanted to keep the mines and steelworks together before he found out the extent of Ruhr claims; NA Reichswerke files, T83 Roll 81, frames 3452359-60, 'Liefergemeinschaft der Eisengruben in Lothringen, 1944'.
46 Case XI, pros. doc. book 113, pp. 1–3, NI-049, Goering decree on the distribution of smelting works in Lorraine and Luxemburg, 5.2.1941; NI-3548, Flick to Göring, 1.11.1940; Case V, Flick doc. book XIB, NI-3539, Flick conference, 16.8.1940, p. 3; NI-2508, Chief of Civil Administration of Enemy Property to Flick, 20.2.1941.
47 Case V, Flick doc. book XIA, NI-5385, Interview between Herr Frohwein and M. Couve de Murville, 4.10.1941.
48 *Ibid.*, Flick doc. book XIB, NI-3542, Flick memorandum, 2.10.1940: NA Reichswerke files, T83 Roll 76, frame 3447887, RWM discussion, 27.6.1941.
49 *Hermann Göring complex*, p. 24.
50 *Ibid.*, pp. 20–1.
51 *Ibid.*, p. 12: on Jugoslavia see R. Schönfeld, 'Deutsche Rohstoffsicherungspolitik in Jugoslawien 1934–1944', *Vierteljahreshefte für Zeitgeschichte*, XXIV (1976), 220–33.
52 Overy, pp. 279–82.
53 M. Riedel, *Eisen und Kohle für das Dritte Reich* (Göttingen, 1973), pp. 305–9. The monopoly was set up, according to Goering's officials, 'to prevent violent competition by German industrial firms for the Russian plants': see Case XI, Pros. doc. book 124, NI-5581, circular of Wirtschaftsgruppe Eisen-und Stahlindustrie, 21.8.1941; Case V, Flick doc. book XIIIC, NI-5262, note of a conversation with Colonel John, for Flick, 13.8.1941.
54 NA Reichswerke files, T83 Roll 81, frame 3452276, Goering decree on the eastern economy, 27.7.1941; Case XI, pros. doc. book 124, NI-10797, memorandum on the founding of Kontinentale Öl AG, 21.1.1941; NI-10162, minutes of the second meeting of the managing board of Kontinentale Öl, 13.1.1942; M. Pearton, *Oil and the Roumanian state* (Oxford, 1971), pp. 228–31.

55 Salzgitter Konzernarchiv (SA), 12/155/4, Paul Rheinländer, 'Vorschlag zur Ausgestaltung der Eisenindustrie im Grossdeutschen Wirtschaftsraum nach dem Kriege', 1941.

56 NA Göring Stabsamt, T84 Roll 7, frames 6704–6, memorandum on trusteeship by Hans Winkler, 21.4.1942.

57 Case v, Flick doc. book xiiib, NI-3665, memorandum of a discussion between Pleiger and Flick, 11.11.1942. Pleiger said he would prefer to exclude the Vereinigte Stahlwerke, and divide up the trustee plants between Flick and the Reichswerke. On VS claims in the region see ibid., NI-5722, Flick memorandum 26.6.1941.

58 Ibid., NI-4500, minutes of a conference, 21.2.1944 and NI-5737, Burkart to Flick, 29.4.1944; Case xi, pros. doc. book 124, NI-2695, BHO Notiz, 17.6.1943 and NI-4437, BHO circular to all trustee firms, 1.11.1943.

59 Case v, Flick doc. book xiiic, NI-3622, letter from Bernhard Weiss to Siemag, 12.12.1942.

60 Ibid., NI-3659, 'Principles of the management of trustee plants of the BHO, Nov. 1942'.

61 Ibid., Flick doc. book xib, NI-1651, Flick file note, 7.5.1941.

62 Case xi, Pleiger doc. book vb, 51–2, minutes of the meeting of the Aufsichtsrat of the Reichswerke AG, 15.11.1944.

63 Borkin, p. 98.

64 Radandt, pp. 79–84, 99–103.

65 Borkin, pp. 100–9.

66 A. S. Milward, The Fascist economy in Norway (Oxford, 1972), pp. 180, 207–8.

67 NA Reichswerke files, Roll 76, frames 3446885–6, letter from Pleiger to Krupp, 8.4.1940; on France see Roll 80, frame 3452713, 'Rationalisierung innerhalb der lothringisch-luxemburgischen Eisenhüttenindustrie', 20.3.1942; on the Sudetenland, Roll 77, frames 3448199–200, Aktennotiz 'Befahrung der Sudetenländische Bergbau AG', 16.7.1943.

68 Overy, p. 289: Case xi, Pleiger doc. book vb, Meeting of the Aufsichtsrat of the Reichswerke AG, 15.11.1944; on reinvestment and depreciation at Vítkovice see ibid., doc. book viia, Extraordinary meeting of the shareholders of the Witkowitzer Gewerkschaft, 28.8.1940, in which it was decided to suspend any distribution of profits in 1939–40 in favour of new investment; on von Krosigk's attitude see TWC, Case xi, 14815–6.

69 Case xi, Pleiger doc. book viia, p. 57, Fiscal report of the Gewerkschaftsvorstand of Witkowitzer Gewerkschaft, 1941.

70 NA Reichswerke files, T83 Roll 75, frame 3446010, Vorschlag Pleiger zum Aufbau der HGW, 9.11.1941.

71 For details on the background to reorganisation see R. J. Overy, Goering: the 'Iron Man' (London, 1984), pp. 144–6, 212–14; Hermann Göring complex, pp. 27–9.

72 NA Reichswerke files, T83 Roll 75, frames 3446008–17, Vorschlag Pleiger zum Aufbau der HGW, 9.11.1941; 3445813, Bericht der Arbeitsgruppe für Verkaufsfragen des Ausschusses für Konzernorganisation, n.d. (June 1941?); TWC trial transcripts Case xi, 14847–8.

73 Hitler's Europe, pp. 205–7: on the activities of the Dresdner Bank see FO 646 460, Office of Military Government of Germany (US), Report on Dresdner Bank investigation, esp. pp. 71–3.

74 NA Reichswerke files, T83 Roll 77, frames 3449374–5, Rheinmetall-Borsig, report on monthly sales, 26.2.1943.

75 Ibid., frames 3449351–8, RFM report 10.9.1940.

76 TWC, Case XI transcripts, 14895: Speer Collection, Imperial War Museum, FD 787/46, Sitzung des Aufsichtsrats der Steyr-Daimler-Puch, 8.9.1944; NA Reichswerke files, T83 Roll 76, 3447016–43, second report of Sudetenländische Treibstoff, 1941/2, September 1942: *Hermann Göring complex*, p. 19: Case XI, Pleiger doc. book VIIA, p. 51; VIIB, pp. 30–4, 51–3; X, p. 65; Riedel, p. 303; Case V, Flick doc. book XIIIA, NI–4332, first report of the BHO, January 1943, p. 3.
77 Radandt, p. 92.
78 NA Reichswerke files, T83 Roll 76, 3447016, second report of Sudetenländische Treibstoff, September 1942; Case XI, Pleiger doc. book VIIA, 51, 5th meeting of Aufsichtsrat, 30.6.1942; doc. book VIII, pp. 58–60, BO to Reichswerke, 24.6.1941.
79 *Hermann Göring complex*, p. 11.
80 Overy, 'Göring's empire', p. 290.
81 For a full list of Reichswerke directors and managers see NA Reichswerke files, T83 Roll 74, frames 3445227–362.
82 Case XI, Pleiger doc. book VIIA, 40, business report for financial year 1940, Witkowitzer Gewerkschaft.
83 *Ibid.*, Pros. doc. book 124, NI-5261, minutes of meeting of BHO Verwaltungsrat, 31.3.1943; Case V, Flick doc. book XIIIA, NI-4332; First report of the BHO, January 1943, pp. 7–8.
84 Salzgitter Konzernarchiv, Braunschweig, SA, 14/150/12, Pleiger to Speer, 11.8.1944.

22 Agribusiness in colonial Zimbabwe: the case of the Lowveld*

EVELYN PANGETI

The literature on agribusiness multinationals and their activities in the developing countries of the Third World has put much emphasis on their negative impact. These multinationals have been accused of, among other things, taking up much of the best productive land; using this land for the production of luxury crops destined for export to the developed countries; using capital-intensive production techniques which do not provide much employment in these countries of mass unemployment; and operating vertically integrated networks of production, marketing and distribution based on their own criteria of economic rationality without reference to the priorities of the host economies.[1] As Barnet and Muller put it, 'through its increasing control of arable land in poor countries, agribusiness is complicating the problem of food distribution. It is good business to grow high-profit crops for export rather than to raise corn, wheat and rice to support a local population without money to pay for it.'[2] Such examples as the ecological destruction of the Brazilian Amazon by agribusiness ranching enterprises or the case of Bud Senegal growing vegetables for the European market in the heart of the famine-ridden Sahel and using a virtually labour-free drip irrigation system can be quoted to support these accusations.[3]

On the other hand, it can and it has been argued that because of their possession of advanced technology, abundant financial resources and management skills, the multinationals are better placed to improve world agriculture and eliminate food shortages, and even 'roll back the desert'.[4]

This paper discusses the agribusiness activities of two multinational subsidiary companies, Triangle Ltd and Hippo Valley Estates Ltd, whose parent companies are both of South African origin. The discussion is set within the context of the above generalisations on multinationals and also within the context of the local environment in Zimbabwe. As capitalist enterprises, multinationals operate specifically for profit, and as such, the political and economic environment in the host country is a major determinant in locating investments. In this case the colonial environment, with its ties

326

with the international economy through the metropolitan power in London, and the influence of a powerful submetropole, South Africa, is of special significance.

The colony of Southern Rhodesia as it was called was occupied under the auspices of the London registered commercial corporation, the British South Africa Company, BSAC. The economic power of this company lay in South Africa, where its founder and patron, Cecil John Rhodes and his associates, had substantial interests in diamond and gold mining. The BSAC had made its initial investments in the colony on the basis of a belief in the existence of a 'Second Rand', hoping to compensate their failure to strike it rich on the South African Rand.[5] By 1907, however, the BSAC had realised that the mineral resources of the colony were not as had been hoped, and so turned to its other asset, the land. This 'white agricultural policy', as Robin Palmer calls it,[6] was based on the planned utilisation of cheap land and labour resources, and substantial capital outlays by the Company State in promoting agricultural development. This 'primitive accumulation' of capital through the forced alienation of land and labour from the indigenous African population demanded the creation of an institutional framework on which it would thrive. The Company thus created 'reserves' for the Africans, the dual purpose of which was to accommodate Africans pushed away from land allocated to white settlers, and to provide a reservoir of cheap labour for the white economy. Surplus expropriated from the Africans through taxes, rents, fines and so on was used to finance the research stations, central farms, specialist services and loan capital, all of which the Company provided in its bid to aid agricultural development. Land was sold to the settlers at nominal rates while the policy of the subsistence wage was established. The company had set a precedent for large farms in the 1890s when much of the land was held by mining companies for speculative purposes, and this tradition was maintained.[7]

The BSAC relinquished political control to the white settlers in 1923, but retained its hold on the economy. The Company was the largest landowner, and owned the railways and mineral rights and was the largest owner of foreign capital in the colony. According to Colin Stoneman the BSAC by 1945 held about half of the total foreign capital in the country (£60 million), half of which was in the railways.[8] On the other hand very little foreign capital entered the economy in the period between 1923 and 1945, while local settler capital accounted for only 30% of productive investment. In the same period, the Settler State increased its participation in the economy to close the investment gap and to promote economic development. A number of State enterprises were set up, such as the Electricity Supply Commission, the Iron and Steel Commission foundries and mills, the Cotton Industry Board mills, raw material processing plants, marketing organisations and the Sugar Industry Board. The State also strengthened the discriminatory measures against African participation in the economy started under Company rule, through such legislation as the Land Apportionment Act of 1930, the Maize Control Act of 1931 and other commodity acts and the Industrial Conciliation Act of 1934.[9] Of these, the Land Apportionment Act was of special significance, as, through its division of land into 'white' and 'African' areas, it significantly reduced the amount of land available to the African majority, making it imperative for the Africans to rely on wage labour for subsistence.

In the period after the Second World War, much foreign capital came into the Zimbabwean economy, mainly because of the flight of capital from Britain and South Africa. This arose from the economic situation in post-war Britain on the one hand and the flight of capital from South Africa after the Nationalist Party came to power in 1948 on the other. The creation of the Central African Federation in 1953 provided a further stimulus for capital inflow, as the Federation created a wider market (Southern Rhodesia was the economic centre of the Federation). As a result, by 1963 about two-thirds of productive investment in the country was foreign controlled, with South African companies dominating agriculture and forestry.

This historical background outlines the political and economic environment in which agribusiness multinationals established themselves. As already shown, this was an environment created by the State in its efforts to promote the development of a capitalist economy; an economy dependent on the exploitation of cheap land and labour, and on foreign capital. The interests of the three partners, the State, local settler and foreign capital, were not in conflict, and thus constituted a 'triple alliance'.

The post-war foreign capital inflow brought in a number of multinationals with world wide interests in agriculture, mining and manufacture. Such giants as Brooke-Bond Liebigs, with large ranching enterprises in South America, South Africa, East Africa, Nigeria, Zambia, Canada, and Britain are involved in ranching and food manufacturing in Zimbabwe, running a 526,000 hectare ranch in the Lowveld. Another ranching giant, Imperial Cold Storage and Supply Co. Ltd, operates through a subsidiary, Nuanetsi Ranch Ltd, and has business connections with Triangle Ltd. Mining giants such as Lonrho and Anglo-American Corporation also have substantial interests in ranching and agriculture; while Tate and Lyle is in the sugar industry, together with the Hulett Corporation of South Africa and Anglo-American Corporation.

The two companies under discussion, Triangle Ltd (with 83,145 hectares) and Hippo Valley Estates Ltd (with 54,200 hectares) are subsidiaries of the Hulett Corporation and the Anglo-American Corporation respectively. The two are basically sugar concerns, but also operate a number of subsidiary activities closely connected with sugar refineries, and have diversified into other branches of production. The Zimbabwean sugar industry in turn is closely connected with the South African sugar industry, in which the Hulett Corporation is a major producer. The Zimbabwean sugar industry is organised under a Sugar Association, ZSA, formed in 1963, to which all sugar producers belong. The two companies Triangle Ltd and Hippo Valley Estates Ltd are the major producers, with a minor contribution from individual planters on the two estates who belong to the Sugar Planters Association. The only other major contributor was Chirundu Sugar Estates in the Zambezi Valley, a subsidiary of Tate and Lyle which was closed down at UDI in 1965 when the whole operation moved to Zambia. The ZSA runs a research station in the Lowveld, with representatives of the producers. The sugar produced is refined for the local market by the Zimbabwe Sugar Refineries Ltd (ZSR), which was formed in 1935 as a subsidiary of the Sena Sugar Estates of Mozambique, but later passed under the control of Tate and Lyle. Tate and Lyle held 50.1% of the shares in ZSR as at 1979. In addition, two marketing companies were formed in 1963; Sugar Distributors (Pvt) Ltd (formerly Sugar Marketing), which handles the local marketing on behalf of the producers; and Sugar Sales (Pvt) Ltd, jointly owned by Triangle and Hippo Valley, which buys all raw sugar for the export market. The exports go mainly to Tate and Lyle in Britain, which handles all sugar imports into Britain for refining,[10] and to the United States.

Within this basic structure of the sugar industry is a maze of interlocking interests through cross-shareholdings and intermeshing directorships, a set-up which gives the multinationals immense power within the economy. A look at the two Lowveld subsidiaries and their parent companies shows the extent of these interlocking interests, which also involve financial institutions, and the parent companies.

The Hulett Sugar Corporation of South Africa owns Triangle Sugar Corporation Ltd, which is a wholly owned subsidiary of the holding company, the Hulett Corporation (Zimbabwe) Ltd, a 100% holding company. Within the Triangle Group are a number of subsidiary companies, all operating in the Lowveld. The Hulett Corporation's shareholding in these subsidiaries is shown together with their activities in Table 22.1. However, the Hulett Corporation in South Africa is a complex amalgam of other South African interests. Starting as a family firm created by Sir J. L. Hulett in 1892, the company has grown to become one of South Africa's largest sugar producers, with interests in Zimbabwe and Swaziland. In 1962, a major reorganisation of the company took place when a consortium of Natal sugar companies obtained a majority holding in it. According to the *South African yearbook* (an organ of the South African Sugar Association), the Tongaat Group obtained a 26% interest and 50% control in Hulett, through Sand T Investments (Pty) Ltd, a holding company; and C. G. Smith Ltd, a subsidiary of C. G. Smith Foods Ltd, obtained a 50% interest in Hulett. On the other hand, C. G. Smith Ltd holds interests in S and T Investments (Pty) Ltd. (The Tongaat Group merged with Hulett Corporation in 1982 to form the Tongaat-Hulett Group.)

Table 22.1 *Structure of the Triangle Group*

Subsidiary	Hulett share (%)	Business
Triangle Ltd	100	Sugar estate, mills and ethanol plant
Lowveld Development Co. Ltd	100	Cane estate
* Mtilikwe Sugar Co. Ltd	51	Cane estate
* Tokwe Development Co. Ltd	51	Cane and other crops
High Syringa (Pvt) Ltd	100	Cane estate
Processing Enterprises (Pvt) Ltd	50.3	Cotton ginning
Triangle Animal Feeds Ltd	75	Stock feeds manufacture
Triangle Trading Co. (Pvt) Ltd	100	Retail trading
Mkwasine Estate	50	Sugar, wheat and other crops

* These two subsidiaries were formed in association with the Imperial Cold Storage and Supply Co. Ltd to develop parts of the Nuanetsi Ranch – owned by Imperial.

Source: Company Files and Annual Reports in Registrar for Companies' Office, Harare

The Zimbabwean subsidiaries of the Hulett Corporation are decentralised under their own management and boards of directors, who are responsible to the parent company for their financial, administrative and industrial policies. This control by the parent company is easily achieved since a number of the directors on the parent company board also sit on the boards of the subsidiaries.

Hippo Valley Estates Ltd is a subsidiary of Anglo-American Corporation of South Africa, controlled through its holding company, Anglo-American (Zimbabwe) Ltd. The structure of the Anglo Group is complex; the company is basically a mining and investment conglomerate. This world empire created by Sir Ernest Oppenheimer in 1917 has investments covering gold and diamond mining, finance and insurance houses and retail motor organisations in South Africa, other African countries, Canada, Australia and Brazil. The 'Oppenheimer Complex' in South Africa is second only to the government as taxpayer and employer, and as such wields immense economic power. The Anglo group consists of a central core with four mining houses, Anglo-American Corporation, De Beers Consolidate, Charter Consolidated and Rand Selection Corporation. The London-based Charter Consolidated (formed through the merger of the BSAC Consolidated Mines and Central Mines Corporation) controls many of Anglo's investments outside South Africa. The four core companies of the group are connected with each other and with their subsidiaries by a complicated pattern of interlocking shareholdings, directorships and management, with each of the four holding over 30% of the shares in each other. According to Lanning and Mueller, Anglo's holding companies are established 'with purely nominal capital, but they can control direct and indirect subsidiaries and affiliates which control much larger financial resources'.[11] In Zimbabwe, Anglo-American Corporation (AAC) has holdings and equity interest of 16.6% in Anglo-American (Zimbabwe) Ltd (AMZIM). AMZIM in turn has a diversified portfolio which includes coal, copper and nickel mining, iron and steel, ferrochrome, engineering industries, rolling stock hire, timber processing, property, merchant banking and finance, plus the agricultural interests in citrus, sugar etc. of which Hippo Valley is a part.[12] Anglo-American has a 40% shareholding in Hippo Valley.

There are several advantages that can be derived by subsidiary companies from being part of a giant group like Anglo-American or Hulett. Firstly, as shown above, both parent companies are involved in the finance business which provides a firm financial backing for the subsidiaries. Hippo Valley, for example, was able to borrow Z$6 million from Anglo-American in 1975. Such 'internal financing' is a major advantage to the subsidiaries as it frees them from external financial control. The subsidiaries can also benefit from the group through technical cooperation, training facilities and management skills. Triangle, for example, benefits from Hulett's experience in sugar production in South Africa, while Hippo Valley benefits from Anglo's resources in finance and technical management.

An interesting feature about the crossholdings is the connection between the two parent companies in South Africa, i.e. the Hulett Corporation and the Anglo-American Corporation. The Anglo-American Industrial Corporation (AMIC), one of the fourteen main companies in the Anglo Group, holds minority shares in the Hulett Sugar Corporation; while the Tongaat Group is an Anglo holding company with a 50% control holding in the Hulett Corporation Ltd. Since the Hulett Corporation merged with the Tongaat Group in 1982, this gives Anglo a substantial holding in Huletts.

Tate and Lyle, the major buyer of Zimbabwean export sugar, have also been involved in the crossholdings between the South African and Zimbabwean sugar industries. As mentioned above, Tate and Lyle had a 50% stake in Zimbabwe Sugar Refineries Ltd. On the other hand, the company also holds a 10% stake in Hippo Valley Estates Ltd, while Tate and Lyle Technical Services Ltd were commissioners to the new Hippo Valley mill in 1964. Tate and Lyle directors have also been at one time or another on the boards of Zimbabwean and South African sugar companies.[13]

The story of the launching of the Zimbabwean sugar industry in 1923 through the efforts of an individual, Tom MacDougall, has been recounted in many ways. Suffice to say here that MacDougall, the original owner of Triangle Ranch, pioneered the growing of cane under irrigation in an area that had been dismissed as good for nothing other than extensive cattle ranching. As mentioned earlier, the government was keen to promote the agricultural sector through either direct participation or the provision of necessary infrastructure. So when MacDougall encountered financial difficulties in 1944, the government, realising the potential of this infant industry, bought him out. A statutory body, the Sugar Industry Board, was formed to run MacDougall's venture, and to carry out research into cane varieties. The Board was expected to prove the viability of the sugar industry, after which it would then sell to private enterprise, and thus continue the cooperation between private and public capital.[14]

In 1953 Triangle made its first profit, thus proving that sugar cane was a profitable proposition. True to its mandate, the Sugar Industry Board sold the estate to a 'syndicate' of Natal sugar farmers in 1954. The syndicate expanded the area under cane, but achieved little progress. In 1957, the Triangle estate was bought by the Hulett Corporation, then called Hulett and Sons Ltd. At the same time, the Hippo Valley Estates were bought by a local settler farmer, Sir Raymond Stockil, in 1956, originally to produce citrus fruits. In the early sixties this estate passed on to the control of Anglo-American Corporation. Hippo Valley turned to sugar cane in 1959 because of the boom in sugar prices in the early sixties, and has since grown to become the major producer in the country.

A major contribution by the government to the sugar industry was the provision of irrigation water. For this purpose, agreements were entered into between the government and the companies for the building of the Kyle and Bangala dams, the major dams in the area. Triangle Ltd contributed some Z$720,000 to the cost of the Kyle dam, which was completed in 1960. The Bangala dam, completed in 1962, was built at a cost of Z$3.8 million, while another dam, the Manjirenji, completed in 1966, cost Z$3.1 million. Having constructed the dams, the government then established another statutory body, the Sabi-Limpopo Authority, constituted on the concept of the American Tennessee Valley Authority. The Sabi-Limpopo Authority was entrusted with the tasks of investigating dam sites, basin surveys, canal alignments, experimenting with various types of crops, and, as with the Sugar Industry Board, establishing the viability of new crops which would then be passed on to private enterprise.[15] One of the Authority's experimental schemes was the Mkwasine project, in which the government heavily subsidised uneconomic winter wheat breeding, rotating it with summer crops of cotton, rice, Sorghum, groundnuts and soya beans. The aim of the Mkwasine project was to establish wheat as a major crop in the Lowveld, and to produce enough for the national needs. Started in 1966, the Mkwasine wheat project had proved successful by 1974, and the estate was sold to a consortium of Triangle Ltd and Hippo Valley. The consortium, however, with the priorities of private enterprise, has since carried out a programme to convert the Mkwasine estate to sugar cane.

The government also concluded agreements with the companies for the settlement of individual cane planters on the estates. The scheme provided for the settlement of approved farmers with some knowledge in cane growing, to be settled on 50 to 400 hectare plots on the company lands. The companies would build houses for the farmers, carry out the initial land preparation, plant the first cane crop and provide other necessary infrastructure. The farmers would then pay the companies back by delivering all their cane to the company mills, the companies retaining 35% of the value of cane milled. A separate scheme was arranged for the Mkwasine estate, where small-scale African farmers were settled on 10 hectare plots, but under the same terms as those on Triangle and Hippo Valley.

Agribusiness in the Lowveld has contributed much to the development of the region and to the national economy. With the backing they have from the financial and other resources of their parent companies, Triangle and Hippo Valley have proved to be among the best sugar producers in Southern Africa, while producing a whole range of other crops and products. It has already been mentioned that the companies are more interested in producing sugar, and the conversion of Mkwasine from wheat to sugar is witness to that. It also shows the differences in priorities between the government, with its national interests, and private enterprise, with its interests in profitable returns on investment. The same profit motives have also been behind the diversification programmes carried out by the two companies during periods of depression on the sugar market.

The first major diversification drive came in the work of the Unilateral Declaration of Independence by Ian Smith and his RF party in 1965, and the subsequent imposition of United Nations sanctions. The result was a partial closure of export markets (especially the British market) on the one hand, and pressure from the UDI government on foreign companies to reinvest their profits and to diversify their operations in a bid to beat the sanctions, on the other. This also coincided with the launching of the Sabi-Limpopo Authority as mentioned above. The second diversification drive was in the mid seventies, caused by the escalation of the liberation war in the country, which disrupted production and took its toll in skilled manpower because of military call-ups.[16] Both companies went into cattle ranching in a big way, using by-products from the sugar mills as cattle feed, while at Triangle, cattle feed manufacturing was established. In the 1978/9 season, Triangle had its greatest area under cotton, a total of 2,800 hectares, processed in the company's own ginnery. At Hippo Valley, however, the citrus section of the estate suffered from marketing difficulties in this period, forcing the management to uproot a greater part of the citrus trees. The citrus factory, which had been producing canned grapefruit segments and orange and lemon concentrates, was also closed down. Part of the reason for destroying the citrus trees was that under the depressed marketing conditions, Hippo Valley could not compete on the local market with other Anglo Group citrus producers at Mazoe and Premier, where citrus growing is the major activity. This again is an example of multinational economic rationale, which ignores host country priorities.

The sugar mills of the two companies have also contributed much to the country's economy through mill by-products. Indeed, it is one of the prides of the sugar industry that nothing is wasted. The cane waste from the mill processing, called bagasse, is used for cattle feed manufacture and for the generation of electricity. In fact both companies produce their own electricity this way. The main by-product of the sugar mill, molasses, is used as a cattle feed supplement, or can be used for the production of industrial ethyl alcohol. Two grades of alcohol are produced, rectified portable spirit, used in the manufacture of spirits such as vodka, gin and brandy; and industrial alcohol, which is used in solvent paint, cosmetics and pharmaceuticals. During the processing of molasses, carbon dioxide is produced, and this is sold either in its solid form (dry ice) for use as a refrigerant, or in cylinders for use in welding, foundry and in fire extinguishers. Carbon dioxide in its liquid form is also used in the manufacture of soft drinks. Hippo Valley produces 75% of the country's alcohol spirit and 75% of the country's liquid carbon dioxide requirements, thus providing useful inputs for the country's manufacturing industries.

At Triangle a major sideline to the sugar manufacturing process was launched with the construction of the first ethanol plant on the African continent. According to Dinham and Hines, the 'success of the Brazilian Proacool programme for turning sugar into ethyl alcohol [ethanol] sparked off excitement among both the sugar companies and sugar-growing countries'.[17] The project at Triangle was started at government request as a foreign currency saving venture at a time when United Nations sanctions were having their worst impact on the besieged economy. The plant, started in 1979, adopted technology developed by the Hermann Brothers of West Germany, a subsidiary of Krupp.[18] The plant was completed in nine months, at a cost of some Z$4 million, that is, disregarding the cost of the established sugar factory and cane fields. As a result of the ethanol plant, sugar production at Triangle fell, as the plant uses about 45,000 tonnes of sugar and 22,000 tonnes of molasses, which account for about 15% of raw sugar produced. Commissioned in 1980 just after the country gained its independence, the plant produces 5,000 litres of ethanol per hour, 120,000 litres per day and 40 million litres per year. The ethanol is then blended with imported petrol in the ratio 15% ethanol to 85% petrol. Apart from saving the country a significant amount of foreign currency (while losing out on sugar exports),

Table 22.2 *Raw sugar production and disposal: 1974–9*

Year	Total production (national) (thousand tonnes)	Disposal (thousand tonnes)		Value of sugar produced (Z$m.)
		Domestic	Exports	
1974/5	292.5	119.0	179.2	31.1
1975/6	284.1	121.5	157.4	18.9
1976/7	302.7	119.7	152.1	20.7
1977/8	310.5	112.9	153.3	22.7
1978/9	299.3	113.0	137.2	25.9*

* This figure, representing the value of total production, can be compared to the figure of Z$51 million in sugar export value in the 1983/4 season, showing the marked rise in production achieved by improved marketing conditions.
Source: Compiled from Agricultural Marketing Authority: *An economic review of the agricultural industry of Zimbabwe: 1980*, 167–8. Drops in production were caused by the reduction of the area under cane to avoid continued stockpiling because of marketing problems. The country achieved self-sufficiency in sugar in 1963.

the plant provides an insurance against fluctuating sugar prices or loss of markets by providing a major alternative use for the sugar. Table 22.2 shows the contribution of the sugar industry to the country's consumption and export needs.

The labour policies of the Lowveld multinational companies have changed markedly over time, in all aspects covering recruitment, accommodation and other facilities, and wages policy. These changes have been made because of economic considerations which necessitated a more humane labour policy, at a time when the government's policies with regard to agricultural workers remained basically unchanged. Production at both Triangle and Hippo Valley has remained very labour-intensive, except for some jobs which are by nature mechanised, such as transportation of cane and the milling processes. As at 1979, Hippo Valley employed some 8,000 workers with about the same number at Triangle. Because of very low wages paid within the agricultural sector in general, the sector has been heavily dependent on foreign migrant workers from the neighbouring countries, Malawi, Zambia, Tanzania, Mozambique and Angola: a situation which has depressed wages and other working conditions for a long time as migrants are generally single males.[19]

Up to 1968, about 90% of the workers at Triangle were migrants, while by that date Hippo Valley had already started on a policy of stabilising its labour by employing more local people. By 1966, 90% of the labour force at Hippo Valley came from the surrounding African areas. Labour conditions at the two estates have generally been bad, in line with national labour conditions in the agricultural sector. Apart from a few minor differences, workers at the two estates were paid low wages, and management–worker relations were generally bad. These conditions were not conducive to high productivity, and by the late sixties management at both estates realised the need for changes in policy.[20] The major drive was towards stabilising the labour force, mainly through raising wages, providing family accommodation and other facilities, and generally improving working relations. Hippo Valley also initiated a Joint Labour Committee in 1968, aimed at standardising conditions and eliminating employer competition, notably with Triangle. Stabilising the labour force meant huge outlays on capital expenditure, mainly on houses. Changes were needed from the slum-like pole and mud huts, to more permanent brick houses with three to four rooms and asbestos roofs. Major housing schemes were started from 1973, both estates adopting a continuous programme of housing improvement. Workers at the jointly owned Mkwasine estate are the joint responsibility of the two companies.

Although wages were improved generally from 1972, the increases cannot be applauded. Wages have been higher in the sugar industry than elsewhere in the agricultural sector (a fact used by management at both estates to exonerate themselves), but that, as D. G. Clarke points out, should not 'ignore the basic issue that wages should be judged in relation to enterprise ability to pay'.[21] The low wage structure can be gauged from a look at a few figures: in 1972, the basic daily rate of pay was 24 cents, plus rations valued at 18 cents daily. In addition, increments of 1 cent for each 6 months worked were given, with cane cutters getting an additional 10 cents daily on cutting days. Within this low wage structure, the companies made a distinction between agricultural workers (those working in the fields), and industrial workers (those working in the factory), with agricultural workers getting the lower wages.[22] The new policy adopted increased wages to a basic 50 cents a day in 1973, which was further raised in 1974, and by 1975, the wages had increased by 80% over 1972 levels.[23]

Low wages aside, the companies have provided a variety of facilities for their workers, mainly from the mid sixties. Both estates accommodate over 40,000 people each, including their workers' dependants, and have done so since the start of the labour stabilisation programme. The companies have therefore had to provide health services, education facilities and recreational facilities in addition to family accommodation. Both companies run modern, well-equipped hospitals staffed with trained doctors and nurses, and run, in association with government, primary and secondary schools. Hippo Valley, for example, runs eight primary schools and a secondary school. Recreational facilities include sporting facilities, beerhalls and clubs. All these facilities demand heavy capital expenditure, but the companies benefit through increased productivity as a result of improved working conditions.[24]

From about 1977, both companies started training programmes for their African workers, mainly because of the loss of skilled white workers caused by military call-up at the height of the liberation war. An industrial training centre was completed at Triangle in 1977, while at Hippo Valley training for all levels of the work force became the policy from 1978.[25] Hippo Valley also benefits in its training programme from its association with the Anglo-American Group, which runs apprenticeship training programmes for all its group companies. The training programmes are a major part of the continuing process of improving conditions and productivity.

From the discussion a number of observations can be drawn. Firstly, the activities of the agribusiness multinationals in the south-eastern Lowveld of Zimbabwe have been shaped to a large extent by the economic policies of the colonial governments. Secondly, this economic environment, in which the state played the role of both midwife and nurse-maid to the economy, created a good investment climate in which foreign companies made handsome profits. Thirdly, while the interests of the multinationals generally coincided with those of the state and local settlers, i.e. in the building of a viable, export-oriented economy, from time to time these interests came into conflict. For example, the multinationals, in reducing the area planted to wheat or uprooting citrus trees, acted more in line with their own long-term economic priorities than in support of the state's priorities for achieving self-sufficiency in food production. In the same way, the multinationals, in improving working conditions and wages for their workers, were acting in the interests of increased productivity and increased profits. Fourthly, it has been shown that the multinationals created highly efficient economic units in an area once seriously underdeveloped, but economic units which, in their organisation, self-sufficiency and isolation are 'enclaves' without much contact with the areas around them except through labour recruitment.[26] However, as shown, the sugar industry does have forward linkages with the manufacturing industry, to which it contributes important inputs. The sugar industry is also an important foreign exchange earner and foreign currency saver. The structure and organisation of the multinational subsidiary, with its vertical integration and the financial backing of the parent organisation, allow it room for flexibility.

NOTES

* The name 'Zimbabwe' is used throughout except where it is necessary to use 'Rhodesia'. The colonial period covers 1890–1980.
I am greatly indebted to the management and staff of Hippo Valley Estates Ltd for their cooperation and hospitality to me during a research visit to the estates.
1 These are the main arguments in books like S. George, *Feeding the few* (1979) and B. Dinham and C. Hines, *Agribusiness in Africa: a study of the impact of big business on Africa's food and agricultural production* (London, 1983) and S. H. Davies, *Victims of the miracle* (1977).

2 R. J. Barnett, and R. E. Muller, *Global Reach: the power of the multinational corporations* (Los Angeles, 1974), p. 182.
3 See Davies (1977) in the case of Brazil, and R. W. Franke and B. H. Chasin, *Seeds of famine* (Totowa, 1980), Chapter 8, pp. 167–97 in the case of Bud Senegal.
4 That the multinationals can contribute to food production in a big way is not denied. See S. George, *How the other half dies: the real reasons for world hunger* (New York, 1977), pp. 155–63.
5 Cf. I. Phimister, 'Rhodes, Rhodesia and the Rand', in *Journal of Southern African studies*, I (1974), 75–6.
6 R. Palmer, *Land and racial domination in Rhodesia* (Berkeley, 1977), p. 81.
7 See *ibid.* for the politics of land (in Rhodesia).
8 C. Stoneman, 'Foreign capital and the prospects for Zimbabwe', *World development*, 4/1 (1976), 25–58.
9 See C. Arrighi, 'Political economy of Rhodesia', in G. Arrighi and J. S. Saul, *Essays on the political economy of Africa* (New York, 1973), pp. 347–8.
10 Information from the Registrar for Companies Office in Harare and in *South African sugar yearbook* – various issues.
11 G. Lanning, and M. Mueller, *Africa undermined: a history of the mining companies and the underdevelopment of Africa* (1979), p. 450.
12 See Anglo-American Corporation Annual Reports.
13 Directorships and structures of the sugar industries of South Africa and the whole of Southern Africa are published in the *South African sugar yearbook*. See also D. Innes, *Anglo-American and the rise of modern South Africa* (London, 1984).
14 This early history can be found in the publications of the companies themselves, the Sabi-Limpopo Authority and other sources on the Lowveld, such as: Sabi-Limpopo Authority, *General development plan 1965–1990* (Salisbury, 1965); Zimbabwe Tourist Board, *Africa calls from Zimbabwe: special issue on the South-Eastern Lowveld* (Sept.–Oct. 1980); and Triangle Ltd, *Green book* (1980).
15 Sabi-Limpopo Authority, *Golden dawn*, (1966), p. 9.
16 Annual Reports of both companies for the 1970s abound with complaints on the disruptive impact of the liberation war on production.
17 Dinham and Hines, *Agribusiness in Africa*, p. 87.
18 G. Shreeve, 'Ethanol energy', in *African economic digest*, vol. I, no. 6 (June 1980), 5.
19 D. G. Clarke, *Agricultural and plantation workers in Rhodesia* (1977) provides a detailed analysis of labour policies, wages and conditions in the agricultural sector.
20 See *ibid.*, pp. 227–48 for labour policies on Triangle and Hippo Valley Estates.
21 *Ibid.*, p. 248.
22 The distinction was unfair, since the agricultural workers are the actual producers of the cane.
23 These wages increases were just enough to cover increases in living costs.
24 Information provided by management in the case of Hippo Valley and from Company Annual Reports in the case of Triangle.
25 At Hippo Valley as from 1978, the management thought it necessary in the interest of increased productivity to give basic training even to the general field workers.
26 The health, education and other facilities at the Estates are specifically for employees and their families only.

23 Multinational companies and the sexual division of labour: a historical perspective

RUTH PEARSON

Introduction

The history of multinational companies is by and large a branch of business history. It relates the strategies, successes and failures of expansionary capital in an age when the drive for accumulation pushed adventurous capital beyond nation state boundaries. It is written largely from the point of view of capital rather than from that of labour, and from the point of view of the home economy rather than that of the country which hosts the foreign operations of multinational companies. Capital, expanding internationally, is seen as the progressive and logical route for the exploitation of western innovation and enterprise. The impact on the economies and societies to which it reaches out is not the concern of the business historian.

Other approaches to charting and analysing the role of the multinational companies and their phenomenal growth in this century have taken a more critical stance (Hymer 1976, Palloix 1978). But very little of even this literature has been concerned with the labour force recruited by multinational companies in their foreign enterprises, or the significance of their specific geographical location. More interest has been shown in the implications of foreign investment for the emergence of an autonomous national bourgeoisie itself able to fulfil its historic mission of accumulation within the national state. And, as I argue below, the one debate in the literature which is concerned with the labour force – the labour aristocracy debate – assumes a male industrial labour force.

What I am concerned with in this paper is the importance of the changing sexual and geographical division of labour in understanding the role of multinationals in the contemporary world economy. I shall argue that the recent phase of the internationalisation of capital, in which multinational companies located production in low wage economies to produce manufactures for exports, reveals the way in which gender, as well as other characteristics, is an important element in understanding how and where multinational companies decide to construct their labour force.

Historians of multinational companies, whatever their specific interest, have to take into account the implications of the freedom or constraints of capital to migrate between different centres of accumulation. Girvan argues that the power of multinational companies derives from five basic concepts of the multinational economy: (1) their large size, particularly in relation to the size of some of the national economies in which they operate, (2) their range of activities over both product lines and countries, (3) the fact that they can operate on the frontiers of technology, (4) the uneven distribution of power and authority spatially across the globe, reflecting the dispersion of subsidiaries and the centralisation of global headquarters, and (5) the fact that 'power in the transnationalised economy also derives from the *collective* characteristics of the community of multinational companies taken as a whole'. In specific industries power is concentrated within an oligopolistic group of large companies which act, according to Girvan, like 'monopolies' vis-à-vis economies in which they have relative power (Girvan 1975, pp. 29–33).

These characteristics of multinationals cited by Girvan focus on the influence that multinational companies can and do have on individual host countries, an influence which is often commensurate, not with the scale and scope of individual company's operations in specific countries, but with the scale and scope of transnational enterprises operating throughout the world. Thus, it can be argued that what constitutes the range of consumer goods available in a given society (Stewart 1977), the kind of technology used in production (Helleiner 1975), the nature and direction of technological change (Cooper 1973), the policies and practices of financial institutions, can be shaped (Edwards 1985), if not determined, by the activities of large corporations organised by decisions made within distant and different host countries relatively immune to the particular priorities or preferences of individual host countries' governments, capital, or population.[1] If one accepts that multinationality carries with it a potential force to intervene in the economies described by Girvan as 'transnationalised' to influence, if not determine the nature and pattern of accumulation, then it is reasonable to suppose that such intervention must affect not only patterns of industry and consumption, financial flows, and technological choice, but also the composition and control of the waged labour force recruited as the basis for accumulation in that economy.

Multinational companies and labour

The literature on multinational companies has, until recently, been concerned with only one issue relating to the labour force employed by the multinational companies operating directly in the third world – the so-called labour aristocracy thesis. This refers to the argument that penetration of third world economies by multinational companies leads to a differentiation of the working class and the emergence of a 'labour aristocracy' on the one hand, and the marginalisation of the bulk of the population on the other (Arrighi 1975, Quijano 1974). This thesis is disputed by other authors who argue that, far from representing a sub-sector of the industrial working class, who are privileged in terms of wages, job stability, skills, etc., the labour force employed by multinational companies in the third world are relatively unskilled, and often paid low wages in a situation in which labour turnover, rather than being stable, is often high as a result of a deliberate strategy of labour control (Humphrey 1979).

This debate recognises an important issue concerning the impact of multinational companies on industrialisation and accumulation in the third world – that the power of multinationals includes the ability to select or construct a labour force with characteristics most consistent with the needs of the valorisation process being undertaken by them. The literature contesting the labour aristocracy thesis specifically focusses on strategies employed to control the labour force. Such strategies include those which are normally part of management–employee relations, such as high wage rates to buy workers' loyalty and frustrate the possibility of radical union organisation (Jenkins 1984: 171), controlled recruitment, job evaluation and promotion strategies. Also included are the practices of building up company-based unions (Henley 1983) and pressurising for government legislation to outlaw unions in industries of national strategic importance (Cardosa Khoo 1978).

Sexual division of the labour force: the missing variable

The labour aristocracy literature focusses on divisions within the working class. However, it is significant that none of the analyses which deals with the labour force recruited by multinationals throughout the import substitution phase of industrialisation makes reference to the sexual division of labour, created as the result of multinational companies' activities in the industrial sector of third world countries. As late as 1983, Henley, writing about multinationals' strategies for labour relations in Kenya and Malaysia, comments that the emphasis on formal qualifications as part of the system of labour force control in Kenya 'credentialism' has historical roots in the 'differentiation of skill by race during the colonial period' (Henley 1983: 122). While this recognises the use of race (and in Malaysia ethnic differences are extremely important) as a basis for dividing and controlling the labour force, the use of sex differences is not alluded to.

This is at one level curious, and at another level completely explainable. Until the mid seventies, when a number of third world countries embarked on a new strategy of industrialisation, export-oriented, which involved foreign companies in a different relationship with third world host economies, the impact of multinationals on the sexual division of labour was to confirm the pattern prevailing in industry in western Europe.

The manufacturing industries which invested in production facilities in the developing countries during the import-substitution phase of industrialisation up to the 1960s were the chemical industry, the pharmaceutical industry, the engineering industry, the steel industry, and the motor industry. These are all sectors which normally employed men as production workers and thus produced in the third world a sexual division of labour no different from that prevailing in those sectors in the first world. Only when women were employed by multinationals in what were normally male industries was the existence of a sexual division of labour ever noticed. For instance, Whitten (1983) records that the Singer Company's Clydebank factory, which was turned over to ammunition production during the First World War, employed a labour force of 14,000 in 1918 'of whom almost 70% were women'. But although Wilkins (1970) heralds the Singer Company as 'the first American international business', no record is made of the sexual composition of the labour force in the Scottish factory when it was established in 1885, employing 5,000 people, nor of the 12,000 employees in its six factories in Europe and the United States.

The assumption must be that this company, like other large firms expanding internationally at the turn of the century, 'normally' replicated the sexual division of labour at home in its foreign manufacturing subsidiaries. There are presumably other examples in the literature which point to instances in which the contrast between the sexual composition of labour in domestic and foreign operations of a multinational company command attention. What would appear to be lacking is any serious attention to the way in which gender and other characteristics of the labour which is available to multinational capital because of the international mobility enjoyed by such firms represents an element in explaining or understanding the geographical patterns of migration at any specific phase of the internationalisation of production.

Multinationals recruit women workers in the third world

The point at which writers started to note the impact of multinational companies' recruitment strategies on the sexual division of labour within host countries was the point at which they visibly and collectively began to recruit women workers. For in industries in which large sections of production have been relocated to developing countries for export production – that is garments and electronics products – the labour force is overwhelmingly female. Much of this production has been located in 'Free Trade Zones' or 'Export Processing Zones', which were specifically designated by host governments to attract foreign investment by a combination of freedom from customs and tariff controls, availability of industrial infrastructure, utilities and communications services, and specifically designed (or abolished) legislation to pre-empt or control labour organisation. 'In the majority of Free Trade Zones, well over 70% of the total employed are women. In Mexico 75% of the workers in the Maquiladoras or "twin plants" along the US border are women. In the Republic of Korea women account for 75% of all workers in export industries...in three export processing zones 80% of the workers are women. In [a] Free Trade Zone in Malaysia 80% of the workers are women and in the export processing zone of Mauritius more than 80% are women' (UNIDO 1980: 6).

Women have become the new industrial workers in an industrialisation strategy which is heavily dominated by multinational companies (UNIDO 1980: 6). Had economists and policy makers taken note of the sexual division of labour in these industries in the industrial countries from which they were relocated, the bias in multinational companies' recruitment would have been entirely predictable. 'In the USA, for example, 90% of all production workers and operators in the two industries which have been most heavily redeployed to developing countries – electronics assembly and wearing apparel – are women' (UNIDO 1980: 6–7).

However, governments actively pursuing export-led industrialisation paid little attention to the sexual composition of the labour force in industry, either in their own third world economies or in the advanced countries from which international capital was migrating. From the theoretical point of view, export-led industrialisation offered third world states a 'third' option of development. Instead of the states' continuing to specialise in the production of primary products for export, or to base an industrialisation strategy on the limited domestic markets, production of manufactures for export offered a way to compete in the world market for manufactured products. From the point of view of third world states, this strategy promised relief to two of their most pressing problems – unemployment and shortage of foreign exchange. Given the lack of analytical interest in the sexual division of labour in the third world, and the consistent under-reporting and under-valuation of women's productive activities in non-wage employment, it is not surprising that few governments predicted that the majority of the new wage earners would be women.

The appeal to nature

In the 1970s both economists and governments did acknowledge that exported industrialisation, far from reducing recorded (male) unemployment, offered employment only to women, which in some cases increased the official level of unemployment.[2] Some state governments used this fact as a positive factor to attract foreign companies to invest in their country rather than one of the dozens of other countries competing for foreign investment. One Malaysian investment brochure which is quoted in the *Far Eastern economic review* (18 May 1979) boasts:

The manual dexterity of the oriental female is famous the world over. Her hands are small and she works fast with extreme care. Who, therefore, could be better qualified by nature and inheritance to contribute to the efficiency of a bench-assembly production line than the oriental girl.

Indeed, from a position of sex blindness about the industrial labour force of multinational companies' overseas operations, economic analysis moved to a position of assuming that women were suited 'by nature' for the kind of work required of them by foreign companies. Curiously, although it is undisputably established that women and children were the preferred labour force in the various textile and garment industries of western countries in the eighteenth and nineteenth centuries (Pinchbeck 1981), an appeal was made, not just to the universal suitability of women for such activities, but to the specific suitability of women workers in different third world locations. Hence the reference to the oriental female quoted above. Even where industrial processes new to the local economy, like electronics assembly, are concerned, the 'natural' abilities of women within the host country culture are inveighed to explain the choice of women rather than male workers:

manual dexterity of a high order may be required in typical subcontracted operations, but nevertheless the operation is usually one that can be learned quickly on the basis of traditional skills. Thus in Morocco, in six weeks girls (who may be illiterate) are taught the assembly under magnification of memory planes for computers – this is virtually darning with copper wire, and *sewing is a traditional Moroccan skill*. In the electrical field, the equivalent of sewing is putting together wing harnesses, and in metal working one finds parallels in some forms of soldering and welding.
(Sharpston 1976: 334, my italics)

How multinationals secure suitable labour power from women workers

The reduction of the incorporation of women into the industrial labour force to their 'natural' and traditional characteristics belies the rational economic choices and management strategies employed by those responsible for this pattern of recruitment. Empirical studies demonstrate that the money costs of employing female labour in world market factories are in general lower than would be the costs of employing men. Kreye found that women's wages in world market factories are in general 20%–50% lower than wages paid for men in comparable occupations (Frobel, Heinrichs & Kreye 1980). But there are exceptions to this; women employed by the multinational electronics companies in Penang Free Trade Zone in Malaysia rank amongst the best paid workers in Malaysia with the exception of those in heavy industry

(Cardosa Khoo 1978). But it is the high rates of productivity achieved by women employed in such factories that explain companies' preference for a female labour force. Direct comparisons are hard to make since so few men are employed in comparable labour–intensive assembly operations. Lim (1978) reports that two multinational electronics firms had, in response to the Malaysian government's call to employ more men, experimented with the employment of a few hundred men as production operators. In both cases the men's productivity was lower than that of women. Comparisons of productivity between workers in foreign establishments assembling or processing products of US origin indicate that productivity is as high or up to several times higher than those in US establishments, while wages show a differential of up to 10:1 with lower and indirect labour costs (USTC 1970).

Women workers are employed by multinational companies in the third world because they represent the labour force offering the lowest unit labour cost in a specific labour process, organised under specific conditions. But it is instructive that to achieve this desired unit cost of labour the multinationals operating in third world export zones do not rely on 'nature' alone. The oft-cited docility of women workers is reinforced by a series of recruitment strategies to eliminate potential trouble-makers, management policies to avoid the development of solidarity and class consciousness (Cardosa Khoo 1978, Henley 1983) and in some cases state-provided prohibitions on unions or other forms of labour organisation. Multinational companies' policies in constructing and controlling their female labour force have been deliberate and consistent. Far from being indifferent to the sexual division of labour in economies in which they operate, they have directly utilised local forms of gender subordination to create a malleable female labour force (Pearson 1984b).

Historical perspective on the sexual division of labour

From a historical perspective this is less of an aberration than might appear. While women constitute less than one-third of the British manufacturing labour force in the 1980s (a proportion which has declined rapidly over the last two decades) (*Department of Employment Gazette*) at earlier stages of Britain's industrialisation women constituted a significant part of the industrial work force.

Many of Britain's female factory workers were employed within the textile, and later garments, sectors, particularly in 'highly differentiated low-skilled repetitive jobs', though it should be noted that in the mid nineteenth century 40% of the female work force in manufacturing were employed not in the textile factories but in the non-mechanised home-based garment and 'toy' trades (Tilly and Scott 1978: 67). However, as is well known, by the mid nineteenth century iron and steel production and the manufacture of machinery and heavy equipment became more important than textile mills as the symbol of Britain's industrialisation.

International location of industry and the sexual division of labour

The sexual division of labour in manufacturing in Britain has only recently become an issue for analysis as the changing structure of Britain's manufacturing sector since the Second World War has corresponded with a change in the demand for different types of labour. And it is not surprising that this period of rationalisation and restructuring has been associated with a significant penetration of foreign capital into Britain's manufacturing sector (Pearson 1984a).

The location by foreign firms of manufacturing in industrialised countries such as Britain, particularly in the peripheral regions of Scotland and Wales, is a location choice increasingly favoured by multinational companies as an alternative to or in addition to location in the third world (Hood and Young 1983). These areas were once the site of traditional nationally owned industries, such as coal mining, shipbuilding and steel mills, now in decline, which employed almost exclusively male labour (Massey 1983). In the sectors which have been involved in large-scale location in the third world, particularly electronics and electrical goods, foreign firms locating in these regions are also selecting women workers for the assembly line or semi-skilled jobs (Pearson forthcoming).[3]

Export manufacturing in the third world also represents options for capital. In the sectors we have been discussing the option is to utilise a low paid segment of the potential labour force in conjunction with minimal fixed capital in the form of machinery and equipment and minimal working capital in the form of wages, wage-related benefits and management costs. This option was neither available nor necessary at previous historical stages of industrialisation and accumulation. Nineteenth-century industrial capital targeted female and child labour employed in the sweatshops and clothing factories of western Europe, where the exploitation of a weak segment of the labour force was a preferable option to investment in mechanisation in garment production.

Indeed, in Britain, as in the third world, a variety of working conditions and systems coexisted to utilise the cheap and productive labour of women workers. While some women, as in the third world factories today, were employed in large-scale mechanised textile factories in unskilled jobs, many others were employed in domestic workshops, or sweatshops. This coexistence of two distinct forms of organisation of production is mirrored in the third world today by the proliferation of domestic workshops and various forms of out-working which characterises sections of the textile and clothing industries in countries which host foreign-owned large-scale factories producing textiles, garments and other products for the world market.

In the eighteenth and nineteenth centuries, as now, the utilisation of female (and child) labour was a response to technical change which usurped the role of the (skilled) male artisan in production. In the twentieth century the technical progress in both manufacturing techniques and international transportation has made the migration of capital to 'cheap' labour environments an option for this particular phase of accumulation. But this option coexists with and is transcended by other options. Cheap female labour is also utilised in domestic workshops in the periphery producing both for the domestic market (Alonso 1983, Schmitz 1982) and the export market (Rivieras Quintero & Gonzales n.d.). It also coexists with the employment of cheap labour within the centres of accumulation which have witnessed a large-scale emigration of capital to less developed regions (both national and international). New York, for example, has witnessed over the last 10 years the proliferation of sweatshops utilising cheap female labour. Significantly the cheap female labour force in this case is available not via the migration of international capital to the cheap labour economies, but through the migration of third world labour to these declining centres of the periphery – from Central America, the Caribbean and Asia (Sassen-Koob). Nor is this range of production relations and organisation of the labour process restricted to the textile and garments sectors, in which it is well established that different forms of production have coexisted since the eighteenth century (Berg, Hudson & Sonescher, 1983). It is reported that subcontracting and out-work of various kinds including women workers using their own domestic cooking equipment is widely used in the electronics industry in California (Katz and Kemnitzer 1984) and in Taiwan (Hu 1984) in association with foreign firms involved in export processing in Free Trade Zones.

Conclusion

What I am arguing in this paper is complex. I contest the view that multinational companies have no significance beyond that of transnational control of assets. On the contrary, I argue that the productive activities of multinational companies, their geographical pattern, their sectoral distribution and the changing trends over time represent and reveal the way in which capital is organising in new and changing structures in a world economy which is itself responding to the past and present actions of multinational capital: that this global process of accumulation is historically specific, and that the role of multinational companies has changed, is changing and will change.

The process of accumulation requires the exploitation of labour power which is available to capital not in an abstract form, but from a labour force which is conditioned by nationality, migrant status, ethnicity and gender.

Where and when multinational companies have targeted young women in the third world as their optimal labour force, this optimality is premised on the feasibility of capital's mobility internationally, the technical possibilities of organising and controlling production processes, and the cooperation and/or cooption of the state, local labour organisation and patriarchal structures in releasing women's labour in the relevant form. But this instance of the gender division of the labour force, and the resulting sexual division of labour in third world export manufacturing, do not stand out as an historical aberration. It must be analysed and understood in the context of the different uses capital has made of women's and men's labour throughout the history of industrialisation in the first world and the third world. And it must also be considered in conjunction with other forms of organisation of production open to capital within the international context, including the increasing use of non-factory production and the flows of foreign investment into the industrialised countries, particularly into the areas where traditional manufacturing and processing industry has declined.

NOTES

1 I am not suggesting that the interests of government, national capital, and peoples coincide, but that the determination of policies may, in specific situations, be more effectively influenced by decisions made by multinational management or international financial institutions than by the articulation of the interests of other agents and groups within the society. This is not to fail to recognise that these groups are in conflict between themselves and that any or all may perceive of their interests as being allied to those of multinational companies.

2 If women are drawn into the labour force by a specific demand for wage labour and if the number of jobs is less than the supply of labour forthcoming, this has the effect of increasing officially measured unemployment statistics (Pearson 1978). The way in which the employment of women by multinational companies in the third world was ignored until the mid 1970s is discussed in Elson and Pearson 1980.

3 It should be noted that the female intensity of labour in sectors in which production has been relocated to the third world does differ between the third world and the first world. This difference is particularly significant when the trends of relocation of production in the European periphery are examined. The female intensity of production in the electronics industry falls from 80%–90% in the third world to 40%–60% in the UK (Pearson 1984a).

BIBLIOGRAPHY

Allen, S., Purcell, A., Waton, A., & Woods, S. (forthcoming), *The changing experience of work*, Macmillan.

Alonso, J. A. (1983), 'The domestic clothing workers in the Mexican metropolis and their relation to dependent capitalism', in Nash & Fernandez-Kelly (eds.) (1983).

Arrighi, G. (1975), 'International corporations, labour aristocracies and economic development in tropical Africa', in Arrighi & Saul (1973).

Arrighi, G. & Saul, J. (1973), *Essays on the political economy of Africa*, MRP.

Berg, M., Hudson, P., & Sonescher, M. (eds.) (1983), *Manufacture in town and country before the factory*, Cambridge University Press.

Cardosa Khoo, J. (1978), *Workings in electronic runaways: the case of Malaysia*, mimeo IDS, Sussex University.

Cooper, C., (ed.) (1973), *Science, technology and development: the political economy of technical advance in underdeveloped countries*, Frank Cass.

Edwards, C. B. (1985), *The fragmented world*, Methuen.

Elson D., & Pearson R. (1980) 'The latest phase of the internationalisation of capital and its implications for women in the third world', Discussion Paper no. 150, University of Sussex.

Frobel, F., Heinrichs, J. & Kreye, O. (1980), *The new international division of labour*, Cambridge University Press.

Girvan, N. (1975), 'Economic nationalists v. multinational corporations – revolutionary or evolutionary change?', in Widstrand (ed.) (1975).

Helleiner, G. K. (1975), 'The role of multinational corporations in the less developed countries' trade in technology', *World development*, vol. III, no. 4.

Henley, J. (1983), 'Corporate strategy and employment relations in multinational corporations: some evidence from Kenya and Malaysia', in Thurley & Wood (eds.) (1983).

Hood, N., & Young, S. (1983), *Multinational investment strategies in the British Isles*, HMSO.

Humphrey, J. (1979), 'Auto workers and the working class in Brazil', *Latin American Perspectives*, no. 23 (winter).

Hu Tai-li (1983), 'The emergence of small scale industry in a Taiwanese rural community', in Nash & Fernandez-Kelly (eds.) (1983).

Hymer, S. (1976), *The international operations of national firms: a study of direct foreign investment*, MIT Press.

Katz, N. & Kemnitzer, D. (1983), 'Fast forward: the internationalisation of Silicon Valley', in Nash & Fernandez-Kelly (eds.) (1983).

Jenkins, R. O. (1984), *Transnational corporations and industrial transformation in Latin America*, Macmillan.

Lim, L. (1978), 'Women workers in multinational corporations in development countries: the case of the electronics industry in Malaysia and Singapore', Women's Studies Program, Occasional Paper no. 9, University of Michigan.

Massey, D. (1983), 'Industrial restructuring as class restructuring', *Regional studies*, XVII.

Nash, J. & Fernandez-Kelly, M. P. (eds.) (1983), *Women, men and the international division of labour*, State University of New York Press.

Palloix, C. (1978), *La internacionalizacion del capital*, Madrid, H. Blume Ediciones.

Pearson, R. (1978), 'Women workers in Mexico's border industries', mimeo IDS, Sussex University.

Pearson, R. (1984a), 'Multinational companies and women's employment in Britain', mimeo, School of Development Studies, University of East Anglia.

Pearson, R. (forthcoming), 'The greening of women's labour in the third and first world', to be published in Allen, Purcell, Waton & Woods (eds.).

Pinchbeck, I. (1981), *Women workers in the Industrial Revolution*, Virago.
Quijano, A. (1974), 'The marginal role of the economy and the marginalised labour force', *Economy and society*, vol. III, no. 4.
Rivieras Quintero, M. & Gonzales, N. (n.d.), 'La industria de la aguja puento invisible en la historia del trabajo feminino en Puerto Rico', mimeo, CEREP.
Sassen-Koob, S. (1983), 'Labor migrations and the new international division of labour', in Nash & Fernandez Kelly (eds.) (1983).
Schmitz, H. (1982), *Manufacturing in the backyard*, Harvester Press.
Sharpston, M. (1976), 'International subcontracting', *World development*, vol. IV, no. 4.
Stewart, F. (1977), *Technology and underdevelopment*, Macmillan, London.
Thurley, K. & Wood, S. (eds.) (1983), *Industrial relations and management strategy*, Cambridge University Press.
Tilly, L. & Scott, J. (1978), *Women, work and the family*, Holt, Rinehart.
UNIDO (1980), 'Women in the redeployment of manufacturing industry to developing countries', UNIDO Working Papers in Structural Change, no. 18, July.
USTC (United States Tariff Commission) (1970), *Economic factors affecting the use of items 807.00 and 8630 of the Tariff Schedules of the United States*.
Whitten, D. O. (1983), *The emergence of giant enterprises 1860–1914*, Greenwood Press.
Widstrand, C., (ed.) (1975), *Multinational firms in Africa*, Scandinavian Institute of African Studies, Uppsala.
Wilkins, M. (1970), *The emergence of multinational enterprise*, Harvard University Press.

24 Transnational corporations and the struggle for the establishment of a New International Economic Order

HORST HEININGER

Demands for the adequate regulation of activities undertaken by transnational corporations have been a major item on the programme for a 'New International Economic Order' ever since an Action Programme and Declaration on the introduction of such order had been passed at the Sixth Special Meeting of the UN General Assembly in 1974. Provisions relating to the right of any national government to regulate the activities of transnational corporations were laid down in Article II of a 'Charter of Economic Rights and Duties of States' adopted by the UN General Assembly in the same year. Discussion about ways to control the activities of transnational corporations has since continued to rank high on the agenda of all important meetings on international economic relations. The issue had been a subject of debates at meetings of UNCTAD, UNIDO, FAO, ILO, and other UN Special Agencies as well as at summit conferences of the non-aligned nations and in negotiations between western industrial states and developing countries, such as the 'North-South Dialogue' in Paris, 1976 to 1977, and the conferences on Lomé I, II, and III.

International efforts towards the regulation of the activities of transnational corporations reached a high point when a UN Commission on Transnational Corporations was set up in 1974, with a working party of that Commission being appointed and asked to draft a Code of Conduct for Transnational Corporations.[1]

I

The process of political independence of a great number of developing countries and their mounting struggles for economic independence, from the early seventies, were accompanied by growing insight to the effect that transnational corporations were in many respects obstacles in the path of full independence.

Transnational corporations, in the first place, have an enormous influence on economic relations among industrialised capitalist countries as well as on relations between these and the developing countries. The turnover figures in 1980 of 382 leading transnational corporations accounted for more than 28% of the GNP of all western industrial states and all developing countries and for about 60% of all trade between those countries.[2] The role played by these corporations in international economic relations is reflected, last but not least, in controlling positions held by them in manufacturing industries in many advanced western industrial states and in numerous developing countries. In the late seventies, for example, they controlled some 25% of the production of manufacturing industries in France, Italy, the Federal Republic of Germany, and the United Kingdom and even 44% in Brazil and as much as 43% in Colombia.[3]

Whenever an appraisal is to be made of the role played by these corporations in international economic relations, with particular reference to developing countries, due consideration should be given to one fact of substantive importance: these organisations are not simply enterprises of a 'multinational' nature but *transnational* corporations. They are, in their overwhelming majority, 'national' corporations of the USA, United Kingdom, the Federal Republic of Germany and so on that are expanding to 'trans-national' dimensions through the establishment of affiliated firms, subsidiaries, purchase of shares and other forms of participation, including 'non-equity arrangements'.

Being transnational corporations, they are closely linked to the social fabric, economy, and government institutions of their respective parent countries. Administrative interference is exercised through a variety of channels all aimed at stimulating private investment abroad, governmental shelter for capital investment with safeguards against political and other risks, preferential treatment in the context of taxation, subsidies, and other measures. The home country's foreign policy is pursued with due consideration of corporate interest and international economic expansion, and corporate policies are even merged with national policy-making.

Finally, there is another aspect of relevance to an assessment of trans-national corporations and the rôle played by them: expansion of these corporations is taking place in the context of a specific international setting in which it proves to cause disorder in international economic relations.

The external expansion of transnational corporations is subject to profit-orientated business strategies. This is the major cause of disorder, since decisions on sites, production profiles, modification of product programmes, investment, export, and other substantial activities of subsidiaries and affiliated firms of a corporation in the investment countries affected are taken solely by the criterion of maximum corporate profit.

Such profit-strategy governed influences on international site choice and division of labour may be in contradiction to the economic development interests of the host countries concerned. Conflict is thus pre-programmed between the economic policies of parent countries on the one hand and the profit strategies of transnational corporations on the other. The situation is exacerbated by the fact that the corporations, because of their intra-firm production, price, and credit relations and their centralised pattern of decision-making, can effectively use economic instruments, such as transfer prices, to evade fully or at least partially governmental control and influence. The growing dimensions of such intra-firm transactions may be seen from the following data: US transnational corporations in 1977 were directly involved in more than 90% of US foreign trade. Thirty-nine per cent of all imports and 36% of all exports were associated with intra-corporate business.[4] Such a more or less autonomous international set-up of the transnational corporations cannot but aggravate the conflict potential in international economic relations.

It is well known that these goals and approaches to the international expansion of transnational corporations are likely to have certain negative political, social, and economic consequences for development in the host countries. Some transnational corporations have resorted to political interference with the internal affairs of host countries. International tension has worsened, last but not least, in the wake of transnational corporate activities in the racist South African Republic. Ideologies, values, and consumption habits alien to host countries concerned have in some instances been introduced at the expense of traditional national values and cultures in developing countries. Transnational corporations have also functioned as levers of their parent countries' foreign policy. Plenty of documentation also has become available on certain social repercussions in the wake of transnational corporations, including harsh exploitation of local labour, brain-drain, discrimination against workers for racist, political, and other reasons, and the like. There is, finally, a wide spectrum of economic consequences, including tax evasion, excessive profit transfer, detrimental effects on host countries' balances of trade and payment, and gross negligence of consumers' interests, environment, and safety, as was drastically shown by the most recent disaster at the chemical complex in Bhopal, India.

II

Control over and regulation of activities of the transnational corporations, therefore, is an absolutely indispensable prerequisite for the introduction of a New International Economic Order and for thorough democratisation of international economic relations. Recognition of unrestricted national sovereignty of any state regarding its own natural resources and economic activities in its own territory is a major demand raised by the developing countries in pursuit of these goals. Their accomplishment should be accompanied at least by a reduction in economic dependence and backwardness, mitigation of plundering, and reversal of the unequal position now held by developing countries versus western industrial states. Accomplishment of this demand, after all, is considered the key to effective control and regulation of the activities of the transnational corporations.

The following more specific demands have been formulated, against that background, over the past ten years in discussions about future structuring of international economic relations and in the debates for the purpose of proclaiming a UN Code of Conduct for Transnational Corporations:

Non-interference by transnational corporations with internal affairs of nations and with inter-state relations;

Streamlining of corporate activities to national development programmes of host countries;

Recognition of human rights by transnational corporations and termination of business in southern Africa;

Regulation of corporate activities and containment of negative practice in the areas of taxation, balance of payments, transfer of technology, financing, property control, conservation and consumer protection, and several additional economic issues;

Briefing of national government and the general public about transactions of transnational corporations;

Right of host governments to nationalisation of corporate property and unobstructed decision-making on compensation;

Unlimited validity of national jurisdiction and rejection of alleged generally accepted modes for international settlement of legal disputes.

Regulation of corporate activities along these lines might be a positive contribution to inter-state relations conducive to justice, equality, and peace at all levels of economic activity and thus help to implement principles for international economic relations on a democratic basis. These demands have been unanimously backed up from the very beginning by the socialist states.

The efforts made by developing countries to get to grips with the problem of transnational corporations have been reflected in all relevant UN documents as well as in all important documents drafted and adopted by the non-aligned movement, including the seventh summit conference at New Delhi, 1983, and its economic declaration (Articles 124 to 128).

III

There is another viewpoint which has been publicised by distinguished economists, politologists, sociologists, and political representatives of leading western industrial states.

They interpret the rapid expansion since the sixties of transnational corporations as a factor of extremely favourable relevance to the network of international relations today: transnational corporations, in their view, are on account of their 'global coverage' vehicles of progress in shaping international relations and prime movers for more cooperation between states, notwithstanding different social systems and standards accomplished in economic development. L. R. Brown, for example, suggested that transnational corporations were likely to reduce the risk of international conflict, since they were as interested as the nation states in a smooth functioning of the international system.[5] Identical and similar views have been disseminated from the sixties in publications by Sidney E. Rolfe, Howard V. Perlmutter, Charles Kindleberger, and other renowned authors on issues of international economic relations. The euphoria regarding the 'peace-making role' of the transnational corporation, which was in full swing in the seventies, has receded somewhat in view of growing economic and political clashes with such corporations, but the concept is still alive.

The importance of transnational corporations to growing 'interdependence between states' is another concept which has been increasingly publicised since the first half of the seventies, the time when developing countries intensified their struggles for a New International Economic Order. Emphasis has been repeatedly laid, in this context, on two aspects for interdependence:

1. Transnational corporations, in the context of world economy, are a decisive or the decisive factor for economic integration in harmony with the objective and inevitable course of economic as well as of techno-scientific progress.

2. National governments and transnational corporations do have a common political interest in the stability of relations, and this has a favourable impact upon international relations at large.

Hence, the concept is one of 'functional harmony of interest' among states with regard to transnational corporations. However, the political ambitions linked to the concept are becoming more obvious, simply because of the fact that from the seventies the claim for interdependence has been increasingly associated with the demand by western governments, primarily on developing countries, for a 'climate conducive to private capital investment' to attract investors from abroad. Ever since we have observed a growing trend towards bilateral investment guaranty treaties under which developing countries are actually forced to grant preferential treatment to investors from abroad. This seems to be a clear indicator of the congruence of interests on major issues of foreign economy and foreign policy between transnational corporations on the one hand, and the governments of home countries on the other.

This concept of a 'progressive role of transnational corporations in an interdependent world' has been continued and further enlarged by a notion according to which *the role of the nation state has become obsolete in international economic relations*. This notion of outdated national sovereignty was backed up by the allegation that the political structure of the world at present, as provided by the majority of nation states and by their great number, could no longer keep pace with the progressive role of international corporations and with global development of production. Nation states had actually outlived their own justified existence and ought to give up at least part of their sovereignty in the future. Here is an extract from a well-known statement made by Charles Kindleberger in 1969: 'the nation state is just about through as an economic unit'.[6] The following proposition was made in 1975 by H. V. Perlmutter in his prognostication on international corporations for the forthcoming decades: 'As it [our global industrial system] becomes more interdependent, nation states must find a balance between *sovereignty-sharing* and *surrender*, and *sovereignty-affirmation* will become quite difficult and painful to achieve.'[7] Other economists and politologists went as far as to complain that the international corporations were 'oppressed' and would be ruined by the nation states if developments went on the same way. Peter F. Drucker, for example, wrote this: 'It is, therefore, entirely possible that the multinationals will be severely damaged and perhaps even destroyed within the next decade.'[8]

Yet it has been interesting to see that those pronounced views on the 'outdated role' of the nation state began to lose momentum in the second half of the seventies and were repudiated to some extent even in countries of the West. The following point was made, for example, by C. Fred Bergsten, Robert O. Keohane, and Joseph S. Nye, renowned US scholars, as early as in 1975: 'With regard to multinational enterprises, some incautious or enthusiastic observers have gone too far in proclaiming the death of the nation state in a world of interdependence. The nonstate actors do not supersede states, although they do affect the system... and create new problems for governments.'[9] Raymond Vernon, too, arrived at a comparable view: 'Neither the multinational enterprise nor the nation state shows much evidence of losing its vitality in the world economy.'[10]

The causes underlying such a change of mind are quite easily disclosed from the reality of international economy and politics in the seventies. Unambiguous evidence was produced to the effect that the role of states in international economic relations was growing rather than diminishing. The correlation between reciprocal dependence of states as a result of growing internationalisation of the economy and state sovereignty proved to be quite different from what had been postulated by the scholars mentioned above. One of the peculiarities of international economic relations was shown to emanate from the fact that the process of economic internationalisation was paralleled by a process of consolidation of national and state independence and accompanied by mounting action for unrestricted sovereignty. This trend has been strongly confirmed by subsequent developments in international disputes for adequate settlement of international economic problems. It has been demonstrated with great clarity by the struggles waged by a great number of young nation states for their economic independence. The use of government authority and full implementation and enforcement of national sovereignty against transnational corporations has proved to be of vital importance to the economic liberation of these states. Incidentally, western industrial states, too, resorted to governmental action to cope with the economic crisis to the benefit of their own transnational corporations, in the context of competition among themselves and against developing countries.[11]

In other words, while the outdated-sovereignty version of the interdependence concept has become less influential, it still is held. It has been recently renewed, to greater effect, by proposals which do not explicitly question state sovereignty: a theory of transnational policies (or transnational relations).

IV

The genesis of this theory dates back to the early seventies. Among its fathers are US economists and politologists, including Keohane, Nye, and Bergsten, who have been quoted earlier.[12] The theory has been substantially enlarged in the mean time by a great number of authors in the USA and western Europe, with a large literature published to date. It is based on the following line of thinking.

The growing strength of transnational relations has been an accompanying phenomenon of 'increasing functional interdependence' and 'globalisation' of problems. There has been a general recession of the 'state component' and, concomitantly, a multiplicity of vital contacts, coalitions, and interactions across state frontiers (and 'below the threshold of state sovereignty'), in other words, transnational relations which have been assuming growing importance as determining factors in international relations.[13]

According to J. Bailey, an advocate of the theory, that trend should be seen as substantial progress as compared with the 'state-centred approach of the past', for the process of transnationalisation had its manifestation in a shift of international relations from the inter-governmental level to a multitude of transgovernmental and transnational interactions which opened up growing opportunities for coalitions between widely different forces. The transnational corporations are thus integrated with this transnational system: 'The transnational approach to politics... actually provides the best imaginable possibility to think of the multinational companies as political actors within the political system.'[14]

Transnational corporations are explicitly distinguished as the most important transnational actors. Their activities across national boundaries, according to the authors mentioned above, could not be checked by centralised authorities in charge of foreign relations under state governments. They acted with relative autonomy, just like other transnational actors, furnished with some sort of a 'substitutional government', and established direct contact with one another across national frontiers, by-passing national governments. Interdependence, consequently, called for the complex interconnection of nation states with international, transnational, and subnational organisations.[15]

This in fact means a substantiation through a theoretical concept of a condition which, as we have noted in section I, has come into existence fortuitously through the international expansion of the transnational corporations. The peculiarities of that expansion and structure, both orientated to profit-making strategies, are now offered as a political blueprint which has originated from the inevitable requirements for the purpose of resolving international problems.

Once the transnational corporations have been introduced as non-state protagonists to the arena of international relations, another step follows to enlarge the theory further: the positions of these corporations are elevated through all sorts of coalitions with sub-units of national governments, other transnational corporations, and international bodies.[16] In all these constellations, a key role is being accorded to transnational corporations as a motor of transnational politics.

For instance, the formation of syndicates is considered to be a promising approach to future problems in international relations. A syndicate, in this context, is defined as an alliance of representatives of transnational and local enterprises and of national governments:

Syndicates of this type may be formed in highly industrialised countries for high-technology research and development projects, say in the context of NATO, or in developing countries for joint national development projects and to open up international markets... In such cases, advance regulation will be possible, and the activities of transnational organisations can be subordinated to coordinated or centralised planning and be made instrumental to a common purpose.[17]

The concept of transnational politics is being further enlarged to the level of an 'interdependence order' that might emerge from 'an OECD core', and this, after all, is followed by a conclusion: 'The UN, being established on a nation state basis, can hardly be considered as a stimulator of development.'[18] The concept is, consequently, boiled down to its original theory of the obsolescence of the nation state and proves to be nothing but an old idea in new dress.

True, not all advocates of the theory of transnational politics have arrived at such wide-ranging conclusions, but they all defend the concept of transnational coalitions and syndicates in which an important or even the decisive role is played by transnational corporations. Hence, non-state actors are made equal partners in international relations and, particularly, in relations between states.

There are three points which are of particular importance, in this context, for they are directly related to the political positions of western government representatives and their approach and attitude towards the function of transnational corporations in international relations. The demand is made, in the first place, that transnational corporations should be *political* actors in international relations. Secondly, they are launched into positions as partners of states and partners 'below the sovereignty threshold' in international relations. Thirdly, the UN is defined as inefficient when it comes to attempted solutions to transnational problems and is thus discredited as far as the transnational corporations are concerned. Such a philosophy is, on account of its political focus, even more disturbing than the mere proclamation of an end to the nation state. It is of a particular political relevance, since without touching formally on legal facts it tries to undercut the reality in which transnational corporations are not subjects of international law and thus cannot act on an equal footing with states in the international arena.

It should be of some interest that the same philosophy is being used to substantiate theoretically political positions in UN debates on a UN Code of Conduct for Transnational Corporations. This has been quite clearly demonstrated in connection with three problems emphasised by representatives of western industrial states:

1. The principles of unlimited national sovereignty over the natural resources of a country and activities within its boundaries are not accepted as long as this means unrestricted validity of national jurisdiction on all issues, including nationalisation and compensation. National jurisdiction must rather be paralleled by so-called norms of customary international law, such as provisions laid down, for instance, in some bilateral investment guaranty treaties.

2. Transnational corporations and their subsidiaries and affiliated companies should be treated by the host country just as local enterprises are and should be granted special status.

3. The Code should provide for a balanced relationship between conduct of transnational corporations and conduct of national governments towards these corporations. It would thus become, at the same time, a code of conduct for governments.

These political positions of industrial states of the West do clearly reveal the role attributed to transnational corporations as transnational actors in international relations 'below sovereignty threshold'. Unrestricted national sovereignty of states in respect of their own natural resources and activities in their territories is rejected, and the transnational corporations are elevated to partner level with states. Some of these demands have even exceeded the limits agreed in bilateral investment guaranty treaties between leading industrial states of the West on the one hand and developing countries on the other. The following reasoning is given by government representatives of western states: 'A state that has accepted foreign investors... ought to treat them in agreement with relevant parts of alien laws as emanating from customary international law.'[19] The delegates of the USA and of other industrial states of the West have made crystal-clear to the UN commission and in numerous publications their continued insistence on these positions.

The examples given in this study are likely to show that the international expansion of transnational corporations has been a crucial aspect of confrontation in international economic relations for more than two decades. The business interests of transnational corporations are shown to be linked to political interests and claims of states and groups of countries. The developing countries and the socialist states, on the other hand, are taking a firm stand against this. It is their established assumption that while international relations cannot be reduced to inter-state relations, the latter are clearly crucially involved. Also, the importance of the economic dimension in politics is growing, and so is the challenge to national governments to be more active in shaping international economic relations. Above all, there can be no equality or equal treatment in the context of international relations of transnational, that is non-state, actors and states. Hence, there can be no doubt that ideas about the control and regulation of activities undertaken by transnational corporations will continue to be involved in struggle for the democratisation of international economic relations in their totality and for the establishment of a New International Economic Order.

NOTES

1 The UN Commission on Transnational Corporations consists of representatives of 48 states appointed as full members by ECOSOC for terms of two or three years. This is done by a predetermined formula providing for 32 developing countries, the People's Republic of China, ten western industrial states, and five socialist countries of eastern Europe. Information on Commission proceedings and results so far achieved, primarily in the context of a Code of Conduct for Transnational Corporations, may be obtained from *CTC Reporter*, a journal issued by the UN Centre on Transnational Corporations, above all from, for instance, no. 12, summer 1982.

2 UN Centre on Transnational Corporations, *Transnational corporations in world development, third survey* (New York, 1983), pp. 46; 366–73.

3 *Ibid.*, pp. 350ff.

4 *Ibid.*, pp. 5–7.

5 L. P. Brown, *World without borders* (New York, 1973), pp. 254ff.

6 Charles P. Kindleberger, *American business abroad: six lectures on direct investment* (New Haven, 1969), p. 207.

7 H. V. Perlmutter, 'A view of the future', in *The new sovereigns: multinational corporations as world powers*, ed. Abdul A. Said and Saiiz R. Simmons (Englewood Cliffs, New Jersey, 1975), p. 168.

8 P. F. Drucker, 'Multinationals and developing countries: myths and realities', in *Foreign affairs* (October 1974), 133.
9 C. F. Bergsten, R. O. Keohane, and J. S. Nye, 'International economics and international politics: a framework for analysis', in: *World politics and international economics* (Washington, 1975), p. 11.
10 R. Vernon, 'Storm over the multinationals: problems and prospects', in *Foreign affairs* (January 1977), 258.
11 Cf. C. F. Bergsten, *Managing international economic interdependence: selected papers of C. Fred Bergsten, 1975–1976* (Lexington, Mass., 1977), pp. 151.
12 Some of these publications are by R. O. Keohane and J. S. Nye; *Transnational relations and world politics* (Cambridge, 1973); 'World politics and the international economic system', in *The future of international economic order: an agenda for research*, ed. C. F. Bergsten (Lexington, 1973); 'Transgovernmental relations and international organisation', in *World politics*, xxvii (1974); *Power and interdependence: world politics in transition* (Boston, 1977).
13 W. L. Bühl, *Transnationale Politik, Internationale Beziehungen zwischen Hegemonie und Interdependenz* (Stuttgart, 1978), pp. 9ff.
14 P. J. Bailey, *Möglichkeiten der Kontrolle multinationaler Konzerne: Die Rolle internationaler Organisationen* (Munich, 1979), p. 6.
15 Bühl, *Transnationale Politik*, pp. 107ff.
16 Bailey, *Möglichkeiten der Kontrolle multinationaler Konzerne*, p. 40.
17 Bühl, *Transnationale Politik*, p. 389.
18 *Ibid.*, pp. 378–9.
19 Ph. Lévy and H. Gattiker, 'Behandlung und Schutz der Auslandsinvestitionen: Konzepte im Wandel', in *Aussenwirtschaft: Schweizerische Zeitschrift für internationale Wirtschaftsbeziehungen*, no. 1 (March 1980), 57.

25 Multinationals in perspective*

ALICE TEICHOVA

I

This paper is not intended to be a summary of the contributions to this volume but, in conclusion, attempts – by looking back – to consider multinational enterprise in historical perspective, many facets of which are discussed in the predominantly empirically based papers contained in the previous pages.[1]

At the time of writing this concluding piece awareness of the rising importance of foreign investment in comparison with foreign trade is a recurrent theme in the economic sections of the daily press. The increasing significance of income from foreign direct investment (FDI) for the leading exporting countries concurrently with growing deficits in their balances of trade is commented on in particular.[2] Historically FDI is closely bound up with the development of international business in general, and can be regarded as the backbone of multinational enterprise in particular. Today the decisive share of the total stock of FDI is owned, controlled and operated by multinational companies whose headquarters are situated in the various parent (or home) countries. Geographically the US, the European Economic Community (EEC) including Britain, and Japan have established a veritable triangular power base which – contrary to what is said in the mainstream of present publications – has so far not been seriously challenged by the emergence of multinational companies in some newly industrializing countries of the Third World.[3]

Estimates of flows of FDI have only recently been more reliably calculated by international organizations such as the United Nations Organization (UNO), the Organization for Economic Co-operation and Development (OECD) and the United Nations Centre on Transnational Corporations. While their results may vary somewhat and the level of precision may be debatable they give an idea of the order of magnitude involved which leaves no doubt about the steep rise in worldwide FDI. From an estimated total of almost $92 billion in 1960 FDI rose to $165 billion in 1971 and to more than $257 billion in 1978, and the rise is continuing in the 1980s.[4] That these

362

increases are dramatic is plain to see if they are compared with the interwar period when the total of all, not only direct, long-term international investments (excluding state loans) of the three main creditor nations (Britain, France and the US) reached its peak of about $34 billion in 1930.[5] There is also general consensus about the rank order of the countries of origin of FDI. Until the 1940s the overwhelming majority of international direct investment originated in Europe, above all in Britain, whose predominance had remained unassailed since the second half of the nineteenth century.[6] By 1967 more than half of the total stock of FDI (55%) came from the US, over a third (34%) from the western European countries, of which 16% was held by Britain, while Japan participated with less than 1.5%.[7] In spite of the distinct tendency of EEC- and Japanese-based FDI to increase in the 1970s, United States investment, predominantly emanating from multinational corporations, has remained at the top in world statistics.[8]

Against this background the term *multinational corporation* gained a firm foothold in the United States in the 1960s[9] and quickly came into common usage around the world. Economists, sociologists, political scientists, politicians and journalists followed by the general public perceived the multinational corporation as a new socio-economic phenomenon originating in and spreading from the USA. Economic and business historians, while using the term in their work, feel unease about the lack of historical consciousness which misleadingly strengthens the tendency to derive the structure of present advanced industrial economies from the 1960s.

In the history of ideas attempts have been made time and again to conceptualize phenomena which were regarded as new without realizing that both the phenomena and their images themselves undergo changes in time. This applies demonstrably to the concept of the *multinational corporation*. It is not difficult to understand that the timing of the origin of the term has been identified chronologically with the rise of multinational enterprise itself and that it was placed in America, for its most intensive and conspicuous expansion has occurred since the 1960s with US companies in the lead. American assets in the world increased incomparably faster than those of any other capital exporting country: between 1950 and 1967 the number of foreign manufacturing subsidiary companies under US control more than trebled (from 988 to 3,646), and between 1959 and 1974 the value of US foreign direct investment almost trebled (from $29.7 billion to $110.2 billion).[10] While before 1914 the US was on balance a receiving economy absorbing more FDI from Europe than was hitherto assumed,[11] American capital export caught up with that of European countries in the 1920s and far outstripped it after the Second World War.[12]

Table 1 illustrates the growth of multinational operations of US- and non-US-based companies by enumerating the manufacturing subsidiaries they established abroad since before the First World War. Multinational

Table 25.1. *Growth of US-, British-, Continental European- and Japanese-based multinational enterprise (pre-1914–1967)*

Period	Numbers of foreign manufacturing subsidiary firms established or acquired by parent companies						
	US	UK	Conti-nental Europe	Europe (incl. UK)	Japan	Total	No. of companies per annum
Pre-1914	122	60	167	227	0	349	—
1914–18 (WWI)	71	27	51	78	0	149	21
1920–38	614	217	361	578	4	1,196	63
1939–45 (WWII)	172	34	44	78	40	290	41
1946–58	1,108	351	377	728	21	1,857	143
1959–67	2,749	1,111	993	2,104	247	5,100	566

Source: Calculated from Lawrence G. Franko, *The European multinationals: a renewed challenge to American and British big business* (London, 1976), Table 1.2, p. 10.

companies distinguish themselves from other types of business enterprises by their main characteristic feature that, as parent companies, they exercise control over subsidiary firms which are scattered over several states.[13] The number of subsidiaries grew continually from the pre-1914 period with obviously slower growth for the duration of the two World Wars. But both post-World War periods register important spurts in the number of subsidiaries as compared to the previous years. The most remarkable expansion occurred in the decade from 1959 to 1967, when more subsidiaries (5,100) were established than the total of the entire previous decades (3,841). If we compare the two periods of rapid expansion by calculating an annual rate of increase from the figures in Table 1, then for the interwar years 63 subsidiary manufacturing firms per annum were established abroad by parent companies as against 566 per annum acquired during 1959 and 1967.

As the above quantitative evidence shows the phenomenon is not new. Indeed, in historical perspective, the short history of the term masks the substantially longer history of the existence of multinational enterprise.[14] Without an acknowledgement that multinational companies have a history and in turn have affected history a deeper understanding of long-term trends impinging upon our time cannot be gained.

Although the most noticeable development took place in the United States during the sixties the cradle of international business such as international cartels and multinational companies is nevertheless to be found in Europe at the end of the nineteenth century.[15] By the 1930s large-scale multinational enterprise had become a crucially important institution in all industrially advanced market economies and in our time multinational companies have become a socio-political commonplace. Economists are seeking to explain this development by constructing theories of multinational enterprise. Historians ask questions about the origin of changes and are looking for a set of patterns. Both lines of thought are reflected in this volume. In the following account an attempt will be made to systematize certain aspects of the manifold approaches to the evolution of multinational business.

II

In historical perspective one of the most significant factors in the rise of multinational enterprise has been the process of concentration.[16] Its pervasive impact on the structure and organization of business became evident from the last quarter of the nineteenth century and was borne out by the growth of large companies which steadily increased their market shares at home and abroad, and stood at the centre of massive merger movements. This process of transformation tends to conform to a pattern which is essentially comparable in industrially highly advanced countries. Economic historians have regarded the changes in economy and society during the late nineteenth century as climacteric, variously assessing them as a shift from a one-nation to a multi-nation industrial system, as the rise of managerial capitalism, as the advent of organized capitalism and as the rise of the corporate economy.[17]

Continually intensifying industrial concentration and rationalization of production within the framework of capitalist market economies were powerfully enhanced in the course of the twentieth century by the growing interactions between science and technology on the one hand and industry, transport and communications on the other. These seminally important relationships still need to be studied in detail, but there can be no doubt that they facilitated normalization and standardization of products as a vital component of the expansion of mass production[18] and thus furthered the creation of oligopolistic and monopolistic formations reaching across national boundaries. Business responded to economic opportunities produced by internal and external factors on domestic and world markets which favoured the growth of the largest concerns into multi-unit, multi-divisional, multi-functional, multi-product and multi-national companies. Writings in business history, not least the heterogeneous examples in this volume, highlight the diverse conditions in individual economies, in different industries and at different points in time, but the common factor which emerges is that multinational companies aim at combining operations and reducing costs on a global scale.[19] During their growth process they have succeeded in obtaining comparative advantages – for which sophisticated technology and organization are essential – from economies of scale to secure a constant flow of production and from economies of scope through product diversification and widening of markets.[20] They have increasingly attempted to manipulate, regulate and replace the market mechanism[21] – shaping or creating markets – thereby gradually changing the structure of the nineteenth-century market economy itself. Consequently, the operations of large economic units led to an ever more administered production, financing, and marketing system.[22]

From the recent proliferation of empirical studies[23] and research in progress on multinational enterprise of which this volume is a representative sample it is possible to recognize certain criteria in chronological sequence and to identify turning points in the path of multinational business expansion. To ascertain whether the number of new foreign subsidiary enterprises established by parent companies clustered in certain periods, different factors were chosen which, singly or in varied combinations, affected the decisions of national firms to operate abroad or of existing multinationals to expand further internationally. They are: firstly, growth due to the application of new technology and of management skills extending effective control and supervision of foreign subsidiaries to marketing, distribution, purchasing facilities, personnel, production units and research and development;[24] secondly, development in marketing and distribution from agents, agencies and/or freestanding companies to production plants;[25] thirdly, changing contractual relations in terms of the hierarchical division of labour;[26] fourthly, the course of the geographical expansion of business operations of firms;[27] fifthly, the different times at which foreign production was substituted for exports;[28] sixthly, multinational expansion in the field of financing production from pre-financing to credit-financing to self-financing of subsidiaries abroad;[29] and finally, the progression in the sphere of finance from the old wealth of private banking houses to the new wealth of investment banking and to multinational banking.[30]

Without, of course, claiming precision the comparison of the time scale of these different factors underlying the foreign expansion of multinational enterprise produced roughly similar results. Three periods of rapid growth clearly emerge. The initial stage of conspicuous expansion fell clearly into the 1880s and 1890s; a further remarkable spurt occurred in the interwar period (the 1920s and 1930s); and the most intensive global reach of multinational companies came about in the 1960s and 1970s. While this is obviously not a surprising result, it tallies with the periodization of other important developments in the economy and society since the 1880s.

On the whole, a credible case can thus be made for a chronological development of multinational enterprise from its origins spreading across national frontiers to its global ramifications. However, the reasons why large companies acquire foreign direct investments are too diverse to be systematized in chronological order. The most that can be said is that access to and control of raw materials and the overcoming of protectionism as well as the breaking out of narrow home markets frequently led to production abroad in the earlier period from the 1880s to 1914, while research and development, diversifying from a common base to reduce costs, differences in labour costs often caused by organized labour, and worldwide trading and financial networks are prominent reasons for FDI from the 1960s onwards. Usually there is a multicausal explanation for almost every case of FDI. Some of the main impulses for operating abroad are mentioned in the different aspects enumerated in the discussion of time sequences above. But, as the detailed work presented in this volume testifies, each foreign subsidiary arises out of a particular set of circumstances which needs to be assessed in the context of the business strategy of the individual multinational companies and in relation to conditions in their respective home and host countries.

Surveyed historically the underlying motive of capitalist enterprise to invest in foreign companies can be traced almost invariably directly or indirectly to the consolidation of acquired markets and to the defence of already occupied market positions or to the penetration and opening up of new profitable markets. Principally, no capital holding is gained and no credit is provided disinterestedly however varied the considerations leading to the decision to place foreign investments may be. Among the most important considerations amply substantiated in this volume are: the control and exploitation of sources of raw material;[31] the strategy of domination of the entire world market or part of it for a certain product or range of products;[32] participation in another country's industrial production in order to evade tariffs which would be imposed were the goods imported, or to comply with local patents laws, or with laws restricting employment to nationals of the host state[33] but also to take advantage of privileges and preferences extended to industrial enterprise in host countries; to shift production to low-wage areas of the world in the desire to achieve cost reductions;[34] to get a foothold in one country by participating in its economic life for further expansion to other countries.[35]

To emphasize the historical perspective again, the increasing importance of capital exports in the form of direct participating investments in enterprises of the receiving countries was part of the process of concentration to which the growth of multinational companies belongs. Many contributions to this book provide evidence that in the wake of this development international economic and political interests became more and more integrated. Multinational companies cannot but include a political component together with financial, organizational, technical and commercial strategies in their economic policy. Only the existence and realization of a business strategy of a widely ramified concern as a whole, which in the course of international competition aims to conquer foreign markets, necessitates mutual relations and cooperation between multinational companies and governments. These would be, firstly, between the business policy of the concern on the one hand and the foreign trade policy and diplomacy of the state in which the concern is headquartered (its home country) on the other, and secondly, between the business policy of the concern's headquarters and those governments in whose countries its subsidiaries operate (host countries). In pursuance of their business policies multinationals establish a network of personal relationships and contacts with the bureaucracy, the ministries, the political and economic associations, interest groups and other elites of those states within their sphere of interest, whether they are home or host countries.

The empirical and comparative studies presented here and elsewhere[36] reveal strong tendencies on the part of large multinational enterprise to adapt to societies with different political, social, cultural and legal systems. However, the basic rules for the decision-making process within the multinational enterprise function essentially undisturbed by heterogeneous legal conditions and institutions, for the exercise of control from a head office over all its subsidiaries wherever they may be situated is central to the operations of a multinational company. The degree to which freedom of action is allowed to individual subsidiary companies varies from one multinational to another; in the last analysis, however, their entrepreneurial policies have to be subordinated to the general business strategy of the core of the concern. Relations within a multinational concern therefore show complicated ties of mutual dependences between the subsidiaries and the head office. Essentially, these relationships are based on direct participation by the parent company in the capital of the subsidiary enterprises, although a large part of the intertwined connexions between capital and credit participations, patent, licence, cartel and other contractual agreements remains opaque. Within the framework of the multinational company the internal entrepreneurial strategies and rules in pursuit of its global aims take precedence over the interests of the individual host states in which the subsidiary enterprises are situated. Consequently, the relationships between governments and multinational companies have perennially been influenced both by conformity and by conflicts of interests.

III

In the 1960s the less developed countries of the Third World, in an attempt to increase their national sovereignty over investment controlled outside their territory, exerted pressure in the United Nations Organization for the implementation of a code of conduct designed to regulate relations between multinational companies and host governments.[37] Their efforts led to the establishment of the United Nations Centre on Transnational Corporations in 1973, the aim of which was to assist 'in the devising of a national and international policy towards multinational companies' which would minimize their 'pervasive influence on domestic political processes in decision-making' and channel their activities into contributing more positively and effectively than hitherto 'to establish a New International Order'.[38] Since the 1960s, concurrent with the unprecedented upsurge of multinational enterprise, the writing on multinational companies has burgeoned.[39] It is sometimes controversial both in its defence and in its opposition to multinational business, but also expresses unease about the increasing control of world markets by multinational companies and about their relations to government in general.

Seen historically, demands for the control of big business and of its international operations in industry and finance are not a new issue. Neither is disquiet about excessive concentration of economic power or concern about the penetration of FDI from leading industrial powers to economically relatively backward states. Indeed, these attitudes can be traced back to the rise of large-scale enterprise, cartels and concentration of production, capital and organization at the turn of the century. How this historical reality was seen previously is documented by the amount of publications on the subject, which has steadily grown since the first book on cartels by Friedrich Kleinwächter published in Innsbruck in 1883. This literature has itself been historically conditioned and it can roughly be divided into three phases.

In the first phase, beginning at the end of the nineteenth century, Kleinwächter described a relatively new phenomenon in the development of business organization. He was followed by authors such as Robert Liefmann[40] and Rudolf Hilferding,[41] who were concerned with the description and classification of cartels, syndicates, trusts and holding companies, ranking them hierarchically into an organizational pattern according to their activity and their degree of concentration. Almost without exception cartels were regarded as part of the process of concentration which as predecessors of mergers and combines accelerated monopolistic formations. If any value judgement was attempted the new trends in business organization and practices were overwhelmingly either regarded as a deviation from the normal course of economic development which the invisible hand of supply and demand would eventually correct, or diagnosed as a sickness of the economic organism, or characterized as a conspiracy against the consumer. Hilferding stands out as an exception since he drew far-reaching theoretical and political conclusions about the origin and growth of banks and industrial enterprises and their interlocking relationships which he terms 'finance capital'. This led on the one hand to the concept which he originated of 'organized capitalism' (which has experienced a recent revival)[42] and, on the other, to V. I. Lenin's theory of 'imperialism as the highest stage of capitalism'.[43] The concept was developed further in studies on 'state monopoly capitalism'.[44]

The second phase of publications and discussion was evoked by the economic crisis of the early 1930s and the Second World War. Concern was voiced about the unprecedented concentration of economic power in a comparatively small number of giant enterprises.[45] One of the results of this apprehension was F. D. Roosevelt's initiative in appointing the Temporary National Economic Committee (TNEC)[46] in 1938, whose task it was to investigate the concentration of power in the US economy and to propose measures in furtherance of competition. The basic assumption underlying the great mass of evidence, reports and monographs which were collected and published was that competition has to be revived against monopolizing forces and that the activities of oligopolies, monopolies and cartels have to be curbed by enforcing existing and/or promulgating new legislation. Consequently, through a contrast between competition and monopoly the first was implicitly considered to be more desirable. This view became fortified when violations of national interest by American-British-German big business during the Second World War were revealed. However, the illusion of the protagonists of a free market economy about the return to a state that had existed in the nineteenth century was at the time, and is even more today, anachronistic.

In the third and present wave of publications on multi- or transnational companies the idea of a return to free market competition as a panacea has virtually disappeared. Since the 1960s a new approach has been gaining consensus which does not ask whether concentration is an inducement or an obstacle to economic development; the main concern of these and subsequent writings is the misuse of economic power. This finds expression in the volumes edited by Helmut Arndt on *Die Konzentration in der Wirtschaft*,[47] but also in the attitudes and debates about a code of conduct with regard to multinational enterprise which have already been referred to.[48]

Approaches based on ideas such as 'competition versus monopoly' or 'concentration of power and its abuse' are of limited value for scientific analysis. For the process of concentration of economic power from cartelization to mergers taking place since the turn of the century has proved to be irresistible.

Competition has not been arrested by increasing numbers of national and international cartels and multinational companies, but the market conditions under which competition operated before the growth of large-scale enterprise have changed. Within the framework of the world market competition as well as cooperation has been carried out effectively among business giants using economic and political means to attain their goals and to defend their interests. Thus multinational companies themselves which dominate markets in their field of production either regionally, nationally or in certain parts of the world enter into cartel agreements with each other, for an effective cartel agreement is an expression of the balance of forces between individual cartel partners.[49] In this way international cartels can temporarily defuse conflict, as they did for instance in the unstable conditions of the interwar period, since they direct competition into agreements about division, control and regulation of markets according to the relative strength of the partners. Contrary to quite widely held views cartels are not necessarily predecessors of large oligopolistic or monopolistic companies; nor are they alternatives to them, but developed concurrently within the process of concentration.

In the historical context the present advanced stage of multinational business structures is the outcome of a century of intensive change in capitalist economies. It has to be seen against the background of scientific and technological developments which made mass production, distribution, employment and consumption on a global scale possible.[50] The vast scale of these continuing transformations involves the whole of human society and in this sense a process of socialization is taking place which qualitatively changes capitalism itself.

NOTES

* This paper draws on knowledge and experience gained during a research project, 'Multinational companies in East Central Europe in the interwar period', with the support of the Social Science Research Council, which is gratefully acknowledged here. It also uses some ideas sketched out in my brief commentary 'Multinationale Unternehmen in historischer Sicht – ein Kommentar', in *Management und Organisation*, Verein der wissenschaftlichen Forschung auf dem Gebiete der Unternehmerbiographie und Firmengeschichte (Vienna, 1984).

1 Contributions to this volume referred to in the footnotes will be cited by the name of the contributor followed by *MNE* (*Multinational enterprise in historical perspective*) and the page numbers where appropriate.

2 E.g. 'Briten kaufen sich im Ausland ein', *Süddeutsche Zeitung*, 9.7.1985. I pointed this out in my book *An economic background to Munich international business and Czechoslovakia 1918–1938* (Cambridge, 1974), p. 9.

3 Cf. Sanjaya Lall (ed.), *The new multinationals: the spread of Third World Enterprises* (Chichester, 1983).

4 J. H. Dunning, 'Changes in the level and structure of international business', cited by Fieldhouse, *MNE*; also Lawrence G. Franko, *The European multinationals: a renewed challenge to American and British big business* (London, 1976), p. 13.

5 Royal Institute of International Affairs, *The problem of international investment* (London, 1937), p. 16.

6 *Ibid.*

7 Franko, p. 13.

8 Philippe Lemaître and Catherine Goybet, 'Multinational companies in the EEC', *IRM multinational reports* (July–September 1984), p. 5.

9 Fieldhouse, *MNE*.

10 Raymond Vernon, *Sovereignty at bay* (Harmondsworth, 1973), p. 62; and *Survey of current business* (United States Department of Commerce, August 1983).

11 Cf. Wilkins, *MNE*; Mira Wilkins, *The emergence of multinational enterprise: American business abroad from the colonial era to 1914* (Cambridge, Mass., 1970), p. 201. In 1913/14 US capital exports amounted to $3.5 billion, while capital imports came to $6.8 billion; *International capital movements during the inter-war period*, United Nations (Lake Success, 1949), p. 2.

12 See Cleona Lewis, *America's stake in international investments* (Washington, 1938), p. 605.

13 This feature is present in all definitions, e.g. J. H. Dunning's simplest characterization cited by Fieldhouse, *MNE*.

14 Fieldhouse, *MNE*.

15 Wilkins, *MNE*; Franko, 'it is clear that even in the mid-1950s neither the condition nor the process of multinationality were unusual to European enterprises'. (p. 11).
16 Leslie Hannah, *The rise of the corporate economy* (London, 1976), p. 2.
17 David S. Landes, *The unbound Prometheus* (Cambridge, 1969), p. 247; Alfred D. Chandler, Jr. and Herman Daems, 'Introduction – the rise of managerial capitalism and its impact on investment strategy in the western world and Japan', in Herman Daems and Herman van der Wee (eds.), *The rise of managerial capitalism* (Louvain, 1974); Jürgen Kocka, 'Organisierter Kapitalismus oder Staatsmonopolistischer Kapitalismus? Begriffliche Vorbemerkungen', in H. Winkler (ed.), *Organisierter Kapitalismus* (Göttingen, 1974); Hannah.
18 Mikuláš Teich, 'Zu einigen Fragen der historischen Entwicklung der wissenschaftlich-technischen Revolution', *Jahrbuch für Wirtschaftsgeschichte*, II (1966), 52.
19 Alfred D. Chandler, Jr., 'Emergence of managerial capitalism', *Business history review*, LVIII (winter 1984), 473–503.
20 Chandler, *MNE*.
21 Chandler and Daems, 'Administrative coordinations, allocation and monitoring: concepts and comparisons', in Norbert Horn and Jürgen Kocka (eds.), *Law and the formation of the big enterprises in the 19th and early 20th centuries* (Göttingen, 1979), p. 28.
22 Teichova, p. xx.
23 Wilkins, 'Modern European economic history and the multinationals', *Journal of European economic history* (1977) and 'The history of European multinationals – a new look', *Journal of European economic history* (1985).
24 Chandler, *MNE*.
25 McKay, Wilkins, H. Schröter, Hertner, Nicholas, *MNE*.
26 Nicholas, Pearson, *MNE*.
27 Hertner, *MNE*.
28 V. Schröter, Lundström, Wilkins, *MNE*.
29 H. Schröter, V. Schröter, Lundström, *MNE*.
30 McKay, Lundström, Kernbauer and Weber, Jones, Rowley, *MNE*.
31 McKay, Chalmin, Pangeti, Ahvenainen and Hjerppe, *MNE*.
32 Church, V. Schröter, *MNE*.
33 Beaud, McKay, Hertner, *MNE*.
34 Nicholas, Brown, Pearson, Overy, *MNE*.
35 Beaud, Wilkins, Landau and Tomaszewski, Hjerppe, and the most blatant and extreme example in Overy, *MNE*.
36 E.g. Horn and Kocka; Alice Teichova and P. L. Cottrell (eds.), *International business and central Europe 1918–1939* (Leicester, 1983).
37 Heininger, *MNE*; Geoffrey Hamilton, 'The control of multinationals: what future for international codes of conduct in the 1980s?', *IRM multinational reports* (October–December, 1984).
38 *Transnational corporations in world development: a re-examination*, United Nations Economic and Social Council, Commission on Transnational Corporations (New York, 1978), p. 131.
39 To cope with the mass of literature the Centre on Transnational Corporations in New York publishes an annual bibliography.
40 Robert Liefmann's publications appeared before and after the First World War and his best-known book is *Cartels, concerns, and trusts* (London, 1932).
41 Rudolf Hilferding, *Das Finanzkapital: Eine Studie über die jüngste Entwicklung des Kapitalismus* (Vienna, 1910), translated into English in 1981.
42 Winkler (ed.).

43 V. I. Lenin, *Imperialism the highest stage of capitalism*, in *Collected works*, XXII (London, 1964).

44 Cf. L. Zumpe (ed.), *Wirtschaft und Staat im Imperialismus: Beiträge zur Entwicklungsgeschichte des staatsmonopolistischen Kapitalismus in Deutschland* (Berlin, 1976); D. Baudis and H. Nussbaum, *Wirtschaft und Staat in Deutschland vom Ende des 19. Jahrhunderts bis 1918/19* (Berlin, 1978); M. Nussbaum, *Wirtschaft und Staat in Deutschland während der Weimarer Republik* (Berlin, 1978).

45 Nussbaum, *MNE*, p. 132.

46 Temporary National Economic Committee, Descriptions of hearings and monographs, 31 volumes and 6 additional volumes, 42 monographs (Washington DC, 1941).

47 H. Arndt (ed.), *Die Konzentration in der Wirtschaft*, 2nd edn. (2 vols., Berlin, 1971).

48 Publications of the Centre on Transnational Corporations at the United Nations Organization in New York.

49 Teichova, chs. 2/2,3/2,4/2 and 5/2; Verena Schröter, *Die deutsche Industrie auf dem Weltmarkt 1929 bis 1933* (Frankfurt, 1984), ch. 3.3; Harm Schröter, *Aussenpolitik und Wirtschaftsinteresse Skandinavien im aussenwirtschaftlichen Kalkül Deutschlands und Grossbritanniens 1918–1939* (Frankfurt, 1983), *passim*.

50 Mikuláš Teich, 'The scientific-technical revolution: an historical event in the twentieth century?', in Roy Porter and Mikuláš Teich, (eds.), *Revolution in history* (Cambridge, 1986).

Index of names

Index of firms

386 *Index of firms*

Index of subjects